Latin American De

MW00655053

More than thirty years have passed since Latin America began the arduous task of transitioning from military-led rule to democracy. In this time, more countries have moved toward the institutional bases of democracy than at any time in the region's history. Nearly all countries have held free, competitive elections, and most have had peaceful alternations in power between opposing political forces. Despite these advances, however, Latin American countries continue to face serious domestic and international challenges to the consolidation of stable democratic governance. The challenges range from weak political institutions, corruption, legacies of militarism, transnational crime, and globalization, among others.

In the second edition of *Latin American Democracy*, contributors—both academics and practitioners, North Americans, Latin Americans, and Spaniards—explore and assess the state of democratic consolidation in Latin America by focusing on the specific issues and challenges confronting democratic governance in the region. This thoroughly updated revision provides new chapters on:

- the environment,
- decentralization,
- the economy,
- indigenous groups,
- and the role of China in the region.

Richard L. Millett is professor emeritus at Southern Illinois University, Edwardsville and vice-president of the American Committees on Foreign Relations.

Jennifer S. Holmes is a professor and head of Public Policy, Political Economy, and Political Science at the University of Texas at Dallas.

Orlando J. Pérez is associate dean of the School of Humanities and Social Sciences at Millersville University. He is a member of the Scientific Support Group for the Latin American Public Opinion Project (LAPOP) at Vanderbilt University and directs the *Americas Barometer* survey in Panama.

Latin American Democracy

Emerging Reality or Endangered Species?

Second edition

**Edited by Richard L. Millett,
Jennifer S. Holmes, and
Orlando J. Pérez**

NEW YORK AND LONDON

First published 2015
by Routledge
711 Third Avenue, New York, NY 10017

and by Routledge
2 Park Square, Milton Park, Abingdon, Oxon, OX14 4RN

*Routledge is an imprint of the Taylor & Francis Group,
an informa business*

Library of Congress Cataloging-in-Publication Data
Latin American democracy : emerging reality or endangered
   species? / Edited by Richard L. Millett, Jennifer S. Holmes,
   Orlando J. Pérez.
      pages cm
   1. Democracy—Latin America.   2. Political participation—Latin
America.   I. Millett, Richard, 1938–   II. Holmes, Jennifer S.
III. Pérez, Orlando J.   IV. Millett, Richard L.
   JL966.L3585 2014
   320.98—dc23
   2014034363

ISBN: 978-0-415-73260-4 (hbk)
ISBN: 978-0-415-73261-1 (pbk)
ISBN: 978-1-315-84895-2 (ebk)

Typeset in Galliard
by Apex CoVantage, LLC

To my wife Denice for her patience and support, and to my daughter Patricia Millett, whose dedication to promoting the rule of law both inspired and informed my work.
RLM

To Patrick, Trevor, Spirit, and Coco for making life fun.
JSH

To my wife and kids, Leyda, Rogelio, and Alexandra, for their constant love and support.
OJP

Contents

Tables and Figures

Tables

Figures

xii *Tables and Figures*

Acknowledgments

As we proceed with the publication of the second edition of *Latin America Democracy: Emerging Reality or Endangered Species?* the editors feel we should first thank Michael Kerns, our editor at Routledge Press, for his continued support and encouragement. The first edition of this volume would not have been successful, nor would a second edition be possible, without Michael's continued support. The idea for the first edition of this book originated with Richard Millett. Thus, Jennifer S. Holmes and Orlando J. Pérez wish to express our gratitude to Richard for asking us to accompany him on this journey. We also wish to thank the contributors to this volume, both the ones who have been with us from the beginning, and those who joined us for the second edition. In no small measure, the success of the volume is due to their intellectual work and dedication. We believe that we have successfully brought together an outstanding group of academics and practitioners—with diverse methodologies and points of view—whose combined efforts provide a unique and comprehensive analysis of the challenges and opportunities facing Latin American democracies today.

The initial conversations for the volume were held at the 2005 meeting of the Midwest Association for Latin American Studies (MALAS) in St. Louis, where a number of scholars and practitioners met to discuss the need for a project to evaluate the challenges facing contemporary Latin American democracies. The intent was to bridge the divide between original scholarship and policy analysis by including as contributors both practitioners and academics. Both the 2006 MALAS meeting in Managua and the 2007 MALAS meeting again held in St. Louis provided opportunities for some of the contributors to meet with the editors and present their papers to a multidisciplinary audience. MALAS continues to serve as a forum for our discussions. Co-editors and some contributors met at the 2012 and 2013 MALAS meetings in Louisville, Kentucky, and St. Louis, Missouri, to discuss ideas for the second edition.

Orlando J. Pérez
Millersville, Pennsylvania

Jennifer S. Holmes
Dallas, Texas

Richard L. Millett
Marine, Illinois

Contributors

Sheila Amin Gutiérrez de Piñeres is vice-president for Academic Affairs and Dean of Faculty at Austin College. Additionally, she holds the rank of Professor of Economics. Her research focuses on economic development and political stability in developing countries and employs a subnational level of analysis. She is the author of *Guns, Drugs & Development in Colombia* (University of Texas Press, 2008) with Kevin M. Curtin and Jennifer S. Holmes. She also is the author or co-author of numerous articles on such topics as development economics, international economics, and Latin America. Her current book project is "Beyond state capacity to services and inclusion: Library parks in marginalized urban areas in Colombia." She is a member of the Dallas Committee on Foreign Relations and a former president of the Midwest Association of Latin American Studies. Piñeres received her PhD in economics from Duke University in 1992, her MA from the University of Chicago, and her BA from Texas A&M.

Gerardo Berthin has nearly twenty years of experience as a program officer/director and/or senior technical adviser for various large and complex policy and governance reform programs. He has worked in nearly forty countries in Africa, Latin America, and Central and Eastern Europe for both the United Nations Development Programme (UNDP) and United States Agency for International Development (USAID) and has extensive experience in anti-corruption, transparency, and accountability policy issues. He has conducted several assessments to incorporate activities into donor and/or government strategies. He is the author and co-author of 12 UNDP national human development reports worldwide and numerous books and journal articles in various governance topics, including transparency and accountability. He is a political scientist with degrees from the University of Chicago, Georgetown University (Washington, D.C.), and the George Washington University (Washington, D.C.).

Julio F. Carrión is associate professor of Political Science and International Relations and director of the Center for Global and Area Studies at the University of Delaware. He previously held positions at Troy State University (Alabama) and the Facultad Latinoamericana de Ciencias Sociales in Ecuador

(FLACSO-Ecuador). He is the editor of *The Fujimori Legacy: The Rise of Electoral Authoritarianism in Peru* (Penn State University Press, 2006), and his most recent publication is "Peru in the Twenty-First Century: Confronting the Past, Charting the Future" (co-authored with David Scott Palmer, in *Latin American Politics and Development, Eighth Edition*, eds. Howard Wiarda and Harvey Kline, Boulder: Westview Press, 2014). He is currently working on a book manuscript on populist governance in the Andes.

Maria del Mar Martinez Rosón has been a post-doctoral fellow of Political Science at Autonomous University of Barcelona since 2012. She also works as a master's thesis advisor at the Centre for Political and Constitutional Studies. She received her PhD from University of Salamanca in 2008 and was a post-doctoral fellow at Tulane University in 2009–2010. Her research focuses on legislative careers, political ambition, representation, and clientelism, in particular, in Central America. Her work has been published in *Política y Gobierno*, *Revista Chilena de Ciencia Política*, and *Revista de Estudios Políticos*.

Rut Diamint is professor at La Universidad Torcuato Di Tella. She is also an independent investigator in the Consejo Nacional de Investigaciones Científicas y Tecnológicas (CONICET). She specializes in defense and international security and has published more than 100 articles and chapters. She has also served as advisor to the Presidencia Provisional del Senado Argentino y Jefe de Gabinete del Ministro de Defensa. She is a member of the Junta Asesora sobre Asuntos de Desarme del Secretario General de las Naciones Unidas (2013–2015) and advisor to Club de Madrid. Her latest books include *El Rompecabezas. Conformando la Seguridad Hemisférica en el siglo XXI*, co-edited with Joseph S. Tulchin and Raúl Benítez Manaut (Bononiae Libris y Prometeo Libros, 2006) and *Democratizar a los Políticos. Un Estudio Sobre Líderes Latinoamericanos* (Los Libros de la Catarata, 2013), co-edited with Laura Tedesco.

R. Evan Ellis is a research professor of Latin American Studies at the U.S. Army War College Strategic Studies Institute with a research focus on the region's relationships with China and other non–Western Hemisphere actors. He has published over ninety works, including *China in Latin America: The Whats and Wherefores* (Lynne Rienner, 2009), *The Strategic Dimension of Chinese Engagement with Latin America* (William J. Perry Center for Hemispheric Studies, 2013), and the *Chinese Companies on the Ground in Latin America* (Palgrave Macmillan, 2014). He has presented his work in a broad range of business and government forums in twenty-five countries on four continents and has given testimony on Chinese activities in Latin America to the US Congress. Ellis holds a PhD in Political Science from Purdue University with a specialization in comparative politics.

Michael J. Ferrantino is lead economist in the World Bank International Trade Unit. Prior to joining the bank, he was lead international economist at the US International Trade Commission. Ferrantino's published research spans a wide array of topics relating to international trade, including non-tariff measures and trade facilitation; global value chains; the relationship of trade to the environment, innovation, and productivity; and US-China trade. He has taught at Southern Methodist, Youngstown State, George-town, American, and George Washington universities. Ferrantino's recent work include: "The Benefits of Trade Facilitation: A Modelling Exercise," prepared for the World Economic Forum's January 2013 report on supply chains; "Enabling Trade: Valuing Growth Opportunities," a chapter on nontariff measures in *The Ashgate Research Companion to International Trade Policy* (2012); and "Evasion Behaviors of Exporters and Importers: Evidence from the U.S.-China Trade Data Discrepancy," with Xuepeng Liu and Zhi Wang for the *Journal of International Economics* (2012). Ferrantino holds a PhD from Yale University

Jennifer S. Holmes is a professor and head of Public Policy, Political Econ-omy, and Political Science at the University of Texas at Dallas. She received her BA from the University of Chicago and her PhD from the University of Minnesota. Her major area of research is political violence, terrorism, and political development with an emphasis on Latin America, especially Colombia and Peru. Her research incorporates both qualitative and quan-titative tools and reflects a sustained commitment to interdisciplinary work. She has also been researching outcomes in US asylum decisions. Her research has been published in numerous journals, such as *Judicature, Small Wars and Insurgencies, Stability: International Journal of Security and Development, Law and Policy, Democratization, Democracy and Security, Studies in Conflict and Terrorism, Journal of Refugee Studies, International Journal of Public Administration, Latin American Politics and Society, PS: Political Science, Bulletin of Latin American Research*, and *Terrorism & Political Violence*. She is the author or editor of six books, including *Guns, Drugs and Development* (with Sheila Amin Gutiérrez de Piñeres and Kevin Curtin) (University of Texas Press, 2008), *Terrorism and Democratic Sta-bility Revisited* (Manchester University Press, 2008), *Immigration Judges and U.S. Asylum Policy* (with Banks Miller and Linda Keith) (University of Pennsylvania Press, 2015), and *Latin American Democracy: Emerging Reality or Endangered Species?* (with Richard Millett and Orlando Perez) (Routledge 2008/2015).

John F. Maisto, Ambassador (Ret.) is a thirty-three-year former career member of the US Foreign Service. He was ambassador to Venezu-ela (1997–2000), Nicaragua (1993–1996), and the Organization of American States (2003–2006). He was senior director for the Western Hemisphere at the National Security Council and, concurrently, Special Assistant to the President (2001–2003). He was foreign policy advisor at the US Southern Command, Deputy Assistant Secretary of State for Cen-tral America, and he served in Argentina, Bolivia, Costa Rica, Panama, and the Philippines. His Philippine service was in Manila as a political officer (1978–1982), and at the State Department as deputy director and then director of Philippine Affairs (1982–1986) during the People Power transition to democracy. He is currently a director of the Miami-based US Education Finance Group and of the Washington-based International Student Exchange Program (ISEP). He is a director of ECI, a Central American-based resort and retirement company. He is also a consultant on global affairs at Arizona State University, a member of the board of advisors of the Washington-based Inter-American Dialogue, and chair of the board of advisors of the American Committees on Foreign Relations (ACFR) in Washington. He writes and speaks on US foreign policy; trade, investment and growth; democratic transitions; Western Hemisphere and East Asia-Pacific regional issues; security and defense matters; and international education. A graduate of Georgetown University's School of Foreign Service, he has a master's degree in Latin American history from San Carlos University, Guatemala.

Richard L. Millett is professor emeritus at Southern Illinois University-Edwardsville and vice-president of the American Committees on Foreign Relations. He has published over a hundred items, including *Searching for Stability*, *Guardians of the Dynasty*, and *Searching for Panama*. He has taught at four universities in Colombia and held the Distinguished Chair of American Studies in Denmark and the Oppenheimer Chair of Warfighting Strategy at the Marine Corps University.

Lorena Moscovich is a political scientist, a researcher, and assistant professor at the Universidad de San Andrés. She holds a PhD from the Universidad de Buenos Aires. She has directed projects and has been awarded with several grants and prizes from the Universidad de Buenos Aires, Brown University, CLACSO (Consejo Latinoamericano de Ciencias Sociales), and LASA (Latin American Studies Association), among others. She has published book chapters and articles in Argentina and abroad. Her topics of interest are the subnational consequences of federal coalition-building strategies, state capacity at the subnational level, economic inequality, and subnational politics in Latin America. She has also worked as a political consultant for public and private organizations, such as the Argentine federal government and the Economic Commission for Latin America and the Caribbean.

Luz E. Nagle is a professor of law at Stetson University College of Law in St. Petersburg, Florida, where she specializes in international law, international criminal law, and national security law. Her career prior to teaching includes having been a judge in Medellín, Colombia; serving as a law clerk to the Supreme Court of Virginia; working as an undercover private investigator in Los Angeles; and pursuing software pirates as a member of Microsoft Corporation's Latin America Copyright Enforcement Practice. Nagle is currently an El Centro Fellow of the Small Wars Foundation and an external researcher in the Strategic Studies Institute of the US Army War College. She has participated in rule of law, judicial reform, and hemispheric security projects sponsored by the US Departments of Defense, Justice, and State and USAID throughout Latin America. Her assignments have included training Argentine judges and Colombian criminal law professors in accusatory criminal justice reform, addressing the deployment of land mines by illegal armed groups in Andean states, and working with the Staff Judge Advocate's Office of the US Southern Command in training Colombian military commanders and staff judges in the application of international humanitarian law and managing humanitarian operations in conflict zones. She has engaged government officials, military commanders, journalists, and human rights advocates from more than fifty countries as a legal expert with the State Department's Distinguished Foreign Visitors Program, and she has been a State Department–sponsored presenter in Colombia, Panama, Venezuela, and Mexico, where she was a visiting lecturer on international humanitarian law and national security in the Diplomat Program in Security and Northern Border Development at the Universidad Autónoma de Nuevo León Faculty of Law and Criminology in Monterrey. An elected member of several learned legal societies, including the American Law Institute, she currently sits on the International Bar Association's Legal Practice Division Council and is a former member of the American Bar Association's Criminal Justice Council. She is also a prominent international voice in the fight against human trafficking and modern-day slavery. Nagle holds an LL.D. from the Universidad Pontificia Bolivariana, a JD from the College of William & Mary, an LL.M. in international law, and an MA in Latin American studies from the University of California at Los Angeles, and two certifications in national security law from the Center for National Security Law at the University of Virginia School of Law.

Orlando J. Pérez is associate dean of the School of Humanities and Social Sciences at Millersville University. He received his BA in political science from Florida International University and a master's degree and PhD in political science from the University of Pittsburgh. He is the author or editor of the following books: *Political Culture in Panama: Democracy after Invasion* (Palgrave-Macmillan, 2011); *Latin American Democracy: Emerging Reality or Endangered Species?* (with Richard L. Millett and Jennifer S. Holmes) (Routledge, 2009); *World Encyclopedia of Political Systems and Parties*, 4th edition (with Neil Schlager and Jayne Weisblatt) (Facts on File, 2006); and *Post-Invasion Panama: The Challenges of Democratization in the New World Order* (Lexington, 2000). His articles have appeared in the *Journal of Interamerican Studies and World Affairs*, *The Latin Americanist*, *Political Science Quarterly*, *Journal of Political and Military Sociology*, and *Revista Latinoamericana de Opinión Publica (Latin American Journal of Public Opinion)*. His current research focuses on the determinants of public support for populist leaders in Latin America, civil–military relations in post-conflict societies, and the transformation of political behavior in Latin America. His forthcoming book is *Civil-Military Relations in Post-Conflict Society: Transforming the Role of the Military in Central America* (Routledge Press, 2015).

Roberta Rice is an adjunct professor in the School of Languages and Literatures at the University of Guelph, Canada, where she teaches in the Master's in Latin American and Caribbean Studies Programme. She also teaches in the Department of Political Science at the University of Toronto. Her research focus is indigenous politics in the Andes. Her work has appeared in *Comparative Politics*, the *Latin American Research Review*, and *Party Politics*. Her book, *The New Politics of Protest: Indigenous Mobilization in Latin America's Neoliberal Era* (University of Arizona Press, 2012), was nominated for the 2014 prize in comparative politics by the Canadian Political Science Association. She is currently working on a comparative research project on indigenous rights and representation in Canada and Latin America.

Francisco Rojas Aravena, a specialist in international relations and international security, earned his PhD in Political Science from Utrecht University. He received his Magister in Political Science and Public Administration from Latin American Faculty of Social Sciences (FLACSO). Currently, he is a rector of the University for Peace. He previously served as secretary general of FLACSO (2004–2012) and director of FLACSO-Chile (1996–2004), taught at Stanford University, Santiago Campus, and was Fulbright Professor at Florida International University, Miami, in Latin American and Caribbean Studies.

Peter M. Siavelis is professor of Political Science and director of the Latin American and Latino Studies Program at Wake Forest University. Siavelis has been published widely, writing on topics including candidate selection, executive-legislative relations, and Latin American politics in numerous journal articles and book chapters, including articles in *Comparative Politics, Comparative Political Studies, Electoral Studies Party Politics, Latin American Research Review*, and *Latin American Politics and Society*. His most recent edited book is *Democratic Chile: The Politics and Policies of an Historic Coalition* (Lynne Rienner, 2014) with Kirsten Sehnbruch.

Laura Tedesco earned her PhD in political science from Warwick University in the United Kingdom. Currently, she is director of the Department of Political Science in Saint Louis University (Madrid Campus). Among her publications are *Democratizar a los Políticos. Un Estudio Sobre Líderes Latinoamericanos* (Los Libros de la Catarata, 2013), co-edited with Rut Diamint; *Alfonsín: De la Esperanza a la Desilusión* (Buenos Aires: Del Nuevo Extremo, 2011); and, with Jonathan Barton, *The State of Democracy* *in Latin America. Post-Transitional Conflicts in Argentina and Chile* (London: Routledge, 2004). She has published articles and chapters relating to the quality of democracy in Latin America, migration in Spain, and urban violence. She has been a consultant to the United Nations Children's Fund (UNICEF) in preparation for their report, *World's Children 2012 — Children in an Urban World.* She has also worked as an associate investigator in FRIDE (Fundación para las Relaciones Internacionales y el Diálogo Exterior) and has published numerous articles in *La Vanguardia* about Latin American politics.

1 Introduction

Democracy in Latin America: Promises and Perils

Richard L. Millett

Mark Twain once observed, "Everybody talks about the weather but no one does anything about it." Today that phrase might be altered to "Everybody talks about democracy, but few seem able to define it." Democracy has become a global buzzword, a concept used to evaluate governments, to condemn those who allegedly subvert or ignore it; democracy is virtually always praised as an unquestionable good. Terrorists, our leaders assure us, hate democracy, while virtually every politician in the Western Hemisphere today proclaims his allegiance to this concept. Even North Korea proclaims that it is "the People's Democratic Republic of Korea." While examples such as this may be scoffed at, attempts to precisely determine what governments are democratic and whether they are becoming more or less so produce little consensus and frequent acrimonious debates, which tell us more about the ideology of the participants than about the nation involved.

Winston Churchill once declared that "[n]o one pretends that Democracy is all wise. Democracy is the worst form of government except for all the others that have been tried" (James 1974, 174). Frequently quoted, but rarely examined, this admission of democracy's weakness and limitations has proved all too true in practice. As a system, it is usually inefficient—at times virtually chaotic—and able to bring forth the worst, as well as the best, characteristics of the human race. It can play upon fears and misconceptions; exploit ethnic, racial, and religious differences; sanctify popular prejudices; and justify denials of justice to minorities. Governments that arrive to power through a democratic process do not necessarily govern democratically.

But if all these dangers exist, the other part of Churchill's quote is also true. Democracy is based upon the assumption that all power should be limited—limited by time, limited by countervailing power, limited by the rule of law. Democracy, as James Madison observed in the *Tenth Federalist*, is designed to promote majority rule with respect for minority rights. It is a system where those who lose today's struggle for power are supposed to be guaranteed another chance tomorrow, and those who exercise power will be held accountable for their actions. Perhaps its greatest strength, at least in theory, is its ability to learn from and rectify mistakes, to adapt to changing conditions.

This volume is designed to build on Churchill's dictum, to examine the progress towards, but also the shortcomings of and dangers to, democratic rule in Latin America. While it generally assumes that progress towards more democratic institutions is desirable, it also accepts that such progress will vary in many ways from society to society, that one size does not fit all. Rather than attempting to impose a single definition and promote a single model, the authors hope to stimulate discussion as to its nature, applicability, strengths, and weaknesses in varied circumstances. In his 1982 volume, *Democracy in Latin America*, Hoover Institute scholar Robert G. Wesson observed:

> In recent decades the contest between democratic and oligarchic tenden-cies has become more complex and has taken on new dimensions. The opposition to democracy has acquired more purpose and confidence and has come to seem more of a concerted tendency, less a mere expression of the hierarchic society or a response to the ineffectiveness of democratic structures.
>
> (Wesson 1982, vii)

In the twenty-first century, this situation has changed dramatically. Rela-tively freely elected governments have been installed everywhere except Cuba, and even there the departure of Fidel Castro from supreme power offers the possibility of a transition to a less authoritarian rule. Polls consistently show strong popular support virtually everywhere for democratic governments. The Organization of American States had adopted the "Democratic Char-ter" pledging member states to the support of democratic rule throughout the hemisphere. In most nations, the media and labor unions are able to operate relatively freely, if not always with adequate personal security. Mili-tary coups seem largely a thing of the past, though events in Honduras raise troubling questions about military collusion with disaffected civilian sectors. Elections are usually monitored by both national and international observers, and despite some controversy, notably in Mexico and Venezuela, the voting process is widely seen as fair and impartial. If not exactly flourishing, electoral democracy seems at least to be in the process of establishing itself as the domi-nant political system in the hemisphere.

However, serious problems remain. As Larry Diamond, co-editor of *The Journal of Democracy*, reminds us, "If democracies do not more effectively contain crime and corruption, generate economic growth, relieve economic inequality, and secure freedom and the rule of law, people will eventually lose faith and turn to authoritarian alternatives" (Diamond 2008, 37).[1] All of these factors are present in today's Latin America. Judicial systems are often weak and/or corrupt, and citizen security has deteriorated in many nations. Incumbent presidents alter and manipulate constitutions to permit their own reelection. Corruption continues to be a serious issue despite the growing transparency of the political process. While security forces have lost most of their political power, their place at times seems to have been taken by organized criminal groups, and military coups at times have been replaced by coups led by angry urban mobs. Latin America's theoretically independent election authorities are increasingly subject to manipulation by governments in power attempting to constrain or eliminate political rivals, manipulate the electoral registry, and inhibit external observations of the electoral process.

Notable progress has been made in incorporating long-neglected and/or exploited groups, notably indigenous peoples and women, into the political process. Women currently hold the presidency in Argentina, Costa Rica, and Chile, while Bolivia has a president who can truly claim to be from that nation's indigenous majority. But these developments have been uneven. Especially in the case of indigenous peoples, access to political power has sometimes further fractured the political system, producing separatists pressures by both indigenous and nonindigenous peoples.

Also disturbing has been the failure of traditional political parties and leaders to exercise effective power once they take office. In many nations, polls indicate that political parties have the lowest or nearly the lowest popular support and credibility of any institution. The greatest threats to democracy often come from within rather than outside the system, from those who proclaim its virtues rather than those who advocate alternative forms of government. As Larry Diamond has observed:

> The problem in these states is that bad government is not an aberration or an illness to be cured. It is . . . a natural condition. For thousands of years, the natural tendency of elites everywhere has been to monopolize power rather than to restrain it—through the development of transparent laws, strong institutions, and market competition. And once they have succeeded in restricting political access, these elites use their consolidated power to limit economic competition so as to generate profits that benefit them rather than society at large. The result is a predatory state.
>
> (Diamond 2008, 43)

Reactions to this take many forms. Some long for a return to the authoritarian regimes of previous decades; others seek to accommodate varying degrees of populism within the democratic spectrum. There are efforts to modify traditional forms of representative government in order to incorporate traditionally excluded or marginalized elements of society. Others see such efforts as being all too easily manipulated by ambitious groups or individuals determined to promote their own agendas. The current situation in Bolivia, Nicaragua, and Venezuela, all of whose governments came to power through elections, exemplifies these issues and makes an examination of the nature and status of hemispheric democracy all the more important.

In summation, Latin American democracy has made significant, but uneven, progress. If the era of military regimes seems ended, other threats remain and, in some cases, seem to be gaining strength. Democracy's future will depend not just on the conditions within individual nations, but on the ability of the hemisphere as whole to effectively join together in its institutionalization. The United States, for good or for ill, will play a central, though diminished, role in this process, but so will global economic and political trends, increasingly beyond the control of any nation-state. The process will be protracted, the ultimate outcome still uncertain, but the result will be crucial in shaping the lives of everyone in the Americas for the rest of the twenty-first century.

Note

1 For a more complete presentation of Larry Diamond's views, *The Spirit of Democracy: The Struggle to Build Free Societies Throughout the World*, NY: Times Books, 2008.

References

Diamond, L. (2008) "The Democratic Rollback." *Foreign Affairs* 87(2) (March/April: 36–48).

James, R.R. (ed.) (1974) *Winston Churchill: His Complete Speeches, 1897–1963.* London: Chelsea House.

Wesson, R. (1982) *Democracy in Latin America: Promise and Problems.* New York: Praeger Publishers.

Section I

The State of Latin American Democracy

2   Democratic Consolidation
in Latin America?

Jennifer S. Holmes

During a time of economic crisis and adjustment, many Latin American countries transitioned from authoritarian regimes to democratic regimes in the 1980s. This was not the first experience with democracy in the region. Since their independence in the 1820s, many Latin American countries "were in the vanguard of international liberalism when they repudiated monarchism, aristocracy and slavery in the past [nineteenth] century, and at least in theory their governments have long rested on the principle of popular sovereignty" (Whitehead 1992, 147), although elections consisted of limited competition among elites. The reality was one of mostly oligarchic or co-optative democracies (Skidmore and Smith 1997, 62), which struggled with the negative colonial inheritances of "a hierarchical society based on class and race, and an economy featuring highly unequal distribution of land and wealth" (Handelman 1997, 26). The evolution of Latin American democracies is unique compared to other regions due to four factors: relatively stable borders, pacted democratization, poorly functioning and long-established market economies, and deep inequalities (Whitehead 1992, 157–58). During the twentieth century, Latin American regimes veered from experiments of expanding suffrage to periods of authoritarian rule. By the early 1980s, most of the authoritarian regimes were liberalizing and becoming more democratic. These "new" democracies continue to face fundamental challenges of creating stable and functional democracies, increasing participation, and providing economic opportunities for their citizens. After discussing the general trends of transitions to democracy and democratic consolidation in this chapter, the focus will change to assessing the broad performance and qualities of these new democracies.

The literature on democratic consolidation has been compared to a "terminological Babel" (Armony and Schamis 2005, 114). Existing attempts to assess national development and processes of democratization suffer from conceptual and measurement challenges. Most definitions of democracy focus on procedural aspects such as elections, without taking into account economic development or the capabilities of those institutions to expedite economic and political development of citizens.[1]

The literature on the definition of democracy is hotly contested. As Kathleen Schwartzman (1998, 161) states, "[T]he debate over the essence of democracy has in no way been resolved in the wave literature." In terms of conceptualization and measurement, there is a lengthy debate.[2] Most studies utilize a definition based upon procedural aspects of democracy and/or political liberties (Collier and Levitsky 1997; Munck and Verkuilen 2002; Bollen and Paxton 2000). This approach is heavily influenced by the work of Robert Dahl (1971) and his seven institutions of polyarchy: elected officials, free and fair elections, inclusive suffrage, the right to run for public office, freedom of expression, existence and availability of alternative information, and associational autonomy.

As Collier and Levitsky (1997) note, among the procedural definitions, the debate revolves around adjectives. They found hundreds of "subtypes" among the different definitions of democracy. Beyond a minimum of free elections, scholars disagree about what additional attributes should be included as part of the minimal standard for democracy (Collier and Levitsky 1997, 433; O'Donnell and Schmitter 1986; Di Palma 1990, 28; Huntington 1991, 9; Przeworski et al. 2000). A drawback of minimalist positions is that they may include authoritarian regimes if they have elections, even if the regimes are not free (Mainwaring, Brinks, and Pérez-Liñán 2001, 41–2). Because of concern over including authoritarian or semi-authoritarian regimes when using a minimalist definition, some advocate including other aspects of procedural democracy, such as civil liberties or an expanded notion of accountability. Without these basic protections, elections can be easily subverted (Mainwaring, Brinks, and Pérez-Liñán, 2001, 43). Scholars such as Mainwaring, Brinks, and Pérez-Liñán (2001); Bollen and Paxton (2000); Diamond (1999); and O'Donnell and Schmitter (1986) utilize this style of concept. For example, in the influential work *Transitions from Authoritarian Rule*, O'Donnell and Schmitter focus on a definition of democracy that builds upon a procedural minimum, including free and fair elections, universal suffrage, and political and civil liberties to define democracy (O'Donnell and Schmitter 1986, 8).

The inclusion of other attributes leads to a further differentiation of the concept, such as concepts of hybrid regimes, electoral democracy, semi-democracy, semi-authoritarianism, etc. (Karl 1995; Diamond 2002; Schedler 2002). According to Frances Hagopian, "[A]s studies of the state evolve beyond being primarily concerned about capacity (a concern of the 1960s) and efficiency (the concern of the 1990s), they should consider whether the state itself is democratic" (Hagopian 2000, 904). Karl (1995) includes aspects such as insufficient control over the military, deficiencies in the rule of law, extensive disenfranchisement, and ineffective checks and balances incorporated into the differentiation of regimes. Scholars such as Schmitter and Karl (1991) and O'Donnell (1996) argue for inclusion of elements of horizontal accountability.

Although the advantages and disadvantages of a minimalist, subminimalist, liberal, and electoral democracy are discussed, rarely does the debate progress to a discussion of deepening the concept beyond proceduralism to incorporate social or economic aspects. In fact, most scholars separate political democracy from social or economic concerns. As Kenneth Bollen states, the "distribution of wealth, work place 'democracy', or the health of the population are not part of the concept. These are important in their own right and should not be confounded with national levels of political democracy" (Bollen 1990, 12–13). Similarly, Schmitter and Karl (1991) separate issue of equity or "social democracy" from their analysis of democracy. As Michael Coppedge warns, "One should not go further into the territory of social and economic democracy and collective citizenship rights, which in my opinion would cross the line into maximalism" (Coppedge 2002, 37). Munck and Verkuilen (2002, 9) similarly warn against maximalist concepts, which can be "so overburdened as to be of little analytical use." Alvarez, Cheibub, Limongi, and Przeworski (1996, 20) wish to "examine empirically, rather than decide by definition" relationships among different attributes of democracy. Many scholars, both within and outside of the traditions of modernization theory or political development, have focused on the possible interrelations among the different aspects or measures of democracy and economic development.[3] In these cases, a minimalist definition would be appropriate.

Alternatives to Minimalism

In general, development concerns are omitted within procedural definitions of democracy. Democracy may become only a set of rules without a corresponding emphasis on quality. Theoretically, Huber, Rueschemeyer, and Stepens (1997) partially address this limitation by introducing participatory and social dimensions to their formal model of democracy. Other scholars, such as Foweraker and Krznaric (2002, 2003) find significant differences among the performance of both established democracies and third-wave democracies, especially in areas of civil and minority rights. Specifically, in the cases of Brazil, Colombia, and Guatemala, "advances made in political rights and parliamentary representation have not been matched by improvements in the record of civil and minority rights" (2002, 37). An alternative is to develop democratic indices to serve as a self-assessment tool for the quality of democracy in a particular country. For example, Boyle, Weir, Beetham, and Klug (1993) developed a self-assessment for the United Kingdom. They built their assessment around two principles: popular control and political equality. They examine four dimensions through a thirty-question survey. The four dimensions are free and fair elections, a democratic society, civil and political rights, and open and accountable government. In addition to problems of creating an equivalent survey in a cross-national study, they acknowledge difficulties in applying this to developing nations and new democracies because it would not necessarily take into account any "stage-like character of democracy's development" (Beetham 1999, 169). As Moore (1966) demonstrated, there may be different paths to democracy.

Many scholars reject incorporating normative aspects into their concepts. For example, Samuel Huntington states, "Fuzzy norms do not yield useful analysis" (Huntington 1991, 9). In a similar vein, Giuseppe Di Palma has stated that the democratic ideal should be separate "from the idea of social progress" if it is to survive (Di Palma 1990, 23). Although much of the field tries to eschew any normative dimensions in analysis, some prominent scholars, such as Robert Keohane, have recognized a duty for political scientists to ask these types of questions. "We need to reflect on what we, as political scientists, know that could help actors in global society design and maintain institutions that would make possible the good life in our descendants. . . . What normative standards should institutions meet, and what categories should we use to evaluate institutions according to those standards?" (Keohane 2001, 1).

Indeed, a focus on procedure alone may quickly produce skeptics among citizens. For example, the increasing disillusionment with democracy, thinly understood, is a growing problem in Latin America (Latinobarometro 2002). Democracy involves much more than just regular, free elections. The incorporation of economic progress, inclusion, and distributional issues are essential to move democracy beyond procedure and development beyond growth. Whereas many scholars exclude "measures of any system of government (e.g. national security, social welfare, protection of the environment, even legitimacy and system support) in favour of values that are intrinsic to liberal democratic government" (Foweraker and Krznaric 2003, 314), citizens seem to include these system-wide assessments when they evaluate their democracies. The reality is that there is a historical precedent for nondemocratic regimes. Other democratic waves have been followed by reverse waves.

Twentieth-century attempts at democracy faced additional strain from foreign interventions, ranging from direct to covert. However, after the Cold War, the international environment became more supportive of Latin American democracies and citizens had embraced (or in some cases at least reluctantly accepted) the new democratic era. Table 2.1 presents one classification of Latin American regimes to provide an overview of the instability characteristic of this time period.

Mainwaring, Brinks, and Pérez-Liñán (2001, 2007) provide a trichotomous classification of Latin American regimes, including the novel category of semi-democratic, which provides greater insight into the gradations of democracy. Although other categorizations of regimes are available, this demonstrates the general pattern of democratization and breakdown. Today, the trend toward democracy appears strong, although the threat of reversion remains. The risk of a return to authoritarianism is real, especially as many citizens become frustrated with the slow pace of improvement. Although democracies have not fallen, many have been shaken. Peru suffered a "self-coup" in 1992, Peruvian president Fujimori fled to Japan in 2000, three Ecuadorian presidents and two Bolivian presidents were forced to resign due to popular pressure since 1997, and Venezuela suffered a coup attempt in 2002. In addition, starting with the resignation of Argentine President de la Rua on December 20, 2001, Argentina experienced a succession of interim presidents and presidential resignations over two weeks, until Caretaker

Table 2.1 Classification of Latin American Political Regimes 1900–2007

Country	Democratic	Semi-democratic	Authoritarian
Argentina	1916–29, 1973–74, 1983–99, 1983–2007	1912–15,1946–50, 1958–61, 1963–65, 1975,	1900–11, 1930–45, 1951–57, 1962, 1966–72, 1976–82
Bolivia	1982–2007	1956–63, 1979	1900–1955, 1964–1978, 1980–81,
Brazil	1946–53, 1956–63, 1985–2007	1954–55	1900–45, 1964–84
Chile	1932–72, 1990–2007	1900–23, 1925–26,	1924, 1927–31, 1973–89
Colombia	1974–89	1910–48, 1958–73, 1990–2007	1900–09,1949–57
Costa Rica	1928–47, 1953–2007	1902–05, 1910–16, 1949–52,	1900–01, 1906–09, 1917–19, 1948
Cuba		1940–51	1900–39, 1952–2007
Dominican Republic	1978–93, 1996–2007	1924–27, 1994–95	1900–23, 1928–77
Ecuador	1948–60, 1979–99, 2001–03	1934, 1944–45, 1961–62, 1968–69, 2000, 2004–07	1900–33, 1935–43, 1946–47, 1963–67, 1970–78
El Salvador	1994–2007	1984–93	1900–83
Guatemala	2000–01	1926–30, 1945–53, 1986–99, 2002–07	1900–25, 1931–44, 1954–85
Haiti	2006–07	1995–98	1900–94, 1999–2005
Honduras	1999–2007	1929–34, 1949–54, 1957–62, 1971, 1982–98	1900–28, 1945–56, 1935–56, 1963–70, 1972–81
Mexico	2000–07	1911–12, 1988–99	1900–10, 1913–87, 1945–87
Nicaragua	1996–2007	1929–35, 1984–95	1900–28, 1936–83, 1945–83
Panama	1956–63, 1994–2007	1904–15, 1918–27, 1932–47, 1964–67, 1990–93	1916–17, 1928–31, 1948–55, 1968–89
Paraguay		1989–2007	1900–88
Peru	1963–67, 1980–82, 1985–87	1912–13, 1915–18, 1939–47, 1956–61, 1983–84, 1988–91, 1995–2007	1900–11, 1914, 1919–38, 1948–55, 1962, 1968–79, 1992–94
Uruguay	1915–30, 1942–72, 1985–2007	1904–14, 1931–32, 1938–41,	1900–03, 1933–37, 1973–84
Venezuela, RB	1947, 1958–99, 2000–01	1946, 1999, 2002–07	1900–1945, 1948–57

Source: Mainwaring, Brinks, and Pérez-Liñán, 2007.

President Duhalde managed to remain in power until elections in April 2003. In January 2009, Honduran President Manuel Zelaya was removed from office and was voted out of office by the Honduran congress. Many scholars do not want to overburden procedural democracy with heightened expectations of improvements in stubborn social and economic challenges. However, some of the issues of regime stability are relevant to whether or not democracies survive.

Despite the current international environment being more favorable to democracy, as Whitehead (1992, 148) points out, many of the Latin American democracies were viewed internally as "second best outcomes" and are in effect "democracy by default." As Mainwaring (2006, 13) points out, there is growing discontent among both elites and the popular sectors with democracy, its leaders, and its institutions in the region. The goal of this chapter is to present a balanced set of measures that evaluates democracies according to more than just procedural aspects, incorporates development aspects, and moves beyond typologies and toward assessment, without defining democratic development as the advanced industrial democracy status quo. There are both theoretical and practical reasons for doing so. Theoretically, assessment implies goals and aims. Practically, a measure that moves beyond procedure is more compatible with citizen expectations.

Holmes and Piñeres (2006) developed a comprehensive concept of democratic development based upon four categories (democratic inclusiveness, democratic health, human capital, and economic and political security). This comprehensive measure of democratic performance is designed to assess the strength and resilience of democracies. The concept is oriented toward evaluation. Most concepts of democratic consolidation and development do not include this evaluative or scorecard approach. As Sartori stresses, "[W]hat makes democracy *possible* should not be mixed up with what makes democracy more *democratic*" (Sartori 1987, 156). However, in terms of understanding citizen satisfaction, democratic stability, and the like, a deeper and broader concept is necessary. This approach to democratic development also includes measures that do not uniquely belong to democracies. Instead, factors that contribute to regime stability are included. The present work considers development to be inclusive of both political and economic progress. Economic progress is not captured by measuring gross domestic product or growth rates alone, but needs to address issues of inclusiveness and breadth of economic growth.

Human Capital

To assess development of the citizen, illiteracy, educational attainment, and government investment in education are examined, in addition to differential mortality rates. These indicators are shown in Table 2.2

Literacy is measured by the rates of literacy of people over the age of fifteen. Sizeable proportions of illiterate citizens exist in Bolivia, Guatemala, El

Table 2.2 Human Capital

	Public spending on education (percent of GDP)	Literacy rate (percent of people 15≤)	Persistence to grade 5 (percent of cohort)	Mortality rates of children under five (per 1,000 live births)	Differential mortality rates of children under five	Tertiary school enrollment (percent of gross)
Argentina	6.26	97.9	94.9	14.2		78.6
Bolivia	6.89	..	89.4	41.4	73	..
Brazil	5.8	90.4	..	14.4	66	..
Chile	4.5	..	98.1	9.1		70.5
Colombia	4.4	93.6	87.4	17.6	23	42.7
Costa Rica	..	96.3	91.0	9.9		44.5
Dominican Republic	2.2	90.1	83.6	27.1	63	..
Ecuador	4.5	91.6	91.7	23.3		..
El Salvador	3.4	84.5	87.0	15.9		25.5
Guatemala	2.9	75.9	75.3	32.0	39	..
Honduras	..	85.1	75.0	22.9		20.4
Mexico	5.2	93.5	96.5	16.2		27.7
Nicaragua	4.6	..	..	24.4	45	..
Panama	3.5	94.1	92.1	18.5		41.8
Paraguay	4.8	93.9	83.8	22.0	37	51.0
Peru	2.5	..	85.1	18.2	52	42.6
Uruguay	4.5	98.1	..	7.2		63.2
Venezuela	..	..	96.0	15.3		..
Year of data	2010–11	2011	2010	2012	various	2010–11

Source: World Bank, Difference in Child Mortality Rate: HDR 2006, Table 8.

Salvador, Peru, and Nicaragua. Countries such as Uruguay and Argentina, which have long, successful experiences with broad education, do well, with illiteracy rates less than 3 percent. Lower levels of educational attainment are captured by looking at percent of kids who started and completed fifth grade. High levels of educational attainment are reflected by tertiary school enrollment. Here, countries such as Argentina and Bolivia show success, whereas others like Costa Rica lag in this area. Public spending as the percent of GDP reflects strong government commitment to education in Bolivia and a relatively low level in Peru and the Dominican Republic. Children's mortality rates vary dramatically in the region, from a low of 7.2 per 1,000 in Uruguay up to more than 41 in Bolivia. Finally, the difference of the under-five mortality rate (per 1,000 live births) between the richest 20 percent and the poorest 20 percent of the population assesses whether there is a significant difference in one of the most fundamental measures of human development. Although many countries do not report this statistic, alarming gaps are evident in Bolivia and Haiti, compared to Colombia.

Democratic Health

This cluster of indicators, presented in Table 2.3, includes measures of popular support and regime characteristics. Popular support for democracy is also important. Latinobarometro asks questions varying from support for and satisfaction with democracy. Support for democracy is greater than 70 percent among Argentineans, Uruguayans, and Venezuelans, whereas only less than half of Mexicans, Hondurans, Salvadorans, Guatemalans, and Panamanians reported support for democracy. Interestingly, satisfaction with democracy is overall lower. The most satisfied citizens are in Uruguay (82 percent) and the least satisfied are in Honduras (18 percent) and Mexico (21 percent).

Corruption can be measured by Transparency International's Corruption Perception Index. Freedom House provides indices of political liberties and civil rights. Although there is a great deal of debate about the advantages and disadvantages of using these indicators, the Corruption Perception Index (Seligson 2002; Lancaster and Montinola 2001; Svensson 2005) and the Freedom House

Table 2.3 Democratic Health

	Support for democracy	Satisfaction with democracy	Corruption perception index score	Political rights and civil liberties
Argentina	73	51	34	2, 2
Bolivia	61	38	34	3, 3
Brazil	49	26	42	2, 2
Chile	63	38	71	1, 1
Colombia	52	28	36	3, 4
Costa Rica	53	35	53	1, 1
Dominican Republic	60	45	29	2, 3
Ecuador	62	59	35	3, 3
El Salvador	49	36	38	2, 3
Guatemala	41	29	29	3, 4
Honduras	44	18	26	4, 4
Mexico	37	21	34	3, 3
Nicaragua	50	52	28	4, 3
Panama	49	44	35	2, 2
Paraguay	50	25	24	3, 3
Peru	56	25	38	2, 3
Uruguay	71	82	73	1, 1
Venezuela	87	42	20	5, 5
Year of data	2013	2013	2013	2013

Sources: Support for Democracy and Satisfaction with Democracy (Latinobarometro) With which of "the following statements do you agree most? Democracy is preferable to any other kind of government/Under some circumstances, an authoritarian government can be preferable to a democratic one/For people like me, it doesn't matter whether we have a democratic or a non-democratic regime. "Answer shown "Democracy is preferable to any other kind of government." Satisfaction with Democracy: "In general, would you say you are very satisfied, fairly satisfied, not very satisfied or not satisfied at all with the way democracy works in (country)?" Answer shown "Very satisfied" plus "fairly satisfied," Corruption index (Transparency International), Political rights and civil liberties (Freedom House)

measures (Scoble and Wiseberg 1981; Banks 1986; Gastil 1990; McHenry 2000) are arguably the best available indicators for evaluating recent trends in corruption and liberties. High scores in the corruption index reflect low levels of perceived corruption. For example, Chile and Uruguay have the least level of corruption in the region, compared to Paraguay and Venezuela, which have the worst corruption. Freedom House measures both political rights (consisting of electoral process, political pluralism and participation, and functioning of government) and civil liberties (consisting of freedom of expression and belief, associational and organizational rights, rule of law, and personal autonomy and individual rights). The lower the score, the more free the country. Chile, Costa Rica, and Uruguay received scores of 1, whereas Honduras received weaker scores of 4 and Venezuela 5, reflecting concerns of Freedom House.

Democratic Inclusiveness

The depth and breadth of participation is also important to democracies. To what extent have women and racial and ethnic minorities been included positions of authority in civil society, civil service, and government? What legal and extra-legal barriers to participation exist? Two widely available measures are available for the region and are presented in Table 2.4. First, the Gender Inequality Index provides an indicator of the "loss of achievement due to gender inequality in three dimensions: reproductive health, empowerment and labour market participation" (HDR 2013, 31). A high value reflects a greater loss of achievement and higher discrimination in areas of employment, health and education. The Latin American country with the best score is Costa Rica and the worst is Haiti, followed by Guatemala. In general, more economically developed countries have a lower index. Comparisons among countries of roughly equivalent levels of economic development are telling. For example, among the wealthiest Latin American countries, Argentina (15,347), Chile (14,987), and Uruguay (13,333), Costa Rica has a significantly better score than all of them, despite their higher GDP per capital (10,863).

Instead of examining differences by gender, the Minorities at Risk project provides readily available measures of access to power of minority groups, political discrimination, and political restrictions. The Political Discrimination Index, based on the years 1950–2003, provides a general coding of public and social policies in erasing or promoting political inequalities. It is based on a scale of 0–4, with 0 being no discrimination and 4 being exclusionary with repressive policies. Low levels of discrimination are found in Bolivia, Costa Rica, and Paraguay. Discrimination is also found in the Dominican Republic (directed toward Haitian immigrants and their descendants).

Economic and Political Security

Security should be measured in both economic and political terms. Table 2.5 presents the indicators. Economically different aspects, including growth rates, distribution, and levels, should be used. To address concerns about

Table 2.4 Democratic Inclusiveness

	Gender Inequality Index (GII)	Group	Political discrimination
Argentina	0.380	Indigenous peoples	2
Bolivia	0.474	Indigenous highland & indigenous lowland	1
Brazil	0.447	Afro-Brazilians	3
Chile	0.360	Indigenous peoples	2
Colombia	0.459	Afro-Americans	2
Costa Rica	0.346	Indigenous peoples	1
Dominican Republic	0.508	Antillean blacks	1
Ecuador	0.442	Afro-Americans	4
El Salvador	0.441	Indigenous highland peoples, indigenous lowland peoples & Afro-Americans	3
Guatemala	0.539		
Haiti	0.592	Indigenous peoples (Mayans)	3
Honduras	0.483	Indigenous peoples & Black Karibs	3
Mexico	0.382	Mayans, Zapotecs, and other indigenous peoples	3
Nicaragua	0.461	Indigenous peoples	2
Panama	0.503	Afro-Caribbean & Chinese	3
Paraguay	0.472	Indigenous peoples	1
Peru	0.387	Indigenous peoples	1
Uruguay	0.367	Indigenous highland peoples, indigenous lowland people	2
Venezuela	0.446	Afro-Americans	3
Latin America & the Caribbean	0.419	Afro-Americans	3
Very high human development	0.193	Indigenous peoples	1
Year of data	2012	2003	

Source: 2013 United Nations Human Development Report, Table 4, Political Discrimination (Minorities at Risk).

comparability across countries, purchasing power parity (PPP) was developed. PPP uses the United States as the basis to figure the cost of an equivalent consumer basket of goods in each country. For example, on average, Chileans have twice the purchasing power of Ecuadorans, who have more than twice the purchasing power of Hondurans and almost three times that of the average Nicaraguan. Countries with the highest gross domestic product (GDP) per capita growth rate include Panama, Peru, and Chile. Colombian and Mexican growth no doubt has lagged due to the persistent internal conflict. El Salvador, Guatemala, and Honduras have had weak growth, while Paraguay

Table 2.5 Economic and Political Security

	GDP per capita growth	GNI per capita, PPP (Constant 2005 international)	Unemployment rate (percent)	FDI net inflows (percent of GDP)	GINI index	Percent children 5< underweight (moderate and severe)	Political stability & absence of violence/ terrorism (score & percentile rank)
Argentina	3.5	15,347	7.2	2.6	44.5	2.3	0.07 (48)
Bolivia	0.0	4,444	3.2	3.9	56.3	4.3	−0.50 (30)
Brazil	4.6	10,152	6.9	3.4	54.7	1.7	0.07 (48)
Chile	2.8	14,987	6.4	11.2	52.1	..	0.35 (59)
Colombia	3.6	8,711	10.4	4.2	55.9	3.4	−1.40 (8)
Costa Rica	2.6	10,863	7.6	5.8	50.7	1.1	0.63 (67)
Dominican Republic	3.5	8,506	13.0	6.5	47.2	7.1	0.23 (55)
Ecuador	1.3	7,471	4.5	0.7	49.3	6.2	−0.60 (27)
El Salvador	0.4	5,915	6.9	2.0	48.3	5.5	0.21 (54)
Guatemala	1.4	4,235	4.2	2.3	55.9	13.0	−0.65 (25)
Haiti	1.8	1,070	7.0	2.3	59.2	17.7	−0.79 (21)
Honduras	2.5	3,426	4.8	5.8	57.0	8.1	−0.40 (35)
Mexico	3.7	12,947	4.9	1.3	48.3	3.4	−0.67 (24)
Nicaragua	8.9	2,551	7.7	7.7	40.5	5.5	−0.37 (36)
Panama	−2.9	13,519	4.5	9.3	51.9	3.9	−0.15 (40)
Paraguay	5.0	4,497	6.3	1.4	52.4	3.4	−0.84 (20)
Peru	3.6	9,306	4.0	6.0	48.1	4.2	−0.86 (20)
Uruguay	4.0	13,333	6.0	5.8	45.3	5.4	0.71 (69)
Venezuela		11,475	7.8	0.6	44.8	3.7	−0.99 (18)
Year of data	2012	2012	2012	2012	2000–2010	2006–2010	2012

Sources: Percent children underweight HDR 2013, Table 7; GINI: HDR 2013, Table 3; GNI per capita HDR 2013; Table 1, unemployment World Development Indicators. World Bank Governance Indicators.

actually had negative per capita growth during this time period. In addition, unemployment rates can be useful to assess the participation in the economy. Reported unemployment is high in countries such as the Dominican Republic and Colombia, and relatively low in Bolivia and Peru. However, since unemployment does not address those outside of the formal sector or structurally unemployed, it is useful to examine other aspects. The percentage of children who are underweight provides a fundamental view to the economic security of children, among the most vulnerable citizens. High rates of child malnourishment are reported in Guatemala (which has a low unemployment rate) and Honduras, while they are very low in Costa Rica and surprisingly high in Uruguay. Inequality should also be examined. The Gini index shows high levels of inequality in Bolivia, Guatemala, Haiti, Honduras, and Colombia, while countries such as Argentina, Nicaragua, and Venezuela have relatively low rates of inequality. Sustainability of growth can also depend on foreign direct investment (FDI). High levels of FDI flows are seen in Chile and Peru, whereas Venezuela and Ecuador have low levels of FDI due to their populist economic policies, portending poor future economic growth.

Finally, a lack of security undermines economic performance and development, thus civil strife and violence need to be examined. High levels of conflict exist, especially in Colombia, followed by relatively high levels of conflict in Venezuela, Peru, and Paraguay. Although difficult to measure cross-nationally, this indicator takes into account different types of internal conflict, ranging from terrorist threats to armed conflict to violent demonstrations to ethnic tensions. Old land conflicts remain divisive, such as in Colombia and Guatemala; police continue to be charged with egregious human rights violations, such as in Brazil; and guerrillas remain active, for example, in Peru and Colombia. Although some scholars may object to an indicator of conflict in a measure of democracy, there are some precedents for this. For example, Mainwaring, Brinks, and Pérez-Liñán (2007) downgrade democracies to semi-democratic if there are parts of the country under an "authoritarian subnational regimes" like when nonstate violent groups control parts of the country.

Conclusion

If we think about consolidation by asking Giuseppe Di Palma's question "At what point . . . can democrats relax?" (Di Palma 1990, 141), it is clear after a broad examination of democratic development that the answer is it is best not to relax. Even the most economically developed and politically stable country, Chile, could improve its performance, especially in regard to it GII (Gender Inequality Index) score. In addition, it has lingering issues with the Mapuche, as reflected in their political discrimination score of 2. Interestingly, Chileans also have mediocre levels of satisfaction with democracy and support for democracy, compared to the rest of the region. Moreover, almost 40 percent of Chileans do not view democracy as necessary for development. Political stability seems deeper in Uruguay. However, its GDP growth per capita was anemic, although FDI inflows and the second-best corruption index score portend stronger economic growth in the future. Some of the most challenged nations include some of the poorest, including Nicaragua, Bolivia, and Ecuador. However, even among the poorest countries, there are signs for optimism, including strong commitment to education in Bolivia. Both Venezuela and Argentina may be sliding into populism. These two wealthy countries have relatively high unemployment rates, potential or increasing instability, and poor corruption scores. Interestingly, citizens in these two countries report some of the highest support for and belief in democracy, reminding observers of a resilience of democracy. This broad view into democratic development identifies both sources of stability and strain within Latin American democracies. One of Juan Linz's key insights into the study of democratic stability is the importance of leadership. Linz asked, "[W]hat causes a regime to move beyond its functional range to become a disrupted or semicoercive regime that ends in repudiation by large or critical segments of the population?" (Linz 1978, 10). He argued against deterministic analysis, instead pointing out that despite opportunities and constraints created by the economic and political situations, leaders still have room for meaningful and often crucial actions. Although few Latin Americans wish to return to an era of harsh dictatorships (*dictaduras*), as the lessons learned from the past experiences become less salient in light of contemporary difficulties or stubborn challenges, it is best not to become complacent about the durability of Latin American democracies. As noted by others in this volume, the promises of progress often are accompanied by undemocratic practices.

Notes

1 There is a large literature that focuses on the relationship between regime type and economic growth. This is an important literature that requires a "thin" definition of democracy devoid of economic development or other factors so that these causal questions can be probed. However, this is not the analytical focus of this work.
2 There are difficulties due to the lack of conceptual underpinnings, teleological assumptions based on the achievement of advanced industrial nations, issues of multidimensionality vs. unidimensionality, and issues of a binary vs. continuous concept (Bollen & Paxton 2000, Waylen 1994, Bollen and Jackman 1985, Sartori 1987, Dahl 1989, Collier and Adcock 1999). Clearly, there is a long history of controversy concerning the measurement of liberal democracy (May 1973, Inkeles 1991, Bollen and Paxton 2000).
3 This theme has a long tradition in the nineteenth century (see Lipset 1992, 2) and in the twentieth century, including the works of Schumpeter (1950), Moore (1966), Skocpol (1979), Berger (1986, 1992), and Stephens (1993). In this tradition, the emergence of democracy is in part a result of a transition to a market economy. More recently, scholars have conducted statistical analyses to examine the precise relationships between them (*Przeworski et al 1995; Helliwell 1994;* Barro 1996; Arat 1988; Londregan and Poole 1996; Przeworski and Limongi 1997). Other work has focused on the relationship between socioeconomic variables and human rights or freedom (for example, *Chalmers 1990;* Huntington 1991; Lipset et al 1993; Inkeles 1991; *Bollen and Jackman 1985;* and Cutright 1963).

20   *Jennifer S. Holmes*

References

Alvarez, M., Cheibub, J.A., Limongi, F., and Przeworski, A. (1996) "Classifying Political Regimes." *Studies in Comparative International Development* 31(2): 3–36.

Alvarez, M., Cheibub, J.A., Limongi, F., and Przeworski, A. (1996) "What Makes Democracies Endure?" *Journal of Democracy* 7(1): 39–55.

Arat, Z. (1988) "Democracy and Economic Development: Modernization Theory Revisited." *Comparative Politics* 21(1): 21–36.

Armony, A.C. and Schamis, H.E. (2005) "Babel in Democratization Studies." *Journal of Democracy* 16(4):113–28.

Banks, D. (1986) "The Analysis of Human Rights Data Over Time." *Human Rights Quarterly* 8: 654–80.

Barro, R. (1996) *Getting It Right: Markets and Choices in a Free Society.* Cambridge, MA: MIT Press.

Beetham, D. (1999) *Democracy and Human Rights.* Cambridge, MA: Polity Press.

Berger, P. (1986) *The Capitalist Revolution.* New York: Basic Books.

Berger, P. (1992) "The Uncertain Triumph of Democratic Capitalism." *Journal of Democracy* 3(3):7–17.

Bollen, K. (1990) "Political Democracy: Conceptual and Measurement Traps." *Studies in Comparative International Development* 25(1): 7–24.

Bollen, K. and Jackman, R. (1985) "Political Democracy and the Size Distribution of Income." *American Sociological Review* 50: 438–57.

Bollen, K. and Paxton, P. (2000) "Subjective Measures of Liberal Democracy." *Comparative Political Studies* 33:58–86.

Boyle, K., Weir, S., Beetham, D., and Klug, F. (1993) "Democracy: Key Principles and Indices." Paper presented at the European Consortium of Political Research Joint Sessions Workshop, Leiden, Netherlands, April 1993.

Chalmers, D. (1990) *Dilemmas of Latin American Democratization: Dealing with International Forces.* New York: Columbia University.

Collier, D. and Adcock, R. (1999) "Democracy and Dichotomies: A Pragmatic Approach to Choices about Concepts." *Annual Review of Political Science* 2: 537–65.

Collier, D. and Levitsky, S. (1997) "Democracy with Adjectives: Conceptual Innovation in Comparative Research." *World Politics* 49(3): 430–51.

Coppedge, M. (2002) "Democracy and Dimensions: Comments on Munck and Verkuilen." In the Symposium on G. Munck and J. Verkuilen (2002) "Conceptualizing and Measuring Democracy: Evaluating Alternative Indices." *Comparative Political Studies* 35(1) 35–9.

Cutright, P. (1963) "National Political Development: Measurement and Analysis." *American Political Science Review* 28: 253–64.

Dahl, R. (1971) *Polyarchy: Participation and Opposition.* New Haven: Yale University Press.

Dahl, R. (1989) *Democracy and Its Critics,* New Haven: Yale University Press.

Di Palma, G. (1990) *To Craft Democracies: An Essay on Democratic Transitions.* Berkeley: University of California Press.

Diamond, L. (1999) *Developing Democracy: Toward Consolidation.* Baltimore: Johns Hopkins University Press.

Diamond, L. (2002) "Elections Without Democracy: Thinking About Hybrid Regimes." *Journal of Democracy* 13: 21–35.

Foweraker, J. and Krznaric, R. (2002) "The Uneven Performance of the Democracies of the 3rd Wave: Electoral Politics and the Imperfect Rule of Law in Latin America." *Latin American Politics and Society* 44(3): 29–60.

Foweraker, J. and Krznaric R. (2003) "Differentiating the Democratic Performance of the West." *European Journal of Political Research* 42(3): 313–40.

Gastil, R.D. (1990) "The Comparative Survey of Freedom: Experiences and Suggestions." *Studies in Comparative International Development* 25: 25–30.

Hagopian, F. (2000) "Political Development, Revisited." *Comparative Political Studies* 33(6/7): 880–911.

Handelman, H. (1997) *Mexican Politics.* New York: St. Martin's Press.

Helliwell, J.F. (1994) "Empirical Linkages between Democracy and Economic Growth." *British Journal of Political Science* 24(2): 225–48.

Holmes, J.S. and Gutiérrez de Piñeres, S.A. (2006) "The Democratic Development Scorecard: A Balanced Method for Assessing National Development in Democracies." *International Journal of Social Economics* 33(1/2): 54–76.

Huber, E., Rueschemeyer, D. and Stepens, J.D. (1997) "The Paradoxes of Contemporary Democracy: Formal, Participatory, and Social Dimensions." *Comparative Politics* 29(3): 323–42.

Human Development Report. (2013) The Rise of the South: Human Progress in a Diverse World. United Nations Development Programme, NY:NY 2013.

Huntington, S. (1991) *The Third Wave: Democratization in the Late Twentieth Century.* Norman: University of Oklahoma Press.

Inkeles, A. (1991) *On Measuring Democracy.* New Brunswick: Transaction Publishers.

Karl, T.L. (1995) "The Hybrid Regimes of Central America." *Journal of Democracy* 6(3): 72–86.

Keohane, R.O. (2001) "Governance in a Partially Globalized World," Presidential Address, American Political Science Association 2000. *American Political Science Review* 95(1):1–13.

Lancaster, T.D. and Montinola, G.R. (2001) "Comparative Political Corruption: Issues of Operationalization and Measurement." *Studies in Comparative International Development* 36(3): 3–28.

Latinobarometro. (2013) Informe de Prensa. Retrieved from www.latinobarometro. Accessed January 12, 2014 http://www.latinobarometro.org/documentos/LATBD_INFORME_LB_2013.pdf

Linz, J. (1978) *The Breakdown of Democratic Regimes: Crisis, Breakdown and Re-equilibration.* Baltimore: Johns Hopkins.

Lipset, S.M. (1992) "Conditions of the Democratic Order and Social Change: A Comparative Discussion," in S.N. Eisenstadt (ed.) *Human Society: Democracy and Modernity.* New York: E.J. Brill.

Lipset, S.M., Seong, K-R., and Torres, J.C. (1993) "A Comparative Analysis of the Social Requisites of Democracy." *International Social Science Journal* 45: 155–75.

Londregan, L.B. and Poole, K.T. (1996) "Does High Income Promote Democracy?" *World Politics* 49:1–30.

Mainwaring, S. (2006) "The Crisis of Representation in the Andes." *Journal of Democracy* 17(3): 13–27.

Mainwaring, S., Brinks, D., and Pérez-Liñán, A. (2001) "Classifying Political Regimes in Latin America, 1945–1999." *Studies in Comparative International Development* 36(1): 37–65.

Mainwaring, S., Brinks, D., and Pérez-Liñán, A. (2007) "Classifying Political Regimes in Latin America, 1945–2004," in Gerardo Munck (ed.), *Regimes and Democracy in Latin America: Theories and Methods* (121–60). Oxford: Oxford University Press.

May, J. (1973) *Of the Conditions and Measures of Democracy.* Morristown, NJ: General Learning Press.

McHenry, D.E. (2000) "Quantitative Measures of Democracy in Africa: An Assessment." *Democratization* 7(2): 168–85.

Moore, B. (1966) *Social Origins of Dictatorship and Democracy.* Boston, MA: Beacon.

Munck, G.L. and Verkuilen, J. (2002) "Conceptualizing and Measuring Democracy: Evaluating Alternative Indices." *Comparative Political Studies* 35(1): 5–34.

O'Donnell, G. (1996) "Illusions about Consolidation." *Journal of Democracy* 7(2): 34–51.

O'Donnell, G. and Schmitter, P. (1986) *Transitions from Authoritarian Rule: Tentative Conclusions about Uncertain Transitions.* Baltimore: Johns Hopkins University Press.

Przeworski, A. et. al. (1995) *Sustainable Democracy.* Cambridge: Cambridge University Press.

Przeworski, A. et al. (2000) *Democracy and Development: Political Institutions and Material Well-Being in the World, 1950–1990.* Cambridge: Cambridge University Press.

Przeworski, A. and Limongi, F. (1997) "Modernization: Theories and Facts." *World Politics* 49:155–83.

Sartori, G. (1987) *The Theory of Democracy Revisited.* Chatham: Chatham House.

Schedler, A. (2002) "Elections without Democracy: The Menu of Manipulation." *Journal of Democracy* 13(2): 36–50.

Schmitter, P.C. and Karl, T.L. (1991) "Modes of Transition in Latin America, Southern and Eastern Europe." *International Social Science Journal* 128(2): 269–84.

Schumpater, J. (1950) *Capitalism, Socialism, and Democracy.* 3rd. edition. New York: Harper and Row.

Schwartzman, K. (1998) "Globalization and Democracy." *Annual Review of Sociology* 24: 159–81.

Scoble, H.M. and Wiseberg, L.S. (1981) "Problems of Comparative Research on Human Rights," in V.P. Nanda, J.R. Scarritt, and G.W. Shepard, Jr. (eds.) *Global Human Rights: Public Policies, Comparative Measures, and NGO Strategies.* Boulder: Westview.

Seligson, M.A. (2002) "The Impact of Corruption on Regime Legitimacy: A Comparative Study of Four Latin American Countries." *Journal of Politics* 64(2): 408–33.

Skidmore, T. and Smith, P. (1997) *Modern Latin America.* Oxford: Oxford University Press.

Skocpol, T. (1979) *States and Social Revolutions.* Cambridge: Cambridge University Press.

Stephens, J.D. (1993) "Capitalist Development and Democracy: Empirical Research on the Social Origins of Democracy," in D. Copp, J. Hampton, and J. Roemer (eds.) *The Idea of Democracy.* Cambridge: Cambridge University Press.

Svensson, J. (2005) "Eight Questions about Corruption." *Journal of Economic Perspectives* 19(3): 19–42.

United Nations. *Human Development Report Technical Note 1, 2007–2008* (355–61).

Waylen, G. (1994) "Women and Democratization: Conceptualizing Gender Relations in Transition Politics." *World Politics* 46: 327–54.

Whitehead, L. (1992) "The Alternatives to Liberal Democracy: A Latin American Perspective," in D. Held (ed.) "Prospects for Democracy," special edition of *Political Studies* 40: 146–59.

3 Measuring Democratic Political Culture in Latin America

Orlando J. Pérez

Introduction

This chapter seeks to analyze the connection between micro-level attitudes and regime stability in Latin America. The connection between political culture and democracy has been a concern of social scientists since Gabriel Almond and Sidney Verba's 1963 breakthrough book, *The Civic Culture*, identified a cluster of attitudes and values that, they argued, led to stable democracies (Almond and Verba 1963). Ronald Inglehart subsequently pioneered cross-national research that built on, and empirically tested, Almond and Verba's assertions. In his model, the prevalence of a few specific individual attitudes and values—overall life satisfaction, interpersonal trust, and a disdain for revolutionary change—strongly increased the likelihood that democracy would persist in any given country (Inglehart 1990). Other scholars such as Edward Muller and Mitchell Seligson argued that Inglehart had it backwards: democratic experience causes the development of civic culture—or at the very least, there is a reciprocal relationship (Muller and Seligson 1994). Parallel to this debate over civic culture, political scientists have also been arguing over the concept of "social capital." In Robert Putnam's 1993 study of regional governments in Italy, he found that what best explains the performance of democratic institutions is not socio-economic development, but rather "civic community": participation in public affairs, conditions of political equality, norms of trust and solidarity, and above all the existence of a vibrant civil society. Taken together, Putnam dubs these individual and collective civic attributes "social capital" (Putnam 1993). For some scholars, however, Latin America lacks the requisite pattern of beliefs to sustain democratic governance (Wiarda 2001).

The chapter will use national probability surveys to examine the pattern of beliefs and attitudes that shape the political culture of Latin Americans. The surveys were conducted by the Latin American Public Opinion Project (LAPOP) as part of the *Americas Barometer* in nations of North, Central, and South America. As nations in Latin America struggle with economic, social, and political problems that strain the public's support for democratic regimes and engender acquiescence—if not outright support—for authoritarian measures, two key questions should be answered: Do Latin Americans possess the requisite political culture to sustain democratic governance? And what factors shape the beliefs and attitudes of Latin American citizens toward democracy and the extant regimes?

The chapter will focus on five specific values: 1. General preference for and satisfaction with democracy; 2. The meaning of democracy for citizens in Latin America; 3. Support for the extant political system; 4. Political tolerance; and 5. Combining system support and political tolerance, the chapter examines attitudes supportive of "stable democracy."

Data

The data used in this study come from the *Americas Barometer* involving face-to-face[1] interviews conducted in nations of North, Central, and South America and the Caribbean between 2006 and 2012. The surveys were all carried out with uniform sample and questionnaire designs under the auspices of the LAPOP at Vanderbilt University. The samples were all national and stratified by region and substratified by urban/rural. For the purposes of our analysis, each national sample has been weighted equally to represent an N of 1500.[2] This unique series of surveys allow comparisons across Latin America and the United States and Canada. As such, it provides an important source of comparative analysis between the two mature and fully consolidated democracies in the region, the United States and Canada, and younger and more fragile democratic regimes.

Do Latin Americans Support Democracy?

Before studying the meaning of democracy, however, we should explore whether Latin Americans indeed prefer democracy as a general concept. It would hardly be worth exploring the "meaning" of democracy if substantial majorities did not support a democratic regime over its alternative. The LAPOP uses a question that asks respondents to what extent they believe democracy, despite its many flaws, is the best form of government.[3] This is commonly referred to as the "Churchillean" concept of democracy, derived from Winston Churchill's statement that "democracy is the worst form of government, except for all those other forms that have been tried from time to time" (Mishler and Rose 1999). Results are presented in Figure 3.1.[4]

Figure 3.1 shows data from 2012. Uruguay, Venezuela, and Argentina exhibit the highest levels of support. In these three countries, citizens average score on support for democracy is above 80 on the 0–100 index. Ironically, the three Latin American countries express higher support for democracy than Canada and the United States. In both Canada and the United States, we find a deterioration of support for democracy between 2006 and 2012, from an average of 87.3 and 91.3 to the results presented in Figure 3.1. Clearly, the global economic crisis had a significant effect on support for democracy in the more developed countries of the Americas, whereas support for democracy in the rest of Latin America remained stable or improved. Hondurans express the lowest support, with only an average of 52.6 on the 0 to 100 index supporting democracy as the best political system. Citizens in nations such as Bolivia, Nicaragua, Ecuador, Peru, and El Salvador, with younger, more fragile, and troubled democratic regimes,

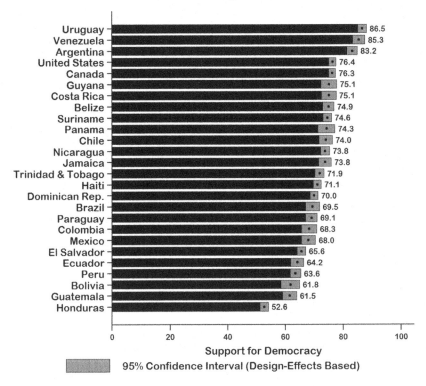

Figure 3.1 Support for Democracy

exhibit less support, although significant majorities even in these countries support the idea that democracy is the best form of government. The good news of these results is that they provide evidence that (1) the majority of citizens in the Americas support democracy, and (2) that despite the economic crisis of 2008–09, Latin Americans continue to express significant levels of support for the notion that democracy is the best possible system of government.

Venezuela presents an interesting case, where the average score on the index is quite high at 85.3 despite the institutional and political changes underway in their country.[5] On the one hand, many Venezuelans supportive of the current government may indeed believe that it is implementing a transformation toward "participatory democracy." On the other hand, opponents of the Chávez regime may express support for "democracy" in contradistinction to the regime's ideals. Together, the two groups would form a wide majority of the Venezuelan population.

Next we can observe that while preference for a democratic regime is widespread, satisfaction with how democracy works is not.[6] Figure 3.2 shows ten countries in the survey below the 50 point mark. The highest satisfaction is found in Uruguay and Costa Rica, and the lowest level is found in Haiti. We find significant gaps between the results presented in Figure 3.1 and those in Figure 3.2.

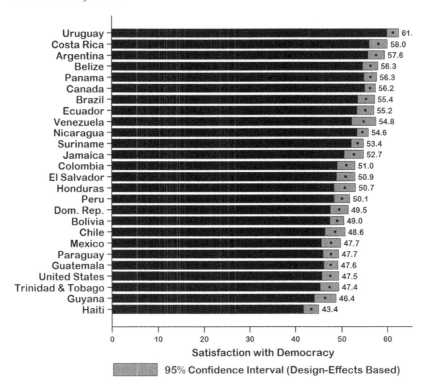

Figure 3.2 Satisfaction with Democracy

For example, in Uruguay, there is more than 20 points difference between support for democracy as a system and satisfaction with how it functions.

In general, levels of satisfaction with democracy in Latin America seem to be correlated with presidential approval rates. Figure 3.3 shows the linear relationship between presidential job approval and satisfaction with democracy. Satisfaction with how democracy works goes from a high of 65.6 for respondents who approve strongly of the job the incumbent president is doing to a low of 34.3 for those who disapprove strongly. Support for the president's job performance is conditioned by a multitude of contextual factors, including economic conditions, political scandals, and the extent to which the president is viewed as an effective leader. The observed relationship between satisfaction with democracy and attitudes toward the president reflect a weakness for democratic governance in Latin America. Since presidential approval is highly variable and subject to significant swings, the relationship makes satisfaction with democracy more volatile.

Another variable that affects satisfaction in a significant way is fear of crime. As shown by the Millett chapter in this volume (Chapter 13), crime and insecurity are major problems facing democratic governments in Latin America. What this analysis shows is that insecurity has a deleterious effect on attitudes toward democracy. Figure 3.4 underscores this link by showing a clear relationship

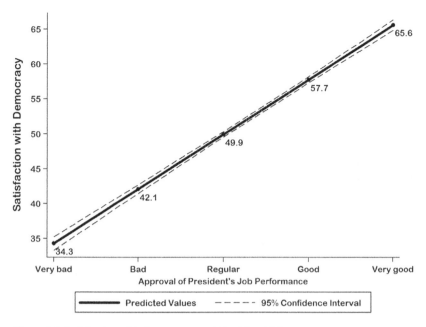

Figure 3.3 Satisfaction with Democracy and Presidential Support

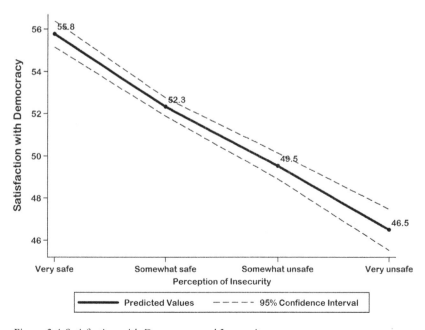

Figure 3.4 Satisfaction with Democracy and Insecurity

between fear of crime and satisfaction with democracy.[7] As citizens' sense of security in their neighborhood declines, so does satisfaction with democracy.

Meaning of Democracy for Latin Americans[8]

I turn now to an analysis of the meaning of democracy for Latin American citizens. Democracy as an ideal seems to have become universally accepted. In today's world, it seems all governments, regardless of their institutional structures, claim to promote some type of democracy. Universal support for democracy, however, takes place at the cost of disagreement over its meaning. Everyone defines democracy according to their own interests. A condensed list could include direct democracy, representative democracy, liberal (or bourgeois) democracy, proletarian democracy, social democracy, totalitarian democracy, industrial democracy, plebiscite democracy, constitutional democracy, associative democracy, pluralist democracy, economic democracy, people's democracy, and participative democracy.

The key institution in a democracy is the election of leaders through competitive elections. In a democracy, people become leaders through elections in which the governed participate. In 1942, Joseph Schumpeter made the most important modern formulation of this concept of democracy. In his pioneering study, *Capitalism, Socialism, and Democracy*, Schumpeter discovered the deficiencies of what he called the "classic theory of democracy," which defined democracy in terms of "the people's will" (source) and "the common good" (purpose). Discarding such suggestions, Schumpeter constructed what he called "another theory of democracy." He pointed out that "the democratic method is that institutional arrangement for arriving at political decisions in which individuals acquire the power to decide by means of a competitive struggle for the people's vote" (Schumpeter 1947).

Following Schumpeter, but widening the categories that define the democratic system, Robert Dahl shows us that democratic governments are fundamentally characterized by their ability to respond to citizens' preferences without establishing political differences between them. For this to take place, all citizens need to have an equal opportunity to (1) formulate their preferences; (2) publicly manifest these preferences among their fellow partisans and before the government, both individually and collectively; and (3) be treated equally by the government. That is, the government should not discriminate in any way regarding the contents and origins of such preferences. These three basic conditions should be accompanied by eight guarantees:

1. Freedom of association
2. Freedom of speech
3. The right to vote
4. Eligibility for public office
5. The right of political leaders to compete for votes
6. Diverse sources of information
7. Free and fair elections

8. Institutions that make government policies depend on the vote and other forms of preference expression

Dahl's definition favors institutional processes that guarantee a level of popular sovereignty in the determination of who governs. In this sense, it does not address concepts of socioeconomic rights or guarantee any conditions of equality among citizens.[9] Therefore, liberal or representative democracy is currently founded on institutions that structure the competition between political elites and guarantees that all citizens participate equally in the country's political processes.

By the end of the twentieth century and the beginning of the twenty-first, the concept of "democracy" acquired a universal acceptance that leaves it, in many cases, without any real foundation. All governments try to legitimize themselves by claiming to be democracies. Citizens "learn" this lesson and tend to "pray before the temple of democracy." But the key question is, does the public know the true meaning of democracy? In addition, what does democracy mean in conceptual terms to citizens? The *Americas Barometer* surveys always contain various questions that measure attitudes about democracy and democratic government. However, given the problems of the concept's universality, for the 2006 survey, we made an effort to measure the different ways citizens conceptualize democracy. For this analysis, the survey asked a series of semi-open questions that required respondents to give up to three different meanings of democracy. I focus here on one particular question that asked respondents to identify which of the meanings they had enumerated is the most important (if only one meaning was given, the analysis focused on this one). Table 3.1 presents a framework for categorizing the various answers.[10]

The idea is that there are definitions that go beyond a rational, profit-maximizing calculus to focus on abstract aspects or political and institutional norms. The people for whom such definitions are more important conceive of democracy as a system based on principles and political processes without hoping for personal or family gain from democratic practices. Logic suggests that as more citizens identify democracy with abstract or normative values, the more stable their support for the democratic political system will be, since this support will not be subject to the ups and downs of the national economy, political scandals, or the weakness of the ruling government.

Obviously, when the public shows greater support for negative or "empty" concepts, the stability and survival of the democratic regime will be in greater danger. It is important to note that even when people have negative or empty opinions of democracy, this does not mean an inevitable breakdown of the democratic order. After all, we are not analyzing the views of the country's political leaders or important political sectors that, ultimately, have the power to cause the breakdown of the democratic political order. Nonetheless, public opinion is important to establish the parameters of what is and is not acceptable for political leaders. That is, if a wide majority of the people do not believe in democracy, political leaders will have the green light to act undemocratically. Figure 3.5 shows the results percentage of respondents that express each conceptualization of democracy. The results are interesting: First, majorities—small

Table 3.1 Analytical Framework for the Various Concepts of Democracy (codes in parentheses)

Normative and intrinsic concepts of democracy	Instrumental concepts of democracy	Empty or non-specified concepts of democracy	Negative concepts of democracy
Freedom (without saying what kind) (1)	Economic freedom (2)	Has no meaning (0)	Freedom, lack of (5)
Freedom of expression, of voting, of electing, of human rights (3)	Well-being, economic progress,growth (7)	Other response (80) Don't know or no response (88)	Well-being, lack of, no economic progress (8)
Freedom of movement (4)	Capitalism (9) Free trade,business freedom(10)		Work, lack of (12)
To be independent (6)	Work, greater opportunities of (11)		Fraudulent elections (16)
Right to choose leaders (13)			Equality, lack of, inequality (22)
Elections, voting (14)			Participatory limits (23)
Free elections (15)			Disorder, lack of justice, corruption (28)
Equality (without specifying) (17)			War, invasions (33)
Participation (without specifying) (24)			

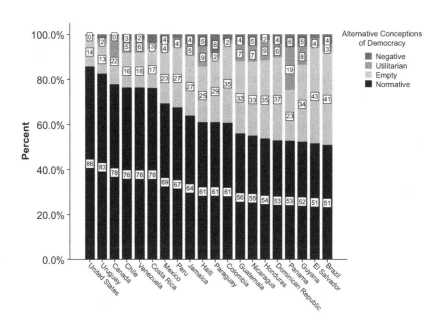

Figure 3.5 Conceptualization of Democracy

in some countries, but majorities nonetheless—support normative conceptualizations of democracy. Second, as shown with previous results, Uruguayans express the highest levels of support for normative conceptions among all Latin American nations, equivalent with citizens of the United States and Canada. Third, the lowest support for normative conceptions is found in Brazil and El Salvador where only 51 percent of citizens express such attitudes. These two countries also exhibit the highest percentage of "empty" conceptions: 41 and 43 percent, respectively.

These results beg the question of what factors affect respondents' choice among conceptualization. For this analysis, I employed a multinomial regression technique.[11] Appendix 3.1 shows the model results. The analysis reveals statistically significant differences in wealth and education between respondents who chose normative versus negative and utilitarian conceptions of democracy. In turn, those who express empty conceptions differ significantly in all demographic variables from those choosing normative.

Figure 3.6 shows the relationship between education and conceptions of democracy. Those citizens who possess greater levels of education are significantly more likely to express normative or intrinsic definitions of democracy than those with lower education. These results point to the importance of education in promoting support for democratic values.

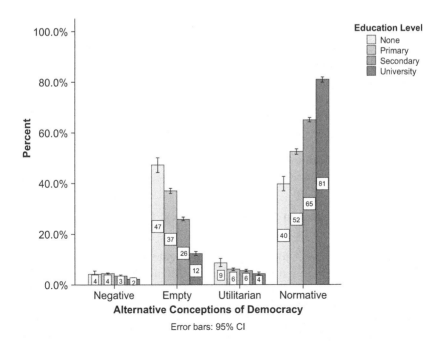

Figure 3.6 Alternative Conceptions of Democracy by Education

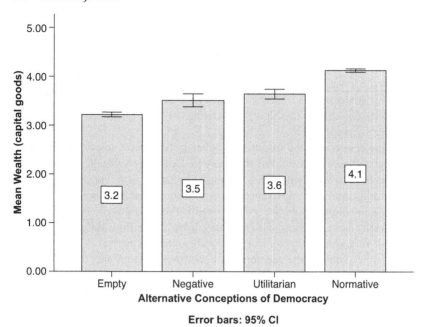

Figure 3.7 Alterative Conceptions of Democracy by Wealth

Figure 3.7 shows the relationship between wealth[12] and conceptions of democracy. As wealth increases, so do normative conceptions of democracy. While education and wealth are related, the results of the regression analysis demonstrate that they act independently of each other.

The analysis presented here provides evidence that individual-level socio-economic and demographic variables do help predict alternative conceptions of democracy: wealthier, more educated, male, urban residents are more likely to hold normative values. While individual national analyses may result in slightly different conclusions, it is clear that education is an important variable in determining the way in which citizens analyze democracy.

Political Tolerance and System Legitimacy: Examining Values Supportive of Stable Democracy

The emphasis on support for democratic stability stems from the premise that although public opinion is not totally determinant in a democratic regime, it is one of the most important factors behind political stability. In large measure, the legitimacy of the system depends on how citizens view it. Juan Linz, in his work on the breakdown of a democratic system, says that legitimacy depends largely on the public believing that existing institutions, despite their problems, are better than the alternatives.[13] We are talking about the political institutions here, not the administration in power. Seymour Martin Lipset defines legitimacy as "the capacity of a system to generate and maintain the belief that the existing institutions are the most appropriate for the society." Lipset's theory is based on the premise that political systems that receive the public's support, and therefore legitimacy, can survive even in the face of an economic or political crisis.[14]

The North American political scientist David Easton, in turn, talks about two important types of support: "specific" support and "diffuse" support. The first refers to the public's support for the ruling government. Although this kind of support is important for those who govern, since it can influence the government's capacity to implement its policies, it is not as important as the second type of support. "Diffuse" support refers to support for institutions, that is, the political system and the institutions that constitute it. The political system can survive when the administration or ruler in power is unpopular, but it is in danger when the institutions lose support and, therefore, legitimacy (Easton 1975).

Political tolerance is one of the most important democratic values. In the previous section, we analyzed political system support. Support for the system is important for political stability, but it does not guarantee the survival of democracy. Therefore, political tolerance, defined as an individual's acceptance of the rights of others to express varied opinions, is key to establishing a stable democratic regime. There is an extensive literature on political tolerance.[15] One of the most debated topics is how to measure tolerance.[16] This study measures tolerance through an index based on the responses to a series of questions (the D series) in the questionnaire. The original scale of these variables goes from 1 to 10.

The following questions were used for this analysis:

(01)	(02)	(03)	(04)	(05)	(06)	(07)	(08)	(09)	(10)	(88)
Strongly disapprove								Strongly approve		Don't know

D1. There are people who always speak badly of [country] form of government, not only the current administration, but the kind of government. How strongly do you approve or disapprove of these peoples' **right to vote**? Please read me the number on the scale: *[Probe: Up to what point?]*

D2. How strongly do you approve or disapprove that these people can conduct peaceful demonstrations in order to express their points of view? Please read me the number.

D3. How strongly do you approve or disapprove that these people can **run for public office**?

D4. How strongly do you approve or disapprove that these people appear on television to **give speeches**?

For our analysis, we recoded the variables to a scale of 0 to 100.[17] The mean of the scale is 54.

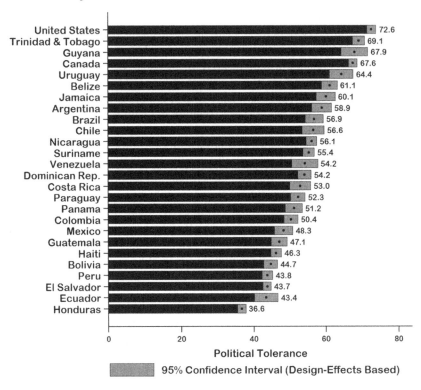

United States ┤ 72.6
Trinidad & Tobago ┤ 69.1
Guyana ┤ 67.9
Canada ┤ 67.6
Uruguay ┤ 64.4
Belize ┤ 61.1
Jamaica ┤ 60.1
Argentina ┤ 58.9
Brazil ┤ 56.9
Chile ┤ 56.6
Nicaragua ┤ 56.1
Suriname ┤ 55.4
Venezuela ┤ 54.2
Dominican Rep. ┤ 54.2
Costa Rica ┤ 53.0
Paraguay ┤ 52.3
Panama ┤ 51.2
Colombia ┤ 50.4
Mexico ┤ 48.3
Guatemala ┤ 47.1
Haiti ┤ 46.3
Bolivia ┤ 44.7
Peru ┤ 43.8
El Salvador ┤ 43.7
Ecuador ┤ 43.4
Honduras ┤ 36.6

0   20   40   60   80

Political Tolerance

95% Confidence Interval (Design-Effects Based)

Figure 3.8 Political Tolerance

Figure 3.8 shows the aggregate level of political tolerance among the surveyed countries. It is important to note that these results represent rankings on the scale and not percentages. The graph indicates that the United States, Trinidad and Tobago, Guyana, and Canada exhibit the highest level of political tolerance in the region. The lowest levels are expressed by El Salvador, Ecuador, and Honduras. Mexico, Haiti, Peru, Bolivia, and Guatemala exhibit tolerance levels below the midpoint of the scale; thus, eight countries surveyed express negative levels of tolerance. The rest of the countries exhibit tolerance levels above the midpoint of the scale (i.e., 50 on the 0–100 scale).

System legitimacy is measured by a scale of support using five questions measured initially by a 1–7 scale, which was transformed to a 0–100 scale for purposes of the analysis.[18] These questions seek to measure "diffuse" support rather than support for the current governments. The mean of the scale is 52.

1	2	3	4	5	6	7	8
None						A lot	NS/NR

B1. To what extent do you trust that the courts in [country] guarantee a just trial?

B2. To what extent do you respect the political institutions of [country]?

B3. To what extent do you think that citizens' basic rights are protected by the political system in [country]?

B4. To what extent are you proud to live under the political system of [country]?

B6. To what extent do you think the political system of [country] should be supported?

The results are presented in Figure 3.9. We find that there are four distinct groups of countries: Belize, Suriname, and Nicaragua express the highest levels of system support well above the mean of the scale. Haiti, Panama, and Honduras express the lowest levels of system support. We find a large group of countries in the middle with varying degrees of system support, ranging from Uruguay, which is relatively high, to Haiti, Paraguay, and Brazil at the low end.

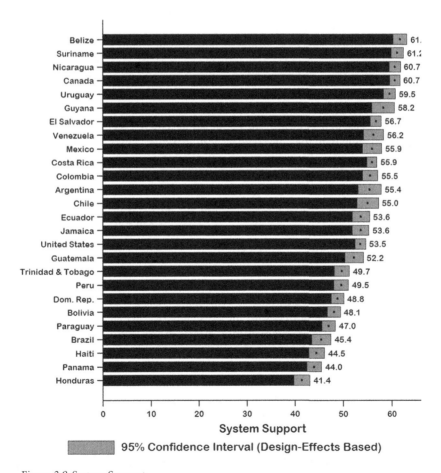

Figure 3.9 System Support

Table 3.2 Theoretical Relation Between Tolerance and Support for the System

Support for the institutional system	*High Tolerance*	*Low Tolerance*
High	**Stable Democracy**	Authoritarian Stability
Low	Unstable Democracy	Democratic Breakdown

Source: This theoretical framework was first presented in Mitchell A. Seligson (2000), "Toward a Model of Democratic Stability: Political Culture in Central America." *Estudios interdisciplinarios de América Latina y el Caribe* 11(2) July–December: 5–29.

Now we will analyze the relation between political tolerance and support for the system. The analysis is based on dividing the tolerance and system support scales in half (50 of 0 to 100) and crossing both variables to obtain a two by two table that shows us the theoretical relation between tolerance and support for the system (see Table 3.2).

It is important to remember that this framework only applies to countries with an electoral democracy, since the effect of high and low levels of both support for the system and tolerance would be very different within an authoritarian system.

Seligson explains the logic of the classifications in the following manner:

> Political systems in which the public shows a high level of support for the system and high tolerance tend to be more stable. This prediction is based on the premise that the system needs strong support in non-authoritarian situations in order to guarantee its stability. By contrast, if people do not support their political system and have freedom of action, this will almost inevitably produce an eventual change in the system.
>
> (Seligson 2002, pp. 51–52)

In cases where tolerance is low but support for the system is high, "the system should remain stable (given the high level of support), but the democratic government might be at risk. Such systems tend to move toward authoritarian (oligarchic) regimes which restrict democratic rights."[19] A situation of low support for the system opens up the possibility of instability in the political system. Where there are high levels of tolerance, "it is difficult to predict if the instability will result in greater democratization or in a period of instability characterized by considerable violence."[20] If the tolerance levels are low, by contrast, "the breakdown of the democratic order would seem to be the most logical result."[21]

However, it is very important to note that public opinion cannot cause the breakdown of a political system. There are innumerable factors that influence such an event, from economic conditions and the geopolitical climate to the policies adopted by the elite and ruling governments. Nonetheless, there is

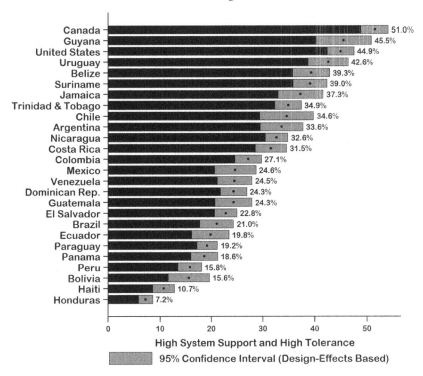

Figure 3.10 High System Support and High Tolerance

no doubt that a political system that has little support and whose citizens are intolerant is more susceptible to a breakdown of democracy.

Figure 3.10 provides the percentages of citizens who fall in the "stable democracy" cell. These individuals express both high tolerance and high system support and would be considered the ideal citizens for sustaining democratic governance. Significantly, only in Canada do a majority of respondents express attitudes supportive of stable democracy. Guyana and Uruguay are the highest among the Latin American countries, and only 45.5 and 42.6 percent, respectively, of citizens in those two nations express high tolerance and high system support. In many nations, less than a third of respondents exhibit such attitudes, and in Honduras, only 7.2 percent do so.

How have attitudes conducive to stable democracy changed over time? Figure 3.11 illustrates the change in stable democracy attitudes between 2010 and 2012. The chart shows that thirteen countries saw an increase in the percentage of individuals who express high levels of system support and tolerance. Guyana is the country with the highest increase, with over 10 percent

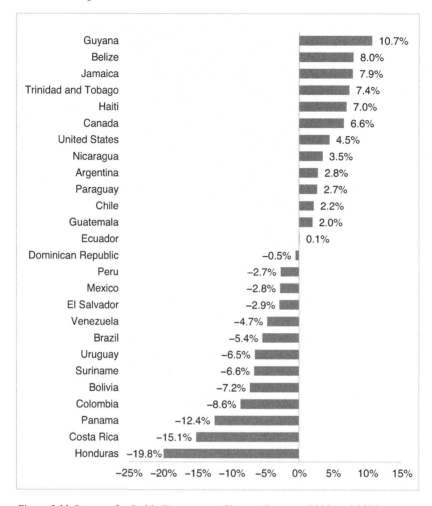

Figure 3.11 Support for Stable Democracy: Changes Between 2010 and 2012

more expressing attitudes supportive of stable democracy. Improvement is also observed in Belize, Jamaica, Haiti, Trinidad and Tobago, Canada, United States, Argentina, Nicaragua, Paraguay, Chile, Guatemala, and Ecuador. In nearly all of these countries the improvement was the result of increased system support rather than political tolerance. The chart shows that countries such as Honduras, Costa Rica, and Panama had the sharpest decline in stable democratic attitudes. In the case of Honduras, the decline was more than 19 percent. The results for Honduras should come as no surprise. The country underwent a traumatic political crisis in 2009 when the armed forces toppled the elected president. The legacy of the military coup has further divided the country politically and socially, and undermined democratic governance. Furthermore, Honduras is the most violent country in the region, with homicide rates reaching 90 per 100,000 inhabitants. In the case of Costa Rica, an unpopular president, Laura Chinchilla, coupled with a decline in the credibility of the political parties and elites, eroded support for the political system between 2010 and 2012, reflected in the decline of attitudes supportive of stable democracy. Panama, too, suffered from a decline in system support due partly to erosion in support for the president as a result of controversial and polarizing policies.

In the end, the problem with stable democratic attitudes lies primarily with the levels of system support. As will be examined in the rest of the volume, the levels of support are, no doubt, linked to a series of institutional, political, social, and economic problems facing many of the nations of the region. These problems stem from weak and fragile institutions, crime and insecurity, poverty, unequal distribution of wealth, and the negative effects of globalization.

Conclusion

This chapter began with a question: Do Latin Americans possess the requisite political culture to sustain democratic governance? I have tried to answer this question by focusing on five specific values: (1) general preference and satisfaction with democracy; (2) alternative conceptions of democracy; (3) support for the political system; (4) tolerance; and (5) attitudes supportive of "stable democracy." The answer, as with much of the analyses conducted about Latin America, is complex and depends on various factors. Latin Americans do generally support democracy as the best form of government. It seems that for many in the region, democracy is truly the only game in town. However, that does not mean that everyone adheres to the same meaning of democracy. Institutionally, we know that in places like Venezuela, Ecuador, and Bolivia leaders are implementing populist and radical left policies that seek to transform the traditional liberal representative notions of democracy. Whether they will succeed or not is a question explored in other chapters in this volume.

While most citizens in the region express support for democracy as the best possible regime, most are unsatisfied with how democracy works. For many, democracy is equated with failed economic policies, rising crime, and corruption. The fact that fear of crime is associated with lower satisfaction is clear evidence of the negative effects that rising criminal activity has, and will continue to have, on support for democracy. Support for democracy also seems to be conditioned on perceptions of the job performed by the incumbent presidents. Given how fragile and volatile presidential ratings can be, it should not surprise anyone that we will continue to witness weak satisfaction with democracy in many countries of Latin America.

Support for attitudes conducive to a "stable democracy" (high levels of political tolerance and system support) seem weak for most of Latin America compared to Canada and the United States. The one exception in 2012 is Guyana, which seems to have rebounded in the levels of system support between 2010 and 2012, to the extent that the percentage of citizens who express stable democratic attitudes is slightly greater than in the United States. The low levels of stable democratic attitudes in the rest of Latin America are primarily due to relatively low levels of support for the political system and weaker levels of political tolerance. While citizens in some nations such as Uruguay exhibit relatively robust levels of support for attitudes conducive to a stable democracy, others such as Honduras and Haiti express alarmingly low levels.

Finally, this chapter has found that many in Latin America have either empty or negative conceptions of democracy—in some cases, higher than 40 percent. However, majorities do still cling to a normative or intrinsic definition of democracy rooted in freedom and political and civil rights. These attitudes are conditioned by a number of demographic variables; among the most important are wealth and education. Education and economic well-being are thus closely linked to an understanding of democracy that is more likely to sustain citizens' support even under economic and political crises. For many less educated, poorer, and rural citizens, democracy is either an empty vessel without real meaning or a failed instrument for obtaining concrete benefits. In both cases, democratic support and stability falters as citizens' needs and expectations are not met. In such circumstances, many are willing to support alternative forms of government or heed the siren call of populism.

Notes

1 The samples in Canada and the United States were conducted by telephone using random digit dialing technique.
2 Additional information may be obtained at www.lapopsurveys.org.
3 The question wording is as follows: Democracy may have problems, but it is better than any other form of government. The answers were transformed into a 0–100 scale for better illustration.
4 Note that the confidence interval is represented by the "I" at the top of each bar. When they overlap between bars, the differences are not statistically significant. The longer the "I," the greater the dispersion about the mean, and thus the greater the variability in the responses.
5 Since coming to power in 1999, Hugo Chávez and his successor, Nicolás Maduro, have dismantled the liberal representative institutions of the previous political system and constructed a regime based on direct popular appeal to the masses through a set of institutions increasingly controlled by the executive. The regime has repeatedly used popular referenda to seek approval for his agenda, along with a set of local institutions to mobilize citizens in support of the regime's aims and ideals. For a fuller description of Venezuela's current political system, see Carrion's chapter in this volume.

6 The question was:. In general, are you very satisfied, satisfied, unsatisfied or very unsatisfied with the way democracy works in [country]? The answers were transformed into a 0–100 scale for better illustration.

7 For additional evidence of the connection between crime and democratic values, see Orlando J. Pérez, "Democratic Legitimacy and Public Insecurity: The Impact of Crime Victimization on Support for Democracy in El Salvador and Guatemala." *Political Science Quarterly* 118(4) (Winter 2003–04): 627–44.

8 This section draws heavily from Orlando J. Pérez, *La cultura política de la democracia en Panamá: 2006, Barómetro de las Américas*, Un estudio del Proyecto de opinión Publica en América Latina (LAPOP), Vanderbilt University, USAID, 2007. The analysis relies on the 2006 round of the *Americas Barometer*, the only year in which the conceptualization question was asked.

9 Critiques of liberal democracy by the political and scholarly left have centered on this phenomenon.

10 The author wishes to thank Dr. Mitchell A. Seligson and his team at the central office of the Latin American Public Opinion Project at Vanderbilt University for developing this framework.

11 For additional explanation of this technique, see Vani Kant Borooah (2001). *Logit and Probit: Ordered and Multinomial Models* (Quantitative Applications in the Social Sciences), 1st edition. New York: Sage Publications.

12 We measure wealth through a scale of possession of capital goods; higher numbers indicate greater wealth.

13 See Juan Linz (1978), *The Breakdown of Democratic Regimes: Crisis, Breakdown, & Reequilibration*. Baltimore, MD: The Johns Hopkins University Press.

14 See Seymour Martin Lipset (1981), *Political Man: The Social Basis of Politics*, expanded edition. Baltimore, MD: Johns Hopkins University Press; Seymour Martin Lipset (1994), "The Social Requisites of Democracy Revisited." *American Sociological Review* 59 (February): 1–22.

15 See Samuel C. Stouffer, *Communism, Conformity and Civil Liberties* (New York: Doubleday, 1955); Mitchell A. Seligson and Dan Caspi, "Arabs in Israel: Political Tolerance and Ethnic Conflict;" *The Journal of Applied Behavioral Science* 19 (February 1983), 55–66; Mitchell A. Seligson and Dan Caspi, "Toward and Empirical Theory of Tolerance: Radical Groups in Israel and Costa Rica," *Comparative Political Studies* 15 (1983b), 385–404; Mitchell A. Seligson and Dan Caspi, "Threat, Ethnicity and Education: Tolerance Toward the Civil Liberties of the Arab Minority in Israel (in Hebrew)," *Megamot* 15 (May 1982), 37–53; John L. Sullivan, James E. Pierson, and George E. Marcus, *Political Tolerance and American Democracy* (Chicago: University of Chicago Press 1982); James L. Gibson, 1993, "Perceived Political Freedom in the Soviet Union." *Journal of Politics* 55: 4 November 936–74; James L. Gibson, 1992a, "Alternative Measures of Political Tolerance: Must Tolerance Be 'Least Liked'?" *American Journal of Political Science* 36: 2 May 560–77; James L. Gibson, 1992b, "The Political Consequences of Intolerance: Cultural Conformity and Political Freedom" *American Political Science Review* 86: 2, 338–56; James L. Gibson, 1988, "Political Tolerance and Political Repression during the McCarthy Red Scare." *American Political Science Review* 82 (June): 511–29; James L. Gibson, 1989, "The Policy Consequences of Political Intolerance: Political Repression during the Vietnam War Era." *Journal of Politics* 51: 13–35; James L. Gibson and R. Bingham, 1985, "The Behavioral Consequences of Political Tolerance," in Gibson and Bingham, *Civil Liberties and Nazis: The Skokie Free-Speech Controversy*. New York: Praeger.

16 For a more thorough discussion of this topic, see the section on political tolerance in Mitchell A. Seligson (2002), *Auditoria de la democracia: Ecuador* (45–6). Pittsburgh: University of Pittsburgh and CEDATOS.

17 The conversion is made by subtracting 1 from each score. Then each score is divided by 9, so that each one is located in a range from 0 to 1. Finally, this score is multiplied by 100.
18 The conversion is made by subtracting 1 from each score. Then each score is divided by 6, so that each one is located in a range of 0 to 1. Finally, this score is multiplied by 100.
19 Mitchell A. Seligson (2000), "Toward a Model of Democratic Stability: Political Culture in Central America." Estudios interdisciplinarios de América Latina y el Caribe 11(2) July–December: 10.
20 Mitchell A. Seligson (2000), "Toward a Model of Democratic Stability: Political Culture in Central America." Estudios interdisciplinarios de América Latina y el Caribe 11(2) July–December: 11.
21 Mitchell A. Seligson (2000), "Toward a Model of Democratic Stability: Political Culture in Central America." Estudios interdisciplinarios de América Latina y el Caribe 11(2) July–December: 11.

References

Almond, G.A. and Verba, S. (1963) *The Civic Culture*. Princeton: Princeton University Press.

Easton, D. (1975) "A Re-assessment of the Concept of Political Support." *British Journal of Political Science* 5: 435–57.

Gibson, J.L. (1988) "Political Tolerance and Political Repression during the McCarthy Red Scare." *American Political Science Review* 82 (June): 511–29.

Gibson, J.L. (1989) "The Policy Consequences of Political Intolerance: Political Repression during the Vietnam War Era." *Journal of Politics* 51: 13–35.

Gibson, J.L. (1992a) "Alternative Measures of Political Tolerance: Must Tolerance Be 'Least Liked'?" *American Journal of Political Science* 36(May 2): 560–77.

Gibson, J.L. (1992b) "The Political Consequences of Intolerance: Cultural Conformity and Political Freedom" *American Political Science Review* 86: 2, 338–56.

Gibson, J.L. (1993) "Perceived Political Freedom in the Soviet Union." *Journal of Politics* 55(November 4): 936–74.

Gibson, J.L. and Bingham, R. (1985) "The Behavioral Consequences of Political Tolerance," in J.L. Gibson and R. Bingham (eds.), *Civil Liberties and Nazis: The Skokie Free Speech Controversy*. New York: Praeger.

Inglehart, R. (1990) *Culture Shift in Advanced Industrial Society*. Princeton: Princeton University Press.

Mishler, W. and Rose, R. (1999) "Five Years After the Fall: Trajectories of Support for Democracy in Post-Communist Europe," in P. Norris (ed.) *Critical Citizens: Global Support for Democratic Governance*. Oxford: Oxford University Press.

Muller, E.N. and Seligson, M.A. (1994) "Civic Culture and Democracy: The Question of Causal Relationships." *American Political Science Review* 88(3): 635–54.

Putnam, R.D. (1993) *Making Democracy Work: Civic Traditions in Modern Italy*. Princeton: Princeton University Press.

Schumpeter, J.A. (1947) *Capitalism, Socialism and Democracy*, second edition. New York: Harper.

Seligson, M.A. (2002) *Auditoria de la democracia: Ecuador*. University of Pittsburgh and CEDATOS.

Wiarda, H.J. (2001) *The Soul of Latin America: The Cultural and Political Tradition*. New Haven: Yale University Press.

Appendix 3.1 Predictors of the Different Conceptions of Democracy Multinomial Regression Analysis Parameter Estimates

Concepciones alternativas de la democracia(a)		B	Std. Error	Wald	df	Sig.	Exp(B)	95 percent confidence interval for Exp(B)	
								Lower Bound	Upper Bound
Negative	Intercept	-2.044	.224	83.468	1	.000			
	Gender	.018	.068	.070	1	.791	1.018	.891	1.163
	Age	.002	.002	.881	1	.348	1.002	.998	1.007
	Education	-.049	.009	30.920	1	.000***	.952	.936	.969
	Wealth	-.137	.018	55.550	1	.000***	.872	.841	.904
	Size of City	-.047	.037	1.630	1	.202	.954	.887	1.026
	Urban/rural	.142	.124	1.312	1	.252	1.153	.904	1.470
Empty	Intercept	.705	.100	49.552	1	.000			
	Gender	.301	.030	99.655	1	.000***	1.352	1.274	1.434
	Age	-.014	.001	182.834	1	.000***	.986	.984	.988
	Education	-.118	.004	840.220	1	.000***	.889	.882	.896
	Wealth	-.145	.008	310.863	1	.000***	.865	.851	.879
	Size of City	-.082	.017	24.152	1	.000***	.922	.892	.952
	Urban/rural	.238	.055	18.680	1	.000***	1.269	1.139	1.413
Utilitarian	Intercept	-2.275	.178	163.028	1	.000			
	Gender	-.014	.054	.066	1	.797	.986	.888	1.095
	Age	.002	.002	1.521	1	.217	1.002	.999	1.006
	Education	-.034	.007	25.018	1	.000***	.966	.953	.979
	Wealth	-.072	.014	24.983	1	.000***	.931	.905	.957
	Size of City	-.052	.030	2.910	1	.088	.950	.895	1.008
	Urban/rural	.460	.100	20.971	1	.000***	1.583	1.301	1.928

The reference category is: Normative. N: 25,290 Pseudo R^2: .099 * sig. < .05 ** sig. < .01 *** sig. < .001

4   The View from the North
The United States and the OAS: What Frustrates the Americans?

Ambassador (Ret.) John F. Maisto

The common view about the Organization of American States (OAS) among "Americans"[1] is that the OAS lacks relevance. The OAS dodges the difficult issues of democracy and human rights in the hemisphere. It permits countries whose governments violate the basic rules of democracy and human rights, as outlined in the 2001 Inter-American Democratic Charter (IADC), to block dealing with them at the OAS.

There is a marked lack of political will among member states at the Permanent Council, which is supposed to be the political action arm of the one-country, one-vote oldest international organization in the world to deal with clear issues of democracy and human rights. In Venezuela, Ecuador, and Bolivia, the only time democracy issues are raised is to receive election observation reports that usually fail to go deeply into how the government in place utilizes its power and resources for election politics. In Honduras, where a coup to oust the elected president was ordered by the legislature and authorized by the Supreme Court, the result was the swift expulsion of Honduras from the OAS and the OAS dealing itself out of the diplomacy that eventually resolved the impasse through an already-scheduled election.

Americans see a double standard: a lack of OAS action regarding leftist authoritarian or authoritarian-leaning governments (Venezuela, Ecuador, Bolivia) over the last years contrasted to any rightist government such as Honduras in 2009. In Honduras, strict application of the IADC was swiftly embraced. In the other three countries, application of the charter was ignored in spite of petitions of democratic opposition and civic groups.

The OAS charter was adopted on April 30, 1948, in Bogotá, Colombia, though multilateral relations among the countries of the Western Hemisphere go back much further. A series of inter-American conferences that began in the 1820s led to the creation of the International Union of American Republics in 1890. Originally created to collect and distribute commercial information, the International Union of American Republics was renamed the Pan American Union in 1910. In 1933, following the launch of President Franklin Roosevelt's "Good Neighbor" policy, the United States and other nations in the hemisphere signed the Convention on the Rights and Duties of States, which formally recognized the equality of states and the principle of nonintervention in one another's internal affairs. Close coop- eration during World War II considerably strengthened hemispheric ties, which were reinforced in the post-war period with the adoption of the Inter- American Treaty of Reciprocal Assistance (Rio Treaty) in 1947. The OAS Charter and American Declaration of the Rights and Duties of Man were signed a year later by the United States and twenty other countries[2] in the region to legally codify the institutions and principles that had come to form the inter-American system. In 1959, the Inter-American Commission on Human Rights was created to carry out the provisions of the American Declaration of the Rights and Duties of Man. During the 1960s, the OAS greatly expanded its economic, social, cultural, scientific, and technological programs, placing a strong emphasis on development following the 1961 launch of President Kennedy's "Alliance for Progress." Abuses by authori- tarian governments prompted the creation of the Inter-American Court of Human Rights in 1978, and growing concern over narcotics trafficking led to the establishment of the Inter-American Drug Abuse Control Com- mission in 1986. The OAS acknowledged the challenges posed by regional and international terrorism by creating the Inter-American Committee Against Terrorism in 1999, and recognized the near-universal commitment to democracy in the region through the adoption of the Inter-American Democratic Charter in 2001.[3]

The United States has always wanted an effective regional organization, for commercial reasons at the end of the nineteenth century, to the Pan American Union and the struggle against fascism, to the Cold War period that ended in 1989. The United States saw the regional organization that became the OAS in 1948 and the inter-American system of agreements and alliances after World War II as bastions of support for the United States in the hemisphere, and throughout the world.

The United States also saw the OAS as a bulwark against any possible communist advance during the 1950s, such as in the Dominican Republic in 1965, and particularly after the Castro revolution in Cuba. In addition, the inter-American system of agreements, alliances, and entities such as the Inter- American Defense Treaty and Board, in which the OAS has played a central role, has been the framework for the US presence in the region. Defense of the Panama Canal was another key element.

The end of the Cold War in 1989 changed the US "Security First" view of the hemisphere. It coincided with the opportunity to make the OAS into a well-grounded community of democracies. The OAS would be the place not only to resolve political differences and territorial issues, but also to advance and strengthen democracy and human rights.

The result was the flowering of OAS entities such as the Inter-American Human Rights Commission (IAHRC). The IAHRC is the most successful and respected independent human rights organization in the world. (Attempts by Ecuador to weaken the IAHRC were thwarted by a coalition of concerned countries at the 2013 OAS General Assembly.) In addition, the OAS houses three entities of horizontal cooperation linking specialized government agencies of member countries to combat the threats to democracy: narcotics trafficking (The Inter-American Drug Abuse Control Commission [CICAD]), terrorism (Inter-American Committee against Terrorism [CICTE]), and corruption (Mechanism to Follow Up on Implementation of the Inter-American Convention Against Corruption [MESICIC]).

The culmination of OAS support for democracy came with the adoption of the IADC in 2001. The charter, with strong bipartisan support, fulfilled a key US objective: an OAS composed of democratically elected governments that subscribe to a common set of representative democracy principles and practices. These values would be key to strengthening institutions and rule of law and fighting corruption, thus enhancing free-enterprise economic systems, including providing for social and economic safety nets.

The US democracy agenda for the hemisphere as the millennium began envisaged an OAS, with the new IADC, as a model—the only regional organization besides the European Union to make democracy its political centerpiece. It soon became clear, however, particularly as Bolivarian Venezuela become more active in its ideological agenda, that the OAS would not take up issues of democracy and human rights in response to the clamor of opposition groups and civil society who invoked the IADC. The reason: the OAS is composed of executive branches, and their OAS representatives were under instructions, citing sovereignty and the principle of nonintervention, to prevent such complaints from being considered at the Permanent Council.

One early example of rejecting a role for the IADC came when Ecuador President Lucio Gutierrez dismissed the entire Ecuador Supreme Court, a clear violation of separation of powers. The attempts to bring the issue to the OAS under the charter were thwarted because Ecuador opposed.

No issue concerning a country can be raised formally at the OAS without that country's consent. This is tradition in the hemisphere, directly linked to sovereignty and nonintervention.

Another example was President Correa's attacks on Ecuador's media.[4] The media's freedom to oppose government is as old as representative democracy itself, and always a legitimate subject of debate. Not debatable, of course, is freedom of the media to take political positions. And the use of state power to suppress this freedom, through taxes, fines, licensing, or a controlled judiciary, is a well-worn tactic of authoritarian regimes of the right or the left. Of course, the IADC was made to deal with such issues.

But perhaps the most serious example of sovereignty trumping democracy is in Venezuela. In early 2014, peaceful student demonstrators protesting government policies were confronted with repression by security forces and attacks by illegal armed groups linked to government parties. Such clashes produced deaths and injuries, and detained students suffered torture and inhumane treatment. Independent media were harassed. Civic protest and democratic opposition were treated as crimes, and opposition leaders jailed, including former Caracas Mayor Leopoldo Lopez, who is still incarcerated and still without trial. These obvious IADC violations were not taken up formally by the OAS because of Venezuela's (sovereignty) objections.

All these instances of IADC violations are protected by outdated principles of sovereignty and nonintervention in internal affairs. Only a plea by an executive branch "member of the club" can get the OAS involved. Such was the case in 2005 when President Bolaños of Nicaragua feared legislative branch takeover, and in response to his request, under the IADC, the OAS responded with a diplomatic mission that headed off a potential violation of separation of powers.

One possible reform of the OAS could entail allowing branches of government in addition to the executive (that is, legislatures, supreme courts, election tribunals) to have access to the Permanent Council in instances involving the IADC. Another would be to allow legitimate opposition groups and civil society organizations the opportunity, when credible evidence of violations of the charter are reported, to be heard at the Permanent Council or by one of its specialized committees. Such suggestions were made in a report by the secretary general to the Permanent Council in 2007, but were never further aired or discussed.

What is, or should be, the role of the OAS in such situations? If there is no consensus among members, what can OAS leadership do? A first response would be to do no harm. However, doing nothing is doing harm. Doing nothing as governments use disproportionate force to quell protest, unleash armed groups to attack, jail democratic opposition leaders, and harass media or dismiss branches of government, and then stand aside to allow them to cite sovereignty to avoid any response under the IADC is doing harm.

These are governments that have the constitutional and legal obligation—in addition to international obligations under the IADC—not to resort to such measures, particularly with regard to civilians exercising their rights.

The OAS—that is, the Permanent Council—with a leading role of the secretary general, can and should describe, report, explore, and debate these situations. When the facts show governments have violated the IADC, it should be reported to the Permanent Council and debated. All this can be done with a view to pursuing solutions, or first steps to solutions.

These are the types of measures that Americans would expect from the OAS, not platitudes wrapped in legal jargon to rationalize doing nothing.

In the midst of the early 2014 events in Venezuela, the secretary general, José Miguel Insulza, called for dialogue as the only path for Venezuelans to take. He was right, of course, for only Venezuelans can ultimately resolve Venezuelan problems. He emphasized "let nobody expect the OAS to issue condemnations, deepen the divide, or reject legitimate protest." He added that people have every right to expect from the OAS unconditional defense of human rights and freedom of expression.

Americans would think that to do that, the IADC can and should be applied, no matter the rejection of any government and their invoking of sovereignty and their cries of nonintervention, given that all the democratically elected governments of the hemisphere have subscribed to international agreements on democracy and human rights conventions and the IADC.

The secretary general also stated that people have the right to expect from the OAS "defense of institutions and the rule of law." Again, the IADC applies, for it is incumbent on democratic governments to do just that. But if a sizeable portion of the population claims that this is not the case, demonstrates in the streets, and is battled disproportionately by state security forces, then Americans would expect that the OAS has a role to play: invoke and apply the IADC whether the government in question accepts it or not. This is not a matter of moral or even political equivalence of the government vs. the opposition and the citizens in the streets. And when the secretary general says it is not incumbent for the secretary general to label a government a dictatorship, or the opposition fascist, it is indeed incumbent on the OAS or the secretary general specifically and emphatically to assert the right of peaceful assembly for citizens in opposition to their government, if they wish to so proclaim.

Americans would think, as well, that the OAS or the secretary general should warn a member government to refrain from labeling all the legitimate opposition forces and, in the case of Venezuela, university students from all over the country, "fascists."

What should US policy be to change these attitudes and practices? The short answer is patient diplomacy, engagement, and seeking coalitions to deal with specific issues (such as in defeating Ecuador's efforts to weaken the IAHRC in 2013). The United States should use every opportunity at the OAS and in our bilateral diplomacy to call attention to the need to utilize the IADC fully to deal with blatant violations of the charter. This should include, when situations warrant, supporting efforts to allow access to the OAS for branches of government beyond the executive, and efforts to create opportunities for access, when situations warrant, for civil society organizations and legitimate political opposition groups

In sum, what frustrates concerned Americans about the OAS is the practice of *not* invoking or attempting to apply the IADC in situations where democratically elected governments violate it. At the same time, such practices, in the view of Americans who care about democracy in Latin America and the Caribbean (and many Latin Americans as well), increasingly make the OAS less relevant, less respected, less dependable, and less of a hope for beleaguered citizens in hemispheric countries who want to believe in the first sentence of the IADC:

"The people of the Americas have a right to democracy and their governments have the obligation to promote and defend it."

The countries of the hemisphere have the opportunity to fix this situation and exert political will to make the OAS much more responsive to threats to democracy. If they move in that direction, they will see enthusiastic support from the United States and the rebirth of a new, more relevant, more respected OAS. If they do not, we will see the slow unwinding of what could have been a truly effective regional organization that is a democratic model for the globalized world of the twenty-first century.

Notes

1 "The Americans" is shorthand for the US administration of either political party, key members of Congress of both parties, important media and think tanks, academics, and in general Americans who follow and care about Latin America and the Caribbean—and the OAS.
2 The OAS has expanded over time. All thirty-five independent nations in the hemisphere have now signed the charter.
3 See: OAS, "Our History," www.oas.org/en/about/ our_history.asp.
4 For an extensive examination of the Ecuadorean political situation under President Correa, see the Carrión chapter in this volume.

5   Latin American Democracy

The View from the South[1]

*Francisco Rojas Aravena, translated
by Leonor Elsner*

The consolidation of electoral democracy has taken place rapidly in Latin America. Politics is important. Political actors are strategic. Advances in Latin American democracy could be reversed if the political culture and the forms and practices of democracy itself are not reinforced. Citizen participation is a key element. Nevertheless, democracy is not reduced to elections alone; it also entails the full (political, civilian, social, and economic) exercise of effective public participation. Without such participation, governance and democratic coexistence is precarious.

The regional political map has changed in an important way since 1999. If before this date the debate was democracy or dictatorship, in the last decade it has become representative democracy versus participatory democracy. The development of democratic governance requires both. Economically, the initial debate was about the role of the state versus the role of the market in the context of neoliberalism. There is currently an important consensus around key aspects of a model of development that strengthens the role of the state and social policies to overcome poverty.

The results of Latin America's elections show the region's difficulty in constructing political majorities, a task that is both complex and difficult. The region must reconstruct national social agreements to guarantee stability and promote opportunities to allow the governments to operate more democratically. Yet in the majority of Latin American countries, fragmentation and polarization are hindering the government's role and the ability of citizens to exercise their rights and citizenship politically, economically, and socially. In this context, Latin America's election results during November 2005 and December 2006, as well as those of 2012 and 2013, show large divisions within each country. Practically everywhere, the citizens' dissatisfaction is expressed in increased abstention.

The legislatures are divided and without clear majorities. A notable exception is the case of Ecuador where the governing party has almost 90 percent of the parliamentary seats. In the election that resulted in Michelle Bachelet's victory in Chile, a majority was achieved in the House of Representatives; however, this majority was less than two-thirds of the House, and did not extend to the Senate. Constant political negotiation is therefore required across the region, which is often fruitless and bogs down the political process. Thus, presidents rule by decree, which creates a situation in which citizens distance themselves from the democratic institutions. Furthermore, presidents routinely encounter difficulties in implementing their legislative program. This often stimulates corruption, perceived as an "easy road" to resolving these difficulties, but that only contributes to and aggravates the situation. It is necessary to create mechanisms for constructing nationwide effective agreements, capable of reflecting the plurality of a society within the framework of democracy. Democratic governance must be guided by the majority while remaining respectful of the minority.

In the present situation, some have argued that Latin America is falling into a "new leftist tendency." However, in reality, there is a search for new options, for roads that may open to new perspectives and redress the exclusion, both political and social, of the majorities; an attempt to overcome and alleviate the negative effects of structural transformations stemming from the era of neoliberalism. The current challenge, in a context of greater political autonomy and international economic spaces, is to advance in development models that will allow growth to overcome poverty and reduce inequality.

Eroded Democracies

Studies conducted in Latin America conclude that democracy is strongly supported. According to the *Latinobarometro*[2] for 2013, 56 percent of respondents support democracy. Yet despite this, an almost equivalent percentage of people reported dissatisfaction with their democratic governments, with 57 percent indicating that the government had not succeeded in resolving the citizens' demands. Only 39 percent reported that they were satisfied with the way democracy functioned. Latin Americans' trust in governments, political parties, and congress has eroded, which naturally affects the legitimacy of basic democratic institutions.

In this sense, it is important to emphasize that democracy in itself is not capable of guaranteeing good government, although it does permit the

Table 5.1 Latin America: Confidence in the Institutions

	1998	2001	2003	2005	2006	2007	2008	2009	2010	2011
Government	28	–	–	36	43	39	44	45	45	40
Judicial System	32	27	20	31	36	30	28	32	32	29
Congress	27	24	17	28	27	29	32	34	34	32
Political Parties	21	19	11	18	22	20	21	24	23	22

Source: Corporación Latinobarómetro. *Informe Latinobarómetro* 2011. Santiago, Chile; 2006: www.latinobarometro.org; In the *Latinobarometro* of 2013, this question is not available.

replacement of bad governments by legitimate processes. Democratic elections allow citizens to voice new viewpoints and create new majorities.

In the last two decades, many Latin American presidents have been replaced outside of the electoral framework. This is not new. It addresses a reality that has existed for years. Since 1991, we find sixteen presidents who have resigned before finishing their term. In the case of Bolivia, two did not finish their presidency; in Ecuador, there were three; and in Peru, one. We should include the unsuccessful coup d'état in Venezuela against President Hugo Chavez and the successful one in Honduras, which displaced President Manuel Zelaya, as well as the parliamentary coup against President Lugo in Paraguay. We have, then, seven cases of instability in the Andes region. The rest occurred in Paraguay in 1999 and 2012; in Argentina in 2001; and previously in Brazil, Guatemala, Haiti, Dominican Republic, and Venezuela. In all of the cases, the replacements were made by strict adherence to constitutional norms, thus avoiding any sanctions from the international community.

In order to understand why such phenomena occur, it is necessary to look at the nature of the region's political systems and the role of the president. Usually in Latin America—contrary to the English-speaking Caribbean—presidential regimes prevail, systems in which the chief of state is crucial. National constitutions place the president at the center of control with extensive powers. Despite this, in many countries, presidents cannot count on congressional majorities.

Table 5.2 Latin America: Interrupted Presidential Mandates 1992–2013

Country	Date	President
Haiti	September 1991	Jean Bertrand Aristide
Brazil	September 1992	Fernando Collor de Mello
Guatemala	June 1993	Jorge Serrano Elías
Venezuela	August 1993	Carlos Andrés Pérez
Dominican Republic	August 1996	Joaquín Balaguer
Ecuador	February 1997	Abdalá Bucarám
Paraguay	March 1999	Raúl Cubas Grau
Ecuador	January 2000	Jamil Mahuad
Peru	November 2000	Alberto Fujimori
Argentina	December 2001	Fernando De la Rúa
Bolivia	October 2003	Gonzalo Sánchez Lozada
Haiti	February 2004	Jean Bertrand Aristide
Bolivia	March 2005	Carlos Mesa
Ecuador	April 2005	Lucio Gutiérrez
Honduras	June 2009	José Manuel Zelaya
Paraguay	June 2012	Fernando Lugo

A review of Latin America's history shows this situation has generated political tensions that are resolved through intervention, open or covert, from the powers that be, principally the armed forces. Currently, military interventions are less viable. The democratic consensus in Latin America is strong, so breaking the constitutional framework brings political-diplomatic isolation and can yield strong economic sanctions. The Inter-American Democratic Charter democratic clauses included in the subregional pacts have fundamentally contributed to avoiding authoritarian regimes. Yet, in themselves, these agreements do not succeed in achieving stability or ensuring democracy. However, we must recognize that they play an important function in establishing incentives for reducing tensions and diminishing the prospects for constitutional ruptures.

Presidential systems have resulted in many cases in a hyper-presidentialism, in which presidents govern by decree, minimizing the role of Congress, and controlling the judiciary. Political systems are led by organizations, which are manifested in governments led by one-party or coalitions. We see this in the formal or informal political alliances that are created by political parties and/or by elected representatives in parliament. These coalitions constitute a block that supports or opposes government-appointed politicians. We refer here to political parties of a formal hegemonic nature, as well as those with lax structures that group distinctive movements and organizations under a common denomination. Historically in Latin America, there have existed political systems founded on a hegemonic party, without a counterweight, the most evident cases being the Institutional Revolutionary Party in Mexico, which lasted for seventy years; Peronism in Argentina; or in different historical periods, the Alianza Popular Revolucionaria Americana in Peru, or the Partido Liberación Nacional in Costa Rica. Often, parties in government admit independent deputies and form a majority without necessarily establishing a coalition. In general, when coalitions are established, they correspond more or less to formal agreements among the various political parties. The parties organize around a common program reflective of the agreements of those in the coalition. One of the most evident examples of this was the Concertación de Partidos por la Democracia in Chile—between 1990 and 2010—which was succeeded by the current coalition, Nueva Mayoría (New Majority).

Latin American presidential systems have strong foundations either in a coalition or in one-party governments. Although one could suppose that coalitions are better able to design legislative programs than are single parties, this is generally not so. In Latin America, we find strong coalitions in governments as much as we find them in parties. For example, in Argentina, Peronism formed the axis of a one-party presidential system led by President Néstor Kirchner, and later Cristina Fernández de Kirchner, against which the opposition party was incapable of designing a successful alternative program. In Chile, on the other hand, a coalition governed, which provided great stability in the country from 1990 to 2008, with an alternation in the period of 2008 to 2012. However, neither single-party governments nor coalitions have been able to assure cohesion or strength for the political system. It is not possible, therefore, to reach a conclusion on this matter. There can be coalitions that strengthen political and democratic systems and their governmental capacities, or there can be one-party governments that secure democratic consistency and stability. There is no general pattern at the beginning of 2014.

Table 5.3 shows that in Latin America at the beginning of 2014 there were five strong coalitions, two weak coalitions, and one neutral coalition. Of the single-party governments in power, six are strong and four are weak; in the case of El Salvador, there was a tie between two political parties with equal levels of support. The only conclusion that can be established, therefore, is the difficulty in constructing majorities that support and reinforce the government's capacity, above all in the context of socially and politically fragmented countries. The results of the elections in the years 2012 and 2013 show that there was continuity in five countries: Chile, Ecuador, Honduras, Dominican Republic, and Venezuela; in three there was alternation and the opposition won: Chile, Mexico, and Paraguay.

Latin American political systems have demonstrated difficulty establishing effective state policies and constructing stable majorities. Democratic governance demands policies that focus on government management, and that are more inclusive in terms of options offered by the coalitions they encounter in government and policies that incorporate different minority and civil society organizations. We are speaking of permanent policies with human resources and finances allocated for their implementation, designed and carried out with extensive public participation.

Table 5.3 Coalitions and Political Parties in the Political Systems of Latin America

Coalitions		*A Party*	
Brazil	Strong	Argentina	Weak
Bolivia	Strong	Ecuador	Strong
Colombia	Neutral	Paraguay	Strong
Chile	Strong		
Peru	Weak		
Uruguay	Strong		
Venezuela	Weak		
Guatemala	Strong	Costa Rica	Weak
		El Salvador	Neutral
		Dominican Republic	Strong
		Nicaragua	Strong
		Honduras	Weak
		Panama	Strong
		Haiti	Weak
		Mexico	Strong

At the national level, in many cases, there is no basic consensus on the formulation of state policies. Consequently, many of the principal demands of the population are unaddressed; political, economic, and social problems are left unresolved; and thus the marginalization of important actors in these societies increases. Moreover, many countries have not resolved institutional political deficits, resulting in further polarization and disaffection, as power is concentrated in the administration. In the economic realm, there is a lack of agreement on growth and development agendas; likewise, there is dissension in how to face insecurity and poverty. These differences generate political and policy polarization. It should be noted that, since 2003, economic growth through the export of primary raw materials has homogenized certain policies in the region.

In the first decade of this century, when presidential candidates won but lacked a majority in parliament, "changing the rules" was the preferred option. This called for constituent assemblies to redefine the political system through constitutional change. Bolivia, Ecuador, and Venezuela have been immersed in these processes. In Colombia, constitutional change allowed presidential reelection. Consensus would allow various actors to construct visions and projects. The political parties, the movements, and other organizational forms looking to exercise power could implement these agreements in governmental programs, which are greatly reflective of national interests in the context of globalization.

It is also important to emphasize that presidential reelection—consecutively or with a gap in between terms, which is permitted in thirteen countries and prohibited in five (Guatemala, El Salvador, Honduras, Mexico, and Paraguay)—allowed six former presidents to be reelected: Lula in Brazil; Uribe in Colombia; Chávez in Venezuela; Alan García in Peru; Oscar Arias in Costa Rica; and Daniel Ortega in Nicaragua in a first stage, later joined by Rafael Correa, Evo Morales, and Michelle Bachelet. Projections indicate that in 2014, Dilma Ruseff, Tabaré Vázquez, and Juan Manuel Santos, and again Evo Morales and Daniel Ortega, will continue this trend.

Poverty and Inequality: A Crucial Challenge

Latin America's principal problems continue to be poverty and inequality. In 1990, 48.3 percent of the population was living in poverty. In 2006, this figure decreased to 38.5 percent. This means that in 2006, there were 205 million people in poverty in Latin America, among which 79 million could be considered in extreme poverty.

Inequality continues to be dramatic. It has deepened social divisions and has increased economic and social differences. Poverty levels have declined slowly, and the gap between the rich and the poor has increased. Speaking particularly to the situation of indigenous peoples, who represent the majority of the population in several countries, Latin America has not

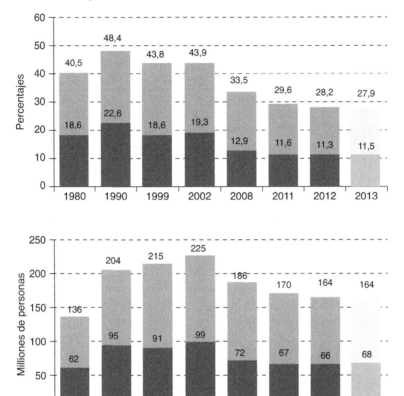

Figure 5.1 Latin America: Poverty and Destitution, 1980–2013

Source: CEPAL. Panorama Social de América Latina. December, 2012.In: *www.eclac.org*. Estimate corresponding to eighteen countries of the region plus Haiti. The figures placed on the sections of the top bars represent the percentage and the total number of poor people (indigents and poor who are not indigents). The figures for 2013 are projected.

succeeded in incorporating systems of effective participation and does not provide adequate access to basic public needs. This is a structural issue that fundamentally affects societies like Guatemala, Ecuador, Peru, Bolivia, and parts of Mexico. A similar situation exists with the Afro-descendant populations.

From 1995 to 2003, many countries reported experiencing negative growth and economic stagnation. After 2003, an increase in growth began. However, there is little to suggest that Latin America can rise above the problems of poverty. Furthermore, one must take into account unemployment rates, particularly those in urban areas and those of the young (a rate that is double

Table 5.4 Latin America and the Caribbean PIB Growth, 2011–2014 (Rates of annual percentage change)

	2011	2012	2013 a)	2014 b)
Latin America and the Caribbean	4,3	3,1	2,6	3,2
Latin America	4,4	3,1	2,6	3,2
Brazil	2,7	1,0	2,4	2,6
Mexico	3,8	3,1	1,3	3,5
Caribbean	0,5	1,2	1,3	2,1

Source: CEPAL. Preliminary Balance of the Latin America and the Caribbean Economies. December 2013.

that of those over the age of twenty-four). On a positive note, inflation has been controlled, and governments now exercise greater responsibility over the economy.

Corruption: A Chronic Evil

Corruption directly affects everyday life, democratic institutions, and economic well-being of a country. Corruption is present at various levels in all the countries and societies of Latin America.[3] When corruption is systematic, it impacts the state's cohesion. In addition, corruption affects the public sector as much as it does the private, and it affects the rule of law. All of this significantly affects citizens' negative perceptions of the political system.

Many of the anticorruption methods applied in Latin America have not yielded the expected results, and there are only a few examples of success. Fighting corruption is difficult, and it requires changing important cultural patterns. Nevertheless, it continues to gain more and more political relevance. In this area, the role of civil society is particularly significant.[4] International financial organizations continue to give attention to transparency and the capacity for citizens to develop institutionalized and systematic mechanisms for accountability. Corruption constitutes, therefore, an essential factor in the delegitimization of political systems and leadership, and it increases disapproval by citizens.

The results reaffirm the striking perspectives portrayed through public opinion polls and by indicators such as those of Transparency International.

The first column in Table 5.5 consists of two countries from the Southern Cone—Chile (22) and Uruguay (19)—and three of the English-speaking Caribbean area—Barbados (15), Santa Lucia (24), and St. Vincent and the Grenadines (33). In the last column are five countries: Guyana (136), Honduras (140), Paraguay (150), Venezuela (160), and Haiti (163).

Table 5.5 Latin America: Ranking of Corruption Perception Index

1–33	34–79	80–130	131–179
Barbados (15)	Dominica (41)	Peru (83)	Guyana (136)
Uruguay (19)	Costa Rica (49)	Trinidad & Tobago (83)	Honduras (140)
Chile (22)	Cuba (63)	El Salvador (83)	Paraguay (150)
Saint Lucie (22)	Brazil (72)	Jamaica (83)	Venezuela (160)
Saint Vincent and the Grenadines (33)		Colombia (94)	Haite (163)
		Panama (102)	
		Ecuador (102)	
		Mexico (106)	
		Argentina (106)	
		Bolivia (106)	
		Dominican Rep. (123)	
		Guatemala (123)	
		Nicaragua (127)	

Source: Transparency International 2013. In: www.transparency.org.

Increase in Violence

Weak rule of law prevails in the democracies of Latin America. There are areas in every country in which state control is nonexistent and where violence is used by nonstate organizations. This affects the ability to govern democratically and inhibits human development. Homicides increase, as shown in Table 5.6, are in part a consequence of small-arms trafficking, which leads to kidnappings. A country that lacks the ability to exercise authority within its borders, to protect human rights, to provide security to the population, and to ensure national order is exposed to social polarization and instability.

The political systems, institutions, and political parties have not succeeded in providing adequate responses to these problems. In all of Latin America's major cities, there are areas in which the authority of the law and the democratic state does not reach. There are sections of cities controlled by criminal organizations. For this reason, urban security is among the highest priorities on the political agenda today. Without an adequate response from political parties, parliaments, and governments, which continually require international cooperation to achieve possible solutions, options will arise that promote "taking the law into one's own hands."

Organized crime is a rising danger, yet Latin American political systems have been reluctant to tackle this issue effectively. For many years it was conspicuously absent from presidential platforms and the goals of political parties. All the while, organized crime and illicit transnational activities have an increasing impact. "Strong Arm" (*mano dura*) responses appear as an immediate reaction linked to a certain judicial populism, for which the solution is related to the increase of punishments and convictions, and taking measures such as reducing

Table 5.6 Percentage of Homicides With Firearms According to Subregions (2010 or recent year available)

Subregion	Value
South America	
Caribbean	
Central America	
Northern America	
South-Eastern Asia	
Southern Europe	
Africa	
Western Europe	
Western Asia	
Northern Europe	
Oceania	
Central Asia	
Southern Asia	
Eastern Asia	
Eastern Europe	

Source: UNDOC. *Global Study on Homicide.* 2011. Trends, Contexts, Data

the age at which a minor can be charged, convicted, and incarcerated. "Strong Arm" policies find their strategy in more repression, including the death penalty, which stand in opposition to international agreements signed by Latin American countries. In those countries that have implemented "Strong Arm" policies, the results have been counterproductive: increasing the number of those in jail—the immense majority without trials or convictions—while failing to decrease crime and homicide rates. In due course, these policies have required that many of those incarcerated be set free due to lack of evidence. The harm and the backward movement that these policies cause in the democratic system are great, especially referring to civil rights and in relation to respecting human rights. Also, they tend to militarize the response not only toward crime, but also toward social issues. The response to crime needs to be as complex as the causes that create them. In addition, there is a growing level of impunity for many types of crimes.

Today, the emerging danger of organized crime is recognized as part of the presidential programs, but continues to be weak in the visions of political parties. In the academic field, there is some progress, but further research, analysis, and theoretical frameworks are still required. However, organized crime and illicit transnational networks have a growing impact. The impact of organized crime is one of the most significant changes in the last decade, especially in Central America, Mexico, and some Caribbean countries.

The adoption of a multidimensional perspective allows tackling complex security phenomena, in which the deciding factors are not military, but new threats. In this sense, the concept of security includes political, economic, social, health-related, and environmental factors.[5] The control and limitation of transnational organized crime demand higher levels of coordination within the state and the development of supranational institutions.[6] The meetings of Ministers of Public

Security of the Americas have established the first steps of coordination in the continent. ,The same is true of Comunidad de Policías de América (AMER-IPOL). To further international cooperation, political parties and governments must approach this issue as a national priority and as a state policy that requires the efforts of the entire political system. Debates about the failure of the "war on drugs" were strongly expressed at the Summit of the Americas in Cartagena de Indias (2012), and the need to consider different options is an opinion that is often expressed with intensity in the region. This is reflected in the report submitted by the Organization of American States (OAS) in 2013.

Surprises and Those That Are Surprised: The Growing Difficulties of Gauging Regional Reality

The use of public opinion polls as instruments of interpretation has been common in the analyses made by social scientists and governments. Many have thought that if polls were properly designed they would possess sufficient forecasting capacity to discern the main emerging national agendas and accurately evaluate the region's leaders. These results were seen as close to political reality, thus allowing for more accurate decision making. However, the most recent elections in Latin America demonstrate that, in general, the processes of public decision making have not advanced. In the region, there appears to be a marked tendency for a hidden vote, and those who wish to ascertain the voting intentions of the public based solely on public opinion surveys will fail. This situation has persisted for more than a decade.

This has consequences that extend beyond elections. The exercise of power and the attempt to find ways to strengthen government strategies have equally been based on the indicators from the polls as a reflection of the citizenry's acceptance of policies or decisions. To develop an agenda solely and exclusively on wavering public opinion can be risky. To respond only to the ups and downs of public opinion polls is to generate policies that are reactive and do not focus on long-term interests. Conversely, it is important to highlight that on the principal issues, public opinion is moved by and conforms to what is broadcast on television. Government policies should be founded on long-term results rather than responding to yesterday's news.

Between November 2005 and December 2006, twelve elections were held in Latin America. Eight presidential elections were held in the years 2012 and 2013. In 2014, seven more took place. Table 5.7 shows that with few exceptions, the results of these elections were unexpected and did not coincide with the predictions made by public opinion polls. This has produced surprises and many surprised observers, and illustrates the necessity of improving the instruments used to capture public opinion and combining them with other indicators and measurements capable of gauging what people are actually thinking.

The electoral results expressed some unforeseen tendencies and some continuations. In these elections, seven were surprises and five were predicted.

Table 5.8 shows that in the new cycle, the majority of the results were predicted; only three results were surprising.

Table 5.7 Elections in 2005 and 2006: Changes in Leadership, Latin America

Honduras	Nov. 2005	Manuel Zelaya	Surprise
Bolivia	Dec. 2005	Evo Morales	Surprise
Chile	Jan. 2006	Michelle Bachelet	Predicted
Costa Rica	Feb. 2006	Oscar Arias	Surprise
Haiti	Feb. 2006	René Preval	Predicted
Peru	Apr. 2006	Alan García	Surprise
Colombia	May. 2006	Reelección Uribe	Predicted
Mexico	Jul. 2006	Felipe Calderón	Surprise
Brazil	Oct. 2006	Reelección Lula	Predicted
Ecuador	Oct. 2006	Rafael Correa	Surprise
Nicaragua	Nov. 2006	Daniel Ortega	Surprise
Venezuela	Dec. 2006	Reelection Chávez	Predicted

Table 5.8 Elections 2007–2013: Change of Leadership, Latin America

Argentina	Dec. 2007	Cristina Fernández	Predicted
Bolivia	Jan. 2009	Reelection Evo Morales	Predicted
El Salvador	Mar. 2009	Mauricio Funes	Surprise
Panama	May. 2009	Ricardo Martinelli	Predicted
Uruguay	Nov. 2009	José Mujica	Predicted
Costa Rica	Feb. 2010	Laura Chinchilla	Predicted
Colombia	Jun. 2010	Juan Manuel Santos (2nd round)	Predicted
Brazil	Oct. 2010	Dilma Rouseff (2nd round)	Predicted
Haiti	Mar. 2011	Michel Martelly (2nd round)	Surprise
Peru	Jun. 2011	Ollanta Humala (2nd round)	Surprise
Nicaragua	Nov. 2011	Reelection Daniel Ortega	Predicted
Dominican Rep.	May. 2012	Danilo Medina	Predicted
Mexico	Jul. 2012	Enrique Peña Nieto	Predicted
Venezuela	2012	Hugo Chavez	Predicted
Ecuador	Feb. 2013	Reelection Rafael Correa	Predicted
Venezuela	Apr. 2013	Nicolás Maduro	Predicted
Paraguay	Apr. 2013	Horacio Cartes	Predicted
Honduras	Nov. 2013	Juan Orlando Hernández	Predicted
Chile	Dec. 2013	Reelection Michelle Bachelet (2nd round)	Predicted

In the 2014 cycle, more continuities than changes or alternations appear as predictable. But, as in previous cycles, the polls do not clarify the tendencies or the central aspects of the reluctance to participate. In this new cycle, there will be three elections in Central America (Costa Rica, El Salvador, and Panama) and four in South America (Brazil, Bolivia, Colombia, and Uruguay). In Costa Rica and Panama, the opposition won. In the other countries the governing party won, either with new leadership, such as in El Salvador and Uruguay, or by reelecting the sitting president, such as Brazil, Bolivia and Colombia.

In the majority of countries, we observe a territorial fragmentation in the voting in which the most neglected regions reject the extant economic and political models. In the same way, in practically all of the elections, significant fragmentation is created in Congress, with the major exception of Ecuador and, to a lesser extent, Chile. All of this creates considerable distrust of the elected presidents. In these cases, very often, the winners achieve power with minimal support and in the presence of a high level of abstention.

Creating Indicators for the New Political Map

Resorting to traditional perspectives of right and left for the purpose of categorizing the Latin American political panorama and its election results proves to be a useless task. These criteria, belonging to the Cold War era, make it difficult to strictly classify political leaders. This is a political prism that has ceased to be useful. In effect, it is as difficult to affirm that Leonel Fernández of the Dominican Republic and Oscar Arias of Costa Rica are from the neoliberal or traditional right, as it is to determine that Lula of Brazil, Kirchner of Argentina, or Bachelet of Chile today represent the traditional left. Left and right do not reflect the essential identities of the new leaders, nor do they represent the changes that are occurring in the world.

It is difficult to think of a political map of the region being totally structured, but we can point to some key elements necessary for its construction. We can rely on a few indicators that will allow us to interpret and understand the current political situation in Latin America. Aside from poverty and inequality, increases in violence, and the rise of corruption, it is necessary to consider new factors. Among the most important are the new geopolitical factors: the division between the north and the south in Latin America, and the trends in the Pacific and the Atlantic. We must also consider the anti-US climate; Latin America's insertion into the global economy and the perceptions of fair trade treaties; political polarization and the lack of social integration; leadership disputes; the tension between populism and responsible politics; the impact of the crisis of representation; and the relationships between the government, the opposition, and civil society organizations.

First, considering the weight of the economy, the influence of the United States, migratory processes, and remittances, two distinct Latin Americas are emerging: one in the north, oriented toward the United States, and another in the south that is more independent. Cultural ties represent the principal bonds between both. In the Latin America of the north, the processes of economic and commercial integration have had better stability, as demonstrated by the North American Free Trade Agreement (NAFTA) and the Sistema de Integración Centroamericana (SICA). At the same time, the free trade agreement between Central America and the United States (CAFTA) reflects the commercial power of Washington and its interest in reinforcing its unilateral weight through an agreement that appears multilateral. Table 5.9 shows that in the Central American region, trade relationship with the United States is very important because the United States receives most of the exports from that area of Latin America. Central America is also a privileged zone for US investments and the development of assembly plants (*maquiladoras*).

Second, the manner in which George W. Bush's government launched the "War on Terror" and the invasion of Iraq generated a strong international rejection of US foreign policy, including from the most important countries in Latin America. The countries of the region have tended to exercise a strong rejection of the unilateral politics of Washington. This was evident in Iraq's case. The arrival of Barack Obama to the White House generated high expectations for a change in the relationship. His speeches at the Summit of the Americas in Trinidad and Tobago and those expressed in the various tours to the region reinforced these expectations; however, many of them have not been met. The link with topics of domestic politics, as in the case of immigration, has generated expectations without effective results. The focus of US priorities in other regions, particularly in the wars in Iraq and Afghanistan, further reduced the presence and interest of the United States in Latin America and the Caribbean. This made it possible for the countries in the region to exercise autonomy and develop new mechanisms for the coordination of regional politics without the presence of the United States.

Third, in South America, one can observe a strong nationalism and criticism of certain aspects of globalization. This is added to anti-US tendencies and the rejection of unilateralism. The largest countries have led international efforts to coordinate policies to achieve a greater degree of autonomy. The main outcomes of these efforts are Bolivarian Alternative for the Americas (ALBA) and Union of South American Countries (UNASUR); the first with a strong anti-American label and the second reaffirming the autonomy of the region.

Fourth, Latin America is divided in terms of the impact of and the way of dealing with the cycles of international finance and global trade. There are different approaches, particularly in relation to trade liberalization and free trade agreements. The countries bordering the Pacific tend to support free trade, while the countries of the Atlantic—Argentina, Brazil, and Venezuela—reject this opening, and particularly those free trade agreements signed with the United States. In reality, this is not related so much with bordering one ocean or another, but with the way in which the economies of those on the Atlantic have more industrial weight: Brazil and Argentina have a domestic industrial base and rely on protectionist policies against imports from the United States. In the economies of the Pacific—Chile, Ecuador, Peru, and possibly Mexico—a very considerable part of their exports are tied to their natural resources: in Mexico, petroleum; in Chile, copper; and in Ecuador and Peru,

Table 5.9 Latin America and the Caribbean: Main Commercial Partners

MERCOSUR 2011	CAN 2012	MCCA 2012	CARICOM 2010	MÉXICO 2013 a)	CHILE 2013
Asia (34.7%)	United States (28%)	United States (33.3%)	United States (39.9%)	United States (78.5%)	China (23.4%)
European Union (23.0%)	European Union (14%)	MCCA (25.2%)	CARICOM (17.7%)	European Union (5.4%)	European Union (15.4%)
MERCOSUR (15.3%)	China (9% c/u)	European Union (14.7%)	European Union (10.7%)	Asia (4.8%)	United States (13.6)

a) January to October 2013. Includes only merchandise exports.

Note: The values presented in each case refer to the percentage of exports to the country or region.

Source: Prepared with IDB information. MERCOSUR report No. 17. February 2013. SIECA. Current status of the Central American economic integration. December 2013. In: www.sieca.int; Secretariat of the Andean Community. Andean Community: Foreign Trade in the Andean Community 2012. In: www.comunidadandina.org DIRECON. Report of Foreign Trade of Chile Third Trimester 2013. In: www.prochile.cl National Statistics Institute, Geography and Computing. Commercial Balance of Mexican goods. Revised information January–October 2013. In: www.inegi.gob.mx; CARICOM. Caricoms trade. A quick reference to some summary data. 2005–2010. Guyana, 2013. In: www.caricomstats.org.

mining. Therefore, commercial liberalization contributes to opening these countries up more effectively to different world markets, particularly those in China. Eleven countries have signed free trade agreements with the United States: Mexico, the Central American nations, and Dominican Republic, and three of the South American Pacific nations: Chile, Colombia, and Peru. The United States does not have existing agreements with Mercado Común del Sur (MERCOSUR) countries, nor with ALBA of South America. The latter have not signed agreements with the European Union either, although at the beginning of 2014, the first steps were taken to open relations with Europe.

To overcome the growing marginality of Latin America in global matters, as much politically as commercially, it is essential to design an agenda of constructive cooperation capable of tackling the weighty issues of interest to the various actors in the region. It is undeniable that a future agenda tying Latin America to major Western powers must incorporate, along with issues of investment, commercial ties, and migration, security issues that demand consideration of the problems of drug trafficking, organized crime, and terrorism.

Fifth, significant social and political polarization is permeating the region. Some countries are marked by deep social divisions that can cause high levels of conflict. Also, there are relatively stable countries with acceptable levels of social integration and cohesion. This is not meant to imply a complete absence of tensions, but comparatively, they are much less serious than those occurring in other Latin American countries. In the countries with greatest conflict, the difficulties of governing are directly related to social divisions and polarization that can lead to clashes and ruptures of democratic stability.

To reflect on the new Latin American middle classes is to address one of the successes in the region: millions of people moving out of poverty. It is an important change in the last three decades. In one decade alone, from the year 2000, inequality diminished in thirteen of seventeen countries of Latin America. As a result, there is a higher social demand for quality education, for more housing, and for better health coverage. The main demand is for economic and social stability, which ensures employment opportunities; but there is also a demand for political change. States increasingly promote policies that help develop the middle classes. In turn, they generate new social and political demands that must be met, and if they are not fulfilled, they generate frustration. Also significant are the protests of these new actors. Political parties fail to capture the essence of these changes. New forms of communication have facilitated the convergence of interests and the coordination of actions. The elites require greater sensitivity to these changes, and academics should capture the particularities of this new force that has broken into the world.

Sixth, competition for leadership stimulates conflicts among Latin American presidents. Trust among heads of state has passed through cycles of high erosion, as reflected in the speeches and criticisms related to "The Great Colombia" (Venezuela, Colombia, and Ecuador). This goes beyond attacks made during presidential campaigns—it is something more serious. In this context, clashes with Hugo Chávez were of particular note. The "CNN effect"—or the impact of the media—increased the resonance and effect of these discourses far beyond the actors directly involved. Chávez sought to strengthen his alternative integration project (ALBA) and his policy proposal, which at times seemed competitive with the interests of Brazil, but there was never an effective challenge. The death of Hugo Chávez had a big impact on the perspectives of regional integration and especially on the ALBA.

The seventh and final question is the debate between populism and pragmatism. The margins of action for Latin American countries in the context of globalization are limited. On the one hand, those who look to insert Latin America into the global system are trying to develop policies defined as "responsible." In some macroeconomic areas, these policies are not substantially different from those of neoliberalism. Nonetheless, they represent profound differences in social policies: their programs seek to improve the quality of citizens' lives, especially the neglected and vulnerable. In Latin America, the advances in social policies are an achievement of all governments in the region. This type of leadership does not make grand promises; it appeals instead to the responsibility of achieving solutions in a context of limited options.

On the other hand, the crisis of representation favors the appearance of "neopopulist" proposals. Eminently political, the neopopulist phenomenon is manifesting itself into a type of leadership in which the role of institutions is very limited, based on a direct communication between the leader and the people. This is facilitated by the media. This public dialogue and the political response have the capacity of generating important mobilizations. Populism can be a detonator of instability and deepen the crisis of representation in democratic institutions. The changing rules, the deinstitutionalization, the concentration of power, and clientelism are transformed into recurring political expressions. The legacies of neopopulism in the political sense, independent of their economic and social results, will demand the reconstruction of institutions, rule of law, and the rights of citizens in the context of polarization. This task will be anything but easy in the context of a disillusioned citizenry who sees their hopes frustrated. To reconstruct political systems after the collapse of populism may take a long time, great effort, and strong political will. Populist policies erase traditional institutional policies; hence, the search for new constitutional frameworks. This new form of policy making transcends the existing institutions and seeks to form a new and direct relationship between the leader and the masses. Populism tends to express itself in various forms of patronage that affect the essential foundations of democratic representation, although at times they "respect" democratic forms. In others, they are performed by mechanisms with low degrees of legality and legitimacy. One of the more complex characteristics of the region is the violence that is expressed, especially in the northern area of Central America, Mexico, and the Caribbean. The lack of security, justice, and rule of law produces pandemic figures of intentional homicide and high levels of impunity. In Latin America, insecurity is one of the central concerns, and violence hinders human development.

It is necessary to add to the aforementioned a last essential element: the deadlines for consultation and negotiation of regional projects are short. Those that are not designed, made, approved, and have immediate implementation capacity will have no future prospects. Future electoral cycles are likely to continue to shape internal dynamics, once again relegating consensus building and regional integration issues to the back burner.

Electoral democracy has taken root in Latin America. Electoral processes are daily becoming more transparent. Those who win the election also win the recount. Acts of coercion are decreasing. Electoral tribunals are becoming more important in all of the countries. Nonetheless, the problems with elections are closely linked to the use of public resources in campaigns, namely those exercised by big communication media, especially television conglomerates. This generates inequality of access. In this context, in relation to elections, money (public and private, legal or illegal) is a strong temptation and an easy way of co-optation by organized crime. Thus, beyond the advances in this field, it is necessary to strengthen the mechanisms of democracy and transparency. The alternation of power through elections demonstrates that democracy advances despite the weaknesses of institutions like political parties or Congress. However, the danger of abstentionism has emerged, even as the dangers of coups d'état have practically disappeared.

The economic growth experienced in Latin America since 2003, and which is projected to continue in the future, is generating the best conditions and opportunities the region has had in more than a quarter century to advance in the direction of designing policies to mitigate poverty. The emergence of the new middle classes will be essential in the development and future of democracy and regional stability.

Latin American democracies have great challenges that their governments must face in a short period. Citizens want efficient and effective responses to various issues on the public agenda. Their patience is short. Therefore, when concrete results are not forthcoming, rapid declines in presidential popularity occur, precipitating changes in government by means of popular protests or "street democracy," as seen between 1997 and 2009. This phenomenon demonstrates that people can achieve results with important popular movements centered in the capital or other urban areas. In this context, the populist temptation of radical processes within weak institutions emerges as a significant threat in many countries of the region.

As transnationalization and globalization, especially in the context of the international financial crisis of 2009–2013, have shown, significant decisions no longer reside at the national level. Yes, the people choose; but governments do not. A direct consequence is that elections and politics in general are devalued. Once again, the need for a more deliberative democracy resurfaces with these dimensions, in particular, with the need for greater international dialogue.

Stable governance in Latin America has but one future: to deepen democracy and make it more efficient. The legitimacy of electoral democracy is beyond doubt. The question is how to go deeper, to take advantage of the prospects of economic development with greater equity. Societal participation in the design and execution of various public policies is essential, as is containing, limiting, and acting against corruption. Corruption is an integral element in the erosion of state democracies and rule of law. The quality of democracy the region is capable of constructing will significantly determine the future stability, prosperity, and peace of Latin America and the Caribbean.

Notes

1 I would like to thank Diana Guardia for her collaboration. An earlier version was published by *Nueva Sociedad* 205(September/October) in 2006.
2 *Corporación Latinobarómetro*.Informe Latinobarómetro 2006. Santiago, Chile. 2006, 2011, and 2013. Retrieved from www.latinobarometro.org.
3 World Bank. *Anticorruption in Transition: A Contribution to the Policy Debate.* Washington, D.C: World Bank, 2000.
4 Transparencia Internacional. *Convenciones Anticorrupción en América, lo que La Sociedad Civil Puede Hacer para que Funcionen.* 2006. Retrieved from www.transparency.org.
5 Declaración sobre Seguridad de las Américas. OEA. México. 2003.
6 FLASCO (2006) *El Crimen Organizado Internacional: Una Grave Amenaza a la democracia en América Latina y el Caribe.* II Informe del Secretario General. FLACSO/ Secretaría General. Retrieved from www.flacso.org.

Bibliography

Archondo, R. (2006) Qué le espera a Bolivia con Evo Morales? *Nueva Sociedad* 202(3–4): 4–12. .
Bernald, M. and Serrano, M. (2005) *Crimen Organizado y Seguridad Internacional, Cambio y Continuidad.* México DF, Mexico: Fondo de Cultura Económica.
Bonilla, A. and Ortíz, M.S. (comp.) (2013) *El Papel Político, Económico, Social y Cultural de la Comunidad Iberoamericana en un Nuevo Contexto Globa.* (p. 306); San José, Costa Rica: SEGIB/AECID/CAF/FLACSO.
Casas-Zamora, K. (2013) *The Besieged Polis. Citizens Insecurity and Democracy in Latin America* (p. 110). http://www.brookings.edu/research/reports/2013/07/08-citizen-insecurity-casas-zamora. Accessed December 16, 2014.
CEPAL. (2006) América Latina y el Caribe: Proyecciones 2006–2007. Serie Estudios Estadísticos y Prospectivos No 42, Santiago de Chile. http://repositorio.cepal.org/bitstream/handle/11362/4743/0600287_es.pdf?sequence=1. Accessed December 16, 2014.
Fernández de Soto, G. and Pérez Herrero, P. (coord.) (2013) *América Latina: Sociedad, Economía y Seguridad en un Mundo Global.* (p. 366). Universidad de Alcalá/CAF, Madrid: Editorial Marcial Pons.
FLACSO (July 28, 2005) La Gobernabilidad en América Latina: Balance Reciente y Tendencias a Futuro, Informe del Secretario General. http://www.flacso.org/sites/default/files/I-INFORME-SG-2005.pdf. Accessed December 16, 2014.
FLACSO (May 2006) El Crimen Organizado Internacional: Una Grave Amenaza a la Democracia en América Latina y el Caribe, II Informe del Secretario General. http://www.flacsoandes.edu.ec/libros/digital/49251.pdf. Accessed December 16, 2014.

FLACSO-Chile (2005) *Agenda Democrática*. http://www.flacsochile.org/publicaciones/agenda-democratica-2o-ed/. Accessed December 16, 2014.

Freedom House. (2003) *Freedom in the World 2013*. Retrieved from www.freedomhouse.org.

Gratius, S. (February 2006) La 'Revolución' de Hugo Chávez: ¿Proyecto de Izquierdas o Populismo Histórico? Fundación para las Relaciones Internacionales y el Diálogo Exterior. Retrieved from www.fride.org/Publications/Publication.aspx?Item=1073.

Guzmán León, J. and Sáenz, S.B. (coord.) (2010) *Voces Latinoamericanas sobre Gobernabilidad Democrática* (p. 214). San Jose, Costa Rica: FLACSO/AECID.

Nogueira, M.A. (2006) *Más allá de lo Institucional: Crisis, Partidos y Sociedad en el Brazil de Hoy*. *Nueva Sociedad* 202(3–4): 31–44.

Osorio, J. (2006) *La Descomposición de la Clase Política Latinoamericana: ¿el Fin de un Periodo?* *Nueva Sociedad* 203(5–6): 15–26 .

Paramio, L. and Revilla, M. (eds.) (2006) *Una Nueva Agenda de Reformas Políticas en América Latina*. Madrid: Fundación Carolina/Siglo XXI.

PNUD (2004) *La Democracia en América Latina. Hacia una Democracia de Ciudadanos y Ciudadanas* (coord.: Dante Caputo), Aguilar/Altea/Taurus/Alfaguara, Buenos Aires. http://www2.ohchr.org/spanish/issues/democracy/costarica/docs/PNUD-seminario.pdf. Accessed December 16, 2014.

PNUD (2013) *Informe Regional de Desarrollo Humano 2013–2014. Seguridad Ciudadana con Rostro Humano: Diagnóstico y Propuestas para América Latina*. (p. 266). New York: UNDP.

Revista Política Exterior (2011) *El Hombre de Obama para América Latina*: *Entrevista a Arturo Valenzuela*. (pp. 158–67). Madrid: Enero/Febrero.

Rodríguez, J.C. (2006) *La Nueva Política Pendular de Paraguay. Entre el Mercosur y el ALCA*. *Nueva Sociedad* 203(5–6): 10–14 .

Rojas Aravena, F. (ed.) (2012) *América Latina y el Caribe: Vínculos Globales en un Contexto Multilateral Complejo*. (p. 510). Buenos Aires: Editorial Teseo/CIDOB/AECID/FLACSO.

Rojas Aravena, F. (ed.) (2012) *América Latina y el Caribe: Relaciones Internacionales en el SigloXXI. Diplomacia de Cumbres y Espacios de Concertación Regional y Global*. (p. 412). Buenos Aires: Editorial Teseo/AECID/FLACSO.

Rojas Aravena, F. (2013) Cambios en el Mapa Político en América Latina y el Caribe, in M. Mesa (coord.), *El Reto de la Democracia en un Mundo en Cambio: Respuestas Políticas y Sociales*. (pp163–81) Madrid: Anuario 2013–2014, CEIPAZ.

Rojas Aravena, F. and Alvarez-Marín, A. (eds.) (2011) *América Latina y el Caribe: Globalización y Conocimiento. Repensar las Ciencias Sociales*. (p. 412). Montevideo, Uruguay: UNESCO/FLACSO.

Rojas Aravena, F. and Guzmán León, J. (coords.) (2011) *La Política sí Importa, la Inseguridad Preocupa y la Violencia Impide el Desarrollo. Estudio de Opinión Latinoamericana 2009–2010*. (pp. 208). San José, Costa Rica: IPSOS/AECID/FLACSO.

Silva, P. and Rojas Aravena, F. (comps.) (2013) *Gobernabilidad y Convivencia Democrática en América Latina: Las Dimensiones Regionales, Nacionales y Locales*. (p. 220). San José, Costa Rica: FLACSO/AECID.

Solís Rivera, L.G. (2006) *Elecciones en Costa Rica: la inevitable transición*. *Nueva Sociedad* 203(5–6): 4–9 .

Villasuso, J.M., Francisco, F.J., and Marco Arroyo, F. (2005) *Corrupción: Más allá de las Percepciones*. San José, Costa Rica: Fundación Friedrich Ebert/Cedal.

Zovatto, D. (2013) *América Latina 2013: Balance Político Electoral*.(p. 22A). San José, Costa Rica: Diario La Nación.

6 The Rule of Law in Latin America

Luz E. Nagle

"The rule of law is conceivable only if institutions tame or transform brute power"

(Teblicock and Daniels 2008, 40)

In the first edition of this chapter, we addressed the nature of the rule of law in Latin America, its historical origins, the distinctions between the rule of law and rule by law as it pertains to government and rule in Latin America, and effect that rule-of-law reform programs has had in the region. This new chapter examines the forces at work in Latin America that shape the development of and impediments to achieving a sustainable rule-of-law paradigm in the region.

Introduction

Significant events have impacted the rule of law in Latin America since the first edition of this chapter was published in 2008. The passing from the Latin American political arena of polarizing figures like Hugo Chávez, Alvaro Uribe, and Felipe Calderón, and the ascendency of populist heads of state like Cristina Fernández de Kirchner, Evo Morales, Nicolás Maduro, and Dilma Rousseff signal a sweeping shift toward leftist-socialist ideologies dependent on rhetoric that appeals to the masses and stricter government control over the private sector. Drug cartels have destabilized many states in Mexico, transnational criminal organizations and international terrorist groups have become entrenched throughout South America, indigenous rights groups have grown more militant against oppressive state policies, and Central American states are increasingly coming under the unsettling influence of China and Russia.

The rule of law is being redefined and in some instances subjugated by the prerogatives of a new generation of liberal politicians and highly educated technocrats who use popular agendas and the dispensation of entitlements to gain and retain power and personal wealth. In tangible ways, nearly all the countries in the region are emerging rapidly from Third World status. But despite progress and increased security in many regions of countries that have been afflicted by violence for decades, Latin American states are still struggling due to the entrenched effects of corruption, lack of government accountability, lack of access to education for all, and a woeful lack of enforcement of and indifference to the laws that embody a civil society. For much of the region, the rule of law, as one scholar notes, is a "fragile path of progress" (Teblicock and Daniels 2008).

This chapter addresses some of the many issues that impact the rule of law in Latin America. These are corruption, dysfunctional judiciaries, shortcomings in legal education, organized crime and terrorism, and the increasing influence of foreign states in the region.

Framing the Rule of Law

When the Organization of American States (OAS) adopted the Inter-American Democratic Charter in 2001,[1] the rule of law was defined as the "effective exercise of representative democracy,"[2] the essential elements of which include "access to and the exercise of power in accordance with the rule of law" and "the separation of powers and independence of the branches of government."[3] To accomplish such goals, the charter stressed, citizen participation must be "ethical and responsible" while complying with the constitutional and legal frameworks of each nation.[4]

Over the last decade, the composition of governments in the region, the conduct of government officials, the attitude of military and law enforcement personnel toward the civilian population, and a feeling among many segments of society that their concerns and issues are ignored by the state call into question whether any of the ambitions of the charter have been achieved or sustained. Crime, violence, protest, and government inefficiency weaken progress in fortifying the rule of law. Indeed, today's images transmitted through social media and broadcast news of protests in the streets of Latin American capitals look little different from the grainy footage of protestors clashing with authorities in the 1960s and 1970s. The irony is that in some countries, the protestors back then are the politicians under fire now.

Understanding the rule of law in Latin America in its present state begins first and foremost by not viewing the region through a monochromatic lens. The stereotype of struggling banana republics run by dictatorial oafs has been replaced by a vibrant collage comprised of highly educated technocrats who can claim many advances in the quality of life for many Latin Americans. Remote villages are now connected to the Internet, and e-commerce portals have brought small-scale coffee growers, weavers, and artisans into direct contact with consumers in First World countries. Where once there were no schools or teachers, children are now educated through distance learning, and medical care that not long ago was left to the local shaman is now provided by teams of dedicated and highly motivated medical professionals. Steps are now being taken to establish and protect property rights for rural inhabitants—a decades-old hindrance to development and enfranchisement—and engineers and scientists are hard at work in many places trying to improve government infrastructure and provide safe drinking water and continuous electrical power.

Establishing the rule of law requires a consistent state presence that can be measured and monitored. The World Bank has established six Worldwide Governance Indicators to determine the state of governance in a country. These indicators include the process by which governments are selected, monitored, and replaced; the capacity of the government to effectively formulate and implement sound policies; and the respect of citizens and the state for the institutions that govern economic and social interactions among them.[5] The markers identified to determine governance are as follows:

- **Voice and accountability** captures perceptions of the extent to which a country's citizens are able to participate in selecting their government, as well as freedom of expression, freedom of association, and a free media;
- **Political stability and absence of violence** measures perceptions of the likelihood that the government will be destabilized or overthrown by unconstitutional or violent means, including politically motivated violence and terrorism;
- **Government effectiveness** captures perceptions of the quality of public services, the quality of the civil service and the degree of its independence from political pressures, the quality of policy formulation and implementation, and the credibility of the government's commitment to such policies;
- **Regulatory quality** captures perceptions of the ability of the government to formulate and implement sound policies and regulations that permit and promote private-sector development;
- **Rule of law** captures perceptions of the extent to which agents have confidence in and abide by the rules of society, and in particular the quality of contract enforcement, property rights, the police, and the courts, as well as the likelihood of crime and violence;
- **Control of corruption** captures perceptions of the extent to which public power is exercised for private gain, including both petty and grand forms of corruption, as well as "capture" of the state by elites and private interests.[6]

These indicators provide an important framework to quantify and isolate critical details about what Latin Americans think of their governments. For example, it is notable that Latin American nations perceived to be among the most corrupt are also states in which a strong leftist/populist form of authoritative government has taken hold in the last decade, such as in Argentina, Bolivia, Nicaragua, and Venezuela. We also learn from such indicators that stabilizing government, maintaining security throughout a state's national territory, and guaranteeing constitutional freedoms are essential to preserving and expanding the rule of law. The modern Latin American state in general seems to understand this, but executing this understanding is still highly problematic due to the many following issues that continually challenge and threaten the rule of law.

Corruption

Corruption runs deeply throughout the cultural, historical, political, and social fabric of Latin America, and emanates from an imbalance of the social, government, and business forces that confer on the ruling elites a virtual monopoly on economic opportunity and upward mobility. Throughout Latin America, corruption is viewed not as a characteristic of political system, but as the system itself (DePalma 1999). A working definition is provided by the United Nations:

> Corruption determines the misuse of Governments' resources by diverting them from sectors of vital importance such as health, education and development. Poor people are therefore deprived of economic growth and development opportunities. The price of public services rises to the point that economically deprived people can no longer afford them. As the poor become poorer, corruption feeds poverty and inequality.[7]

The Corruption Perceptions Index,[8] maintained by Transparency International, underscores the extent to which corruption threatens the rule of law in Latin America. In 2012, of 176 nations represented in the index, only Chile and Uruguay fall within the top twenty countries perceived to be the least corrupt in the world. Costa Rica and Cuba ranked at 48 and 58, respectively. Of the remaining Latin American nations, nearly all rank in the lower half, with Venezuela occupying the ignominious rank of being the 165th most corrupt country in the world (tied with Haiti).

World Bank research paints a discouraging picture of failure to establish and sustain the rule of law in Latin America. Throughout the 1990s and the first decade of the new millennium, foreign governments and private corporations pumped billions of dollars in aid into Latin America in a sweeping array of reform projects geared toward development, security, and institution building. Yet, only three of eighteen Latin American states showed progress in the rule of law midway through the last two decades (Teblicock and Daniels 2008, 37–8)

Some scholars apply a strict economic analysis to explain why the rule of law has been impeded, noting three categories of impediments to establishing the rule of law. First, there is a lack of human capital and technical know-how that impairs institution building despite the presence of political will (Teblicock and Daniels 2008, 38). Second, "social-cultural-historical factors" render rule-of-law development impotent (Teblicock and Daniels 2008, 39). Third, economy-based factors such as a "lack of effective political demand for reforms" impede rule-of-law development (Teblicock and Daniels 2008, 39). Any number of analyses can account for why the rule of law struggles to take hold and to be retained in the Latin American morass, but in my mind, it all boils down to one factor: corruption.

From corruption, failures of state and good intentions flow. It can be a matter of intentional and willful corruption, or passive corruption, which entails corrupting a system simply by doing nothing to improve it. Laissez-faire can be as debilitating to the rule of law as positive acts to commit bribery, graft, other white collar criminal acts, or violent acts of a political nature.

Let us look at the three impediments noted earlier in the context of corruption in Latin America.

Lack of human capital and technical know-how that impairs institution building. A random Internet search of professionals in various disciplines, from engineering, to economics, to law, indicates that Latin America is vibrant with a new generation of highly educated technocrats. Many in the private sector and in academia have advanced degrees from outside Latin America. Among twenty-five law partners listed in the Martindale-Hubbell law firm directory for just one law firm in Sao Paolo, Brazil, sixteen hold advanced law degrees (LL.M.), and thirteen of the sixteen degrees are from foreign universities, including Cambridge University, the University of London, the University of Chicago, New York University, and the University of Paris. In one of the leading Central American law firms, five of the seven partners in the San José, Costa Rica, office hold LL.M. degrees from Georgetown University, New York University, and the University of Houston, respectively. At the University of Antioquia in Medellín, Colombia, several members of the engineering faculty hold Ph.D. degrees from abroad, including one professor holding a degree from the University of Troyes in France. Two engineering professors from the National University in Medellín received Ph.D. degrees in Argentina and in Wisconsin, respectively, while an economics professor at EAFIT University (Escuela de Administración, Finanzas y Tecnología) in Medellín holds a PhD from the University of Illinois. Throughout academia and in the higher levels of government anywhere in Latin America, one can find highly educated individuals whose educations have taken them beyond Latin America to expose them to other cultures, other political systems, and other attitudes about work, progress, and development.

In many cities in Latin America, the economy is strong, like in Medellín and Panamá City, Panamá, where billions of dollars from decades of drug trafficking and money laundering have pumped up the formal economy and created a construction boom that has enriched thousands of businessmen and reduced unemployment to record lows. In Peru, the national economy grew at a robust 6.4 percent annually from 2002 to 2012 (Neuman 2013), employment was strong, imported goods were flowing into the country, and people were spending money on luxury goods.

Such indicators could be construed to contradict this first impediment to the rule of law because while there is plenty of human capital and technical know-how throughout Latin America, institutionalized corruption is always pegged to prosperity and development. It persists like a cancer, constantly attacking what should otherwise be a healthy body politic and a vigorous economic and commercial constitution. When one speaks to highly skilled and highly educated professionals making their way through life anywhere in Latin America, common concerns and frustrations rise to the top like froth on a café latte.

For example, promotions to higher positions of authority are often based on personal connections rather than merit, with the result that individuals in positions to make important decisions are often incompetent to do so. Licensing, permitting, and satisfying a maze of inexplicable regulations and requirements is a lengthy and exhausting process, such that bribery and quid pro quo business arrangements become the only means to get anything accomplished quickly. Business people expect it, and bureaucrats rely on it.

Being older and more experienced is now becoming a liability as younger technocrats, intoxicated by the arrogance of youth, move into the business world and forcibly move older executives aside. The loss of business acumen, technical skill, and wisdom of older colleagues has a negative impact on the collective knowledge of any organization and renders that organization less competent and "seasoned." Ethical conduct in business is considered anathema of the older generation, and corporate governance becomes little more than an interesting topic for panelists at annual conferences in Orlando or New York.

Bureaucratic malaise impedes getting anything accomplished day in and day out in most government offices, and layers of red tape and an inexplicable and unaccountable gauntlet of staffers and minor functionaries slow the pace of work to a snail's crawl. Even the acquisition of scientific apparatus for academic research is subject to bureaucratic chokepoints that encourage under-the-table dealing in order to get the equipment necessary to engage in research and development enterprises (Pérez and Bashirullah 2000, 273). A pair of scientists from Venezuela put this quite succinctly when they wrote that an inefficient bureaucratic system reigns in most Latin American academic institutions as well as in government. Most universities employ more administrative staff than faculty and squander budgets on unnecessary paperwork to justify the positions created within divisions that have task-specific designations, such as "purchasing," "budget," "finance," and "control" (Pérez and Bashirullah 2000, 273).

> The simplest transaction, for example, payment of expenses to attend a scientific meeting, will probably not be completed until the event is over, unless the researcher personally tracks the file from desk to desk. Every four years, the authorities change and the new ones introduce their own systems, allegedly for efficiency but in fact to justify hiring new people. So a new bottleneck is created. This growth of administration can come only at the expense of research and teaching.
>
> (Pérez and Bashirullah 2000, 273)

The scientists concluded, "Drastic measures are required to minimize bureaucracy and improve efficiency, but university authorities (which are elected) will not risk their popularity" (Pérez and Bashirullah 2000, 273). This preservation of the bureaucratic status quo is a form of corruption that impedes the sustainability of a rule of law, not just in legal matters and governance, but also in the norms that bind the civil society.

Taken in another view, the academics' concerns underscore a long-standing authoritarian pragmatism in Latin America, that is to say, rule by law rather than rule of law, that is intended not for the benefit of all society, but for the sake of preserving bureaucratic systems and for preserving the livelihoods of bureaucrats who become lazy and indifferent. Not only is the preservation of bureaucracy corrosive to the Latin American state and its institutions, but at some point, individuals grow so exhausted confronting the bureaucracies that they resort to bypassing the system through illegal or unethical means, which further reinforces corruption and further weakens the prospects of achieving the rule of law.

Circumventing corrupt bureaucratic systems, pushing out individuals perceived as being past their prime, and disregarding the aspirations of technocrats who wish to accomplish good and encourage progress and development all create a climate of corruption that encourages illegality, or at the least, unethical behavior, and no amount of human capital and technical know-how can overcome those individuals who have conceded to the forces of corruption simply because they hold bureaucratic authority to do essentially whatever they want to do with impunity.

Social-cultural-historical factors render rule-of-law development impotent. Political scientists and legal historians attach labels to eras of development in order to delineate the evolution of sociopolitical systems in Latin America. Schor (2003) has pointed out, for instance, that a thorough examination of the legacies at play in the hemisphere is central to understanding the political and social tensions that affect nation building, development, and security in the region. If one peels back the onion of social, cultural, and historical factors, fundamentally, the modern Latin American state is the embodiment of a centuries-old patronage system in which a ruling elite maintains control by manipulating interaction among and within the three branches of government in order to preserve the status quo of a ruling class composed of large landowners in control of vast natural resources, and a powerful merchant class capable of manipulating trade and commerce to influence the political landscape.

Following independence from Spain, the nascent Latin American republics teethed their way through oligarchies, autocracies, dictatorships, liberalism, fascism, corporatism, socialism, populism, and now, neopopulism. All these political movements, regardless of what was accomplished, have one common component that persists down through the decades: that a minority of like-minded individuals imposes itself on the majority for the sole purpose of preserving their own prerogatives as political elites. The well-being of the democratic state and its citizens has little to do with anything, and indeed, reactions by those disaffected by the imposition of the political elites have resulted in internal armed conflict and civil war in most Latin American states at some point or another. In fact, but for isolated hostilities between Latin American countries, like the War of the Pacific[9] and the War of 1941,[10] violent conflict in Iberoamerica since liberation from European powers has been primarily internal armed conflicts and civil wars.

In such a crucible of political tension and historical turmoil, the rule of law has almost no chance of emerging, and even in this new decade, we see populist democratic movements propelling authoritarian leaders into power in places that are by no means failing Third World backwaters. This has occurred in Argentina, Brazil, Colombia, Ecuador, Nicaragua, and Venezuela, to name a few. While the new populist leadership may claim that their democratic election into office proves that the rule of law is healthy and respected, once in office, their policies become those of rule *by* law rather than rule *of* law. One highly respected liberal journalist with many years of experience in Latin America recently reported that this new batch of authoritarian populists has amassed vast powers to marginalize their opponents and the media, manipulate the system to their advantage, and "erode the checks and balances" (Forero 2012).

Nowhere has this become more evident than in Argentina where socialist President Cristina Fernández de Kirchner rode a wave of populist support into office and promptly resorted to time-honored dictatorial tendencies such as ruling by decree without any legislative input, imposing state controls of all sorts on the private sector, seizing pension funds, and printing money in order to blunt rapid inflation. She has justified these actions as being for the good of the people who, she seems to feel, have no idea what is good for them. In the process, she has quietly amassed a personal fortune through blatant corruption estimated to be in the many tens of millions of dollars (Mount and Sherwell 2012).

If history is bound to repeat itself, then the example of Fernández de Kirchner is little different from the activities of long-gone Latin American dictators who ruled by fiat and enriched themselves while in office. Social, cultural, and historical factors do play an important part in rendering the rule of law impotent. But when citizens seem willing to elect and reelect modern-day robber barons, should the question become not "is there a rule of law in Latin America?" but rather, "does the rule of law even matter?" Another factor, at once social, cultural, and historical, is that the majority of Latin Americans are simply resigned to the fact that the rule of law simply does not exist for them and is of such an abstract and ephemeral character as to be meaningless.

Lack of Effective Political Demand for Reforms Impede Rule-of-Law Development

Latin American politicians and government officials tend not to do anything to upset their own "rice bowls" when it comes to instituting reforms. Some legislative and judicial branches in Latin America are little more than a rubber stamp for authoritarian executive branches that rule by decree rather than by democratic dialog and debate. The legislative branches also tend to ignore the wishes of their constituency in favor of preserving the political prerogatives of the ruling elites, such that any level of citizen support and commitment for rule-of-law reforms is "unlikely to translate into effective political mobilization for reforms" (Teblicock and Daniels 2008, 39).

Moreover, all three government branches tend to be rife with patronage and cronyism, and those politicians and government bureaucrats who derive their livelihoods and a host of benefits from the status quo of corruption are reluctant to institute reforms that fortify and advance the rule of law (Teblicock and Daniels 2008, 39–40). From a private-sector perspective, all three branches of government exist to create economic prosperity and enrichment for the political elites. For example, the executive branch decrees favorable treatment for a large energy project by a corporation that will cut the president and his or her cronies in on a piece of the pie. The legislative branch, whose members will also receive their share of the pie, imposes or rescinds through legislative acts laws that remove environmental regulations that may adversely affect the exploitation of resources, or enact legislation that reduces labor rights and union representation so that the corporation can maximize profit. The judiciary protects the corporation and the corrupt politicians by tying up for years any legal challenges to the project, and throws out of court claims for damages by populations adversely impacted by the project. The rule of law, then, becomes little more than a political platitude to extort when the need to be self-righteous arises—for instance, when international aid organizations like the World Bank and the Inter-American Development Bank and foreign governments propose development and reform projects.

On the other hand, some Latin American judiciaries have taken activist positions to confront excesses in the executive branch or to take the initiative away from the legislative branch when that branch vacillates on key issues that impact the rule of law. We saw this in recent years in Colombia, where the Colombian Constitutional Court's relations with then President Alvaro Uribe deteriorated over various constitutional rights issues to the point that the executive launched a stunning smear campaign of personal attacks against several of the court's judges in retaliation in an effort to cow the judiciary to Uribe's will.[11] That he did not succeed was a stunning rebuke to the hubris Uribe displayed over the course of his unprecedented tenure as an autocratic president of Latin America's oldest representative democracy.[12] In this rare instance of an executive branch failing to bend the judiciary to its will, the manifestation of the rule of law, while ephemeral at best, was present in that moment in recent Colombian history.

Law enforcement throughout Latin America cannot be said to enjoy the full confidence and support of the civil society. In Mexico, for instance, 80 percent of the Mexican population believes that police are generally corrupt (Cevallos 2009) and that at any time a police officer might attempt to extort citizens in some way. Mexican children learn early on from older family members not to trust police or any Mexican authorities (Samuels 2005). Even American tourists in Mexico have known for decades that carrying extra money specifically to pay off police officers who may detain them is a requisite for travel south of the border. It does not help the perception of citizens toward law enforcement when, contrary to the United States where television and film portray police officers and detectives as larger-than-life heroes and guardians of society, Mexican police have long been portrayed in telenovelas and on the big screen as corrupt and incompetent oafs or sinister antagonists. Stereotypes, whether justified or not, contribute to negative perceptions that adversely impact the status of the rule of law.

Dysfunctional Judiciaries

The judicial branch in Latin America has long been viewed as the Cinderella of government (Nagle 1999), forced by many factors to play a subservient role in the functions of government. The judiciary has been plagued by many maladies that impact the rule of law, and unfortunately, the solutions prescribed have in many cases succeeded only in making matters worse. Throughout Latin America, the independence of the judiciary, a key requirement for a tripartite government, is undermined by self-serving interests and subterfuge within the other political branches.[13] If the meaning of the rule of law also includes sustaining *formal or procedural justice*, then the justice system must be predictable and certain, and those working with the judiciary must be accountable and their work transparent. Each year, judiciaries in nearly every Latin American nation come under harsh criticism for incompetence, corruption, and failure to deliver justice. More alarming still is that several of the judiciaries most troubled are those that have transitioned to an accusatorial justice system imposed by the United States throughout the last two decades.

In Honduras, the judicial system suffers from inadequate funding, poor staffing, lack of resources, low wages for judicial officials, and lack of performance standards that make judicial officials susceptible to bribery, patronage, political influence, and interference by power special interests in the outcomes of court proceedings (United States State Department 2012, 7–8). Public distrust of the judicial system is widespread. Although Honduran law "provides for the right to a fair public trial, permits defendants to confront or question witnesses and present witnesses and evidence on their behalf, and grants defendants access to government evidence relevant to their cases," these rights frequently are not respected (United States State Department 2012, 7–8).

Among other problems associated with a weak and failing judicial branch are:

- Extrajudicial killings by members of the police that go unpunished
- Arbitrary and summary executions committed by vigilantes and former members of the security forces that continue with near impunity
- Beatings and other abuse of detainees by security forces

- Impunity for human rights violations
- Failure of the judiciary to provide due process of law and to reduce lengthy pretrial detentions (United States State Department 2005)

The judiciary in El Salvador barely functions by any standard, and the rule of law continues to be violated. The Immigration Refugee Board of Canada's report on El Salvador in 2012[14] presents a demoralizing picture of weak government and failing institutions that support the judicial functions, and the US State Department considers El Salvador one of the most violent countries in the world (USAC 2012). Citizen security is under constant threat by gangs and international organized crime[15] due to "inadequate training, insufficient government funding, lack of a uniform code of evidence, and isolated instances of corruption and outright criminality" among the Salvadoran National Police.[16] The judiciary itself is reported to be inefficient, corrupt, and prone to political interference. Impunity of criminals is high; law enforcement officers, victims, and witnesses are intimidated and murdered; judges are subject to outside intimidation and influence; and the criminal conviction rate has been abysmal.[17] The Salvadoran human rights organization, Instituto de Derechos Humanos de la UCA (IDHUCA), has reported that oral testimony takes precedence in judicial proceedings and that scientific evidence is rarely used.[18] Witness protection in judicial proceedings is broken. One newspaper reported in 2011 that in one instance, "six hours after a witness had testified without a voice distorter, two of his family members were attacked resulting in one of them being killed."[19]

Peru fares little better with a judiciary that is debilitated by corruption, misconduct, and incompetence from the start of police investigations up through the senior judges trying cases. The judiciary's conversion to an accusatorial system at the behest of the United States has greatly complicated the prosecution of complex organized crime cases. The specialized judges that once handled such cases under the inquisitorial system have been replaced by jury trials, which according to one report, "demands a higher burden of proof and causes prosecutors to have to work harder to build their cases. Few prosecutors are currently capable of this."[20]

The effective delivery of justice throughout Latin America has been severely compromised by the introduction over the last decade of the Anglo-American adversarial system imposed by the United States in a manner that can only be described as paternalistic.[21] Rather than preserving the inquisitorial processes of Latin American legal institutions by fixing specific problems in weak and failing judiciaries, the United States sent forth teams of so-called rule-of-law experts that were convinced that the civil law judicial processes are inferior to the common law milieu of the Anglo-American legal system. These "experts" took the sledgehammer approach to gutting and replacing the judicial systems without any apparent regard to the social, cultural, and historical background of Latin America's centuries-old continental legal traditions.

The results have been mixed at the least and disastrous at worst. Rather than helping to improve the delivery of justice and reinforce the rule of law, the judicial reform efforts have deterred meaningful and enduring change and have caused discontent, confusion, and animosity toward reform projects and deter rule-of-law ends.[22] No doubt serious reform of the judicial institutions in the Americas was needed. But there were also clear risks, as one legal scholar pointed out, in using Anglo-American models to fix the legal "insufficiencies" without "due regard to the particular needs and contexts of the Southern 'receiving' societies" (Thome 2000).

Organized Crime and Terrorism

The United Nations has long recognized that organized crime is one of the major threats to development, security, and sustaining the rule of law.[23] The presence of domestic and transborder criminal organizations and terrorist groups pose a clear and present danger to regional stability and strengthening of the rule of law throughout Latin America. Organized crime and terrorist groups take hold and proliferate where governance is weak and corruption is the norm. They exploit corruption in state institutions by infiltrating weak and failing political systems, by asserting economic criminality—for instance in the form of money laundering and illegal exploitation of resources—and by imposing influence throughout all levels of Latin American society, particularly where government authority is impotent or not present at all. Transnational organized crime also impacts the rule of law in the entire region because it transcends national boundaries and exploits gaps in international law enforcement cooperation.

Organized crime both feeds and benefits from underdevelopment and conflict.[24] Farmers from developing countries produce illicit crops because they are not given a sustainable alternative by their government. Public servants, those mostly responsible for the deterrence of corruption, are no longer able financially to support their families. There is also a direct link between development and illicit arms trafficking, especially in post-conflict situations. Illicit trafficking and the trade of counterfeited consumer goods take great advantage of the diminution of state-enforced restriction on exchanges across borders. The deregulation of financial markets makes money laundering possible on a global scale.[25]

We see this occurring in Lima, Peru, where money laundering and other illegal business practices now have a significant impact on the formal economy of this booming metropolis. Current reports are that $7 billion in illegal funds are being moved through the Peruvian economy annually.[26] Not only has Peru now overtaken Colombia as the world's leading producer of cocaine, but the favorable conditions for carrying out illegal business activities have attracted Russian, Mexican, and Colombian transnational crime syndicates.[27] What is occurring in Lima mirrors what happened in Medellín, Colombia, in the last decade. Both are booming cities, both have been rendered more secure by a strong executive branch that reduced crime and subdued terrorism and internal armed conflict. Yet, while lower crime rates and security are indicators of establishing the rule of law, white collar criminal activities, mainly in the form of money laundering, have skyrocketed. Casinos proliferate in both cities, both cities are major destinations for sex tourism, empty hotel rooms are reported as full as a means of laundering money, and designer boutiques in upscale shopping malls are little more than money-laundering fronts for drug cartels and transnational criminal organizations. In such conditions, can the rule of law be said to be present?

The tropical resort island of Isla de Margarita just off the coast of Venezuela was once famous as a world-class windsurfing destination. In the last decade under the rule of President Hugo Chávez, it became a world-class destination for money laundering and allegedly a safe haven for Islamist organizations like Hezbollah (Mahjar-Barducci 2011). In fact, the US Treasury Department blacklisted the number-two Venezuelan diplomat in Syria in 2008 "for fundraising and logistical support to Hezbollah" and running a network that "raises and launders money and recruits and trains operatives to expand Hezbollah's influence in Venezuela and throughout Latin America" (Mahjar-Barducci 2011). The terrorist organization Hamas is also involved in nefarious activities in Isla de Margarita, and both organizations used the island as a staging base to infiltrate its operatives in the United States and elsewhere throughout Latin America.

Hezbollah is also present in the triborder region of Argentina, Brazil, and Paraguay. This essentially lawless region has been an ideal safe haven for terrorists for decades and is often referred to as the United Nations of Crime (Levitt 2013). Terrorist cells are believed to have staged out of the triborder to launch attacks on the Israeli embassy and a Jewish community center in Buenos Aires in the early 1990s (Library of Congress 2003). In Paraguay, the Hezbollah is known to be heavily involved in a four-story shopping center, Galeria Page, in Ciudad del Este, Paraguay. The US Treasury Department has long considered the Galeria Page the center of money-laundering operations and counterfeiting of US dollars operations in Paraguay (Levitt 2013, 78).

The fragility of the rule of law in South America has allowed these criminal organizations to flourish. The problem has grown so severe that organized crime in the region has spilled beyond the Western Hemisphere, embracing alliances and associations with criminal organizations as far flung as the former Soviet bloc, the Middle East, and China (Library of Congress 2002). While the reasons may be many, organized crime in Latin America has flourished primarily due to the rigidity and excessive formalism of certain national laws and differences in the laws from one jurisdiction to another, which together pose a daunting obstacle to fighting international criminal organizations. Combined with a lack of cooperation in the investigation, prosecution, and/or extradition of such groups, the current situation in Iberoamerica is one in which organized crime overwhelms the rule of law in the Americas, despite many efforts and the promulgation of multilateral mechanisms (Nagle 2002).

Legal Education

The American Bar Association's (ABA) Rule of Law Initiative, known as ROLI, has undertaken many efforts to improve the delivery of justice and fortify the rule of law throughout the world. One of the ABA's goals has been to use legal education reform to influence development of the rule of law by "assisting law schools in introducing new courses and practical training that better meet the needs of tomorrow's legal professionals, and promoting a rule of law culture through civic education campaigns on the rule of law and citizens' rights."[28] Latin America's path to achieving the rule of law begins with educating lawyers to be ethical stewards of the law and selfless stakeholders in the delivery of justice.

But Latin America has long been known to have one of the highest ratios of inequality and social exclusion in the world. "In this region, where education, and especially higher education, is the privilege of a few, lawyers play a crucial role in shaping society and its institutions" (Montoya 2010). Yet, many critics of legal education in Latin America despair that the traditional methods and pedagogy in legal education leaves lawyers poorly prepared to confront the many imposing challenges afflicting the region (Montoya 2010).

In a critique of Latin America's legal education, a Colombian law professor wrote recently:

> Latin American schools have focused on professional education to the exclusion of general education and basic research; faculties have been highly independent; and studies show they have suffered from credentialism, an obsession with degrees, diplomas, and other academic trappings. These institutions also have become enamored with their elitism, as they see themselves molding and educating the region's political elite.

The professor's trenchant statement reflects the manifestation of other impediments to the rule of law we have discussed in this chapter. Latin America, too, is lost in dogmatic pedagogy, in which the lawyers are taught legal subjects without being challenged to probe and understand the norms and social policies underpinning the law. Again, as noted earlier, without peeling back the onion, it is difficult to understand the foundations that establish and sustain the rule of law.

In Mexico, for example, legal education focuses on antiquated theoretical legal models taught from outdated books, which makes it difficult for future lawyers to understand how the law relates to modern society (Montoya 2010). Mexican legal education shares several general features with legal education elsewhere in Latin America. For example, as is common in countries having a continental civil law legal system, some law degrees are the equivalent of an undergraduate education, and students enter legal training directly out of high school (Montoya 2010). Classes are in a lecture format, and students learn through memorization and deductive reasoning through the study of logic

(Nagle 2000, 1097). Exams are administered orally, often by a tribunal of faculty experts in the topic being examined (Nagle 2000, 1098).

While we tend to think of law schools in the United States and Europe as being centers of legal research, in Mexico, fewer than 20 percent of the institutions that offer the law degree are involved in research or other scholarly activities, (Montoya 2010, 548), and students rarely engage in intellectual discourse with their professors during classes. Also, as is the case throughout much of Latin America, most Mexican law faculty practice law as full-time practitioners (Nagle 2000, 1098).

In Colombia, law school entails five years of study offering a generalist and continental legal education. Critics stress that this doctrinaire approach to training lawyers "covers too much with too little depth and does not allow students to pursue alternative professional options" (Nagle 2000, 1098). Such a curriculum is outmoded in today's legal terrain in which changes in the law and globalization of legal practices now occur at lightning speed through the digital domain. Moreover, neglecting to train future lawyers in legal reasoning and interpretive analysis cannot but have a debilitating impact on the future legal landscape in Latin America and a chilling effect on the rule of law.

Latin American law schools should take a fresh look at their missions to train lawyers in the new millennium. Courses should be added to the curriculum that cover corruption and how to combat corruption. The course should include teaching about anticorruption laws, and comparative analysis with international conventions and the laws of other nations should be part of the topics covered. International organizations, such as the International Bar Association, could prove helpful by endorsing efforts by Latin American legal scholars to develop model anticorruption curriculums. If the goal is to sustain and fortify the rule of law in Latin America, then it is incumbent upon law schools in Latin America to train the students to become aware of their duties to change the political environment that has allowed corruption to endure for so long.

Influence of Foreign States in the Region

The concept of the "rule of law" identifies a vital component of a Western tradition with roots in Roman antiquity that centuries later fully developed during the birth of liberal constitutionalism. It is best characterized, in the words of Max Weber, as "legal domination" (Li 2000). If we talk about the rule of law, we are talking about a concept in which the law is autonomous from the government. Because it is autonomous from the government, the institutions, and the codes, the rule of law is supposed to include checks and balances in implementations that are going to curb the government's power.

So the two concepts of rule of law and rule by law are absolutely different, and when we consider the role played in democracy building by such entities as the United States Agency for International Development and the World Bank, it can be argued that the rule-of-law projects imposed upon Latin American governments in the name of mutual assistance, foreign aid, economic development, and regional security are little more than reform regimes designed for recipient governments throughout the region to continue ruling *by* law and not by rule *of* law.

While international organizations such as the United Nations and the OAS attempt to create a compass for Latin American nations to steer by, Latin America's burdens hinder forward progress. Institutionalized corruption and persistent underdevelopment are strident impediments to change (Nagle 2001). Yet, reformers give the impression that external institutions are perfect and invulnerable and should be almost sacrosanct models for solutions to every problem in Latin America. Reform promoters are true believers in their work, and as such, they are susceptible to overlooking that the very institutions upon which reform regimes are modeled are themselves susceptible to corruption, abuse, and political machinations, particularly within the judicial process.

The United States, which spearheads much of the rule-of-law reform agendas in Latin America, seems to overlook the fact that its legal culture is different from those of Latin America. "Legal culture is often considered as a given feature of the local environment to which proposed legal reform projects must adapt; many argue that legal and judicial reform programs must be tailored to fit local legal culture or they will fail."[29] Most advocates of rule of law reform truly do mean well, but strengthening the rule of law is something that must come from within each individual Latin American state and not be a process that is imposed upon it by another nation, particularly one that has a long and checkered history of interference and exploitation in the Americas. Moreover, reforming all institutions may not be essential to rule-of-law reform and "can even impede it, by insisting on a model that is either unnecessary or unsuited to the political and cultural landscape" (Kleinfeld Belton 2005, 18).

The promotion of rule-of-law initiatives in Latin America began in earnest in the mid-1980s (Carothers 2003, 5). Yet, despite the promise of being a cure-all elixir, many rule-of-law programs have resulted in far more problems than they address, and at times, rule-of-law reformers have operated on dissimilar directives and "overlapping and sometimes conflicting goals" (Thome 2000). What is happening in the region can be summarized with the statement, "We know how to do a lot of things, but deep down we don't really know what we are doing" (Carothers 2003, 5).

Many rule-of-law programs reveal a lack of knowledge at numerous steps throughout the formation, development, and evaluation process, and even more shortcomings in the follow-up monitoring stage. Programs seem to suffer from a lack of coordination, and there is "uncertainty about the essence of what the rule of law actually is—whether it primarily resides in certain institutional configurations or in more diffuse normative structures" (Carothers 2003, 5). International assistance and its effectiveness in rule-of-law agendas appear ambiguous when each Latin American nation has promoters and aid workers focusing on different fields, using different strategies, and with many and at times contradictory goals. In some instances, there are multiple rule-of-law programs addressing the same issues in one country as in another, but with no sense of coordination or communication to learn what is working and what is not working. There has also been a tendency for rule-of-law consultants to apply a one-size-fits-all program from country to country without regard for the political, social, historical, cultural, and institutional nuances and intricacies unique to any given Latin American state. This mentality toward finding practical and specific solutions causes confusion and frustration and renders the promises touted by some rule-of-law reforms unfulfilled.

Conclusions

The rule of law is a misused, misunderstood, and at times maligned term. Is the rule of law a term to describe due process, justice, and equality before the law? How do we determine the extent to which a state possesses the rule of law? Or does the rule of law refer to an even and equal manner in which government institutions deal with its citizens? Are we referring to how fair and just the system is? Are we talking about how much discretion a government has over its citizens? Does the rule of law assist economic growth? Does it protect human rights? Is the rule of law an essential precondition for democracy? Are we referring to the rules and procedures by which the state enforces its laws, and do we assume that the rule of law entails that the state is transparent, public, clear, and explicit, and not arbitrary or subject to political exploitation by the state?

The rule of law depends entirely on stable institutions that are effective and accountable to the civil society and committed to confronting deeply entrenched corruption and emerging from centuries of rule by patronage and exceptionalism asserted by the elites. In this regard, the effective rule of law in Latin America remains ephemeral and elusive.

There is great wisdom in the observations of two authors who wrote:

> To develop a positive conception of the rule of law one must start with political forces, their goals, their organization and their context. . . . When power is monopolized, the law is at most an instrument of the rule of someone. . . . Rule of law emerges when self-interested rulers willingly restrain themselves and make their behavior predictable in order to obtain sustained, voluntary cooperation of well-organized groups commanding valuable resources.
>
> (Teblicock and Daniels 2008)

Achieving the rule of law requires government leaders to communicate with their own citizens—from all sectors of the society—and make them participants (stakeholders) in the reforms.[30] They must be transparent and accountable, and they must take a stand on corruption. Achieving these goals is central to helping Latin America sustain the rule of law.

Notes

1 *Carta Democratica Inter-Americana* (Democratic Charter), OEA/Ser.G/CP-1. Retrieved from www.oas.org/OASpage/esp/Publicaciones/CartaDemocratica_spa.pdf.

2 Article 2 of the Democratic Charter. Retrieved from www.oas.org/OASpage/eng/Documents/Democractic_Charter.htm.

3 Article 3 of the Democratic Charter. Retrieved from www.oas.org/OASpage/eng/Documents/Democractic_Charter.htm.

4 Article 2 of the Democratic Charter. Retrieved from www.oas.org/OASpage/eng/Documents/Democractic_Charter.htm.

5 See "Frequently Asked Questions about Worldwide Governance Indicators." Retrieved from http://info.worldbank.org/governance/wgi/index.aspx#faq.

6 See "Frequently Asked Questions about Worldwide Governance Indicators." Retrieved from http://info.worldbank.org/governance/wgi/index.aspx#faq.

7 See United Nations Interregional Crime and Justice Research Institute website at www.unicri.it/topics/organized_crime_corruption/.

8 See "Transparency International, Corruption Perceptions Index 2012." Retrieved from www.transparency.org/cpi2012/results.

9 Fought between Peru, Chile, and Bolivia from 1879 through 1883, which resulted in Bolivia losing its access to the Pacific coast.

10 Fought July 5–31, 1941, between Ecuador and Peru over border conflicts.

11 See, for example, Hugh Bronstein, "Colombian President Calls for Replay of Tainted Re-election," Reuters, June 28, 2008.

12 In 2007, the Washington Office on Latin America urged the US Congress to press President Uribe on resolving unsolved assassinations of hundreds of labor unionists, questions about his involvement with paramilitary activity, and the displacement of Afro-Colombians prior to voting on a trade agreement with Colombia. See "Uribe Must Act on Impunity, say U.S. Congressmen," Washington Office on Latin America (May 4, 2007). Retrieved from www.wola.org/news/uribe_must_act_on_impunity_say_us_congressmen.

13 For a thorough review of presidential hubris in Latin America, see Human Rights Watch's report on judicial independence. Retrieved from www.hrw.org/reports/2004/venezuela0604/2.htm.

14 UNHCR. El Salvador: Crime and State Efforts to Combat Crime; State Protection Programs for Victims and Witnesses; Requirements to Access Programs; Statistics on Granted and Refused Applications for Protection; Duration and Effectiveness of These Programs. Retrieved from www.refworld.org/docid/5035f9602.html.

15 Ibid (citing to the Council on Hemispheric Affairs report of Feb. 16, 2012).

16 Ibid (according to a US State Department report of April 8, 2011).

17 Ibid.

18 Ibid (citing *Instituto de Derechos Humanos de la UCA*).

19 Ibid (according to the *La Prensa Gráfica* newspaper, a Salvadoran newspaper, *La Página*, reported that in 2010, "at least 100 witnesses were murdered in 2010 across the country").

20 See "Lima the New Las Vegas." *Tenácitas International* (Sept. 24, 2013). Retrieved from http://tenacitas-intl.com/lima-the-new-las-vegas/?utm_source=September+Investigative+Report&utm_campaign=September+2013&utm_medium=email.

21 For an in-depth analysis of the conversion of the Colombian judiciary to an accusatorial system, see Luz E. Nagle (2008) "Process Issues of Colombia's New Accusatory System." *Southwestern Journal of Law & Trade in the Americas* 14: 223.

22 According to Belton, depending on how law reforms are implemented, institutional reforms can undermine the rule of law. See Rachel Kleinfeld Belton, "Competing Definitions of the Rule of Law: Implications for Practitioners." Rule

of Law Series Working Papers No. 55, Carnegie Endowment for International
Peace, 2005. Retrieved from www.carnegieendowment.org/files/CP55.Belton.
FINAL.pdf.
23 See United Nations Interregional Crime and Justice Research Institute website at
www.unicri.it/topics/organized_crime_corruption/.
24 Ibid.
25 Ibid.
26 See "Lima the New Las Vegas." *Tenácitas International* (Sept. 24, 2013). Retrieved
from http://tenacitas-intl.com/lima-the-new-las-vegas/?utm_source=September
+Investigative+Report&utm_campaign=September+2013&utm_medium=email.
27 Ibid.
28 ABA Rule Law Initiative (2013) "Promoting Justice, Economic Opportunity, and
Human Dignity." Retrieved from www.americanbar.org/content/dam/aba/direc-
tories/roli/misc/aba_roli_2013_program_book_web_email.authcheckdam.pdf.
29 See "Legal Culture and Judicial Reform." World Bank Law and Justice Institutions.
Retrieved from http://web.worldbank.org/WBSITE/EXTERNAL/TOPICS/
EXTLAWJUSTINST/0,,contentMDK:23115500~menuPK:2035153~pagePK:2
10058~piPK:210062~theSitePK:1974062~isCURL:Y,00.html.
30 See US Army Peacekeeping and Stability Operations Institute (2004) "Rule of Law
Conference Report" (July 6–9, 2004). Retrieved from http://stinet.dtic.mil/cgi-
bin/GetTRDoc?AD=ADA428140&Location=U2&doc=GetTRDoc.pdf.

References

ABA Rule Law Initiative, Promoting Justice, Economic Opportunity, and Human Dig-
nity. (2013) Retrieved from www.americanbar.org/content/dam/aba/directories/
roli/misc/aba_roli_2013_program_book_web_email.authcheckdam.pdf. Accessed
11/3/14.
Carothers, T. (2003) "Promoting the Rule of Law Abroad: The Problem of Knowledge."
Rule of Law Series Working Papers No. 34, Carnegie Endowment for International
Peace. Retrieved from http://www.carnegieendowment.org/files/wp34.pdf.
Cevallos, D. (June 7, 2009) "Police Caught between Low Wages, Threats and Bribes."
Inter Press News Service. Retrieved from http://ipsnews.net/print.asp?idnews=
38075. Accessed 11/3/14.
DePalma, A. (Feb. 15, 1999) "How a Tortilla Empire Was Built on Favoritism."
New York Times. Retrieved from www.nytimes.com/1996/02/15/world/how-a-
tortilla-empire-was-built-on-favoritism.html?pagewanted=all. Accessed 11/3/14.
Forero, J. (July 22, 2012) "Latin America's New Authoritarians." *Washington Post.*
Retrieved from http://interamericansecuritywatch.com/latin-america%E2%80%99s-
new-authoritarians/. Accessed 11/3/14.
Human Rights Watch (2004) Judicial Independence. Retrieved from www.hrw.org/
reports/2004/venezuela0604/2.htm. Accessed 11/3/14.
Kleinfeld Belton, R. (2005) "Competing Definitions of the Rule of Law: Implications
for Practitioners." Rule of Law Series Working Papers No. 55, Carnegie Endowment
for International Peace. Retrieved from www.carnegieendowment.org/files/CP55.
Belton.FINAL.pdf. Accessed 11/3/14.
Levitt, M. (2013) "South of the Border, a Threat from Hezbollah." *Journal of Inter-
national Security Affairs* 77(Spring 2013).
Li, B. (2000) "What Is Rule of Law?" *Perspectives* 1:5.

Library of Congress (May 26, 2002) "A Global Overview of Narcotics-Funded Terrorist and Other Extremist Groups: A Report Prepared by the Federal Research Division." Retrieved from www.loc.gov/rr/frd/pdf-files/NarcsFundedTerrs_Extrems.pdf. Accessed 11/3/14 .

Library of Congress, Terrorist and Organized Crime Groups in the Tri-Border Area (TBA) of South America. (July 13, 2003) Retrieved from www.loc.gov/rr/frd/pdf-files/TerrOrgCrime_TBA.pdf. Accessed 11/3/14.

"Lima the New Las Vegas" (Sept. 24, 2013) *Tenácitas International*. Retrieved from http://tenacitas-intl.com/lima-the-new-las-vegas/?utm_source=September+Investigative+Report&utm_campaign=September+2013&utm_medium=email. Accessed 11/3/14.

Mahjar-Barducci, A. (July 21, 2011) "The Holiday Island of Isla de Margarita, Venezuela, Hosts Hezbollah Militants." Gatestone Institute International Policy Council. Retrieved from www.gatestoneinstitute.org/2285/isla-de-margarita-venezuela-hosts-hezbollah. Accessed 11/3/14.

Montoya, J. (2010) "The Current State of Legal Education Reform in Latin America: A Critical Appraisal." *Journal of Legal Education* 59: 545.

Mount, I. and Sherwell, P. (Feb. 12, 2012) "The Argentine President and Her Empire in the South." *Telegraph*. Retrieved from www.telegraph.co.uk/news/worldnews/southamerica/argentina/9076133/The-Argentine-president-and-her-empire-in-the-south.html. Accessed 11/3/14.

Nagle, L.E. (1999) "The Cinderella of Government: Judicial Reform in Latin America." *California Western International Law Journal* 30: 345.

Nagle, L.E. (2000) "Maximizing Legal Education: The International Component." *Stetson Law Review* 29: 1091, 1097.

Nagle, L.E. (2001) "E-Commerce in Latin America: Legal and Business Challenges for Developing Enterprise." *American University Law Review* 50: 859.

Nagle, L.E. (2002) "The Challenges of Fighting Global Organized Crime in Latin America" *Fordham International Law Journal* 26: 1649.

Nagle, L.E. (2008) "Process Issues of Colombia's New Accusatory System" *Southwestern Journal of Law & Trade in the Americas* 14: 223.

Neuman, W. (Aug. 19, 2013) "As a Boom Slows, Peru Grows Uneasy." *New York Times*. Retrieved from www.nytimes.com/2013/08/20/world/americas/as-a-boom-slows-peru-grows-uneasy.html?pagewanted=all&_r=0. Accessed 11/3/14.

Pérez, J.E. and Bashirullah, A.K. (May 18, 2000). Letter to the Editor: "Bureaucracy Strangles Latin American Research" *Nature* 405: 273.

Samuels, L. (Dec. 29, 2005) "In Mexico, Culture of Corruption Runs Deep." *San Luis Obispo Tribune*.

Schor, M. (2003) "The Rule of Law and Democratic Consolidation in Latin America." Paper prepared for the 2003 meeting of the Latin American Studies Association, Dallas, Texas, March 2003. Retrieved from www.umass.edu/legal/Benavides/Fall2005/397U/Readings%20Legal%20397U/14%20Miguel%20Schor.pdf. Accessed 11/3/14.

Teblicock, M. and Daniels, R.J. (2008) *Rule of Law Reform and Development: Charting the Fragile Path of Progress*. Cheltenham: Edward Elgar.

Thome, J.R. (2000) "Heading South But Looking North: Globalization and Law Reform in Latin America." *Wisconsin Law Review* 691, 701.

United Nations Interregional Crime and Justice Research Institute. Retrieved from www.unicri.it/topics/organized_crime_corruption/. Accessed 11/3/14.

USAC Report (Apr. 7, 2012) El Salvador 2012 Crime and Safety Report. Retrieved from www.osac.gov/Pages/ContentReportDetails.aspx?cid=12336. Accessed 11/3/14.

US Army Peacekeeping and Stability Operations Institute, Rule of Law Conference Report (July 6–9, 2004) Retrieved from www.au.af.mil/au/awc/awcgate/army-usawc/pksoi_rule_of_law.pdf. Accessed 11/3/14 .

US State Department, Bureau of Democracy, Human Rights, and Labor. 2005 Country Report on Honduras. Retrieved from www.state.gov/j/drl/rls/hrrpt/2005/61732.htm. Accessed 11/3/14.

US State Department. Honduras Country Reports on Human Rights Practices for 2012. Retrieved from www.state.gov/documents/organization/204670.pdf. Accessed 11/3/14.

Section II
The Status of Institutions

7 Executive-Legislative Relations and Democracy in Latin America

Peter M. Siavelis

Introduction

With the consolidation of democratic regimes across Latin America during the last thirty-five years, analysis of democratic transitions has given way to a concern with the actual functioning of democracies and, in particular, with the influence of democratic institutions like the presidency, congress, elections systems, political parties, the courts, and bureaucracies. ⎤ ~LMP

This has certainly not always been the case. These institutional elements of democratic politics were overlooked in the past for many reasons, some practical and some theoretical. In practical terms, during the mid-1970s, few countries in the region were democracies. Analyses, therefore, largely focused on the role of militaries, the origins of authoritarian rule, and later, transitions to democracy. In theoretical terms, the predominant approaches to understanding Latin American politics during the 1960s and 1970s focused on societal and cultural variables, the importance of economic modernization, dependency, or the influence of international actors. Institutions were largely viewed as a by-product of one of these other variables or as simply epiphenomenal, rather than important independent variables in their own right. Even with the return of democracy across the region, institutions remained largely overlooked, as governments were more concerned with addressing deep social and economic problems.

An incipient institutional focus began in the 1990s, with widespread analyses of Latin American presidencies. Certain institutions, and especially legislatures, remained underanalyzed. This is the case because the latter were usually seen as rubber stamps for overly powerful executives. Morgenstern notes that Latin American legislatures were viewed as "at best irrelevant to the policy process, if not venal and destructive" (Morgenstern 2002, 1). Latin American legislatures and the nature of legislative power when analyzed were also misunderstood, with scholars fundamentally viewing legislative power as a zero-sum relationship, with legislative power simply a function of executive power. Indeed, Needler notes "in the sense of the formal constitutional attributions of power, the legislature is stronger where the president is weaker" (Needler 2002, 156).

Many of these practical and theoretical realities have now changed. Recent analyses recognize that institutions and executive-legislative relations are central to understanding the quality of democracy in the region, and indeed, critical to understanding whether democracy succeeds or fails. As democracy became consolidated and militaries faded in importance as the ultimate arbiters of politics, there have been dramatic demonstrations of the centrality of the executive-legislative equation. These include instances of impeachment or attempted impeachment, dramatic constitutional reforms aimed at transforming the nature of executive-legislative structures, and ample evidence that legislatures do matter in shaping policy (Morgenstern and Nacif 2002, 394–449).

This chapter analyzes the evolution of thinking about executive-legislative relations in Latin America and the performance of its presidential regimes since the widespread transitions toward democracy began thirty-five years ago. It explores the generally negative reputation of presidentialism as a regime type in the first literature on the subject and evaluates how this reputation has changed over time. Given the reality that fundamental regime reform is unlikely, the chapter explores arguments that have been advanced for improving presidentialism as a system. The chapter concludes with a discussion of the functioning of executive and legislative relations on the ground in Latin America, pointing to significant trends. Overall, this chapter argues that the performance of Latin American presidentialism has been mixed, as is the evidence that the institutional structure of presidentialism itself is responsible for this mixed record.

The Perils of Presidentialism

Despite many studies of the US presidential system, the study of presidentialism in Latin America remained overlooked until recently. This is paradoxical because Latin America in many senses is the continent of presidentialism, with the largest concentration of presidential systems in any region in the world. Presidentialism took root very early in Latin America. As the region's revolutionary leaders sought potential models for structuring nascent governments, they looked to the two great political revolutions that could provide models of their time: the US and the French. By the time most Latin American countries achieved independence in the 1820s, however, the United States remained the sole revolutionary inspiration, with France having already descended into the disorder of the Napoleonic era. The US system was essentially copied by Latin American countries, given their leaders' admiration for the revolution and their fraternity with US revolutionaries.

Despite copying its general political model, however, efforts to reproduce the success of the United States in consolidating democracy proved elusive, and the region has often been characterized by instability and violence. Despite long periods of democratic politics in some countries (and particularly Chile, Uruguay, and Costa Rica), scholars looked to explanations beyond simple regime structure as the root causes for the instability that engulfed most of the rest of the region.

However, increasing concern with institutions in general, and presidentialism in particular, actually grew out of scholars' efforts to understand the democratic breakdowns that occurred during the 1970s. A path-breaking article by Juan Linz hypothesized that rather than just an artifact of Latin America's historic effort to copy the US system, presidentialism might actually be central to an explanation for persistent problems of instability in Latin America (Linz 1994, 3–87).

In particular, Linz argues that presidentialism's separation of powers creates problems of dual legitimacy, because both legislators and the president have *int.* a claim to legitimate authority. This problem does not exist in parliamentary *)* systems where the executive and legislative branches are fused. Further, the direct and separate election of legislators and presidents is likely to produce double minority presidents, or those who are elected with only a plurality of the popular vote and who lack majority support in the legislature. The potential executive-legislative deadlock produced by this situation is exacerbated by presidentialism's rigidity, or the inability to remove an unpopular or moribund president. In parliamentary systems, of course, this can be done with a simple vote of no confidence. However, beyond the extreme measure of impeachment (which is reserved for illegal acts), the rigidity of presidentialism prevents the removal of presidents in situations of deadlock or where presidents are extreme lame ducks.   ~Very true

While presidentialism has been relatively successful in the United States, the country's ideological homogeneity, moderate politics, two-party system, and the historic willingness of its parties to cross the aisle in congressional voting helped underwrite success. However, as Linz points out, in Latin America, we face a distinct political context, and the region's more common multiparty systems create a completely different political dynamic. All of these features combined, and the reality that presidentialism lacks the institutional exits provided by parliamentarism (and principally the vote of no confidence), make presidential systems more prone to military intervention given their lack of institutional mechanisms to solve problems of executive-legislative deadlock. — Fascinating

Subsequent country and theoretical studies confirmed many of Linz's contentions. Valenzuela underscored presidentialism's contribution to the dramatic breakdown of democracy in Chile in 1973 (Valenzuela 1994, 91–150). Indeed, Valenzuela established Chile as the virtual poster child for the problems of presidentialism, given how executive-legislative deadlock during the administration of socialist Salvador Allende, coupled with the inability of the Congress to impeach him, precipitated the violent military intervention of 1973 and initiated a brutal seventeen-year dictatorship. Hartlyn went on to underscore the problems presidentialism caused in Colombia, and Lamounier recommended a shift to parliamentarism in Brazil (Hartlyn 1994, 220–53; Lamounier 1994, 179–219).

Mainwaring echoed Linz's argument and provided further theoretical backing for it, stressing the problematic combination of multipartism and presidentialism. He underscored the tendency of this combination to result in immobilizing executive-legislative deadlock, which can destabilize democracy (Mainwaring 1993, 198–228). He adds that polarization of politics is more likely in multiparty presidential systems than where two parties are the norm. This is the case primarily because in multiparty systems presidents are less likely to be able to rely on majorities of their own parties. Finally, this combination for Mainwaring provides disincentives for the type of coalition building that can facilitate democratic governability. Similarly, Stepan and Skach argued that parliamentarism was superior because it better generates policy-making majorities, facilitates cross-party deals in the context of multiparty systems, provides fewer incentives for executives to violate the constitutions, allows for the easier removal of unsuccessful executives, and provides career paths that better contribute to the type of long-term party and government careers that can facilitate governability (Stepan and Skach 1994, 119–36). By the mid-1990s, presidentialism had quite a sullied image.

Is Presidentialism Really that Perilous?

These works quickly generated a flurry of critiques. Shugart and Carey underscored that a simple dichotomy between presidential and parliamentary systems fails to capture the many ways to structure executive and legislative relations, and that certain types of presidential systems might be more likely than others to produce the types of problems of democratic governability identified by Linz and his followers.[1] In particular, they suggest that the question may not be the simple existence of one or another system, but whether presidential systems are properly crafted. They contend that presidentialism can function well as long as several aspects of its design are taken into account. Presidential systems that resist providing excessive legislative powers to presidents may prove more stable if coupled with other elements of institutional design, like an election system that encourages fair representation of all parties and produces incentives for the formation of pre-electoral coalitions. Properly crafted presidentialism, they contend, provides numerous benefits when compared to parliamentarism, including greater accountability, identifiability, mutual checks on authority, and the existence of a natural and well-positioned arbiter that can strike bargains and facilitate compromise.

Mainwaring and Shugart echo and build upon many of the arguments set out by Shugart and Carey (Mainwaring and Shugart 1993). They argue that the variations within presidential systems may be more important than the distinction between parliamentary and presidential systems. In particular, they argue that presidential power, the nature of the party system, party discipline, and the format of the election system can have an important effect on the potential for success of presidentialism. Somewhat counterintuitively, Mainwaring and Shugart find that presidents with weaker power over legislation may actually tend to function better, because the president is forced to deal, negotiate, and reach compromises with the legislature. In addition, they stress that the party makeup of the legislature is extraordinarily important in determining whether the perils associated with presidentialism emerge. While majority support of a president's own party in the legislature may be optimal, it is not necessary. Rather, what is important is whether the president can rely on a sizable legislative contingent within the context where relatively disciplined parties can craft agreements and coalitions. With respect to the election system and the timing and sequencing of elections, any measures that can be taken to ensure that presidents will be able to rely on such legislative contingents are, in the view of Mainwaring and Shugart, desirable. *Go over*

Because presidentialism can perform better where sizable and disciplined majorities reign, scholars turned to the obvious question of how such majorities could be encouraged. Jones argues that electoral rules have an important effect on the nature of legislative majorities and that majority runoff presidential elections have a spillover effect on the party system, encouraging fragmentation (Jones 1995). This is the case because in lowering the hurdle for victory in the first round of the election, such systems encourage the proliferation of presidential aspirants. In addition, two-round elections often eliminate the benefits of concurrent legislative and presidential elections. Presidents chosen in the second round face a legislature elected in the first round—so second-round presidents will be unable to rely on the usual correlation of party forces between the president and congress that congruent elections are valued for producing. In essence, then, these types of systems tend to produce presidents without majority mandates. Jones argues that a full-scale switch from presidentialism to parliamentarism is unrealistic, and that presidentialism can provide some concrete benefits. He suggests that creative design of electoral institutions can ameliorate many of the problematic aspects of presidentialism identified by its critics. Jones considers plurality elections for president, combined with concurrent legislative elections, as such an institutional formula.

Indeed, newer literature even takes issue with the very distinction between presidentialism and parliamentarism. Cheibub et al (2011) argue that the conventional distinction between the two categories of regimes is largely based on stereotypes regarding each one. In essence, they find that there is a great deal more heterogeneity within each category and a larger number of shared similarities in characteristics across categories. Albert (2009) echoes this contention, demonstrating how discussions of the structural differences between the two regime types actually obscure more than they reveal about their functional dynamics. These accounts suggest that it may have been a mistake to build so much scholarly literature around categorizations that are presumably inaccurate.

Linz and his followers revitalized the study of democratic institutions in Latin America by underscoring the institutional elements that may contribute to democratic breakdown or underwrite successful democratic governance. While open to accusations of overstating the case, critics of presidentialism succeeded in bringing analysis of institutions back into the picture at the very time institutional approaches were regaining traction in the social sciences.[2] These studies were accompanied by a rebirth in interest in the institutional makeup of newly democratic regimes, and scholars increasingly viewed Latin America's presidential democracies as useful laboratories for the study of federalism, electoral systems, executive power, political parties, and party systems. However influential the argument was in reinvigorating the study of institutions, it had little practical effect in inciting fundamental regime change. Despite recommendations for a widespread shift toward parliamentarism, no government (with the exception of Brazil, whose 1993 plebiscite on the question of regime structure yielded a resounding desire to maintain presidentialism) has seriously considered the adoption of a parliamentary system. Practical realities limit such a switch. Though presidentialism was copied from the United States, the weight of tradition has induced Latin Americans to identify it as a system that conforms to their political culture. In addition, most Latin American publics (and the US public for that matter) fail to understand the basic differences between the two types of regimes. The most significant reality that advocates of a switch to presidentialism ignored was that politicians are simply loath to change the political structures that bring them to power. Indeed, it makes no sense for them to do so.

Why Does Presidentialism Work and How Can Successful Presidentialism Be Built?

While the formal aspects of executive-legislative relations had been well accounted for in the literature by proponents of Linz's arguments and its critics, there remained gaps in our understanding of the interbranch equation. What is more, cases that played very prominently in the debate as the poster children for the ills of presidentialism actually turned out to function quite well after returning to democracy (Brazil, and especially Chile). Because a widespread shift to parliamentarism was unlikely, analysts turned their attention to two interrelated tasks. The first was to explain why, in the light of such damning arguments to the contrary, presidentialism sometimes worked so well. The second was to account for ways that successful presidentialism could be built.

To answer these two questions, four new elements were introduced into analysis of the executive-legislative equation. First, analysts began to consider the possibility that successfully managing interbranch relations likely had much more to do with the nature of the legislature than had been supposed. Second, scholars increasingly abandoned the underlying assumption that the branches of government were locked in a power struggle. Increasingly, they analyzed when presidents and legislatures choose to forgo the exertion of their full range of powers, exert powers other than those set out explicitly in the constitution, or choose not to exert power at all. Third, they recognized the potential for building coalitions principally through the crafting of multiparty cabinets. Finally, scholars shifted away from a primary focus on the formal constitutional and partisan powers of each branch of government to recognize the importance of informal institutions in affecting the conduct and quality of executive-legislative relations.

The *Legislature* as a Player

Responses to Linz's critique of presidentialism professed to be about executive-legislative relations. However, the executive still ended up playing the starring role, and there was little analysis of the powers and influences of legislative branches beyond references to the necessity of malleable legislative majorities for presidents. Even before Linz's critique, legislatures in Latin America were usually depicted as, at best, rubber stamps, and, at worst, obstructionist bodies. Numerous studies emerged attesting to the myriad ways that legislatures are influential in the policy process.[3] The frequent depiction of legislatures as simple rubber stamps was often due to a misunderstanding of the more subtle ways they influence politics. The country studies in Morgenstern and Nacif's collected volume showed that legislative influence is often exerted through informal channels, the bureaucracy, or by way of strategic agenda setting (Morgenstern and Nacif 2002). Legislatures can also compel executives to withdraw proposals if they are not expected to pass, in the process exercising substantial influence and leaving little trace of it.

Similarly, Cox and Morgenstern demonstrate that presidential and legislative power oscillate, and rather than being locked in a zero-sum power struggle, each branch adjusts its strategy to meet the strategy of the other. That is to say, presidents decide which prerogatives to use, or not use, depending on what type of legislature they face and the extent of their political powers (Cox and Morgenstern 2002). Cox and Morgenstern note that when presidents are politically weaker (in partisan terms), they tend to resort more to the assertion of unitary powers (those that can change policy without the influence of the legislature, i.e., decrees, regulatory changes, and vetoes), while when politically stronger, they rely less often on these powers. However, in this equation, legislatures are clearly influential and have more of an effect on the success of presidentialism than had been supposed.

A Zero-Sum Game

In the Linzean tradition, presidents and legislatures were often depicted in a zero-sum power struggle, with each branch maximally exerting its prerogatives to thwart the power of the other. However, the decision to employ or not employ presidential power is sometimes counterintuitive and can affect the prospects for success of presidentialism. With a clear, disciplined, and decisive majority, presidents may be tempted to bypass Congress and rely on party discipline to simply initiate executive policy with little input from Congress. Alternatively, with an intransigent opposition in both houses, presidents may be tempted to use the full powers granted by the constitution (or exceed them).

This may include ample use of powers of exclusive introduction, decree, and urgency provisions. In this sense, in both conditions of partisan strength and partisan weakness, presidents may act unilaterally with little concern for the legislature. Congress may, indeed, seem powerless in both of these situations.

However, where presidents lack a partisan majority, the decision on how far to push executive power is more complex. The paradoxical reality is that a divided (though not intransigent) congress may provide the president a strong incentive to avoid the potentially damaging and/or controversial use of the extreme unitary presidential powers, actually providing the legislature with more influence. Presidents who have sizable legislative contingents can often best achieve their goals through negotiation, cajoling, convincing, and accommodating the opposition, rather than imperiously imposing their constitutionally vested authority (Mainwaring and Shugart 2002).

With respect to the strategic exercise of power, it is also important to note that, at times, presidents strategically choose not to exercise power. It is theoretically as important to understand the decision not to assert power as it is to understand the excessive assertion of power. Weldon shows that despite the wide-ranging formal and partisan powers of Mexican presidents, at least in budgetary matters, they often avoided the imposition of unilateral powers, decree authority, or late presentation of the budget to force fast-track consideration (Weldon 2002, 225–58). This is the case because successive presidents found that in forgoing such options, the chamber was more likely pass the budget and pass it more quickly and was less likely to insert pork or particularistic appropriations.

What is more, legislating is an iterated game for presidents who must return to face Congress again. Therefore, this negotiated strategy allows presidents to achieve their goals while simultaneously avoiding poisoning the legislative well to which they must return. These realities provide support for Cox and Morgenstern's conclusion that presidential strategies toward the legislature are partially a function of the extent of pro-government support in the legislature, though this is certainly not a linear relationship. Jones' and Siavelis' analyses of Argentina and Chile, respectively, provide additional evidence to support this contention (Jones 1997; Siavelis 2002). Jones shows how Argentine President Carlos Menem succeeded in passing his neoliberal reform program early in his first term by building on the plurality of support he could rely on in his own Partido Justicialista (PJ) and peeling away some votes from the opposition.[4] Siavelis demonstrates that the first post-authoritarian Chilean presidents avoided controversial use of their many unilateral powers to better build long-term support within their own Concertación coalition and to avoid alienating the opposition in order to legislate—mostly because presidents could rely on a majority in the Chamber of Deputies, but had to build one in the Senate.

Just as presidents sometimes choose not to employ their powers, legislators do the same based on strategic cost-benefit analyses of whether legislating is worth the trouble, or if delegation to the executive branch or bureaucracy better serves their interests. So, while presidential strategies of the nonexertion of power usually involve a calculated trade-off between the use of more or fewer of their formal or unilateral powers, the most common path for legislators is to delegate powers to other institutions. Epstein and O'Halloran argue that legislatures will prefer to make policy where the political benefits they obtain outweigh the costs (Epstein and O'Halloran 1999). Where they do not, legislators will prefer to delegate power to the executive. Though based primarily on US politics, Epstein and O'Halloran's study is relevant to Latin American legislatures, with some adjustment, and with an eye to the goals of particular legislators. The important point is that similar cost-benefit analyses govern the decisions of Latin American legislators to delegate their powers or not, albeit within the context of distinct incentive structures.

For example, Samuels analyzes a paradox where legislators acted to curtail their own formal powers, but did so strategically to enhance their ability to promote their own agendas and interests (Samuels 2002, 320, 315–40). When the Brazilian budgetary amendment process was established in the late 1980s, only individual members of Congress could submit amendments. However, the plethora of individual amendments, combined with the chaotic process that resulted, often held up the ultimate approval of the budget, meaning everyone lost. It also spread already thin resources over far too wide a range of particularistic projects, endangering the approval of many. Therefore, in the succeeding decades, legislators acted to curtail their own involvement in the amendment process and agreed to allow only amendments initiated by members of organized groups, in particular, state legislative delegations. Ironically, this curtailment of formal power permitted legislators to more successfully and consistently bring back pork to the state, which, as Samuels notes, is so crucial to building later careers in the states. Thus, the common depiction of a zero-sum executive-legislative struggle by Linz and his critics was not empirically borne out.

Coalitions through Cabinet Building

The centrality of forming and maintaining governments in multiparty parliamentary systems provides strong natural incentives for coalitions and alliance, not least of which is the desire of all involved parties to stay in government. There are fewer incentives for the formation of coalitions in presidential systems, a supposition that was often the rationale for contending that presidential systems produced an incentive structure that was antithetical to cooperation (Mainwaring 1993). However, critics of presidentialism failed to recognize how purposeful efforts of presidents to build coalitions could counteract the negative incentives structures for cooperation created by presidential systems.

Though not as widespread as under parliamentarism, multiparty cabinet governments have been surprisingly common in Latin America (Cheibub, Przeworski, and Saiegh 2004). By appointing multiparty coalitions to their cabinets, presidents can build coalitions that are useful for both hammering out cross-party agreements and for insurance that cabinet members will be able to deliver votes from their legislative parties.

something US. should do?

The building of such alliances may avert some of the potentially destructive forms of behavior identified by critics of presidentialism and result in the kind of workable legislative majorities that have been deemed so important to its success. Amorim Neto's cross-national study of 106 cabinets from thirteen Latin American countries provides evidence that presidents who eschewed decree powers and relied on normal legislative means to implement their policies consistently laid the groundwork for legislative support through the use of cabinet appointments to instill loyalty (Neto 2006, 415–40). However, those presidents who more forcefully employed unilateral and/or decree strategies tended to appoint cabinets with less of an eye towards coalitional proportionality and that were more likely to be composed of technocrats and cronies. Membership in a cabinet also implies some access to resources in exchange for support of the government. Morgenstern suggests that this membership conditions the loyalty and unity of legislative agents on which presidents depend for the passage of legislation (Morgenstern 1994). In this sense, presidents can strategically use this tool to overcome their partisan weakness. Of course, the ability of presidents to do so depends on the nature of the party system. Cohesive agents may be willing to cross ideological lines at the direction of high-level party officials and ministers, or they may be more motivated by ideology and be less willing to offer legislative support in exchange for cabinet posts.

I like that

Informal Institutions

Presidents can construct informal institutions and engage in informal activities in order to build legislative coalitions or promote their own agendas and at the same time avoid some of the purported problems of presidentialism. The notion of "informality" has a long trajectory in analyses of Latin American politics. Most often, informality is expressed in terms of the negative consequences of nepotism, patron-client relations, corporatism, and patrimonialism.[5] Lauth notes that these problems are especially disadvantageous in "fledgling democracies" (Lauth 2000, 21–50). Less critical and normative treatments of informal institutions are not as prevalent in the literature. This dim view of informal institutions finds its roots in a general tendency to view politics in the developing world as somehow dysfunctional if they do not conform to the norms of political processes in developed countries. The long trajectory of concepts like clientelism, patrimonialism, and nepotism in the Latin American literature has led to the somewhat indiscriminate lumping together of any form of informal institution along with these more negative ones. *— sad but true*

Increasingly, informality has been recognized to potentially play a positive role. Helmke and Levitsky's work is the most important contribution to this emerging recognition.[6] In particular, they recognize that certain types of informal institutions can be beneficial—albeit, at times, with a cost in terms of representation. However, their work also raised some knotty problems and particularly the difficulty of separating informal institutions from other informal activities (or simple "ways of doing things"). To deal with this problem,

explain

they differentiate informal institutions from simple informality by contending that informal institutions are "socially shared rules, usually unwritten that are created, communicated, and enforced outside officially sanctioned channels."[7]

Siavelis shows that informal institutions were perhaps more important than formal institutions when it came to the legislative success of presidents and democratic governability in post-authoritarian Chile (Siavelis 2006, 33–55). Presidents oversaw a series of informal institutions that allowed them to govern. For example, in order to hold together multiparty coalitions, Chilean presidents established an informal institution known as the *cuoteo* which provided for the widespread distribution of cabinet seats among members of the governing Concertación coalition. Chilean presidents have distributed cabinet portfolios among the coalition's governing parties in line with a power-sharing formula based on the relative electoral weight of each party. What is more, vice-ministers usually represent different parties than the minister. Despite the lack of formal agreement, this informal institution provided widespread party input into ministerial decision making and has provided an incentive for coalition maintenance, which extended into the legislature, and in turn, allowed presidents to successfully govern and pass legislation. Siavelis goes on to analyze a whole range of informal institutions that allowed Chilean presidents to overcome the "difficult combination" of presidentialism and multiparty systems.

Informal institutions can also facilitate presidential use of extra-parliamentary social actors to buttress executive power, authority, and influence in the legislative process. Crisp recounts how, despite the relatively limited formal powers of pre-Chavez Venezuelan presidents, executives were really the most important legislators in the country, given their informal powers.[8] In particular, Venezuelan presidents used their nonlegislative decree powers to create "high-profile commissions" that brought "executive branch authorities and the representatives of interest groups together to study issues of the president's choice."[9] At the policy formation phase, these commissions were often charged with drafting legislation that the president planned to present to Congress, which naturally reflected the president's preferences. Venezuela's hyper-institutionalized parties (Coppedge 1994), rather than acting as a check on the president's legislative power, actually helped solidify it. Venezuelan parties' extreme discipline made the courting of individual legislators futile. In addition, given the importance of simple party voting, the Congress had no infrastructure for the development of expertise of deputies, nor a committee structure that would allow legislators to actually study and seriously debate legislation. Party elites simply instructed legislators how to vote.[10]

Legislators can also employ informal mechanisms to facilitate intra- and interbranch legislative cooperation and the success of presidentialism. Mejia Acosta finds that the Ecuadorian public is adverse to the establishment of formal cross-party coalitions based in the legislature because they are perceived as the product of illicit deal making.[11] Therefore, the construction of informal legislative coalitions shaded from the public allows legislators to achieve their goals through vote trading and the acquisition of particularistic pork, while at the same time allowing presidents to build governing coalitions. The enforcement mechanism related to these coalitions defines their status as informal institutions. The threat to "go public" provides a powerful tool to assure compliance. Therefore, in the absence of formal incentives for cooperation, other informal institutions may facilitate coalition building and the success of presidential government.

Thus, in each of these ways, many of the problems of presidentialism are ameliorated. Beyond basic regime structure, a number of formal and informal institutions and activities by presidents and legislatures transform the stark incentive structure set down by Linz.

Evaluating Executive-Legislative Relations in Latin America's Presidential Systems: Six Trends

Clearly then, there has been a dramatic evolution in thinking about executive-legislative relations and democracy in Latin America. Much of this theory developed, however, without the empirical referents that long-standing, functioning democratic regimes could provide. However, it has now been thirty-five years since the wave of democratization began in Latin America, providing sufficient experience to step back and ask how presidential democracy has fared. The record is decidedly mixed. Although intercountry variation in performance is undeniable, six distinct trends have emerged.

The Marginalization of the Military as an Arbiter in Executive-Legislative Conflict —You have to see it

On the positive side, it is undeniable that there has been a transformation in the region's politics. While 37.5 percent of changes of government in Latin America between 1930 and 1980 took place by way of military coup (or 104 out of 277), from 1980 to 1990, only seven of thirty-seven changes of government took place by way of military intervention, and according to Valenzuela, only two "can fairly be described as having an anti-democratic intent" (Valenzuela 2004, 5). Further, these seven coups were confined to Bolivia, Haiti, Guatemala, and Paraguay. In 2000, there were coup attempts in Ecuador, Paraguay, and Peru, and in 2002, there was an attempted coup to unseat President Hugo Chávez in Venezuela. A successful coup also unseated Haitian President Jean-Bertrand Aristide in 2004. However, the most dramatic example of a return to a Latin America's coup-ridden pattern of politics was the successful military coup against Manuel Zelaya in Honduras in 2009. In both Honduras and Haiti, power was turned back over to civilian authorities. Thus, despite attempts, no coup has successfully placed a military president in power since the 1976 Argentine coup, and no military leader has come to the presidency in the region by way of a coup. This record represents a decidedly positive shift away from overt and direct military influence in politics. It also undoubtedly suggests that international unwillingness to accept military governments has provided additional incentives for militaries to stay out of politics. However, it does not suggest that presidentialism is necessarily functioning well.

Successful Governments with Party Backing

It is important also to mention recent strides in governing in Latin America and the numerous successful presidents who have governed with the backing of traditional parties or with relatively well-institutionalized newer parties. Much was made during the mid-2000s of the leftward trend in Latin American politics, as well as the triumph of anti-system presidents. Unfortunately, analysts and news reports presented the standard lists of such victories, lumping together very different types of presidents. However, such lumping together of disparate presidents and candidates is very deceiving. Though all were leftists, only a few represented anti-system or anti-party candidates. Moderate leftists who worked within the party system and with broad party backing included Chile's Michelle Bachelet (reelected in 2013), Argentina's Nestor Kirchner, Brazil's Inácio Lula da Silva (whose equally moderate successor Dilma Rousseff was easily elected in 2010), and Uruguay's Tabaré Vazquez. These presidents differ markedly from those presidents and candidates who were more populist, nationalist, and anti-system leaders (Venezuela's Chávez, Bolivia's Evo Morales, Nicaragua's Daniel Ortega, Peru's Ollanta Humala, and Mexico's Manuel López Obrador). What is less clear is how to categorize Argentina's Cristina Fernandez who has tended to oscillate between the two camps. Humala has also pursued a more moderate course since winning the presidency in 2011.

It is among the former moderate leftists ruling with party backing that one finds hope in Latin America's presidential systems. Though varying month by month and from policy to policy, the popularity of most of these presidents and/or the coalitions they represent remained relatively high, and each was able to build the kind of legislative coalitions that have been able to fend off the usual problems associated with presidentialism. In addition, Chávez's 2013 death has created a good deal of uncertainty regarding the future of the populist socialism he espoused and the support he provided for his like-minded allies on the continent. What is more, if we look beyond the left, those presidents who have been victorious as representatives of traditional parties or parties of the right also have proved successful in building legislative coalitions (the most dramatic being conservative Colombian president Alvaro Uribe).

Increasing Use of Presidential Impeachments

While the instances of military coups or attempted coups have decreased dramatically across the continent, impeachments have become more common. Impeachment proceedings or presidential resignations under threat of impeachment occurred in Brazil in 1992, in Venezuela in 1993, in Ecuador in 1997, in Peru in 2000, and in Paraguay in 1999, 2002, and 2012. Indeed, in Paraguay, impeachment is coming disturbingly close to being the standard method to remove presidents. This trend can be interpreted in two ways. On the one hand, an increasing number of impeachments may point to a disturbing trend of ineffective presidentialism, where impeachments have simply displaced coups as the new model of regime change and legislatures have assumed the "role previously exercised by the army" (Huneeus, Berrios, and Cordero 2006, 405). In line with this view, the end of the Cold War and the international repudiation of military involvement in politics have prevented a resurgence of the old-style form of military regime change, but the underlying political processes remain essentially dysfunctional. On the other hand, impeachments can be interpreted in a more positive light. In a region where institutions and legality are purportedly flouted, at the very least, problematic presidents are called to heel and replaced through institutional rather than extra-institutional means. The trend also challenges previous assertions that legislatures were simply rubber stamps, incapable of holding presidents accountable (Pérez-Liñan 2007).

Interrupted Presidencies

Others who are less sanguine that presidential democracy has turned a significant corner contend that despite the relative absence of overt military influence in politics, presidentialism remains a significant stumbling block to successful democratization. What is clear is that the tendency for presidential systems to produce interbranch conflict has not been significantly ameliorated with the return to democracy. Though there have been no dramatic coups of the type that brought governments down in Argentina and Chile in the 1970s, Valenzuela argues that the negative characteristics of presidentialism continue to manifest themselves (Valenzuela 2004). He argues that fourteen presidential administrations have collapsed between 1985 and 2004 through early removal by impeachment or forced resignation, while a fifteenth (Peruvian President Alberto Fujimori) shuttered the legislature, abruptly interrupting the country's constitutional order. Indeed, after Valenzuela's study, presidencies were interrupted twice in Bolivia during 2005 and once in Ecuador in the same year. For Valenzuela, these "interrupted presidencies" confirm his very early concurrence with Linz that the basic problem with Latin American presidentialism is the regime structure itself. He dismisses subsequent critics of his and other Linzean arguments as having somehow missed the point by focusing on factors that may facilitate the functioning of presidentialism in discrete circumstances but do not alter its fundamentally negative incentive structure. For Valenzuela, presidentialism remains at the center of all that is wrong with democracy in Latin America.

Low-Quality and Anti-Party Presidencies

The negativity of other analysts grows less from the regime type in particular and rests more with the generally low quality of democracy in the region. In the mid-1990s, Guillermo O'Donnell's argument concerning the sources of this low-quality democracy in the region gained wide currency (O'Donnell 1994, 55–69). O'Donnell contended that a new type of democracy had emerged in Latin America, which he called "delegative democracy." In this form of democracy, the style of presidential rule rests "on the premise that whoever wins election to the presidency is thereby entitled to govern as he or she sees fit, constrained only by the hard facts of existing power relations and by a constitutionally limited term of office."[12] O'Donnell's argument concerning the causes of delegative democracy was not tied directly to regime structure in the tradition of Linz and Valenzuela. Rather, he notes the problem grew out of three interrelated tendencies: the absence of effective horizontal accountably (that is to say oversight from Congress, the courts, or other powerful high-level governmental institutions), a politically isolated form of technocratic decision making, and a pattern of evolution from omnipotent to almost powerless presidents as presidential terms wore on.

O'Donnell's argument proved problematic on a number of counts. While O'Donnell traced the roots of delegative democracy to a lack of mechanisms of horizontal accountability, there was a tacit suggestion that the governed public was somehow to blame for the emergence of such systems. This assumption proved wrong, both in the frequent assertion of legislative power aimed at presidential impeachment and in the power of social movements and mobilizations, which were often tied directly to precipitating impeachment.[13]

Despite uncertainty as to the causes, the issue of the quality of presidents remains problematic. Recent presidential elections in Latin America reveal a trend toward the election and candidacy of anti-party politicians and outsiders with often widespread citizen support (at least initially). What is more, some anti-party presidents have sidestepped or violated commonly accepted democratic practices. The leader of the 1992 coup attempt in Venezuela, Hugo Chavez, was elected president in 1998 and moved to consolidate his authority by questionably democratic means. Peruvian president Alberto Fujimori came to power lacking ties with any established parties and parlayed initial popularity into an *autogolpe* (or self-coup) to reinforce his own power and to successfully win presidency in 1995 and again in 2000. Bolivian President Evo Morales rode a wave of discontent and protest to successfully wage an anti-party presidential campaign and assume the presidency in 2006 as head of a loose confederation of cocoa farmers known as the *cocaleros*. While the party vehicle created by Morales to support his candidacy has gained seats with each election, its orientation consistently challenges the power of traditional parties. Ollanta Humala's victory in the first round of the 2006 Peruvian presidential election represented another challenge to traditional parties.

Other events in the hemisphere also point to a disturbing trend, which might enhance the likelihood of additional low-quality and anti-party presidencies. Chile, traditionally the model for institutionalized parties with high levels of citizen identification, has experienced dramatic erosion in the level of citizen identification with parties, beginning with the student movements of 2006 that have endured off and on until 2014. In addition, despite indications of solidifying party institutionalization in Brazil during the early 2000s, in 2013, massive anti-government protests have emerged that call into doubt the trend of stable presidencies backed by political parties with widespread popular support. While neither of these examples can be characterized as anti-party presidencies, they leave open the door for the emergence of such candidates, given the low level of esteem in which citizens hold parties.

Despite a general rise in anti-party sentiment across the region, it is especially intense in Brazil and Chile. In addition, while some dispute remains with respect to whether parties provide the best vehicle to represent popular social movements, it is undeniable that parties remain essential instruments to structure representative democracies. What is more, outsiders who come to the presidency without party backing are likely to face difficulties in governing because they lack the party base in the legislature around which they can build the working party majorities identified as crucial to the success of presidentialism. Finally, the anti-party orientation of these leaders, in turn, further encourages their anti-system orientation, threatening commonly accepted democratic practices.

Conclusion: Presidents, Legislatures, and Democracy in Latin America

Latin America remains the continent of presidentialism, and it is unlikely that the political will for significant regime transformation will take place. It is clear that some of the system's structural characteristics have created serious problems of governability across the region, and in some cases, have contributed to regime breakdown. However, in other cases, presidential systems have prospered and presidents have been successful in building what seem unlikely coalitions for success. What is more, many crises have been tied to legislative/executive conflict, while many have not. In this sense, the record of presidentialism in Latin America is decidedly mixed, as have been efforts to successfully tie regime structure to patterns of instability. It is clear that both with regard to the performance of Latin America's presidential democracy and with regard to arguments concerning the perils of presidentialism, successful design is crucial to assuring that presidentialism performs well. It is also clear that theoretical and governing success is tied to variables not directly related to regime type, such as election systems, the extent of presidential and legislative powers, and the timing and sequencing of elections. The task for theorists remains to further explore what makes presidentialism either functional or dysfunctional, and the task for reformers and politicians is to adjust these findings to national realities in disparate political systems to design presidential systems that can work.

Notes

1 Matthew S. Shugart and John M. Carey (1992) *Presidents and Assemblies: Constitutional Design and Electoral Dynamics.* New York: Cambridge University Press. Although Shugart and Carey's study predates that of Linz with respect to

publication date, it is a response to Linz whose essay was in extensive circulation in the late eighties and early nineties.

2 For a review of the so-called new institutional literature, see Thomas Koeble (1995) "The New Institutionalism in Political Science and Sociology." *Comparative Politics* 27 (1995): 231–43.

3 For useful reviews of the state of the study of Latin American legislatures, see Mark Jones (1992) "Legislator Behavior and Executive-Legislative Relations in Latin America." *Latin American Research Review* 37(3): 176–88 and Brian Crisp and Felipe Botero (1994) "Multicountry Studies of Latin American Legislatures: A Review Article." *Legislative Studies Quarterly* 24(3): 329–56.

4 While Menem technically had a majority of PJ legislators during his first term, a few of those formally on PJ lists actually belonged to other parties, and Menem lost a few of his own party's legislators as a result of the neoliberal content of his economic reforms. These relations also deteriorated quickly with Menem's increasing reliance on questionably constitutional decree power. See Javier Corrales (2002) *Presidents without Parties: The Politics of Economic Reform in Argentina and Venezuela in the 1990s.* University Park, PA: The Pennsylvania State University Press.

5 Richard Hillman (1994) *Democracy for the Privileged: Crisis and Transition in Venezuela.* Boulder, CO: Lynne Reinner; Frances Hagopian (1993) "After Regime Change: Authoritarian Legacies, Political Representation, and the Democratic Future of South America." *World Politics* 45: 464–500; and Howard Wiarda and Harvey Kline (1996) *Latin American Politics and Development.* Boulder, CO: Westview Press.

6 Gretchen Helmke and Steven Levitsky (1996) "Introduction," in G. Helmke and S. Levitsky (eds.), *Informal Institutions and Democracy: Lessons from Latin America* (1–32). Baltimore: Johns Hopkins University Press.

7 Ibid, 5.

8 Crisp, Brian. "Presidential Behavior in a System with Strong Parties: Venezuela, 1958–1995," in Mainwaring and Shugart (eds.), *Presidentialism and Democracy in Latin America* (160–98). New York: Cambridge University Press (1997)

9 Ibid, 175.

10 Crisp, Brian. "Presidential Behavior in a System with Strong Parties: Venezuela, 1958–1995," 175.

11 Mejia, Acosta, "Crafting Legislative Ghost Coalitions in Ecuador," in Helmke and Levitsky (eds.), *Informal Institutions and Democracy: Lessons from Latin America* (69–86).

12 Ibid, 59.

13 See Pérez-Liñán, *Presidential Impeachment and the New Political Instability in Latin America.*

References

Albert, R. (2009) "The Fusion of Presidentialism and Parliamentarism." *The American Journal of Comparative Law* 57(3): 531–77.

Cheibub, J.A., Elkins, Z., and Ginsburg, T. (2011) "Latin American Presidentialism in Comparative and Historical Perspective." Public Law and Legal Theory Working Paper Series, Law School of the University of Chicago.

Cheibub, J.A., Przeworski, A., and Saiegh, S. (2004) "Government Coalitions under Parliamentarism and Presidentialism." *British Journal of Political Science* 34: 565–87.

Coppedge, M. (1994) *Strong Parties and Lame Ducks: Presidential Partyarchy and Factionalism in Venezuela.* Stanford: Stanford University Press.

Cox, G.W. and Morgenstern, S. (2002) "Epilogue: Latin America's Reactive Assemblies and Pro-active Presidents," in S. Morgenstern and B. Nacif (eds.), *Legislative Politics in Latin America*. New York: Cambridge University Press.

Epstein, D. and O'Halloran, S. (1999) *Delegating Powers: A Transaction Cost Politics Approach to Policy Making Under Separate Powers*. Cambridge: Cambridge University Press.

Hartlyn, J. (1994) "Presidentialism and Colombian Politics," in Linz. J. and Valenzuela, A. (eds.), *The Failure of Presidential Democracy*. Baltimore: Johns Hopkins University Press.

Huneeus, C., Berríos, F., and Cordero, R. (2006) "Legislatures in Presidential Systems: The Latin American Experience." *The Journal of Legislative Studies* 12(3–4): 204–225.

Jones, M. (1992) "Legislator Behavior and Executive-Legislative Relations in Latin America." *Latin American Research Review* 37(3): 176–88.

Jones, M. (1995) *Electoral Laws and the Survival of Presidential Democracy*. South Bend: University of Notre Dame Press.

Jones, M. (1997) "Evaluating Argentina's Presidential Democracy: 1983–1995," in S. Mainwaring and S.S. Matthew (eds.), *Presidentialism and Democracy in Latin America*. New York: Cambridge University Press.

Lamounier, B. (1994) "Brazil: Toward Parliamentarism?" in J. Linz and A. Valenzuela (eds.), *The Failure of Presidential Democracy*. Baltimore: Johns Hopkins University Press.

Lauth, H.J. (2000) "Informal Institutions and Democracy." *Democratization* 7(4): 21–50.

Linz, J. (1994) "Presidential or Parliamentary Democracy: Does It Make a Difference," in J. Linz. and A. Valenzuela (eds.), *The Failure of Presidential Democracy*, vol. II. Baltimore: Johns Hopkins University Press.

Mainwaring, S. (1993) "Presidentialism, Multipartism, and Democracy, The Difficult Combination." *Comparative Political Studies* 26(2): 198–228.

Mainwaring, S. and Shugart, M. (2002) "Conclusion: Presidentialism and the Party System," in S. Morgenstern and B. Nacif (eds.), *Legislative Politics in Latin America*. New York: Cambridge University Press.

Morgenstern, S. (1994) *Patterns of Legislative Politics: Roll-call Voting in Latin America and the United States*. Cambridge: Cambridge University Press.

Morgenstern, S. (2002) "Towards a Model of Latin American Legislatures," in Morgenstern, S. and Nacif, B. (eds.), *Legislative Politics in Latin America*. New York: Cambridge University Press.

Morgenstern, S. and Nacif, B (2002) (eds.) *Legislative Politics in Latin America*. New York: Cambridge University Press.

Needler, M. (2002) "Conclusion: The Legislature in a Democratic Latin America," in Close, D. (ed.), *Legislatures and the New Democracies in Latin America*. Boulder, CO: Lynne Reinner.

Neto, O.A. (2006) "The Presidential Calculus: Executive Policy Making and Cabinet Formation in the Americas." *Comparative Political Studies* 39(4): 415–40.

O'Donnell, G. (1994) "Delegative Democracy." *Journal of Democracy* 5(1): 55–69.

Pérez-Liñán, A. (2007) *Presidential Impeachment and the New Political Instability in Latin America*. Cambridge: Cambridge University Press.

Samuels, D. (2002) "Progressive Ambition, Federalism and Pork-Barrelling in Brazil," in S. Morgenstern and B. Nacif (eds.), *Legislatures and Democracy in Latin America*. New York: Cambridge University Press.

Siavelis, P. (2002) "Exaggerated Presidentialism and Moderate Presidents: Executive-Legislative Relations in Chile," in S. Morgenstern and B. Nacif (eds.), *Legislative Politics in Latin America*. New York: Cambridge University Press.

Siavelis, P. (2006) "Accommodating Informal Institutions and Chilean Democracy," in G. Helmke and S. Levitsky (eds.), *Informal Institutions and Democracy: Lessons from Latin America* (33–55). Baltimore: Johns Hopkins University Press.

Stepan, A. and Skach, C. (1994) "Presidentialism and Parliamentarism in Comparative Perspective," in J. Linz. and A. Valenzuela (eds.), *The Failure of Presidential Democracy*. Baltimore: Johns Hopkins University Press.

Valenzuela, A. (1994) "Party Politics and the Crisis of Presidentialism in Chile: A Proposal for a Parliamentary Form of Government," in J. Linz. and A. Valenzuela (eds.), *The Failure of Presidential Democracy*. Baltimore: Johns Hopkins University Press.

Valenzuela, A. (2004) "Latin American Presidencies Interrupted." *Journal of Democracy* 15(4): 5–19.

Weldon, J. (2002) "The Logic of Presidencialismo in Mexico," in S. Morgenstern and B. Nacif (eds.), *Legislatures and Democracy in Latin America*. New York: Cambridge University Press.

8 Women and Politics in Latin America

María del Mar Martínez Rosón

In the spring of 2014 there were three women serving as presidents of their country in Latin America: Cristina Fernández in Argentina, Dilma Rousseff in Brazil, and Laura Chinchilla in Costa Rica. They are not the first to win a presidential election. Before them, Michelle Bachelet in Chile, Mireya Moscoso in Panama, and Violeta Barrios in Nicaragua were elected as presidents in open and free elections. But even though the presidency is the most important and more visible political office in a country, there are other levels of government where the presence of women has increased in recent years. The aim of this chapter is to analyze the participation of women in Latin American politics, describing their political background and experience, as well as comparing their political interests with their male colleagues. Here I will focus on legislative members from eighteen Latin American countries. Other scholars have attempted to research women representation beyond legislatures and have looked at executive cabinets (Escobar-Lemmon and Taylor-Robinson 2005, 2011), political parties (Roza et al 2010; Llanos and Sample 2008), and local-level institutions (Llanos and Sample 2008b; Krook 2009). Different analyses show that women legislators in many countries in Latin America are gaining seats, and even though they face difficulties, women are willing to enter politics. However, in some countries, the representation of women has not made any progress.

Women and Politics: The Numbers

The first question that scholars have tried to answer is how many women occupy positions of political power. Figure 8.1 shows the progression of the presence of women in three different institutions of representation for the last twenty years. As can be seen, the incorporation of women into politics at different levels of representation is quite variable. Although the percentage of seats held by women has exceeded 20 percent in legislative chambers and municipal councils, the number of women in mayoral positions is still very low in the Latin American region. Unfortunately, the percentage of women does not exceed 25 percent for any of the government levels. However, the positive reading of Figure 8.1 is that, over time, the participation of women in all

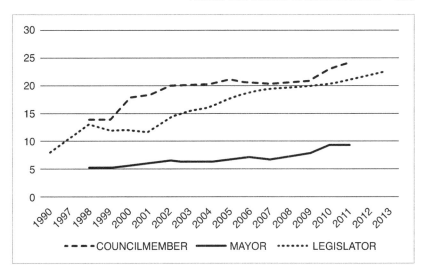

Figure 8.1 Women in Office Between 1990 and 2013 in Latin America (percentage)

Source: CEPAL Database.

*http://*estadisticas.cepal.org/cepalstat/WEB_CEPALSTAT/Portada.asp

levels of political decision making has been increasing, especially in collective bodies. This slow advance without setbacks can help to normalize the presence of women in political positions.

Beyond the aggregate trends in the region, the comparison between countries shows very important differences in the number of women in political office. Table 8.1 reveals the percentage of seats held by women in lower houses, upper houses, positions in executive cabinets, party membership, and leadership positions within parties for each Latin American country. The percentage of women elected in Latin American parliaments varies from more than 40 percent in Nicaragua, the country with the highest percentage, up to less than 10 percent in Panama's legislature. The Inter-Parliamentary Union[1] ranking also locates Brazil, Uruguay, Colombia, and Guatemala in the lower posts with less than 15 percent of women parliamentarians. Along with Nicaragua, Ecuador, Costa Rica, Argentina, and Mexico are well placed in the world ranking, with more than 35 percent of women. For those countries with upper houses, variation is also present. Bolivia almost achieves gender parity with 47 percent of female senators.[2] At the other extreme, the upper house of the Dominican Republic comprises less than 10 percent of women.

Unfortunately, it has been more difficult for scholars to gather together data for the executive branch, and no updated information is available for all the Latin American countries. In spite of this, it can be said that, as in other areas, significant progress has been made in recent years. In the executive, the

Table 8.1 Women in Power Positions in Latin America

IPU Rank Sep. 1 2013	Country	Lower or Single House			Upper or Senate House			Council members	Mayors	Ministers	Party National Executive Committees	Party Leadership	Party Membership
		Elections	Total Seats	% W	Elections	Total Seats	% W	% W 2011	% W 2011	%W 2007	%W 2009	%W 2007	%W 2009
18	Argentina	10 2011	257	37.4	10 2011	72	38.9	n.a.	10.2	25.0	17	29.5	52
44	Bolivia	12 2009	130	25.4	12 2009	36	47.2	13.4²	7	31.3	40	n.a.	n.a
121	Brazil	10 2010	513	8.6	10 2010	81	16.0	12.5	9.2	14.3	16	n.a.	n.a
94	Chile	12 2009	120	14.2	12 2009	38	13.2	23.2	12.5	36.4	13	20.0	48
106	Colombia	3 2010	165	12.1	3 2010	100	16.0	14.5	9	23.1	34	27	n.a
15	Costa Rica	2 2010	57	38.6	—	—	—	38.6	12.3	37.5	41	43.9	n.a
66	Dominican Republic	5 2010	183	20.8	5 2010	32	9.4	33.3	7.7	17.6	14	14.0	36
14	Ecuador	2 2013	137	38.7	—	—	—	28.6	6.3	32.0	17	20.1	n.a
43	El Salvador	3 2012	84	26.2	—	—	—	25.2	10.7	15.4	25	15.8	n.a
99	Guatemala	9 2011	158	13.3	—	—	—	8.8¹	1.8	25.0	16	18.2	54
72	Honduras	11 2009	128	19.5	—	—	—	22.4	3.4	25.0	38	34.6	n.a
19	Mexico	7 2012	500	36.8	7 2012	128	32.8	38.5	5.9	20.0	23	30.6⁴	47
9	Nicaragua	11 2011	92	40.2	—	—	—	24	8.6	31.2	20	24.3	n.a
122	Panama	5 2009	71	8.5	—	—	—	11.1	9.3	21.4	13	18.8	n.a
81	Paraguay	4 2013	80	17.5	4 2013	45	20.0	21.9	7.5	10.0	16	18.9	47
63	Peru	4 2011	130	21.5	—	—	—	27.4	3.9	26.7	31	25.5	48
106	Uruguay	10 2009	99	12.1	10 2009	31	12.9	17.8	24.7	30.8	19	12.5	n.a
83	Venezuela	9 2010	165	17	—	—	—	18.2³	18.2	18.5	21	n.a.	n.a

Source: Data for Lower and Upper Houses from Inter-Parliamentary Union database (www.ipu.org). Council members and mayors' data come from CEPALSTAT. Percentage of women in ministerial cabinets and party leadership data come from Llanos and Sample (2008). For party membership and national executive committees data, see Roza et al (2010).
¹ data for 2010, ² data for 2009, ³ data for 2006, ⁴ data for 2004.

number of female ministers, on average, has moved from 5 percent in 1980 to 7 percent in 1990 to 18 percent in 2003 (Escobar-Lemmon and Taylor-Robinson 2005) to 24 percent in 2007 (Llanos and Sample 2008). In a more recent study of Escobar-Lemmon and Taylor-Robinson (2011), these authors calculated an average of 20 percent of female ministers in Argentina (between 1999 and 2011), 35 percent in Chile (between 2000 and 2010), 24 percent in Colombia (between 1998 and 2010), and 25 percent in Costa Rica (between 1998 and 2010). In 2007 (see Table 8.1), Costa Rica and Chile were the executives with the higher percentage of minister portfolios held by women—above 35 percent. Conversely, Paraguay and Brazil executives have fewer than 15 percent of female ministers.

In the local arena, the differences are also very clear, and again Costa Rica and Mexico have the best percentage of councilwomen and Guatemala and Panama the lower. In addition, Uruguay has the larger percentage of female mayors (24 percent), and Guatemala data shows the lack of women in these positions (2 percent).

Within political parties, the status of women at different levels depends on the degree of power that is exercised at that level. Where data are available, it can be seen that women represent nearly half of the membership, but when we look at leadership positions and executive committees, the presence of women clearly decreases. On average, 23 percent of the executives of the parties are composed of women, while Bolivia, Costa Rica, and Honduras have around 40 percent. Similarly, on average, women in leadership positions within the party occupy 23 percent of the posts (see Table 8.1).

The comparison between council members and mayors, and also between party membership and leadership positions, shows a notable contrast in the presence of women in the most important offices within institutions. Access to multimember institutions is possible, but access to single-member posts is much more difficult. This reveals that there is still a long way to go to normalize women's access to political decision-making positions and representation and also to achieve gender integration, although some countries led the way, others are just at the beginning.

The second question that researchers have studied is the variation between countries and the quantitative evolution within each country. Many authors have tried to explain the reasons why some countries have a larger female presence in politics than others. The number of women in politics has been explained by cultural, socioeconomic, and political factors in an analysis of advanced Western democracies[3]: more egalitarian cultures and early women's enfranchisement (as cultural factors), the level of women's participation in the public sphere and a strong social democratic tradition (as socioeconomic factors), and finally, proportional electoral systems (as political factors) are said to be positively correlated with higher numbers of women (Childs and Lovenduski 2013, 496). However, none of these factors appears to be either necessary or sufficient conditions of women's representation (Dahlerup and Freidenvall 2010).

Although the presence of women in politics is still low, in recent years there has been a significant increase, as shown in Figure 8.1. Buvinic and Roza (2004, 3–6) explain the increase of women's presence in politics in Latin America based on five variables. First, the increase in girls' educational levels helped to reduce gender inequalities in employment and in politics. Second, international women's movements and the effects of globalization have contributed to a cultural change in terms of women's public participation. Third, the democratization process opens up a space to new political preferences and political expression, and diverse citizen movements have been allowed to emerge. Fourth, the expansion of women's rights through international conventions and treaties, and domestic legislation have helped women to enter and remain in politics. Finally, the implementation of affirmative action measurements, such as quota laws for party electoral lists, has increased women's presence, especially in the legislatures.

But not all authors agree with these statements. For instance, more specific studies have found no relationship between the number of women and education level. Escobar-Lemmon and Taylor-Robinson's (2005) work analyzes the number of women in Latin American executive cabinets, and their results show that a higher percentage of women in the legislature and presidents from leftist parties increases the chances that a woman would receive a cabinet position. But increasing the number of women with education and workforce experience does not have the expected positive impact on representation of women in the executive branch, nor does time since women began to win elections to the legislature. Finally, they found that international pressure—which produced a diffusion effect—appears to be a powerful factor in explaining the percentage of women ministers in Latin America (2005, 840). Although the increase in education level may be an important factor, it is not able to explain the presence or lack of women in certain posts and institutions. Other scholars argue that quotas are the factor that better explains representation of women in Latin American legislatures (Htun and Piscopo 2010), even though this measure is not infallible and the use of gender quotas is not a guarantee, as the next section will try to show (Childs and Lovenduski 2013, 496).

Quotas

The interest in increasing the number of women in politics aims to do more than improve the legitimacy of a political system. Actually, the idea behind the quantitative goal is to achieve a qualitative change. One apparently simple and fast way to increase the number of women, especially in parliaments, is the establishment of affirmative action as quotas. Gender quotas were designed to remove the institutional and cultural mechanisms that cause women's under-representation, shifting the responsibility from individual woman to the institutions, from "equal opportunity" to "equality of results" (Dahlerup 2005). But the effects of quotas go beyond the increase of women's percentages. As Franceschet et al (2009) point out, quotas also "increase diversity among the types of women elected, raise attention to women's issues in policy-making processes—altering the form and content of policy-making—change public attitudes about women and politics, and inspire female voters to get more politically involved" (2009, 2).

There are different classifications of quotas, but basically, gender quotas can be mandatory or voluntary.[4] Mandatory quotas can be established by the constitution or by electoral law. Voluntary quotas are adopted by political parties in their statues. Moreover, quotas may affect different stages of the pathway to power, from the recruitment to the selection of candidates. Even when mandated quotas could be seen as more powerful compliance measures than voluntary party quotas, there is no evidence that those measures are either sufficient or necessary to increase the number of seats held by women in parliaments (Dahlerup 2005; Franceschet et al 2009; Piscopo 2006).

Currently, there are fifteen countries in the region that have established gender quotas by a national law for legislative elections. El Salvador and Nicaragua have been the last countries to introduce a quota, and it will be applied in the next elections in 2015 and 2016, respectively. Two countries, Chile and Guatemala, do not have quotas. It is also important to note that Venezuela established a legal quota in 1997, but this was declared unconstitutional in 2000. Moreover, in countries without legal quotas, some of the parties have voluntarily introduced quotas in their statutes. It is also worth noting that most of the legal quotas were adopted in a very small period, between 1996 and 1997.

Despite the problems that may arise in the application of quotas and their effectiveness, scholars argue that this affirmative action does raise women's legislative presence faster over time in Latin America. From 1995 to 2004, countries with gender quotas experienced an average increase of 9.5 percent, whereas non-quota countries experienced an average increase of 4.1 percent (García Quesada 2005, 3). Today, however, the comparison between quota and non-quota countries does not reveal a similar difference. In Latin American lower chambers, woman share, on average, 22.9 percent of the seats in parliament with quotas, and 22.2 percent in non-quota countries[5]. The difference is larger if we take Nicaragua out (the average decreases to 17.7 percent). As shown in Table 8.2, Nicaragua is the country with the highest percentage of women in the legislative chamber (40.2 percent) for the entire region, but has not applied a gender quota. This gives us a clear example of how quotas are not a necessary condition for achieving gender balance. Within countries that have a quote, women's representation ranges from 38.7 percent in Ecuador to 8.5 percent in Panama. Panama data show that the adoption of quotas—50 percent in this specific case—does not increase the percentage of women in parliament automatically[6].

The effectiveness of quota laws depends on the combination of different factors, including the sanctions for noncompliance, the mandate for the rank order of candidates, the wording, the electoral system, the perceived legitimacy, and the political will of the party elites (Dahlerup 2005, 2006;

Table 8.2 Gender Quotas in Latin America

Country	Year	Quota 2013	Lower Chamber	Upper Chamber	Regional or Local	Voluntary Party Quotas
Argentina	1991	30	Yes	Yes	Yes	Yes
Bolivia	1997	50	Yes	Yes	Yes	Yes
Brazil	1997	30	Yes	Yes	Yes	No
Chile	No	—	No	No	No	Yes
Colombia	2011	30	Yes	Yes	Yes	No
Costa Rica	1996	50	Yes	—	No	Yes
Dominican Republic	1997	33	Yes	No	Yes	No
Ecuador	1997	50	Yes	—	Yes	No
El Salvador	2013	30	Yes	—	Yes	Yes
Guatemala	No	—	No	—	No	Yes
Honduras	2000	30	Yes	—	Yes	No
Mexico	1996	40	Yes	Yes	Yes	Yes
Nicaragua	2012	50	Yes	—	Yes	Yes
Panama	1997	50	Yes	—	No	No
Paraguay	1996	20	Yes	Yes	Yes	Yes
Peru	1997	30	Yes	—	Yes	No
Uruguay	2009	33	Yes	Yes	Yes	Yes
Venezuela	1997	30	In 2000, was declared unconstitutional			

Source: www.quotaproject.org

Franceschet et al 2009; Piscopo 2006; Krook 2009; Jones 2009). A few examples show why quotas are not as effective as expected. In Colombia, the quota established that the 30 percent minimum of each gender applies just for those electoral lists where five or more candidates are chosen. In Panama, lists for internal elections and primaries should be at least 50 percent women, but parties are allowed to fill vacant candidacies with men if not enough women participate. In Mexico, the party list requires at least 40 percent women candidates, but parties who elect their candidates democratically are exempt. That means that those parties with primaries are not obliged to reach the gender quota. Something similar happens in Honduras, where the two main parties celebrate open primaries to select the candidates for presidential and legislative elections. When citizens decide with their vote, the final candidate list does not allow parties to comply with the quota, since the control of names that go on the ballot are now in citizens' hands.

The electoral system is also an important factor that affects quota effectiveness. Women's representation in parliaments is higher in proportional electoral systems than in plurality systems (Dahlerup 2005; Norris 2004). The reason behind this difference is the strategy followed by the party in the nominating process of candidates in the anticipation of the voters' reaction. In proportional representation systems with multimember districts, every party list can allocate more than one candidate, and the design of the ballot tries to attract as many voters as possible. In a plurality system, usually there is just one candidate for each district, and males are considered a safer option than are women candidates (Dahlerup 2005, 28).

The will of party elites is also an important variable that can contribute to internalizing the integration of woman and achieving gender quotas. For example, in the candidate selection process in Costa Rica for the 2006 legislative elections, presidential candidate Oscar Arias had the chance to directly nominate ten of the fifty-seven candidates. Arias appointed eight women and two men who were at the top four spots on the electoral list of San José and the top one for the other provinces (Martínez Rosón 2013). By locating women at the top positions of the ballot, the leader of the party sent a clear message to all the party members who had to select the rest of the candidates and also support women leadership within the party, since those were the safer positions on the electoral list.[7]

But not all scholars support the establishment of affirmative action as gender quotas for recruitment processes, elections to public offices, or internal party positions. It has been argued that gender balance in politics will be achieved gradually as society develops and women's political resources equal men's (Dahlerup 2005). As Dahlerup said, "Some consider quotas to be a form of discrimination and violation of the principle of fairness [and merit], while others view them as compensation for structural barriers that prevent fair competition" (2005, 20). Those against quotas are focused on what kind of woman will be elected. "Opponents have expressed concerns that quotas will facilitate access for elite or 'unqualified' women, bring women to office with little interest in promoting women's concerns, reinforce stereotypes about women's inferiority as political actors, and deter ordinary women's political participation" (Franceschet et al 2009, 3). In the next sections, I will address the analysis of these questions in terms of Latin American women legislators.

Representation

In order to address the study of the real changes, scholars have pay special attention to two different aspects: descriptive representation and substantive representation. Pitkin's (1967) work divides political representation into four different components: authorized representation (the politician is legally empowered to represent and to act for another), descriptive representation (the representative shares similar characteristics such as gender, religion, or ethnicity with his constituents), symbolic representation (the meaning that a representative has for those being represented), and, finally, substantive representation (politicians represent a group's policy interest and issues). Here I will focus on descriptive and substantive representation in order to answer what women are elected to positions of power and what interests they defend.

Descriptive Representation

Besides the number of women elected, other questions need to be answered. What kinds of women are elected? Do they share the same political and sociodemographic characteristics with their male colleagues? Previous research offers opposite results. On one hand, some studies suggest that quotas primarily promote women with ties to powerful men, high levels of education, and close loyalties to their political parties. On the other hand, other scholars argue that quotas lead to the recruitment of women from marginalized groups, low levels of education, lower-status occupations, relatively young, and those with less political experience (Franceschet et al 2009).

Table 8.3 shows a few pieces of information about the political background and sociodemographic characteristics of Latin American representatives. These data have been collected by the Latin American Parliamentary Elites Project of the University of Salamanca (Alcántara, Dir.). Since 1994, personal interviews are carried out with parliamentarians whenever parliaments are renewed after elections. Table 8.3 shows the data from more than 5,000 interviews conducted between 1998 and 2012 in eighteen Latin American countries (see Annex I).[8]

Women represent, on average, close to 17 percent of the interviews, and if we compare their sociodemographic characteristics, several differences are statistically significant. First, women representatives, on average, are younger than their male colleagues. Even though this two-year difference is statistically significant, it is not a huge difference. On the contrary, marital status differences are statistically and theoretically significant. While 84 percent of the male deputies are married or live as a couple, on average, only 58 percent of the women are in this situation. Moreover, the country analysis reveals that this difference is statistically significant in seventeen of the eighteen countries included. These results should make us reflect on the compatibility of family life and political life. Although we do not know the direction of the cause, if family life complicates politics or politics makes family life difficult, the data make clear that family and politics are more difficult to make compatible for women than for men.

Table 8.3 also includes the percentage of parliamentarians who have a college degree or postgraduate education. Some scholars are afraid that quotas would lead to the entry of less educated women, but in Latin America, the data do not support this idea. Aggregate data in the region show a slight difference between men and women, but only in four (Brazil, El Salvador, Honduras, and Peru) of the eighteen countries is the lower educational level of women relative to men's statistically significant. Actually, there are many more cases where the female representatives' level of education is greater than men's: Argentina, Chile, Colombia, Costa Rica, Dominican Republic, Ecuador, Guatemala, Panama, Uruguay, and Venezuela. These two lists include both countries with quotas and without quotas. So in the Latin American region, quotas are not a determining factor on the different levels of education between men and women representatives.[9]

Table 8.3 Background and Political Careers of Legislators: Differences Between Women and Men

	Latin America	Argentina	Bolivia	Brazil	Chile	Colombia	Costa Rica	Dominican Republic	Ecuador	El Salvador	Guatemala	Honduras	Mexico	Nicaragua	Panama	Paraguay	Peru	Uruguay	Venezuela
Gender																			
Men	83.3	69.8	83.5	88.1	89.0	88.7	70.6	84.9	82.0	86.4	89.9	84.4	76.5	82.1	89.3	92.5	80.6	89.2	90.8
Women	16.7	30.2	16.5	11.9	11.0	11.3	29.0	15.1	18.0	13.6	10.1	15.6	23.5	17.9	10.7	7.5	19.4	10.8	9.2
Sig.	***	*																	
Age																			
Men	48	52	45	56	48	45	48	48	46	47	47	49	45	47	48	45	49	49	48
Women	46	50	45	54	47	43	49	47	42	46	46	48	43	43	50	45	45	47	47
Sig.	***	*							***				**	*			**		
Studies[1]	76.1	60.4	66.9	81.3	85.8	91.1	80.3	73.9	86.4	67.0	68.9	65.9	84.8	86.4	84.7	65.5	88.5	57.0	78.0
Sig.	**	***	***	*	***	***	***	<	***	*	***	*	***	**	**	***	***		
Men	76.3	59.2	67.2	83.9	85.1	90.5	79.6	72.4	86.4	69.0	67.9	68.3	85.6	87.7	84.6	66.8	91.5	55.9	77.1
Women	75.1	63.4	65.7	62.5	91.8	95.3	82.1	82.4	86.8	54.7	77.8	53.0	82.5	80.6	85.7	50.0	76.5	66.7	86.7
Married[2]	79.9	75.5	78.3	73.6	83.0	72.3	76.0	83.1	84.1	77.9	84.2	89.4	76.7	78.6	79.0	85.5	79.4	80.1	78.6
Sig.	***	***	***	**	***	***	***	***	***	***	***	**	***	**	**	***	***	***	***
Men	84.2	80.1	81.2	79.3	85.9	75.2	85.4	85.0	90.0	82.5	87.4	91.3	84.5	84.2	82.2	87.4	85.2	83.6	80.4
Women	58.2	64.5	59.6	31.7	59.4	51.6	53.8	72.0	57.2	48.6	56.1	79.1	52.1	52.7	52.4	60.6	54.6	50.2	61.5
Family in politics	51.7	46.1	46.5	56.3	51.1	55.4	50.8	51.1	52.0	48.1	52.9	63.8	49.0	62.9	65.3	58.0	42.8	44.8	52.2
Sig.	**	*																*	
Men	51.0	45.7	46.8	54.7	50.3	55.4	47.8	50.5	50.6	47.2	52.4	64.1	47.8	60.8	65.1	57.2	40.2	43.5	51.6
Women	56.6	47.3	63.3	68.2	57.1	57.0	57.7	54.2	58.0	53.9	58.1	62.2	53.6	72.8	66.7	68.0	53.5	56.1	58.1
Amateur	66.2	68.1	79.3	36.3	41.1	63.3	87.5	69.7	66.5	50.3	65.0	59.3	77.6	75.4	60.2	80.4	71.1	61.5	57.9
Sig.	***	**					<		***	<		<						<	
Men	64.2	63.8	80.3	37.5	39.9	62.9	84.9	69.1	62.2	48.3	63.8	57.3	76.1	73.6	58.3	80.0	70.1	59.8	58.5
Women	75.5	77.3	80.3	27.5	50.9	65.7	93.6	71.7	85.4	62.1	74.9	69.9	80.8	83.6	76.2	88.8	75.1	75.4	52.5

(Continued)

Table 8.3 (Continued)

	Latin America	Argentina	Bolivia	Brazil	Chile	Colombia	Costa Rica	Dominican Republic	Ecuador	El Salvador	Guatemala	Honduras	Mexico	Nicaragua	Panama	Paraguay	Peru	Uruguay	Venezuela
Representation experience	39.4 ***	53.8 ^	32.8 ^	79.2	34.5 *	69.3 *	31.9 *	21.8	40.6	27.6	28.7 *	25.7	53.9 **	26.5	24.5	41.0	35.2	45.3	50.9
Men	40.5	56.5	34.8	78.8	36.6	71.4	38.6	22.3	38.8	28.9	30.4	26.9	57.4	24.6	23.4	42.2	37.0	46.1	50.8
Women	33.6	47.4	22.2	81.5	19.6	53.5	21.0	20.1	47.3	20.0	13.8	19.7	41.3	35.3	33.3	25.5	27.5	39.4	52.1
Designated positions	36.3	44.8	23.2	58.8	23.3	48.6	31.3	65.9	49.8	17.9	41.7	20.3	46.0 ^	27.5	29.7	12.5	24.7 ^	36.1	–
Men	37.0	41.5	24.7	60.5	23.5	49.8	26.1	67.2	44.5	19.3	43.6	20.0	50.1	31.6	30.5	11.3	27.9	36.6	–
Women	33.8	51.0	15.9	46.1	21.7	40.8	39.5	59.7	59.8	11.5	30.0	21.4	35.3	8.3	20.0	20.0	15.5	32.6	–
Party positions	63.7	65.6	25.3	81.7	70.5	23.2 ^	73.2	89.0	50.3	85.7	81.4	58.8	75.4	91.2	75.0	37.5	54.1 **	87.2	–
Men	64.4	67.9	26.0	81.0	71.5	23.9	75.4	87.2	54.0	86.0	79.6	61.4	76.4	91.1	76.3	35.5	59.7	85.4	–
Women	61.2	61.3	21.8	87.3	63.6	17.7	69.8	97.2	43.5	84.6	92.5	50.0	72.8	91.7	60.0	50.0	37.0	100.0	–
Full–time dedication	59.0 ***	69.3	71.2 **	66.6	75.8	83.6 ^	64.1 ***	42.4 *	62.9	49.1 ***	42.7 **	16.5 ***	68.5 ***	39.8	34.7 **	44.1	76.5 *	67.2	61.2
Men	55.8	67.1	67.6	63.0	74.0	82.6	54.6	40.1	60.7	45.3	40.3	12.8	64.8	38.3	31.4	42.7	74.2	66.6	59.4
Women	74.2	74.7	87.3	92.4	90.0	93.8	87.0	53.9	73.8	73.5	63.8	36.7	81.1	46.9	61.9	59.9	86.3	71.8	79.1
Future positions	89.2	95.3	84.6	–	94.1	95.3	85.2	95.8	81.7	88.7	–	78.8	88.0	–	94.8	–	86.6	93.6	–
Men	89.2	92.5	83.3	–	93.3	94.8	84.8	96.3	78.9	87.8	–	76.6	93.8	–	96.2	–	85.7	92.7	–
Women	89.1	100	89.5	–	100	100	85.7	93.7	86.9	92.3	–	85.7	73.5	–	80.0	–	89.0	100.0	–

Source: PELA (1994–2015). ^p<0.100, *p <0.050, **p<0.010, ***p<0.001

[1] Percentage of legislators with university degree or more. [2] Percentage of married legislators or those in a free union.

Moving from sociodemographic variables to other characteristics about their political career, I will try to find out if women representatives have less political experience, different backgrounds, or less political ambition. In a recent study about women ministers in four Latin American countries (Argentina, Chile, Colombia, and Costa Rica) between 2000 and 2010, Escobar-Lemmon and Taylor-Robinson found evidence of women's integration. Women ministers have similar political backgrounds, connections, and experience to men, except in the economic portfolios. Even though women are no longer limited to posts in the economic area, women ministers in this sector are less likely than men to have policy expertise in this field (2011, 29).

Many scholars emphasize the family connections of many female presidents, especially the presence of the husband as a significant political figure (Gutiérrez de Piñeres 2008). Are women in the Latin American parliaments also more dependent on their family status or political connections? Data collected show that, on average, 56 percent of women have or have had other members of their family in politics, but this percentage is 51 percent for male representatives. This difference is statistically significant for the entire region and in Bolivia and Peru. This may be due to two factors. On the one hand, only women with enough political contacts have the self-confidence and the political socialization needed to enter into politics and run for office. On the other hand, women have more difficulties with access to elected institutions, and only through family connections is it possible to remove those barriers.

This family dependency could influence political motivations for joining a party and generate differences between males and females. Fox and Lawless (2005) studied the nascent political ambition among citizens. Their analysis points out that the gender variable affects motivations that are found in the beginnings of a political career. Being a woman influenced the initial decision to run for office and discouraged political interests. Even though gender has an impact among citizens in the initial decision to run, these effects have not been detected among politicians. In a previous work on Central American countries (Martínez Rosón 2011), ideology was found to be the most important motivation for joining the party. The second aspect that drives the political representatives is the party's political program. At the other end, family is the less important cause. Moreover, the results of the analysis show that there is no difference between men and women in the weight that the ideology and the party program have as reasons to enter the party. Parliamentarians in general joined their political party for similar reasons; females and males do not have different motivations.

Even though women in parliament have more difficulties than their political male colleagues in obtaining campaign funding and face limited media coverage (Del Campo 2005) the evidence in Latin America tells us that women's ambition is as powerful as men's, at least among politicians. The 89 percent of the parliamentarians, males and females, would like to continue in politics in the same or a different position. The level of women's political ambition in each country, where the data are available, is greater than men's except in

Mexico, Panama, and Dominican Republic, where a higher percentage of men than women wish to continue a political career. This data do not support previous findings that suggest that women have less political ambition and lack the will to participate, at least among Latin American representatives.

As one might expect, given the fact that there has been a rapid increase of women representatives, the percentage of women who serve for the first time in the parliament is larger than males, and this difference is statistically significant for the region and in Argentina and Ecuador. More than 75 percent of the women are newcomers, but just 64 percent of male representatives are amateurs. In addition, women have less political experience: in designated positions, in formal party positions, and even in other representative public offices like local institutions or upper chambers—only this difference between men and women is statistically significant. These data come without surprises considering that woman do not exceed 25 percent of the party positions even though they constitute between 40 percent and 50 percent of the affiliates (Del Campo 2005) and 19 percent of the executive party committees (and 51 percent of the affiliates) according to Roza et al (2010).

Another important and statically significant difference between female and male parliamentarians is the amount of time dedicated to politics. More men than women have other economic activities besides the parliament. On average, 74 percent of women are dedicated to their position full time, whereas just 55 percent of men are. This difference is consistent in all the cases and is statistically significant in twelve of the countries. Previous research also found that women legislators in Costa Rica dedicate more time to legislative activities than do men (Figueres 2002), but these data confirm it for the entire Latin American region. If men and women do not devote equal time to political work, this may affect the way in which they perform parliamentary functions or the type of functions in which they specialize. That will be the subject of attention in the next section.

Substantive Representation: Representation of Gender Interests

Feminist literature usually claims "that women's political presence will engender women's substantive representation" (Childs and Lovenduski 2013). These two components are highly related in the literature. The important idea here that connects both concepts is the critical mass, which was established around 30 percent. The critical mass means that once women constitute a certain size, politics will be transformed because it will be possible to introduce women's issues in the political agenda and impose changes that favor women's interests (Dahlerup 2005; Studlar and MacAllister 2002; Childs and Lovenduski 2013).

However, there is not a consensus about what representing gender interest means. As Childs and Lovenduski (2013) point out, for some scholars, substantive representation occurs when the political debate includes women's perspectives; for others, when the debate includes a diversity of women's perspectives, or even just when the interests of the representatives are con-gruent with the interests of the represented.[10] Moreover, the representation of women's interest is not guaranteed by the women's presence in legisla-tures (Weldon 2002) because even when women may change the legislative agenda and initiate bills on feminist issues, this does not mean that women will be succeed in passing the law (Schwindt-Bayer 2006; Franceschet and Piscopo 2008).

Many scholars have shown in Western democracies that female legislators have different policy priorities—specifically, they are more interested in issues related to women. The Costa Rican experience suggests that women have dif-ferent leadership styles. Because they are more focused on constituency work and parliamentary committees and spend more time dedicated to these activi-ties, their success rate in passing laws is 81 percent, whereas male legislators pass only 48 percent of their initiatives (Figueres 2002). However, this is not the only side of the story. Schwindt-Bayer (2006) examined legislators' policy priorities and bill initiation behavior in three Latin American countries (Costa Rica, Colombia, and Argentina).[11] She found no significant differences in atti-tudes toward education, health, or economy, but woman place greater priority on children and family issues. However, significant gender disparities appear when examining bill initiation with women marginalized from the traditional men's domain. Another study of six Latin American countries argued that even when the number of women in the legislatures increases, male legislators marginalize female legislators to social committees and keep them away from the economic committees (Heath et al 2005).

Unfortunately, there is no information available about the roll call voting or legislative initiatives for the entire Latin American region, but survey data from the legislatures since 1994 are available and allow us to compare attitudes toward issue priorities between female legislators and their male counterparts. This survey also provides information about legislative work and the decision-making process.

As found in previous research, female officeholders in Latin America have a different focus on representation (Table 8.4). But unlike previous findings, they are not more interested in constituency work than men. In fact, less than 30 percent of women take into account their constituents in making decisions, while more than 36 percent of men do. Female representatives seem to be more aware than men of the public opinion (34 percent) and the positions of interest groups (7 percent), relative to men, when they come to any political decision.

This difference is also evident in Table 8.5. When we ask deputies whom they represent, most of them respond that they represent all citizens, and the second option, with more responses, is that they represent the voters of their district. In this case, the differences are clear and statistically significant, but go in an opposite direction of previous literature findings. Male representatives are more focused on the electors of their district, relative to women, while female representatives are more focused on the general citizenry, relative to

Table 8.4 Opinions That Are Taken Into Account When Making Decisions (percentage)

Multi-response	Men	Women
Constituents of My District	36.6	29.4
National Party Leaders	8.3	9.6
Regional Party Leaders	3.5	2.2
General Public Opinion	31.6	34.0
Party Affiliates	2.1	2.0
Mass Media	1.1	0.9
Other Representatives from My Party	1.1	2.2
Interest Groups	3.7	6.9
Voters of My Party	7.8	7.2
The Government	4.2	5.5
Total (n)	100 (1742)	100 (429)

Source: PELA (1994–2015).

Table 8.5 Representation (percentage)

***	Men	Women
All Party Electors	9.3	8.4
All Electors of My District	39.9	32.5
My Political Party	3.7	5.2
All Citizens	46.6	53.4
A Specific Group of Citizens (Social, Economic, or Religious)	0.6	0.5
Total (n)	100 (4388)	100 (921)

Source: PELA (1994–2015). *p <0.050, **p<0.010, ***p<0.001

men. Accordingly, for women, representing the nation is more important than it is for men. Women have a widespread or general commitment as representatives, whereas men understand representation more narrowly, more connected to their district.

In terms of parliamentary work, the most important task is to elaborate bills (see Table 8.6). The second most important task for men is to represent their district's interests (21 percent), whereas for women, it is to solve their country's problems (21 percent). The function where the difference in percentage is higher is representing the nation—this is more important for women legislators (19 percent) than for men (16 percent). As in the previous table, it seems from these data that women have a more general vision of political activity while men seem to be focused on their constituents.

Table 8.6 More Important Legislative Activities (percentage)

Multi-response	Men	Women
Represent the Nation	15.6	18.6
Elaborate Bills	26.3	26.8
Resolve Country's Problems	20.4	21.3
Control Government's Activities	11.0	8.6
Defend the Interests of My Party	2.0	1.8
Elaborate the Budget	3.4	3.6
Represent My District's Interests	21.3	19.4
Total (n)	100 (6183)	100 (1391)

Source: PELA (1994–2015).

Table 8.7 Reasons That They Were Elected (percentage)

Multi-response	Men	Women
Leader's Image	12.2	13.5
Electoral Campaign	18.0	15.9
Party's Program or Manifesto	15.3	16.1
Family Tradition	3.1	2.2
Personal Charm	18.2	16.1
Party's Ideology	11.6	13.4
Previous Experience in Public Office	18.5	19.9
Previous Management as Deputy	1.7	1.6
Because None of the Other Options Convinced the Voter	0.7	0.7
Other Responses	0.7	0.7
Total (n)	100 (10060)	100 (2009)

Source: PELA (1994–2015).

When deputies are asked for the reasons why they believe they were elected, the two main reasons are the same for men and women: personal experience and personal charisma (see Table 8.7). Surprisingly, despite the importance of parties in the Latin American region, parliamentarians offer explanations based on their personal aspects (personal vote) rather than those related to their party. We have to look at the third and fourth reasons to see differences between women and men. In these positions, the order is reversed, with the campaign being more important for men than the party program, and for women, the program is more important than the campaign they run in order to be elected.

Table 8.8 Role of the State (mean)

	Men	Woman	Total
The state should be the owner of the country's most important companies	3.34	3.68	3.41*
n	759	191	949
The state should be responsible for ensuring people's well-being	5.40	5.42	5.41
n	758	189	947
The state should be primarily responsible for creating employment	4.29	4.57	4.35*
n	754	190	944
The state should implement policies to reduce income inequality	5.91	6.00	5.93
n	755	190	944
The state should be primarily responsible for providing retirement pensions	4.96	5.23	5.01*
n	755	187	942
The state should be primarily responsible for providing health care	5.43	5.82	5.51**
n	751	186	937
The state should be primarily responsible for providing university education	5.10	5.63	5.20***
n	751	187	938
The state should implement public policies to reduce gender inequalities	6.02	6.28	6.07
n	456	112	568

Source: PELA (1994–2015). The scale ranges between 1 "strong disagreement" and 7 "strong agreement."

*p <0.050, **p<0.010, ***p<0.001

Women also have a different position on policy priorities relative to men in terms of the role to be fulfilled by the state. Female legislators seem to be more concerned with issues traditionally associated with women, such as education and health, and believe that the state should intervene in these matters more than male legislators do. Besides these issues, women demand greater involvement of the state in job creation and the provision of pensions than do men.

However, women's demand for greater involvement of the state in education and health care does not necessarily imply a demand for increasing public

Table 8.9 Preferences on Public Spending (percentage)

Multi-response	Men	Women
Infrastructure	13.2	9.6
Health Care	28.1	31.0
Public Security	10.3	10.1
Education	37.9	37.1
Defense and Armed Forces	1.0	0.8
Housing	2.6	2.3
Pensions	1.6	2.7
Environment	1.9	1.8
Gender	0.1	0.4
Economic and Social Inclusion	3.2	4.0
Total (n)	100 (3721)	100 (970)

Source: PELA (1994–2015).

spending for these items. Both male and female legislators believe that their country should spend more money on education and health. But looking at the data in greater detail, slight differences can be found. More women legislators advocate increased public spending on health (31 percent vs. 28 percent), while more male legislators believe that it is better to increase public spending on infrastructure (13 percent vs. 10 percent). However, both male and female legislators believe that education is the highest priority for government spending.

Conclusions

The incorporation of women in elected institutions in Latin America has increased over the last twenty years, even though the number of women in politics is still very low, especially in the local level, where the access to the mayor position is a man's domain. Most of the countries have adopted quotas to increase the presence of women in the legislatures, but not all of them have been as effective as can be expected. Currently, there are fifteen countries in the region that have established gender quotas for legislative elections. Two countries, Chile and Guatemala, do not have quotas, and in Venezuela, the quota was declared unconstitutional. Paradoxically, in 2014, the Latin American legislature with more women representatives (Nicaragua) has not applied a gender quota, and the country with the lower number of legislative seats held by women (Panama) has a 50 percent quota. In 2014, the comparison between quota and non-quota countries does not reveal an important difference like in the past. In Latin American lower chambers, woman share, on average, 22.9 percent of the seats in parliament in countries that have quotas, and 22.2 percent in non-quota countries.[12]

Regarding descriptive representation, women legislators have a higher education level than their male colleagues. Only in four countries are women less educated. Female representatives also have the same motivations to enter politics and they keep the same level of political ambition as men, but family political connections seem to be more important for women. Moreover, women's political careers show that they have less political experience, inside and outside of the chamber, and time dedication and marital status clearly show that reconciling politics and family has been difficult for women.

In a few aspects, women understand substantive representation differently than men. Women have a widespread or general commitment as representatives, whereas men understand representation more narrowly, more connected to their district. Female legislators seem to be more concerned with issues traditionally associated with women, such as education and health, and believe that the state should intervene in these matters more than do male legislators. These differences have no reflection on their attitudes on public spending or the relevance of the several functions that they carry out. In these aspects, women and men legislators are similar.

Some scholars are optimistic and expect that "younger men might adapt more rapidly to women's presence than older men and as new generations enter Latin America's democratic institutions, gender disadvantages might slowly disappear" (Piscopo 2006, 55). They argue that the feminization of Latin American politics will continue because citizens have positive opinions of women's performance in politics and a high number of electors are willing to vote for women candidates (Buvinic and Roza 2004). That might be true for most of the countries, but a few Latin American cases have made very modest advances and women are a minority even in the parliament.

Notes

1 This ranking is available at www.ipu.org/wmn-e/classif.htm.
2 About gender parity in Bolivia, see Htun and Ossa (2013). About gender and race in Brazil, see Htun (2003).
3 Inglehart et al (2002), for example, try to explain what factors influence the percentage of women on a parliament, taking into account the level of modernization and democratic and cultural variables (for the modernization factor, they use GDP per capita, religion as the cultural factor, and Freedom House scores for the level of democracy). The test results show that by itself, the degree of modernization of a country is able to explain only 30 percent of the variance in women's parliamentary representation. The cultural factor explains 46 percent of the variance, but combining these two factors explains 70 percent of the variance, even though modernization is not statistically significant. According to Inglehart et al (2002), the cultural factor seems a more powerful explanatory factor.
4 For a complete explanation of the different kinds of quotas, see Krook (2009), Norris (2004), Dahlerup (2006, 2007), Matland (2006,) or Franceschet et al (2009).
5 El Salvador, Nicaragua, and Uruguay are analyzed as non-quota cases since the adopted quotas have not been applied yet.
6 For a specific analysis of the effectiveness of quotas in Panama, see Jones (2010).
7 For a complete explanation of the effectiveness of quotas, see Jones (2004), Piscopo (2006), and Matland (2006).

8 Databases, questionnaires, and more information about the project can be found at http://americo.usal.es/oir/Elites/index.htm.
9 A comparison of education before and after quotas could address a better understanding of whether quota affects education of those women who enter the legislature.
10 Franceschet and Piscopo's (2008, 395) work divides the concept of substantive representation into two different aspects: substantive representation as a process (changing legislative agendas) and substantive representation as an outcome (changing policy outcomes). For other explanations on why it has been difficult to integrate women perspectives into public policy making, see Fanceschet et al (2009).
11 For Argentina, see Jones (1997).
12 El Salvador, Nicaragua, and Uruguay are analyzed as non-quota cases since the quotas have not been applied yet.

References

Alcántara, M. (dir.) Parliamentary Elites in Latin America (PELA) Project. University of Salamanca. (1994–2015).

Buvinic, M. and Roza, V. (2004) "Women, Politics and Democratic Prospects in Latin America." Sustainable Development Department Technical Papers Series. Washington: Inter-American Development Bank.

Childs, S. and Lovenduski, J. (2013) "Political Representation," in G. Waylen, K. Celis, J. Kantola, and L. Weldon (eds.), *The Oxford Handbook of Gender and Politics* (489–513). Oxford: Oxford University Press.

Del Campo, E. (2005) "Women and Politics in Latin America: Perspectives and Limits of the Institutional Aspects of Women's Political Representation." *Social Forces* 83(4): 1697–726.

Dahlerup, D. (2005) "Strategies to Enhance Women's Political Representation in Different Electoral Systems." Isis Monograph Series 1(1): 12–33.

Dahlerup, D. (2006) "What Are the Effects of Electoral Gender Quotas? From Studies of Quota Discourses to Research on Quota Effects." Paper presented at the International Political Science Association World Congress, Fukuoka, July 10–13.

Dahlerup, D. (2007) "Electoral Gender Quotas: Between Equality of Opportunity and Equality of Result." *Representation* 43(2): 73–92.

Dahlerup, D. and Freidenvall, L. (2010) "Judging Gender Quotas: Predictions and Results." *Policy & Politics* 38(3): 407–25.

Escobar-Lemmon, M and Taylor-Robinson, M. (2005). "Women Ministers in Latin American Government: When, Where and Why?" *American Journal of Political Science* 49(4): 829–44.

Escobar-Lemmon, M. and Taylor-Robinson, M. (2011) "Pathways to Power in Presidential Cabinets: Do Men and Women Appointees Differ?" Paper presented at the Quality and Professionalization of Politicians in Latin America Conference. University of Salamanca, September 26–27.

Figueres, K. (2002) "El camino hacia la igualdad. Las mujeres costarricenses en el parlamento," in M. Méndez-Montalvo and J. Ballington (eds.), *Mujeres en el parlamento: Más allá de los números*. Stockholm: Institute for Democracy and Electoral Assistance (IDEA).

Fox, R. and Lawless, J. (2005) "To Run or Not to Run for Office: Explaining Nascent Political Ambition." *American Journal of Political Science* 49(3): 642–59.

Franceschet, S., Krook, M.L., and Piscopo, J.M. (2009) "The Impact of Gender Quotas: A Research Agenda." Paper presented at the Annual Meeting of the American Political Science Association. Toronto Canada, September 3–6.

Franceschet, S. and Piscopo, J.M. (2008) "Gender Quotas and Women's Substantive Representation: Lessons from Argentina." *Politics & Gender* 4(3): 393–425.

García Quesada, A.I. (2005) "Conditions Determining the Level of Representation of Women: The Experience of the Quota System in Latin America." Prepared for the United Nations Expert Group Meeting on the Equal Participation of Women and Men in Decision-Making Processes. October.

Gutiérrez de Piñeres, S.A. (2008) "Feminism in Latin America," in R.L. Millett, J.S. Holmes, and O.J. Pérez (eds.), *Latin American Democracy: Emerging Reality or Endangered Species?* New York: Routledge.

Heath, M.R., Schwindt-Bayer, L.A., and Taylor-Robinson, M. (2005) "Women on the Sidelines: Women's Representation on Committees in Latin American Legislatures." *American Journal of Political Science* 49(2): 420–36.

Htun, M. (2003) "Dimensions of Political Inclusion and Exclusion in Brazil: Gender and Race." Technical Paper Series of the Sustainable Development Department. Washington, DC: Inter-American Development Bank.

Htun, M. and Ossa, J.P. (2013) "Political Inclusion of Marginalized Groups: Indigenous Reservations and Gender Parity in Bolivia." *Politics, Groups, and Identities* 1(1): 4–25.

Htun, M. and Piscopo, J. (2010) "Presence without Empowerment? Women in Politics in Latin America and the Caribbean." Paper prepared for the Conflict Prevention and Peace Forum. Global Institute for Gender Research (GIGR).

Inglehart, R., Norris, P., and Welzel, C. (2002) "Gender Equality and Democracy." *Comparative Sociology* 1(3–4): 321–45.

Jones, M.P. (1997) "Legislator Gender and Legislator Policy Priorities in the Argentine Chamber of Deputies and the United States House of Representatives." *Policy Studies Journal* 25(4): 613–27.

Jones, M.P. (2004) "Quota Legislation and the Election of Women: Learning from the Costa Rica Experience." *The Journal of Politics* 66(4): 1203–23.

Jones, M.P. (2009) "Gender Quotas, Electoral Laws, and the Election of Women. Evidence from the Latin American Vanguard." *Comparative Political Studies* 42 (1): 56–81.

Jones, M.P. (2010) "La representación de las mujeres en la Asamblea Nacional de Panamá: diagnóstico, buenas prácticas y propuestas de reforma," in H. Brown *Las reformas electorales en Panamá: claves de desarrollo humano para la toma de decisiones.* Panama: Programa de las Naciones Unidas para el Desarrollo.

Krook, M.L. (2009) *Quotas for Women in Politics: Gender and Candidate Selection Reform Worldwide.* New York: Oxford University Press.

Llanos, B. and Sample, K. (2008) "From Words to Action: Best Practices for Women's Participation in Latin American Political Parties." Stockholm: International Institute for Democracy and Electoral Assistance (IDEA).

Llanos, B. and Sample, K. (2008b) "30 Years of Democracy: Riding the Wave? Women's Political Participation in Latin America." Stockholm: International Institute for Democracy and Electoral Assistance (IDEA).

Martínez Rosón, M. (2011) "Ambición inicial: Motivaciones para iniciar una carrera política." *Postdata* 16(2): 259–80.

Martínez Rosón, M. (2013) "Selección de candidatos en Costa Rica," in M. Alcántara and L.M. Cabezas (eds.), *Selección de candidatos y elaboración de programas en los partidos políticos Latinoamericanos.* Valencia: Tirant Lo Blanch.

Matland, R. (2006) "Electoral Quotas: Frequency and Effectiveness," in D. Dahlerup (ed.), *Women, Quotas, and Politics.* New York: Routledge.

Norris, P. (2004) *Electoral Engineering: Voting Rules and Political Behavior.* Cambridge: Cambridge University Press.

Piscopo, J.M. (2006) "Engineering Quotas in Latin America." Ciclas Working Papers 23. University of California, San Diego: California Digital Library.

Pitkin, H.F. (1967) *The Concept of Representation.* California: University of California Press.

Roza, V., Llanos, B., and Garzón de la Roza, G. (2010) *Partidos políticos y paridad: La ecuación pendiente.* Stockholm: International Institute for Democracy and Electoral Assistance (IDEA).

Schwindt-Bayer, L. (2006) "Still Supermadres? Gender and the Policy Priorities of Latin American Legislators." *American Journal of Political Science* 50(3): 570–85.

Studlar, D.T. and McAllister, I. 2002. "Does a Critical Mass Exist?" *European Journal of Political Research* 41(2): 233–53.

Weldon, L. 2002. "Beyond Bodies: Institutional Sources of Representatives for Women in Democratic Policymaking." *The Journal of Politics* 64(4): 1153–74.

Annex I. Countries and legislatures included in the analysis

	Legislature	Legislature	Legislature	Legislature	Legislature	Legislature	n
Argentina	95–97	97–01	03–07	07–11	09–13		481
Bolivia	93–97	97–02	02–06	06–10	10–13		447
Brazil			03–07	07–10			129
Chile	93–97	97–01	02–06	06–10	10–14		446
Colombia		98–02	02–06	06–10	10–14		381
Costa Rica	94–98	98–02	02–06	06–10	10–14		265
Dominican Republic	94–98	98–02	02–06	06–10	10–16		455
Ecuador	96–98	98–02	02–06	07–08	09–12		377
El Salvador	94–97	97–00	00–03	03–06	06–09	09–11	388
Guatemala	95–99	00–04	04–08	08–12	12–16		360
Honduras	94–97	97–01	02–06	06–10	10–14		422
Mexico	94–97	97–00	00–03	03–06	06–09	09–11	722
Nicaragua		96–01	01–06	07–11	12–16		199
Panama		99–04	04–09	09–13			196
Paraguay	93–98	98–03	03–08	08–13			240
Peru	95–00	01–06	06–11	11–16			359
Uruguay	95–00	00–05	05–10	10–15			306
Venezuela	93–98	00–05					169
Total							6342

9 Decentralization and Local Government in Latin America[1]

Lorena Moscovich

Introduction

From environmental problems to physical violence, local governments are the first stop for addressing many of the problems and experiences of citizens' daily life. Local governments are also crucial arenas for broader processes, influencing, for instance, the fate of democratization, the chances to achieve fiscal equilibrium, or the success of policy making. In Latin America, local arenas are also new spaces for citizen participation, policy innovation, provision of public goods and services, and the platform for new leaders in national politics. Behind these changes are the transitions from authoritarian regimes to democracies in all Latin American countries, two decades of decentralization, and the transference of authority from central to local governments, as well as the consensus regarding the need to share fiscal responsibilities across the different levels of government to balance public accounts.

Local governments and subnational politics have lasting effects in nationwide politics. For instance, in Mexico, municipalities were arenas for the relegitimization of the Partido Revolucionario Institucional (PRI) regime (Seele 2012, Hiskey 2012). The national orientation of political parties, along with the success of the opposition at subnational levels in the process of democratization, resulted in lower levels of fragmentation of party politics at the federal level. In Brazil, the persistence of local elections during the years of military rule and the few opportunities for legislators to pork barrel, created incentives for politicians to compete at local levels (Samuels 2000). While the first pattern of transition strengthened the centralized nature of Mexican politics, at least during a brief period, the local arena in the Brazilian transition to democracy contributed to the fragmentation of Brazilian federalism (Samuels and Mainwaring 2004). Several decades later, subnational politics in Argentina, Brazil, and Mexico still has a significant influence on the nature of national democracy. Sometimes, this is due to the persistence of subnational authoritarian enclaves (Gibson 2005; Borges 2007; Ardanaz et al 2013), and in other situations, is due to the emergence of new leaders and arenas for competition at state levels. Governors are important players, both at subnational and federal levels. They are veto players in federal politics and policy making, particularly in Brazil and Argentina (Stepan 2004).

The interplay between local and national politics in Mexico and Brazil is also comparable in relation to policy innovation. Both countries have headed the distribution of new conditional cash transfers (CCTs) later emulated by several developing countries (Fizbein and Schady 2009; Sugiyama 2011). In the case of Mexico, the federal government implemented Programa Nacional de Solidaridad (PRONASOL), providing a number of chances for policy innovation and political participation at the local level (Hiskey 2012). In Brazil, Bolsa Escola, the CCT created by Governor Cristovan Buarque, was first implemented at the federal level by President Fernando Henrique Cardoso. Bolsa Escola was later the base, along with three other programs, for a new CCT, Bolsa de Familia, which is known for its contribution to the electoral success of President Ignacio Lula da Silva (Hunter and Power 2007).

Decentralization processes are complex—they interact with several economic and political variables, and their results are many times unexpected or contradictory. In the last decade, subnational expenditure grew, but at the same time, local governments became more dependent on the central government. Devolution of political authority to local governments sometimes results from centralization pressures in which the president seeks to counterbalance the influence of the intermediate levels of government or powerful national players.

New roles of local governments, as a result of decentralization processes and more generally the interplay with national politics, cohabit with old problems, such as the lack of their own resources and policy-making capabilities; the subordination to the central government; the uneven rule of law across territories; and the persistence of poverty, inequality, and violence, among others. It is very important to stress that the diversity and heterogeneity of local governments in Latin America give place to the uneven distribution of wealth, power, and chances for effective political representation and participation.

My goal in this chapter is to show at a glance the present situation of local governments, with some reference to subnational politics, and the main decentralization processes in Latin America. In this chapter I will give some examples of key decentralization measures in different Latin American countries. Also, using data on expenditure and income, I will track the evolution of the subnational public sector during the last decade and assess its influence on the general government public sector. Next I will revise some of the main theories that explain the reasons for the success of the decentralization in the region and offer some conclusions.

The Unevenness of Local Governments in Latin America

The main features of Latin American local governments is the unevenness in terms of resources, state capacity, and democratization, and their relative strength and autonomy in relation to the central government as a result of the de facto and de jure distribution of power. Huge variations exist not only between local governments in terms of population and wealth, but also in political environments and players, and in the way in which social relations are regulated by the state within local government territories. In this section I will focus on just some aspects related to this, particularly in terms of attributions, population, and fiscal capacity.

Spanish Urban Cabildos set the precedent for local governments that initially lacked authority, but that later in the nineteenth century became arenas of civil life and public participation for the *creoles*. In the past, local governments have been mainly related to people's daily life in rural areas. Urbanization and the quick migration from rural areas to big cities created new challenges for urban local governments, which faced problems such as poverty, pollution, regulation of industry, and rise of crime and violence. Natural resources and the struggle for a better life anchored in connection with the environment and natural resources are the main problems in rural areas. These areas are also threatened by violence (guerrilla, illegal drug trade, gold traders, etc.), displacements, and the advance of mining and agriculture, which expels inhabitants from formerly state-owned lands.

The capacity of the state to regulate private relations by means of its policies and laws is defined by Michael Mann (2006) as the infrastructural power of the state. The within-country distribution of this infrastructural power depicts different conditions of stateness across subnational territories. The seminal work by Guillermo O'Donnell (1993) suggests that the differences can be illustrated on a map with different colors: the blue areas show where states have both material presence and relevant social relations for public matters channeled through regulations, and the green areas are those in which states have buildings and personnel but fail in regulating an important number of social relations. Last, the well-known brown areas are the ones in which states have no physical presence and, as a result, there are no public regulations for an important number of social interactions. This unevenness affects basic rights such as access to justice or public defense (Smulovitz 2012). The lack of regulations and unfair or unequal law enforcement practices, depending on social status, are also relevant features of the rule of law at local levels in Latin America (O'Donnell 2007).

The number of municipalities per country greatly varies in Latin America. It ranges from 75, 81, and 89 municipalities in Panama, Costa Rica, and Uruguay, to 5,564 in Brazil (Nickson 2011). The average population per municipality goes from around 14,089 in Peru to 85,322 in Venezuela. All countries in Latin America elect their mayors, and almost all also elect officials at the intermediate level of government, with the exception of Chile and Suriname (see Falleti 2010). The most populated countries in Latin America—Argentina, Brazil, Mexico, and Venezuela—are federations.[2] Bolivia, Chile, Colombia, Ecuador, Paraguay, Peru, Uruguay, and the Caribbean are unitary countries with great diversity regarding attributions, fiscal responsibilities, and expenditures of local and intermediate governments. For instance, Colombia has undergone a deep process of decentralization, giving automatic revenues to departments and municipalities, decentralizing education, and allowing popular elections of mayors and governors (Falleti 2010). Conversely, Venezuela is a federation that recently experienced a recentralization process giving more power to the president (Eaton forthcoming).

Many constitutions advocate municipal autonomy and decentralization. Municipalities were recognized as federal autonomous units in Mexico (1999) and were given responsibilities in Brazil (1988). Colombia (1991) and Paraguay (1992) were defined as decentralized countries in their constitutions. New municipal codes were also passed in Peru (1984), Bolivia (1985), El Salvador (1986), Colombia (1986), Nicaragua (1988), Venezuela (1988), Guatemala (1988), Honduras (1990), Chile (1992), and Paraguay (2010) (see Nickson 2011, 6–7). However, legal autonomy does not always mean actual independence, unless the other levels of government are willing to enforce it. The Brazilian constitution of 1946 had a deep municipalist rhetoric that was never put into practice until the reform of 1988, when municipalities got their present status (Samuels 2000), and Mexico never completely enforced the constitutional reform of 1999 (Seele 2012). In Argentina, municipal autonomy depends on provincial constitutions. Municipalities in the province of Buenos Aires, for instance, are some of the most important in the country due to their electoral and political weight. However, they don't have autonomous status. In Chile, it wasn't only the autonomy of municipalities that allowed them to be competitive in political arenas in 1992; before that, a set of incremental reforms during the previous years gave them the necessary leverage for this decentralization (Eaton 2004b). In most countries in the region, municipalities have few responsibilities. Brazilian local governments are among the more autonomous in terms of resources, attributions to pass laws, and policy making.

Later, I'll expand upon this issue, but let me move ahead with fiscal matters in order to illustrate the variation in the wealth of municipalities. According to the Inter-American Development Bank (IADB) (2013), the distribution of resources collected for each level of government is also very uneven. For instance, in Bolivia, four cities (La Paz, Santa Cruz, Cochabamba, and El Alto) collect almost three-quarters of the total municipal tax revenues. In the same vein, five cities in Colombia (Bogotá, Medellin, Cali, Barranquilla, and Cartagena) gather two-thirds of the total local taxes. While in Ecuador, 50 percent of the tax revenues come from Quito and Guayaquil; Buenos Aires province and Buenos Aires city, both in Argentina, collect almost two-thirds of the total subnational income. At the state level, a similar share is collected by the four big states of Sao Paulo, Minagerais, Rio de Janeiro, and Rio Grande do Sul. Going back to municipalities, in Peru, Lima gets two-thirds of municipal tax revenues (Corbacho et al 2013).

There are also great differences regarding the number of people who are able to pay but who are not taxed at the subnational level. For instance, in Colombia, only 30 percent to 46 percent of the potential tax payers from industry and commerce paid taxes. In Campeche, 2 percent of the potential tax payers contributed, while in Mexico DF, that figure was 90 percent. According to Artana et al (2012) (in Corbacho et al 2013), the fiscal effort to collect taxes in Catamarca, Formosa, and Tucuman is higher than in Entre Ríos and Santa Fe (all Argentine provinces). Also, tax revenues in Brazil vary greatly; across the northeast states, the revenues collected from taxes are lower than in the southwest states.

Enormous variation regarding territorial regimes, attributions, and material conditions characterized local governments in Latin America. Neither territorial regimes, unitary or federal, nor the level of expenditure at local levels are the only proxies to assess the level of decentralization (Rodden 2004). Instead, reforms and attributions must be analyzed together with several variables, such as the features and history of institutions and local bureaucracies, the relationship among government levels, and the influence of other players such as markets, criminal organizations, or international actors.

Decentralization: Tensions Around Devolution

All the countries in the region underwent different kinds of decentralization processes during the last decades. Some of them were organized according to decentralization laws or reforms based on constitutional reforms or participatory laws. The experience shows that the success of decentralization was mainly an outcome of the balance of power between other levels of government and availability of fiscal and bureaucratic resources to enforce these measures.

The balance of power and responsibilities among local, intermediate, and national governments is not uniform across countries or over time. Decentralization—that is, the devolution of responsibilities and functions from central to intermediate and local governments—evolves in three dimensions: **political**, through the devolution of political authority or by activating or opening new spaces for political representation; **fiscal**, empowering lower levels of government to collect new or higher revenues, and **administrative**, related to the provision of public services and more generally responsibilities for policy making in different fields (Faletti 2010). Many Latin American countries experienced decentralization processes in the post-developmental economy period during the 1980s and 1990s, and in this section I will give some examples of these different measures

The last two decades were fruitful in decentralization experiences in the region. In Central America, several reforms and decentralization measures were enacted during the 1990s and during the first decade of the new century, and show the limitations of some of these experiences. In Guatemala, in 2001 there was a forum on the reform of the legal frameworks for decentralization. Also, the Solidarity Fund for Community Development (FSDC) was a new source to finance municipalities. While the former failed to give clear responsibilities and could not rely on a developed civic society or party system, the latter failed in establishing clear and visible distribution procedures (Bland 2002). Along with a number of administrative and fiscal reforms adopted in El Salvador in the 1990s, first in 1998 and then in 2005, there were adjustments to the transfers given to municipalities. In 2007, a new national decentralization law was passed with the aim of giving incentives for investments, to increase civic participation, and to reduce the environmental vulnerability of municipalities (CGLU 2008). In Costa Rica, where mayors have been elected since 1998, several policy areas include participatory spaces at the subnational level, and a comprehensive institutional plan was designed in order to modernize municipalities, promote decentralization, and give fiscal attribution to local governments (Meoño Segura 2008; Mora Alfaro 2009).

Beyond their differences, the big three federal countries in the region also underwent decentralization processes. Like Chile, in Mexico and Brazil, decentralization was somehow related to the constellation of political relations built during military regimes previous to the transition to democracy. According to Samuels (2000), in Brazil decentralization is explained by the local nature of political careers, thanks to the persistence of competitive local political arenas during the military rule and the urban interests that grew around a number of flourishing cities. Both variables reveal the new tools given by central governments to local politicians and explain the achievements of local players thanks to civil society mobilizations. The preeminence of local interests led to political and fiscal decentralization first, with the election of governors in 1980–1982, and the increase of transfers to states and municipalities in 1983 (Falleti 2010). Later in 1988, a new reform of the tax revenue system also increased the transfers to subnational governments. In the same year, the health system was decentralized and a constitutional reform recognized municipalities as autonomous federal units. With the presidency of Fernando Henrique Cardoso there was a strengthening of the power of the president, and Ignacio Lula da Silva's new alliances partially weakened governors and recentralized power after the implementation of the federal conditional cash transfers (Hunter and Power 2007; Fenwick 2009).

In Mexico, decentralization was seen as a way to renew the legitimacy of the PRI regime. Municipalities were recognized as autonomous and were allowed to collect taxes in the constitutional reform of 1983, and they started to play new roles in policy making in the reform of 1999 (Seele 2012). However, the main impact of decentralization was experienced during the presidency of Carlos Salinas who created the PRONASOL in 1988, a social program strongly focused on municipalities from which, later in 1997, a new budget line was created for local governments. Transfers to municipalities grew from 2 percent to 9 percent in 2006 (Seele 2012). A number of measures and agreements finally resulted in the decentralization of education for all the states in 1992 and the complete political autonomy of the Mexico DF in 1996 (Falleti 2010). Today, Mexican municipalities face many challenges particularly due to the spread of organized crime, illegal drug trade, rise of violence, and the lack of both their own resources and bureaucratic capacity to cope with them (Seele 2012).

Decentralization in Argentina favored provincial governments more than municipalities. Still during the military regime, in 1978, management of primary schools was given to provinces; later in 1992, secondary schools were also transferred to them. A new revenue-sharing regime was passed in 1988, and the complete autonomy of Buenos Aires City, the federal district, was achieved in the period 1994–1996 (Falleti 2010). Municipal autonomy is regulated by provincial laws. There is a complex variety of status of local governments and municipalities. Some of them are defined by territorial frontiers; others instead change their status depending on the number of inhabitants (Cao 2008). Although responsibilities did not suffer deep changes in terms of decentralization from other levels of government, local expenditure increased and reached 8 percent of the total public expenditure (Iturburu 1999). Municipal responsibilities are related to health, public child care, regulation of public services, and, very exceptionally, police.[3] Also, beneficiaries of federal and provincial social programs are chosen at local levels in Argentina (Iturburu 1999).

In Bolivia, the Law of Popular Participation, enacted in 1994, doubled the rents received by municipalities from central governments, and new municipalities were created. Also, ownership over education, health, and irrigation services were established, but staffing and salaries remained responsibilities of the central government (Faguet 2012). After forty years of centralizing tendencies, the quick enactment of this decentralization law seems to have benefited smaller municipalities and increased the level of responsiveness to local needs (Faguet 2012). Also, the decentralization measures seem to have contributed to the political and institutional vacuum and the political instability that followed the collapse of the party system in Bolivia (Jemio et al 2009). Later, politicians at the subnational level and opposition leaders succeeded in resisting several recentralization attempts from the central government (Eaton forthcoming). Colombia is one of the unitary countries with higher levels of decentralization. Among the most important measures taken in this country are more transfers given to municipalities in 1983, mayors elected since 1986 and governors since 1991 (the same year when automatic transfers were increased), and decentralization of education by 1993 (O'Neill 2003, 2005; Falleti 2010). The set of reforms resulted in greater levels of autonomy for the subnational units. In Ecuador, the first attempt to decentralize failed in 1997; later, the constitutional reform of 1998 increased the scope of subnational elections and regulated the previous fiscal reform in order to apply the lagged transfers of revenues for local governments (O'Neill 2003, 2005). In Venezuela, mayors and governors have been elected since 1989, and later in 1990, a new law of decentralization gave administrative responsibilities and fiscal transfers to states (O'Neill 2003, 2005). In Ecuador and Venezuela, opposition parties were unable to prevent the process of recentralization, which has undermined the success of decentralization (Eaton forthcoming).

Also in Peru there was tension between decentralizing and recentralizing trends. Mayors have been elected in Peru since the constitutional reform of 1980 in which fiscal transfers also were given to local and regional governments (governors have been elected since 1989). There was an impasse during 1992, and when elections were re-established in 1993, fewer resources and higher levels of discretion were given to municipalities (O'Neill 2003, 2005). According to Dickovick (2006), decentralization in Peru was based on electoral considerations in order to strengthen the power of presidents, which deliberately favored municipalities regardless of regions. Between 2002 and 2004, eleven laws and regulations were passed in order to give a coherent and gradual approach to decentralization in Peru. However, the success of this reform depended upon the failed creation of macro-regions, and the process was not completed. Asymmetries between regions, problems related to the distribution of the canon of natural resources within regions, and failures in the quality of public service provisions are present challenges of Peruvian decentralization (World Bank 2010). The case of Peru shows that the sequence of decentralization measures affects the incentive for politicians to enforce them, thus undermining their success.

While in unitary countries, decentralization has been mainly done in favor of municipalities, in federal countries, the intermediate level of government introduces variations in the constellation of players and in the bargaining for resources and responsibilities (Chhibber and Somanathan 2002). Another important issue to consider is urban politics. Metropolitan areas tend to concentrate most of the country's populations. There are countries with several densely populated big cities, such as Brazil, Mexico, or Colombia; in others like Argentina and Chile, the population is highly concentrated in one area. If unevenness is one of the features of local governments in Latin America, big cities and metropolitan areas will share some important features such as problems of coordination. Some shared problems of cities and local governments of metropolitan areas are crime, public transport, housing for the poor, and environmental pollution. Also, it is expected that cities are more autonomous thanks to informed voters, mobilized civil societies, and higher tax revenues. Sometimes, big cities are bastions of the opposition and urban politics are highly visible to the rest of the country. The long processes of decentralization, which resulted in the autonomy of federal districts of Mexico and Buenos Aires City, illustrate the fears of the central government to decentralize in favor of this potential cradle of opposition leaders.

Decentralization measures give more responsibilities to subnational levels of governments, and their outcomes vary greatly depending on their interaction with electoral rules, political environments, party systems, resources available (economic and in terms of state capacity), and the incentives of politicians to enforce these measures. In the entire region, the success of these policies was closely connected with the relationship between government levels and the ability of subnational players to resist recentralization trends and with the success in getting more resources from the central government. Given the importance of resources and the dependence of local governments on central transfers, it is crucial to give a general overview of the fiscal performance of the subnational sector in the region.

Decentralization in Numbers: Incomes, Expenditures, and Fiscal Imbalance[4]

Higher levels of expenditure do not necessarily mean that a country is more decentralized or a subnational government is more autonomous. For Rodden (2004), it is very important to consider the origins of the transfers, whether they come from local or national sources. If they come from the central government, it is also crucial to see if the rents are delivered thanks to formula grants or with discretion. There are also going to be differences depending on the origin of incomes, whether they are from taxes, loans, royalties, etc., within a number of variables that affect subnational provision, policy making, and political autonomy. Fiscal data for 2002–2009 in ten Latin American countries show that subnational levels depend upon transfers from the central governments. The level of dependence has been increasing, mainly due to higher levels of expenditure, which weren't accompanied by higher levels of income from local origins. Actually, there is an enormous variation regarding how many resources belong to the subnational public sectors and how much of these are transfers. Moreover, within subnational sectors, sometimes municipalities collect more revenues, and in other cases, the intermediate level of government (regions, states, provinces) gathers higher shares of resources.

When local governments assume more responsibilities, they also need more resources in order to attend to these new functions or for the provision of new services. The functions devolved to subnational levels do not always come with more resources from central governments or with more capabilities to collect new taxes at the local level. The experience shows that administrative decentralization rarely means fiscal decentralization. As a result, decentralization processes affect relations among government levels—the more decentralized a country, the higher the odds that local governments will depend upon the transfers of the central government. The degree of autonomy of subnational levels deeply affects provision of public goods and services, and political relations. Wealthier and autonomous cities in Bolivia also host opposition leaders. President Hugo Chavez was successful in subordinating mayors thanks to the reduction of transfers. In Argentina and Brazil, governors are powerful, but presidents ally poorer and subordinated (and in Argentina also overrepresented) states.

According to the IADB (Corbacho et al 2013), in Latin America, fiscal imbalance doubles that experienced by Eastern Europe and is three times that of Asia. Fiscal imbalance—that is, the difference between expenditures and revenues[5]—has been growing in many Latin American countries and in none of them has it decreased during the last decade. While it tended to be constant in Brazil over the last decade—around 8 percent— Argentina experienced higher levels of fiscal imbalance at the end of the decade than during the previous years; however, in this country, the figure was similar to that of 2000, around 9.3 percent. Bolivia, Colombia, Ecuador, Peru, and Mexico also experienced higher levels of fiscal imbalances in 2009. Within the unitary countries, the more decentralized ones are also more dependent upon central government revenues.

It can be seen that while income from revenues tends to remain constant, the increases in the fiscal imbalance were due to higher levels of expenditures. I already mentioned Colombia, but also in Bolivia, Ecuador, and Peru, the subnational expenditure grew over the last decade. In Ecuador, for instance, the money spent by subnational governments went from 2.3 percent in 2000

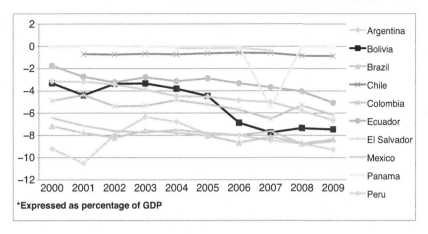

Figure 9.1 Fiscal Imbalance: Selected Latin American Countries 2000–2009*

to 6.2 percent in 2009; in Peru, the money spent at the subnational level in 2009 doubled that amount in 2000, and in Mexico the expenditure grew as well.[6]

Regarding subnational public-sector incomes in Latin America, how much was from their own resources vis-à-vis central government transfers? The distribution of incomes across levels of government is mainly an outcome of the particular combination of fiscal decentralization, tax and revenue sharing systems, and discretional grants. An average for 2000–2009 (Corbacho et al 2013) shows considerable variation regarding the sources of income across government levels. While in Mexico, the subnational sector collected 83.1 percent revenues and Panama 5 percent, Brazil had 40 percent of internal resources. Interestingly, in Bolivia, Peru, Venezuela, and Ecuador, roughly 64 percent to 84 percent of subnational incomes are collected at the local level. As seen earlier, these averages hide enormous within-country variations.

Not only are there differences among countries regarding the money collected by the subnational public sector in relation to central transfers, there are also different patterns in relation to the share collected at local or intermediate levels of government (provinces, states, regions). In federal countries, states collect more than municipalities—this is the case of Mexico, Argentina, and Brazil. In this sense, Venezuela is the exception, where more resources are collected at the local level, 74 percent, than in the unitary but highly decentralized Colombia, with 69 percent of local government revenues. In Bolivia, Peru, and Ecuador, municipalities gather from 81 percent to 92 percent of the total subnational revenues.

During the last decade, Latin American countries have shown enormous variations in terms of how much money is collected at the subnational level in relation to central government transfers, the concentration of taxation across cities, and regarding which level of government is responsible for subnational incomes. Overall, during the last decade, subnational governments have increased the level of expenditures, and higher levels of fiscal imbalances show higher dependence upon central governments. However, this data tell us little of the weight of subnational governments in relation to the general government income and expenditures. I am going to address this issue in the next section

The Weight of the Subnational Public Sector[7]

During the last decade, most countries showed higher subnational expenditures parallel with higher levels of fiscal imbalances. In this section I will give evidence on the within-country variation of the subnational accounts in relation to the total public sector. In Argentina, for instance, while fiscal imbalance and subnational expenditure remained constant (when measured as a share of gross domestic product [GDP]) the data show that the subnational public sector had less weight in 2009 than in 2000. Both income and expenditures at the subnational level have decreased in relation to their national counterparts. On the other hand, Brazil has the highest subnational expenditure in relation to the total public sector. Incomes were never less than 34 percent, and expenditure never dropped below 50 percent. In 2009, subnational expenditure represented 57 percent of the total public expenditure.

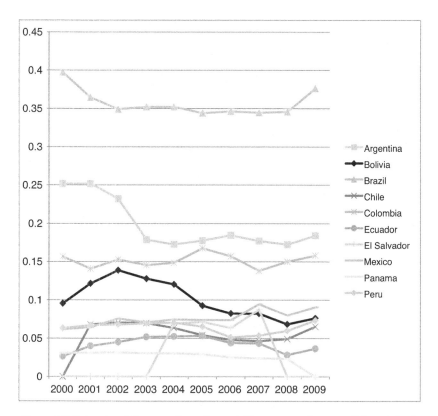

Figure 9.2 Subnational Income Over General Government Income, Selected Latin American Countries 2000–2009.

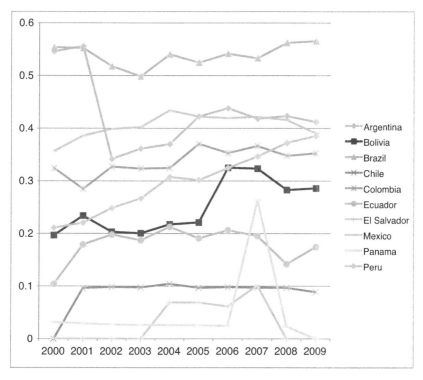

Figure 9.3 Subnational Expenditure Over General Government Expenditure, Selected Latin American Countries 2000–2009.

The weight of subnational income and expenditure on the total public sector in Bolivia has not followed a uniform pattern during the last decade. Overall, from 2000 to 2009, subnational income declined and subnational expenditure grew. In Chile, local expenditure remained at 10 percent and income was around 6 percent as a share of general government expenditure and incomes.

Fiscal imbalance in Colombia varied more than the share of the subnational sector in the general government public sector. The weight of subnational incomes went from 14 percent to 17 percent and expenditures from 28 percent to 37 percent. Ecuador was similar to Colombia—the subnational income hardly varied as a share of the total public income, but expenditures of the government in general went from 10 percent to 21 percent. The same pattern is followed by Mexico, although the gap between the weight of subnational income and expenditure is the greatest. The Peruvian subnational sector also experienced a deep gap between income and expenditure over the total public sector and doubled the weight of subnational expenditures.

Almost all countries analyzed ended the decade with higher shares of subnational spending in relation to the general government, with the exception of Argentina. New responsibilities for subnational governments resulted in an increase of the share of subnational public spending in the total public spending. Although much has been said about trends toward the recentralization process toward presidents, at least considering this proxy, the evidence is not completely straightforward. A higher level of subnational expenditure can be understood as a trend toward more decentralization, but tells us little about the balance of power between presidents, governors, and mayors, and recentralization trends must be analyzed on a case-by-case basis. Moreover, even in the case of Argentina in which the central government has increased its weight in the last decade, this may be due to recentralization trends but also to the increase of expenditures in some policy areas that are exclusively its competence, such as infrastructure or research. This is why it is very important to focus on the internal political processes within countries. Beyond information on income, spending and weight of the subnational public sector, decentralization measures, their outcomes, and more generally the balance of power across government levels can also be understood as an outcome of features of the regimes, alliances (Moscovich 2012), and political relations.

The Politics of Decentralization: Devolution as Strategy: Decentralization from Below, Decentralization from Above, and Recentralization

Decentralization processes in Latin America have been explained by a number of hypotheses. While some of the reasons suggested were related to the spread of pro-market reforms, the consensus of international organizations or the intention to improve political representation through the multiplication of points of access to political power, there is a set of studies that stresses variables related to within-country political relations.

Using the taxonomy of political, fiscal, and administrative decentralization, Faletti (2010) developed a sequential theory. She explored the cases of Argentina, Brazil, Colombia, and Mexico and suggested that the balance of power between national and subnational players in the reformist coalition explains what kind of decentralization comes first and whether the next stages of decentralization will be incremental or, instead, will adopt a reactive pattern of policy making. Coalitions in which subnational interests prevail will try to retain more political power and secure fiscal revenues, while national coalitions will try to devolve administrative functions and resist the fiscal and political decentralization as long as they can.

Not only coalitions, but also more generally different political players, can influence the chances and the degree of decentralization. One of the main proxies for decentralization is fiscal revenues and the share of internal resources that local governments manage vis-à-vis those transferred to them by central governments. These equilibriums are governed by revenue-sharing agreements and by their rules. For Garman, Haggard, and Willis (2001), the main variable behind the level of fiscal resources managed at the municipal level are the political parties' structures. Studying the cases of Argentina, Brazil, and Colombia, they show that more centralized political parties will favor tighter control over fiscal revenues; conversely, less control of political parties will favor higher levels of decentralization.

For the cases of Andean countries, O'Neill (2003, 2005) persuasively shows that determinants of decentralization can be explained by a combination of tenure and the subnational electoral success of the national ruling party. If a ruling party at the national level has better electoral performance at the subnational level and expects to remain in power, it has incentives to decentralize in order to secure the comparative advantages of its success in those constituencies. Decentralization may not be the consequence of a set of measures; instead, sometimes it is the outcome of the accumulation of incremental reforms, which in different political settings can be used by the players in order to retain more power at the subnational level.

In line with the argument of O'Neill, I will use an original dataset of subnational spending to test for the drive to decentralize responsibilities to governors in Brazil and Argentina. Results show that in the 2003 elections in Argentina, President Néstor Kirchner significantly underperformed the governors of his party, with an average loss of 17 points.[8] The sum of the vote difference shows that the governors overtook the president by 400 points, which should have facilitated decentralization in favor of subnational political leaders in order to improve the odds of presidential success in future elections. Four years later, in the national election of 2007, the president also lagged behind the governors, but with a considerable smaller difference: approximately –2 percent. The sum of the differences was –42 percent, again leading to higher levels of decentralization if O'Neill's hypothesis holds. If we consider subnational spending as a share of total public spending and a proxy for decentralization, we see that it grew from 37 percent in 2003 to 42 percent in 2004 and 44 percent in 2006. After the 2007 elections, no variations of the share of subnational spending were observed.

In Brazil, President Ignacio Lula Da Silva got an average of 10 percent fewer votes than the governors of his alliance in the presidential election of 2002. Vote differences reached –260 points favoring subnational leaders. Lula was very successful in reverting his lag for the next elections, when he got, on average, 19 percent more votes than his subnational allies. Notably, the sum of the vote difference benefited Lula by 503 percent. However, the share of subnational expenditure in total expenditure grew from 50 percent in 2000 to 57 percent in 2009. One reason that can explain this variation is that in O'Neill's model, the president was willing to decentralize when his party was likely to be in office for a number of terms. Lula had no assurance regarding his tenure in office, at least during the first years of his presidency; also his party relied on a number of loose alliances at subnational levels and he could not take for granted that these alliances would endure. In addition, given that Lula experienced a higher level of popularity than his electoral alliance (Hunter and Power 2007), it made sense for him to deliver more resources during the last part of this second presidency in which he had to support his successor, Dilma Rousseff.

In Chile, during the dictatorship, more responsibilities were assigned to municipalities (Eaton 2004b). Although this devolution should not be understood as a decentralization process because local officials and delegates of the central government were appointed, after the democratic transition, new responsibilities and the creation of new regional and subnational actors, such as the Subsecretary for Regional and Administrative Development (Subsecretaría de Desarrollo Regional y Administrativo, SUBDERE) within the Interior Ministry and the Association of Chilean Municipalities (Asociación Chilena de Municipalidades, ACHM), gave the necessary leverage for the transformation of municipalities into competitive political arenas from which new political leaders projected themselves to the national level.

If analyzed in a long-term perspective, the equilibrium of functions and resources across government levels has varied over time. Trends to decentralization are not irreversible—just the opposite. The research of Eaton (2004a) shows that in different periods central governments in Latin America have attempted to decentralize in favor of subnational governments, and parallel to these processes (or later when coping with some of their negative outcomes) reversal trends to recentralization were followed. For Eaton, behind these trends is the combination of political economy and regime changes. Regarding decisions of economic policy, during periods of statism, no room for the subnational government is expected. The economic liberalization, for instance, that followed the economic crises of the 1980s, encouraged decentralization trends that favored the reduction of the size of the central state and the delegation of fiscal responsibilities to the lower levels of government. On the other hand, democratization also results in decentralization when subnational elections result in the demand for more resources and responsibilities for the newly elected mayors and governors.

The reverse trends of decentralization processes are usually the result of new attributions of the central government. Recentralization means the reduction of autonomy previously given by the central government to subnational units. Instead of annulling the former subnational functions, recentralization is often made by the accumulation of reforms that give more power to the president. For Dickovick (2011), institutional layering may have two contradictory effects: it can make institutions more rational or it can undermine their performance, in both cases changing the relative equilibrium between levels of government.

Sometimes, decentralization can be seen as a central government strategy to retain power or to undermine the power of some particular actors (i.e., intermediate level of governments). Eaton (2004b) shows the decentralization strategies aimed at undermining the power of some powerful politicians based in Santiago. Moreover, in some cases, decentralization in favor of one level of government may pursue the effect of weakening another. Following Dickovick (2006), the municipalization strategy during the 1990s in Peru, Brazil, and South Africa can be understood as an attempt to undermine the power of the intermediate levels of those governments. As was already said, different tools such as CCTs can also be used by presidents to retain power and bypass governors—this seems to be the case in Mexico (Seele 2012) and Brazil (Fenwick 2009).

Political environments, institutions, players, and power relations are behind the main reasons for decentralization and more generally variations in the balance of power among government levels. Decentralization can be understood as a policy-making tool to achieve better quality of provision or to balance public accounts in the context of economic liberalization. Also, it can be the outcome of democratization and in this context, political alliances, party systems, and electoral performances change the structure of incentives for the central government to push for higher levels of decentralization or, conversely, for a reconcentration of power in presidents' hands. While there is no single theory of decentralization that applies to all countries and times, there are many studies that give us insights regarding which political variables are worth looking at when trying to explain the fate of experiences of devolution of functions and authority to subnational governments. Certainly, the balance of power among government levels and the role of subnational players are among the most important variables to consider (Montero and Samuels 2004).

Conclusions

Local governments in Latin America show deep variations in terms of wealth, law enforcement, and social and political environments. In this chapter I gave evidence of some common features related to the weaker legislative and policy-making attributions in municipalities when compared with intermediate levels of government (particularly in federal countries) and with central governments. However, this does not mean that municipalities are unimportant; sometimes, local governments are sources of policy innovation and arenas for higher levels of political competitions. In other examples, subnational governments are the bastions of authoritarian enclaves, which hinder the odds for nationwide democratization.

During the last decades other common trends have been the decentralization processes that have opened new political arenas for electoral competition and delivered administrative and/or fiscal responsibilities to subnational and local governments. These processes nevertheless have been very uneven in terms of their enforcement by central governments and have shown to have reverse trends of recentralization, sometimes also benefiting municipalities and presidents and at the same time counterbalancing intermediate levels of governments. Data show enormous variation in terms of fiscal capacity across municipalities. Overall, the subnational public sector has been increasing its influence on general governments' income and spending, but is also more dependent on the delivery of central government transfers.

Decentralization processes have been widespread in the region in relation to the balance of public accounts and the increasing need to improve bureaucratic processes and state capacity. However, this chapter has shown that electoral considerations and political alliances and balance of power across government levels appear as more powerful variables to the understanding of the fate of decentralization and the role of local governments in Latin America.

Notes

1 I would like to thank Ernesto Calvo, Marcelo Leiras, Guido Sandleris, and Mariano Tommasi for their insights and suggestions. Tomas Bieda and Sabrina Moran contributed with invaluable research assistance. The final results are entirely my responsibility.
2 Venezuela is the only federal country in the world without a chamber representing the states.
3 There are no data regarding which municipalities have their own police; most don't and in those that do, the police are not allowed to carry guns.
4 The data used in this section come from the IADB, the IMF, and Corbacho et al (2013).
5 That rents from the revenue-sharing system are considered internal income for the level of government that receives it (Artana et al 2012).
6 Data of expenditure, revenues, and fiscal imbalance are measured as share of the GDP. Source: IADB.
7 The data of subnational income and expenditure as a percentage of the total national public sector are based on my own calculations dividing national income and expenditure as a percentage of the GDP over subnational income and expenditure as a percentage of the GDP. Subnational data come from IADB and National IMF. For most countries, the data cover the 2000–2009 period.
8 For the 2003 presidential election, the Peronist party ran split with three different candidates.

References

Ardanaz, M., Leiras, M., and Tomassi, M. (2013) "The Politics of Federalism in Argentina and Its Implications for Governance and Accountability." *World Development* 53: 26–45.
Artana, D., Auguste, S., Cristini, M., Moskovits, C., and Templado, I. (2012) *Sub-National Revenue Mobilization in Latin American and Caribbean Countries: The Case of Argentina*. IDB Working Paper Series No. IDB-WP-297. Washington DC: IDB FIEL.
Bland, G. (2002) "Decentralization in Guatemala: The Search for Participatory Democracy." *Woodrow Wilson Center Update on the Americas* 3.
Borges, A. (2007) "Rethinking State Politics: The Withering of State Dominant Machines in Brazil." *Brazilian Political Science Review* (Online) 2.
Cao, H. (2008) "La Administración Pública Argentina: Nación, Provincias y Municipios." Presented at the XIII Congreso Internacional del CLAD sobre la Reforma del Estado y de la Administración Pública, Buenos Aires.
Chhibber, P. and Somanathan, E. (2002) "Are Federal Nations Decentralized? Provincial Governments and the Devolution of Authority to Local Government." Mimeo: Berkeley.
Ciudades y Gobiernos Locales Unidos. (2008) *La Descentralización y la Democracia Local en el Mundo. Primer Informe Mundial*. Cataluña: CGLU.

Corbacho, A., Fretes Cibils, V., and Lora, E. (eds.) (2013) *Recaudar No Basta. Los Impuestos Como Instrumento de Desarrollo*. Washington: BID.

Dickovick, T. (2006) "Municipalization as Central Government Strategy: Central Regional-Local Politics in Peru, Brazil, and South Africa." *Publius: The Journal of Federalism* 37(1): 1–25.

Dickovick, T. (2011) "Recentralization in Latin America: Institutional Layering and Presidential Leverage," Presented at the Annual Meeting of the American Political Science Association, Seattle.

Eaton, K. (2004a) *Politics Beyond the Capital. The Design of Subnational Institutions in South America*. Cambridge: Cambridge University Press.

Eaton, K. (2004b) "Designing Subnational Institutions Regional and Municipal Reforms in Postauthoritarian Chile." *Comparative Political Studies* 37(2): 218–44.

Eaton, K. (forthcoming) "Recentralization and the Left Turn in Latin America: Diverging Outcomes in Bolivia, Ecuador, and Venezuela." *Comparative Political Studies*.

Faguet, J.P. (2012) *Decentralization and Popular Democracy: Governance from Below in Bolivia*. Ann Arbor: University of Michigan Press.

Faletti, T. (2010) *Decentralization and Subnational Politics in Latin America*. Cambridge: Cambridge University Press.

Fenwick, T. (2009) "Avoiding Governors. The Success of Bolsa Família." *Latin American Research Review* 44(1): 102–30.

Fiszbein, A. and Schady, N. (2009) *Conditional Cash Transfers Reducing Present and Future Poverty*. Washington: The International Bank for Reconstruction and Development.

Garman, C., Haggard S., and Willis Fiscal, E. (2001) "Decentralization: A Political Theory with Latin American Cases." *World Politics* 53(2): 205–36.

Gibson, E. (2005) "Boundary Control: Subnational Authoritarianism in Democratic Countries." *World Politics* 58(1): 101–32.

Hiskey, J. (2012) "The Return of 'The Local' to Mexican Politics," in R. Ai Camp (ed.), *The Oxford Handbook of Mexican Politics*. Oxford: Oxford University Press.

Hunter, W. and Power, T. (2007) "Rewarding Lula: Executive Power, Social Policy and the Brazilian Elections of 2006." *Latin American Politics and Society* 49(1): 1–30.

Iturburu, M. (1999) *Municipios Argentinos. Potestades y Restricciones Constitucionales para un Nuevo Modelo de Gestión Local*. Buenos Aires: INAP.

Jemio L.C., Candia F., and Evia, J.L. (2009) "Reforms and Counter-Reforms in Bolivia." IDB Working Paper Series No. IDB-WP-103. Washington, DC: Inter-American Development Bank.

Mann, M. (2006) "El Poder Autónomo del Estado: Aus Orígenes, Mecanismos y Resultados." *Revista Académica de Relaciones Internacionales* 5: 1–43.

Meoño Segura, J. (2008). *Descentralización Integral para el Desarrollo de Costa Rica. Fundamentos Teórico-prácticos para Valorar la Viabilidad Política de los Ámbitos Territoriales no Centrales, Hacia un Mejor Gobierno*. Costa Rica: Universidad de Costa Rica.

Montero, A. and Samuels, D. (2004) *Decentralization and Democracy in Latin America*. University of Notre Dame: University of Notre Dame Press.

Mora Alfaro, J. (2009) *El Sinuoso Camino a la Descentralización y el Necesario Fortalecimiento del Gobierno Local*. San José: FLACSO.

Moscovich, L. (2012) "From Top to Bottom (and Back to the Top Again): Federal Spending, Sub-national Coalitions, and Protests in Argentina, 2002–2006." *Journal of Politics in Latin America* 4(1): 35–72.

Nickson, A. (2011) "Where Is Local Government Going in Latin America? A Comparative Perspective." *International Centre for Local Democracy.* Working Paper No. 6, 1–36.

O'Donnell, G. (1993) "Acerca del Estado, la Democratización y Algunos Problemas Conceptuales. Una Perspectiva Latinoamericana con Referencias a Países Poscomunistas." *Desarrollo Económico* 130(33): 163–84.

O'Donnell, G. (2007) "Las Poliarquías y la (In)efectividad de la ley en América Latina," in *Disonancias. Críticas Democráticas a la Democracia.* Buenos Aires: Prometeo.

O'Neill, K. (2003) "Decentralization as an Electoral Strategy." *Comparative Political Studies* 36(9): 1068–91.

O'Neill, K. (2005) *Decentralizing the State: Elections, Parties, and Local Power in the Andes.* New York: Cambridge University Press.

Rodden, J. (2004) "Comparative Federalism and Decentralization: On Meaning and Measurement." *Comparative Politics* 36(4): 481–500.

Samuels, D. (2000) "Reinventing Local Government? Municipalities and Intergovernmental Relations in Democratic Brazil," in P. Kingston and T. Power (eds.), *Democratic Brazil. Actors, Institutions, and Processes.* Pittsburgh: Pittsburgh University Press.

Samuels, D. and Mainwaring, S. (2004) "Strong Federalism, Constraints on the Central Government, and Economic Reform in Brazil," in Edward Gibson (ed.), *Federalism and Democracy in Latin America.* Baltimore: John Hopkins University Press.

Seele, A. (2012) "Municipalities and Policymaking," in R. Ai Camp (ed.), *The Oxford Handbook of Mexican Politics* (op. cit.). Oxford: Oxford University Press.

Smulovitz, C. (2012) "Public Defense and Access to Justice in a Federal Context. Who Gets What, and How in the Argentinean Provinces?" Presented at the Annual Meeting of the American Political Science Association. New Orleans.

Stepan, A. (2004) "Electoral Generated Veto Players in Unitary and Federal Systems," in E. Gibson (ed.), *Federalism and Democracy in Latin America* (op. cit). Baltimore: John Hopkins University Press.

Sugiyama, N.B. (2011) "The Diffusion of Conditional Cash Transfer Programs in the Americas." *Global Social Policy* 11(2/3): 250–78.

World Bank. (2010) *Perú. The Decentralization Process and Its Links with Public Expenditure Efficiency.* Washington: World Bank.

10 The State, the Military, and the Citizen

New Security Challenges in Latin America

Rut Diamint and Laura Tedesco

Introduction

Immediately after the return to democracy, Latin American governments focused on establishing and maintaining civilian control over the armed forces. However, the emphasis has changed gradually. Democratic governments have been trying to give a role to their armed forces within the democratic rule of law. In this process, Latin American countries have found different paths and the picture is quite heterogeneous.

We begin from the assumption that one of the main pillars of a democratic state is the full civilian control of the armed forces. The control over all the defense and security-related institutions—that is, the absence of any degree of armed forces' autonomy—marks the level of political maturity of a civilian, democratically elected government. Likewise, political maturity is also expressed through the government's capacity to articulate a national defense policy. This control implies a power relation that obliges the armed forces to accept their subordination to the civilian government and its politics. However, as we will argue in the chapter, the Latin American countries offer different scenarios and there is still military autonomy in some nations. In fact, here we argue that none of the countries that underwent democratization since the 1970s has achieved an *effective* democratic civilian management of defense. By this, we mean a full and operative control by the democratic government over the activities of the armed forces, its budget, and the design and implementation of defense policy. This is the result of two issues: (1) democratic governments have been unable to formulate and implement their defense policy, and thus the armed forces have an important degree of autonomy; or (2) the military have become strong political partners of civilian governments.

There are undoubtedly improvements in the level of control that civilian authorities have over the military. However, in 2013, we can still point to the fact that the military institutions in the region have neither finished their reform process, nor fully incorporated the democratic principles within their internal structures. Recently, the armed forces, and most specifically the army, have increased their internal activities, in some cases replacing the police, which has meant a militarization of public order (Diamint 2013; Zaverucha

2008, 133–36). Latin American countries have experienced an increase in urban violence and organized crime. Thus, many countries have started to use the armed forces to fight these problems.

We have identified two main risks. On the one hand, to involve the armed forces in the fight against organized crime or the implementation of social policies represents a rollback to the pre-democratization scenario in which the armed forces were involved in domestic security problems. On the other hand, these new missions have a regional impact since they have promoted subregional agreements and have provoked the redefinition of the enemy, as is evident with the new relationship between the armed forces and the protection of natural resources. Review

This chapter analyzes these new challenges. The first section presents the different roles the armed forces have taken on board at the domestic level. The second section presents some of the debates about the control of regional scenarios. The third section points out some of the main positive outcomes in establishing civilian control over the armed forces since the transition to democracy. Finally, the last section concludes with the new roles the armed forces are developing and their likely impact.

Back to Domestic Politics

It is important to remember that the domestic security system is aimed primarily at the prevention of crimes or their punishment. Public security is enforced by the penal code, and security depends primarily on the justice ministry. The defense system is targeted at responding to attacks against the state's integrity and sovereignty, and it depends on the foreign affairs and defense ministries, the national congress, and multilateral entities such as the United Nations and the Organization of American States (OAS).

With the democratization processes, the countries of the region, especially those in the Southern Cone, established a separation between internal security and defense policy, which helped to limit the military's participation in internal matters, concentrating their role in the area of international affairs. Therefore, there was a tendency to avoid using the military politically at the domestic level.

Increasingly, it is more difficult to establish the difference between internal and external threats, which we argue is crucial for the establishment of the rule of law. It is ever more difficult due to the incapacity of national governments to organize efficient security policies and also by the pressure of the United States. The US Southern Command Strategy 2016 proposes a single military command to interact with agencies from Latin American countries, which may result in the US military working with Latin American police, generating more confusion about the role of each institution.

Inside this new conceptual framework, issues such as extreme poverty or environmental concerns are included as security problems. This leads to the *securitization* of the development agenda, the militarization of public life, and the undermining of civilian control. The combination of the concepts of regional security, defense, and public security influences national domestic politics. It implies a transformation of the role of the armed forces and second, and considering the authoritarian past of the countries of the region, it could promote an increase in human rights violations and an undermining of democratic institutions. Thus, despite the fact that the separation between defense and public, internal security exists in Southern Cone countries, a closer analysis shows that it is often not clear.

Brazil, Peru, Mexico, and Bolivia have used the military to solve problems related to internal security. Brazil used the army to stop urban violence related to drug trafficking, and the military developed a new doctrine to use troops in activities related to public security—these were named Operations to Guarantee Law and Order (OPGLO) (Zaverucha 2007). In order to satisfy the security environment for the Soccer World Cup 2014 and the Olympic Games of 2016, the armed forces increased their activity in the shanty towns of Rio de Janeiro. The army's involvement is not limited to public security, but also involves other public goods such as natural resources and highway construction.

Mexico has included the armed forces in internal matters, specifically in the fight against organized crime and drug trafficking. So far, the results have not been encouraging and, as the Mexican case shows, the move to include the armed forces in this fight seems to be very complex. Benítez Manaut points out that the war against narco-trafficking involves "approximately 25 percent of officials of the Mexican armed forces" (Benítez Manaut 2013, 43). He found two main problems. On the one hand, there is impunity with respect to human rights violations. On the other, the military are trained to deal with the armed activity of the cartels, but they are not prepared to implement "preventive measures, and less, to work in remaking the social fabric" (Benítez Manaut 2013, 47).

In this context, military values could again permeate society. Likewise, society begins to accept an increase in violence, especially that exerted by the military, as a need to stem the tide of criminal activity. Civil society could look the other way as people take justice into their own hands, and citizens who previously had supported the return of democracy would now support the implementation of harsh policies (*mano dura*) potentially damaging the rule of law.

Moreover, internal intelligence remains in military hands, allowing armed forces surveillance on political and social activists. Their involvement in the fight against organized crime is a perfect excuse to maintain this activity. In 2012 in Argentina, thirteen officers were convicted, with sentences ranging from six months to a year and a half, for espionage in violation of the laws of homeland security, national intelligence and national defense (CELS 2012).

Despite the institutionalization of intelligence activity in all countries of the region and the establishment of new regulations and civil intelligence departments, most of these intelligence agencies combine interior, exterior, and counterintelligence functions. Furthermore, the Brazilian Intelligence Agency (ABIN), the Ecuadorian National Secretariat of Intelligence, or the Secretary of State for Strategic Intelligence (SIE) of Guatemala have indeterminate functions and maintain a strong military presence. A particular case is that of the former Administrative Department of Security of Colombia (DAS) replaced by President Juan Manuel Santos in 2011 with the Administrative Department of National Intelligence. The former DAS had excessive power, justified because of the conflict with the guerrillas and the paramilitaries, which allowed covert actions coordinated by the military and police intelligence agencies, a tradition that has not ended with the new institution (Swenson and Lemozy 2009, XVIII–XXI).

A recent assassination in Paraguay was the rationale behind a government decision to unify the work of the armed forces and the police. Two days after the new president of Paraguay, Horacio Cartes, took power, five private guards were killed in the province of San Pedro. The police and the government believe that the killings were done by the Paraguayan People's Army (EPP). The outcome was that the National Anti-Drug Secretariat, the armed forces, and the national police have been allowed to work together in the north of the country, especially in the departments of Concepción, San Pedro, and Amambay (El País 2013). The fear that emerged among Paraguayans is that Minister of Defense Bernardino Soto Estigarribia militarized the north of the country in search of EPP guerrillas. It is interesting to recall that Soto Estigarribia is a former general and was a member of the presidential guard of former dictator Alfredo Stroessner.

Another sign that shows overlaps between the armed forces' internal and external activities was the decision taken by President Evo Morales to send military troops to confront peasant groups that were threatening to close down the gas transportation system to Brazil. In March 2012, Morales also used troops to repress social protests. More recently, Morales ordered the military to be prepared to fight against the American empire and defend national sovereignty (Los Tiempos 2013; El Mercurio 2013).

In 2006, twenty people were hurt in Ecuador in a clash between the armed forces and indigenous groups and social organizations in a demonstration against the Free Trade Agreement with the United States (Red Globe March 17, 2006). In 2012, faced with mining conflicts, President Ollanta Humala of Peru employed the armed forces to repress and persecute environmental leaders, declaring a state of emergency. The militarization of the streets and abuses by the security forces resulted in the deaths of seventeen people during those protests (La Razón July 22, 2012). In 2013, the Honduran congress approved the creation of the Military Police of Public Order as part of a series of measures to combat crime. This new body will include the best members of the army to provide security to the population (Prensa Libre 2013). Also in Guatemala, the military has the power to repress social protests (Schepers October 15, 2012). In May 2012, Guatemala President Otto Perez Molina imposed a thirty-day state of siege in four southeastern towns. In announcing the state of siege, President Perez Molina, a former army general, claimed that the crackdown had nothing to do with opposition protests against mining operations, but rather was directed against "organized crime" (BBC September 28, 2012).

The militarization of politics in Venezuela due to the incorporation of military officers in running many institutions of the state creates a peculiar situation in the country. Former military officers are governors in eleven states, out of the twenty states that are in the hands of the United Socialist Party of Venezuela. Likewise, President Nicolas Maduro created a new economic council composed of civilians and military, aimed at being, in the words of the president, "the governing body for the popular defense of the Venezuelan economy" (Prensa Latina October 3, 2013).

In the case of Ecuador, the Comprehensive Safety Plan (Public Safety Act of 2009) modified the concept of public forces; consequently, the police were no longer executing auxiliary functions with the armed forces. Therefore, the police were left outside of the tutelage of the military. After this plan, the police's main aim was to ensure citizens' safety (Perspectivas No. 1 2013). According to Rafael Correa's government, the objective of this decision was to face the new challenges provoked by drug trafficking, organized crime, and international terrorism and to help to obliterate the divisions between security and defense. However, this transformation did not mean to reduce other internal activities that the armed forces have in Ecuador, such as economic and environmental issues. Following a similar path, Venezuela's president launched the "Fatherland Secure Mission" (*Misión Patria Segura*), a new public safety plan that incorporates the armed forces in street patrols (El Universo May 6, 2013).

These examples show a general tendency in the region. Indeed, with the exception of some of the Southern Cone countries—specifically Argentina, Chile, and Uruguay—most of the countries are using the military to fight domestic insecurity and/or organized crime.

We argue that the involvement of the armed forces in domestic security matters, rather than solving the issue, has the potential to aggravate it. Their involvement militarizes public security, undermines civilian control, damages the civil administration of defense policies, creates the overlapping of functions between different agencies, postpones the upgrade of police institutions, limits individual guarantees, decreases the efficiency of resources, and increases fiscal expenditure. In sum, the police role of the armed forces is only a palliative to confront insecurity, but, in the long term, it represents a challenge to the institutionalization of the democratic system.

Cooperation Within Tensions

With the return to democracy, Latin America has increased its regional cooperation. The Union of South American Countries (UNASUR), Bolivarian Alternative for the Americas (ALBA), Pacific Alliance, Central-American Integration System (SICA), and lately The Community of Latin American and

Caribbean States (CELAC, created on February 23, 2010) are clear signals of a stronger regional integration. Paradoxically, at the same time, the region is politically fragmented. The emergence of the Bolivarian road to socialism shook regional politics. The failure of the neoliberal project in the late 1990s, together with the need to elaborate more pragmatic policies that would combine market mechanisms with larger degrees of public regulation and social participation, led to a general turn to the center-left. Despite political differences and difficult relations with some of his neighbors, Hugo Chávez was a strong promoter of Latin American regional integration, and this may be his most enduring legacy.

However, border tensions between Ecuador and Colombia reappear from time to time. Colombia and Nicaragua have not been able to solve border issues. Refugees and forced migration create rivalries between some nations and populations. The illegal arms traffic supplies transnational organized crime networks. Even Costa Rica, a country without a military and a history of democratic stability, is mired in conflict with its neighbor to the north, Nicaragua.

Moreover, military expenditure is increasing in South America from its lowest point reached in 1997. The exact amount of the increase cannot be determined because many of the purchases are not included in defense budgets, but instead are derived from transfers and extra-budget allocations. While García Belaunde, Peru's former foreign secretary, said that the massive purchase of armament affects the region's military balance and is a genuine reason for concern (Adnmundo.com April 19, 2007), most politicians do not seem to worry about this increase. Nevertheless, it is important to highlight that Latin America is the region of the world that still assigns the fewest resources as a percent of gross national product (GNP) to defense budgets, approximately 1.4 percent. In Central America's case, no country invests more than 1 percent of their GNP—El Salvador and Nicaragua are the countries that spend the most.

According to the International Institute for Strategic Studies (IISS), the Center for Latin America's Liberalization and Development (CADAL), and the Stockholm International Peace Research Institute (SIPRI), the military expenditures in the continent increased 7.2 percent between 2005 and 2006. In 2012, military expenditure in South America increased by 3.8 percent. Brazil accounted for just over half of the regional total. Some countries have increased their expenditure dramatically. For instance, in 2012, military spending increased in Paraguay by 43 percent and in Venezuela by 42 percent. The latter's government agreed to a US$4 billion loan from Russia. Colombia also increased its military spending, but by only 11 percent. Argentina, Chile, and Peru made significant increases. Argentina has now increased its military spending by 132 percent since 2003, despite having made few major arms purchases. According to SIPRI arms transfer data, Argentina was the eighty-second largest importer of major conventional weapons for the period 2008–2012. As SIPRI points out, in 2012, Brazil was eleventh in the world in military expenditures (Perlo-Freeman et al 2013). The official explanation refers to the replacement of obsolete materials. Chile has also increased its spending. According to Zibechi (2007), a report in *Military Power Review* affirms that Chile has risen from fourth to third place in the military capacity ranking for South America, displacing Argentina and approaching Peru, which continues to occupy second place. In terms of purchases, Chile has purchased weapons valued at US$2.785 billion, Venezuela at US$2.200 billion, and Brazil at US$1.342 billion (Zibechi 2007). These purchases reveal a growing climate of regional mistrust and evidence the effects of populism, which appeals to xenophobic nationalism. One of the main features of populism is the polarization of society. The new wave of populism in the region is currently polarizing not only Venezuelan, Bolivian, and Argentine civil society, but also regional politics.

In this context, the issue of militarization becomes crucial. We are referring here to a remilitarization without militarism. It is, moreover, a double remilitarization of the Americas, both because of the increase in military spending as well as the militarization of police functions.

The possibilities of changing this agenda are very limited, mainly because the United States insists in exporting its domestic agenda—fights against drug trafficking, terrorism, migration, and organized crime—to its backyard. Instead of consistently working for improvement of police forces, transparency and independence of the judiciary, and the professionalization of the customs and migration offices, the United States grants resources only when the strengthening of the military instrument is needed. In "The Politics of Defense for the Western Hemisphere," which the United States presented at the Conference of Defense Ministers in Uruguay in 2012, they explained that in Latin America, the United States is looking to find "partners" to become "security exporters." According to the US Defense Department, the effects of "current threats to regional peace and stability arising from the spread of drug trafficking and other forms of trafficking, gangs and terrorism, (. . .) can be exacerbated by natural disasters and unequal economic opportunity" (Zibechi 2012). While these risks are real, and every Latin American nation has to adopt policies to curb the violence and insecurity, to establish links between US armed forces and police forces in the region, as has happened in the last twenty years, this will not prevent or reduce the threats. Moreover, it will not bring more effectiveness to public safety institutions.

These tensions can also be found in issues related to energy. The provision of energy has become a crucial global security issue. Following the invasion of Iraq, the never-ending volatile situation in the Middle East, the increasing demand for energy from China and India in order to maintain their economic dynamism, and the instability in Central Asia, energy and security have become deeply interrelated. This new international scenario influences Latin America. On the one hand, more protectionist measures have been implemented at the domestic level. For instance, in April 2012, the Argentine government sent to the congress a project for the expropriation of 51 percent of the Spanish oil company Repsol, which was approved a month later. The president of Bolivia, Evo Morales, decreed the nationalization of Transportadora de Electricidad

(TDE), a subsidiary of Red Eléctrica of Spain, which holds 74 percent of the electricity transmission lines in the country. President Morales asked the commander in chief of the armed forces, Tito Gandarillas, to take over the administration and operation of TDE (El País May 1, 2012). Likewise, it is important to highlight that recent discoveries in Brazil and Argentina, together with the oil reserves in Venezuela, have made <u>Latin America second only to the</u> <u>Middle East in terms of oil reserves.</u> —(rubal

The energy policies of Venezuela and Bolivia have provoked national and regional conflicts. Both countries have redefined the role of the state in their domestic economy and have transformed the legal framework by reversing the privatization policies of the nineties. Venezuela promoted the renegotiation of the contracts established for the exploitation of oil and gas, and Ecuador and Bolivia soon followed.

Bolivia is using the military to protect natural resources. President Morales has sent the armed forces to the borders with the aim of reinforcing the state's sovereignty and protecting natural resources such as copper, gold, lithium, iron, and semiprecious stones. As Idón Moisés Chivi Vargas, general director of studies and projects of the Ministry of Communication, said: "The armed forces must protect and preserve natural resources as a source of wealth and just redistribution for the people" (Prensa Indígena August 27, 2013).

[Protecting natural resources as a main role for the military, an idea developed by the Brazilian army, became a common concern of South American countries.] The former Brazilian defense minister Nelson Jobim pointed out that "Latin America possesses the largest reserves of water in the world, as well as the greatest production of energy and foodstuffs" (Ramalho da Rocha 2008). Also, Argentinean President Cristina Fernández de Kirchner expressed at the reception for members of the Security Council of UNASUR: "I stated . . . in 2008 that the issue of natural resources will become an issue—and it is—strategically throughout our region" (Fernández undated).The former minister of defense of Uruguay also confirmed this idea, saying: "The next war, if any, will be for resources and we have resources. We must prepare to defend and prepare together, because a single country cannot defend" (La República 2013).

The academic debate about future conflicts over natural resources is not new since Homer-Dixon published his book *Environment, Scarcity, and Violence* (2001), a classic on the subject. More recently, and linked to the expansion of security challenges, commonly called the new threats, other authors have developed concepts about fighting in space, the ultra-space, and strategic resources (Clunan and Trinkunas 2010).

Despite the substantiated doubts about the relevance of military training for natural resource wars, it must be recognized that the idea has taken root in the subregion—so much so that the former secretary general of UNASUR, Maria Emma Mejia, said:

> I see the American Armies, 20 or 30 years from now, protecting natural
> resources as part of a new notion of sovereignty . . . The region has

27 per cent of the continent's freshwater, eight million square kilometers of forest and three of the countries of UNASUR have the greatest biodiversity. All this has to do not only with the defense of resources, but with the protection of food reserves held by the region.

(Gualdoni 2011)

Is there a Framework for Regional Defense?

In 2008, UNASUR members approved the South America Defense Council (CDS). The CDS was formally created at the Heads of State and Government meeting in Salvador de Bahía, Brazil, on December 16, 2008. March 2009 was the first meeting of ministers of CDS, which also approved an Action Plan 2009–2010. In July 2011, the Working Group of the CDS held its fourth meeting in which they discussed the Protocol of Peace, Security and Cooperation of the Union of South American Nations. This text, imbued with the principles of opposition to the threat or use of force and respect for territorial integrity and sovereignty of each of the member countries of UNASUR, expresses support for the peaceful settlement of disputes and intraregional measures of cooperation and confidence.

While its objectives are to cooperate, consult, and coordinate various aspects of defense policy, the main results have been declarations and documents. Some of the measures approved by the CDS are the exchange of information and transparency in the security system and military spending of each country, control and border surveillance, joint actions to prevent the presence of armed groups, guaranteeing measures such as declaring South America a nuclear weapon–free zone, and refusal to use military force against a sovereign state and its territorial integrity (Flemes et al 2011, 109–10). Nevertheless, no member has changed its defense posture based on the criteria agreed to by the council.

In the meantime, there is debate over the development of a South American Defense School (ESUDE). Although the school was created in September 2013, there still is no decision regarding its regulatory regime, the place where it will be located, or how it will work to integrate the militaries of the eleven members in a common doctrine and operational structure.

Other promising results achieved in order to avoid mixing the military with internal security matters was the creation of the South American Council on Citizen Security, Justice, and Coordination Actions against Transnational Organized Crime of UNASUR (CES), established in Lima in November 30, 2012. The first meeting of CES adopted an Action Plan 2013/2017 divided into three main areas: security, justice, and coordinated actions against transnational organized crime.

Also, we need to recognize that there are positive developments at the regional level regarding the UN Stabilization Mission for Haiti (MINUSTAH). Latin America, as Rosario Green, former Mexican minister for foreign affairs argues, has a *complex multilateralism*, ready to help its neighbors by promoting mutual trust when facing natural disasters or political conflicts (Green 2003). This is the logic of cooperation and has promoted a regional commitment to help resolve the Haitian crisis. MINUSTAH's mandate is to promote and protect human rights and the rule of law. In Haiti, as in most peace operations, the armed forces were involved in confrontations with the civilian population. In the context of peace operations, this type of conflict must be resolved peacefully. The region organized a security group to homogenize defense policies and international security measures. The Latin American group, the so-called G9 or 2 + 9, attempts to achieve consensus through shared values and interests. Thus, Latin American countries are making a specific contribution so that MINUSTAH is viewed as a humanitarian mission rather than an invasion force. It is crucial to highlight that this regional experience is an attempt to achieve consensus despite an absence of hierarchical structures. It is also crucial that the mission has focused on the social and economic problems facing Haiti.

The experience of MINUSTAH shows that Latin America can become a *rule maker*, leaving its historical role of *rule taker*, as Tulchin and Espach argue (Tulchin and Espach 2004, 14). Nevertheless, recognition of this regional leadership will be enhanced by a clear commitment to multilateralism and international principles that allow the region to avoid a new arms race and promote the responsible use of energy resources.

Conclusions

Democracy is now a feature of the region despite weaknesses and deficits in the distribution of its benefits. However, the democratic state is still permeated by weak rule of law and persistent institutional deterioration. Regional integration has become crucial, but also demonstrates clear vulnerabilities.

As far as defense policies are concerned, democracy is still more absent than present. The challenge to control and administer defense, to maintain the separation between the police and the armed forces, and to reinforce civilian capabilities are all important in order to promote the rule of law.

What is the reason why governments have failed to establish successful civilian control? There are several arguments. David Pion Berlin believes that in a context of low regional conflict without a decisive role in global security, the best decision of the Latin American government is to involve the armed forces to improve public safety (Pion-Berlin 2010). Also, there are those who say that while civilian control was a fundamental requirement of the transition to democracy, it has now become obsolete as the concerns of governments are aimed at integrating the armed forces in the production model (Bruneau and Mattei 2008). In other cases, presidents without a political party and with a populist focus could turn to the military as a supporter, so there is little interest in traditional civilian control (Diamint 2013). In general, one could argue that political leaders, once they are confident the military is not challenging the government, have little incentive to exert a continuous and efficient management of the defense system.

However, this could also be the dream scenario for the military. In situations where the military is politicized or where they become an economic agent, military institutions get power, economic resources, and administrative positions in government without having to bear the costs of government. So, they participate in internal decision making without social accountability. This scenario would represent the best of all possible worlds for the armed forces: autonomy, authority and legitimacy from political power. In the end, the replacement of authoritarian states with democracy, or the move from subregional rivalries to cooperative integration, will not happen automatically through regime change.

Finally, there are two contradictory and complementary tendencies in Latin America. On the one hand, there is increasing regional cooperation, especially in the field of defense. On the other hand, the emergence of an agenda steeped in nationalism, which raises the defense of natural resources as a strategy to position the region in the world, could not only weaken the integration process, but also launch Latin America as an actor into the global arena, with uncertain consequences for regional security and democratic stability.

References

Adnmundo.com (April 19, 2007) Preocupa a Perú Carrera Armamentista de Chile. Retrieved from www.adnmundo.com/contenidos/politica/preocupa_peru_compra_aviones_guerra_chile_armas_19_04_07_pi.html. Accessed 9/27/13.

BBC (May 3, 2012) Guatemalan Town Under State of Siege After Clashes. Retrieved from www.bbc.co.uk/news/world-latin-america-17939035. Accessed 9/28/13.

Benítez Manaut, R. (2013) "México. Violencia, Fuerzas Armadas y Combate al Crimen Organizado", in C. Basombrío (ed.), *¿A Dónde Vamos? Análisis de Políticas Públicas de Seguridad Ciudadana en América Latina*. Washington, D.C.: Woodrow Wilson International Center for Scholars.

Bruneau, T. and Mattei, F. (2008) "Towards a New Conceptualization of Democratization and Civil-Military Relations," *Democratization* 15(5): 909–29.

CELS (2012) Informe Anual 2012 – La situación de los Derechos Humanos en Argentina, CELS, Buenos Aires, agosto 2012.

Clunan, A. and Trinkunas, H. (eds.) (2010) *Ungoverned Spaces: Alternatives to State Authority in an Era of Softened Sovereignty*. Stanford, CA: Stanford University Press.

Diamint, R. (2013) "Latin America and the Civil-Military Question Re-examined," in Mares, D. and Martínez, R. (eds.), *Debating Civil-Military Relations in Latin America*. Sussex: Academic Press.

El Mercurio (July 18, 2013) Evo Morales Pide a FF.AA. Alistarse Contra la Conspiración. Retrieved from www.emol.com/noticias/internacional/2013/07/18/609830/evo-morales-pide-a-ffaa-bolivianas-prepararse-contra-la-conspiracion-y-la-agresion.html. Accessed 10/1/13.

El País (May 1, 2012) Evo Morales Nacionaliza la Filial de Red Eléctrica de España en Bolivia. Retrieved from http://economia.elpais.com/economia/2012/05/01/actualidad/1335887717_799794.html. Accessed 9/29/13.

El País (August 19, 2013) El Ataque de un Grupo Guerrillero Causó Cinco Muertos en Paraguay. Retrieved from www.elpais.com.uy/mundo/ataque-grupo-guerrillero-causo-cinco.html. Accessed 9/29/13.
El Universo (May 6, 2013) Maduro Ordena Desplegar Militares para Combatir Inseguridad en Venezuela. Retrieved from www.eluniverso.com/noticias/2013/05/06/nota/905121/maduro-ordena-desplegar-militares-combatir-inseguridad. Accessed 9/28/13.
Fernández, C. (n.d.) Palabras de la Presidenta de la Nación Cristina Fernández en el Acto de Recepción de los Integrantes del Consejo de Defensa Sudamericano y los Ministros de Defensa de los Países de UNASUR, en la Galería de los Patriotas Latinoamericanos, en la Casa Rosada. Retrieved from www.presidencia.gob.ar/discursos/25103-acto-de-recepcion-de-los-integrantes-del-consejo-de-seguridad-de-unasur-palabras-de-la-presidenta-de-la-nacion. Accessed 10/9/13.
Flemes, D., Nolte, D., and Wehner, L. (2011) "Una Comunidad de Seguridad Regional en formación: la UNASUR y su Consejo de Defensa". *Estudios Internacionales* 170: 105–27.
Green, R. (2003) "Un Nuevo Regionalismo Latinoamericano para un Orden Multilateral Alterado". Paper presented to the Conferencia Internacional: Paz, crisis regional, y política exterior de Estados Unidos´, FLACSO-Chile, Santiago, August 28–29, 2003.
Gualdoni, F. (June 23, 2011) Veo a los Ejércitos Sudamericanos Protegiendo los Recursos Naturales. Retrieved from www.elpais.com/diario/2011/06/23/internacional/1308780007_850215.html. Accessed 10/3/13.
La Razón (July 22, 2012) Humala Emplea la Fuerza Militar para Frenar Conflictos Antimineros. Retrieved from www.la-razon.com/mundo/Humala-emplea-militar-conflictos-antimineros_0_1655234463.html. Accessed 9/28/13.
La República (2013) Las Malvinas son "Base de la OTAN". Retrieved from www.republica.com.uy/malvinas-base-de-la-otan/. Accessed 9/26/13.
Los Tiempos (August 2, 2013) Ejército Ensaya Maniobras para Eventual Invasión. Retrieved from www.lostiempos.com/diario/actualidad/nacional/20130802/ejercito-ensaya-maniobras-para-eventual-invasion_222984_481048.html. Accessed 10/4/13.
Martínez, J. (2013) 'Gobierno Venezolano Procura Estabilizar Frentes Económico y Eléctrico,' *Prensa Latina*, Oct. 3,. Retrieved from www.prensa-latina.cu/index.php?option=com_content&task=view&idioma=1&id=1918001&Itemid=1. Accessed 9/23/13.
Perlo-Freeman, S. Sköns, E. Solmirano, C., and Wilandh, H. (2013) "Trends in World Military Expenditure." *SIPRI Fact Sheet* April.
Perspectivas No 1/2013 (May 2013) Los Militares en la Seguridad Interna: Realidad y Desafíos para Ecuador. Quito, Ecuador: Grupo de Trabajo en Seguridad Regional (GTSR). Retrieved from http://library.fes.de/pdf-files/bueros/la-seguridad/10063.pdf. Accessed 9/27/13.
Pion-Berlin, D. (2010) "Civilian Praetorianism and Military Shirking During Constitutional Crises in Latin America," *Comparative Politics*, Volume 42, Number 4, July 2010.
Prensa Indígena (August 27, 2013) Bolivia: Discurso del Presidente Evo Morales sobre Doctrina de Defensa del ALBA. Retrieved from www.prensaindigena.org.mx/?q=content/bolivia-discurso-del-presidente-evo-morales-sobre-doctrina-de-defensa-del-alba. Accessed 9/18/13.

Prensa Libre (Sept. 15, 2013) Honduras Anuncian Inicio de Nueva Policía Militar. Retrieved from www.prensalibre.com/internacional/Honduras-anuncia_inicio-Policiamilitar_0_993500835.html. Accessed 11/5/14.

Ramalho da Rocha, A.J. (2008) "Prioridades Claras, Necessidades Ocultas e o Plano Estratégico Nacional de Defesa". *Revista Liberdade e Cidadania* 1(2) October–December. Retrieved from www.flc.org.br/revista/arquivos/121543798793361.pdf. Accessed 9/9/13.

Red Globe (2006) Fuerzas Armadas Ecuatorianas Reprimen Levantamiento Indígena. Retrieved from www.redglobe.org/index.php?option=com_content&task=view&id=494&Itemid=45. Accessed 3/17/06.

Schepers, E. (Oct. 15, 2012) "Indigenous Protesters Killed in Guatemala." *People's World*. Retrieved from www.peoplesworld.org/indigenous-protesters-killed-in-guatemala. Accessed 9/11/13.

Swenson, R. and Lemozy, S. (2009) "Presentación," in L.R. Swenson and S. Lemozy (eds.), *Democratización de la Función de Inteligencia. El Nexo de la Cultura Nacional y la Inteligencia Estratégica*. Washington, D.C.: National Defense Intelligence College.

Tulchin, J.S. and Espach, R. (eds.) (2004) *América Latina en el Nuevo Sistema Internacional*. Barcelona: Edicions Bellaterra.

Zaverucha, J. (2007) "The 'Guaranteeing Law and Order Doctrine' and the Increased Role of the Brazilian Army in Activities of Public Security." Prepared for delivery at the 2007 Congress of the Latin American Studies Association, Montréal, Canada, September.

Zaverucha, J. (2008) "La Militarización de la Seguridad Pública en Brasil". *Nueva Sociedad* 213(Jan/Feb).

Zibechi, R. (July 23, 2007) "Chile and Venezuela: Myths and Realities of the Arms Race." Americas Program, Center for International Policy. Retrieved from www.cipamericas.org/archives/1002. Accessed 4/9/08.

11 Democracy and Populism in the Andes

A Problematic Coexistence*

Julio F. Carrión

Introduction

Populism is a recurrent feature of Latin America's political experience. In the Andes, a subregion that includes Bolivia, Colombia, Ecuador, Peru, and Venezuela, it seems to be a particularly ingrained form of political representation. While populism may indeed find fertile ground in the Andes, it competes with the efforts and desires of many who want to establish democratic forms of governance in the region. It would be excessive optimism to state that populism is in decline whereas democracy is on the rise in the Andes, for populism continues to exert a persistent attraction, but recent events seem to suggest that its heyday may have been reached. In this chapter I discuss the resurgence of populism and chronicle its success in changing the rules of the political game. At the same time, I discuss the surprising resilience of democracy in post-Fujimori Peru and Colombia, countries that have successfully transitioned from authoritarianism (in Peru) and political violence (both in Colombia and Peru).

While the reemergence of populism has a certain democratic component, as it stresses mechanisms of direct democracy, it also poses serious risks for the continuation of democratic politics in the Andes. In Bolivia, Ecuador, and Venezuela, populist leaders have used their considerable public support to run roughshod over representative institutions that, however defective they might be, in the end guarantee the continuation of competitive, liberal, and democratic politics. But democracy is, indeed, deficient in the Andes. Nonpopulist presidents may have avoided the authoritarian excesses of their populist counterparts—and deserve praise for that—but they have failed to seriously address their countries' deficits of democratic governance and social inclusion. Populism may have been averted in twenty-first-century Peru and Colombia, but this is no reason for complacency, for democracy remains fragile, especially in Peru.

What Is Populism?

There is an ongoing and vibrant debate on populism. The concept is quite amorphous and has been employed to describe a wide range of phenomena, including economic policies (Dornbush and Edwards 1991), ideologies

(Albertazzi and McDonnell 2008; Mudde 2004), discourses (Hawkins 2010; Laclau 2005), and political parties (Taggart 1995), among others. Moreover, the proliferation of populist presidents of different political persuasions has generated a few adjectives to qualify them. We now speak of "classical populism," "neopopulism," "radical populism," and "left-wing populism." Given the many meanings associated with it and the clear lack of consensus on what populism is and is not, some have proposed to abandon the term altogether (Roxborough 1984). This proposal seems too radical, as it is unrealistic to wish away a concept that tries to grapple with both an important and recurrent political phenomenon. For others, populism in Latin America is a concept inherently associated with a particular phase of Latin American history, namely import-substituting industrialization (Malloy 1977; Novaro 1996; Quijano 1998; Schamis 2013). Those who see the utility of using this concept to describe contemporary phenomena tend to follow two general lines of inquiry to understand the roots of its appeal. The first focuses on the institutional deficiencies and crises of representation that lead people to abandon traditional parties and turn to populist outsiders who promise a radical alteration of the political landscape (Mayorga 2006; Panizza 2000; Roberts 2007, 2013). The second line of inquiry stresses the discursive elements of populism, seeking to understand why these rhetorical appeals and strategies are so attractive to the masses (de la Torre 2010; Hawkins 2010; Laclau 2005).

Populism is increasingly seen as a political strategy or style (Knight 1998). Weyland (2001, 14) nicely articulates this view when he strips it of its historical, economic, or sociological connotations and defines it as "a political strategy through which a personalistic leader seeks or exercises power based on direct, unmediated, uninstitutionalized support from large numbers of mostly unorganized followers." This emphasis on populism as a political strategy or leadership style is embraced by many scholars who note its successful rhetorical appeal to the masses, usually accompanied with an "us versus them" mentality and a strong anti-status quo discourse (Boas 2005; Cammack 2000; Dugas 2003; Panizza 2000). Others add that the personalistic characteristics of populism lead to a weakening of representative institutions (Navia and Walker 2008) in order to perpetuate the power of the leader (Barr 2009). Indeed, populism as governance is profoundly anti-institutional. Taggart (2000, 106) writes that "[a]t the best of times populists regard institutions with distaste, but at times of crisis they begin to see them as malignant." Some might see in its privileged use of mechanisms of direct democracy a redemptive force that is not always incompatible with liberal democracy (Arditi 2007; Canovan 2005). Others see the delegitimization of the political opponent that populism nurtures as an inherent threat to democracy (Abts and Rummens 2007).

I propose here a definition of populism that builds on the extensive literature on the topic (in addition to the cited texts, see Burbano de Lara 1998; de la Torre 2010; de la Torre and Arnson 2013; de la Torre and Peruzzotti 2008; Hermet, Loaeza, Prud'homme 2001; Ionescu and Gellner 1969; Panizza 2005; Vilas 1994). I see populism as a form of political representation that has four constitutive elements: (1) a style of leadership that is highly personalistic; (2) an unmediated or poorly institutionalized leader/mass relationship that privileges mechanisms of direct democracy rather than representative democracy; (3) a political discourse or mentality that divides the world between "us" and "them"; and (4) a general distrust of institutional checks and balances that would limit the power of the leader.

The four constitutive elements of populism listed here are combined in a "familiar resemblance" fashion (Collier and Mahon 1993; Goertz 2006). This means that not all elements need to be present with the same intensity. Any combination of two or more of these elements will strongly signify the presence of a populist government. In fact, the manner in which they combine could provide for different variants of populism. For instance, the intensity with which populist leaders undermine checks and balances would allow us to distinguish between democratic and authoritarian populism. In similar fashion, the organizational features that actualize the relationship between mass and leader could allow us to differentiate between neopopulism, which relies on very little or no organization, and classical populism, which exhibits stronger organizational life (Roberts 1995; Weyland 1996, 2001). Weyland (2001) correctly stresses the fact that populism falls within the domain of politics, but to assert that populism exhibits one single domain does not imply that it lacks multidimensionality. Those who see populism exclusively as a political strategy or leadership style underplay its governance attributes, particularly its problematic attitude toward institutional checks and balances and conflict resolution (Carrión 2013).

Populism in Latin America confronts an alternative type of political representation that can be generally labeled as traditional representative democracy. Traditional representative politics, unlike populism, exhibits a pluralist mentality that refuses to delegitimize political opponents, thus eschewing the "us versus them" discourse that is so dear to populism. In dealing with conflict resolution, populism embraces a governance style that is confrontational and uncompromising, whereas traditional representative democracy values accommodation and judicial adjudication. Nonpopulist parties and leaders strive to build broad-based coalitions in an effort to compensate for their less-than-impressive electoral support among the poor. Given their emphasis on accommodation and broad-based representation, these leaders prefer to rely on the existing institutions of liberal democracy, such as congresses and the courts, rather than mass mobilization. In so doing, they largely accept institutional checks and balances, even if they voice—sometimes loudly—their displeasure with them.

While traditional representative politics revolve around the institutions of representative democracy, populism tends to privilege mechanisms associated with direct democracy, such as plebiscites and referenda (Canovan 1999). The direct appeal to the masses serves a crucial role in the populist project for it allows populist leaders to bypass or overrule representative institutions and judicial review. Without mass support and the partial acquiesce from key political actors—as I will show—the populist project is hardly possible. The use of plebiscites has become the preferred mechanism through which populist leaders enhance and consolidate their power, not only in the Andes and Latin America, but also in the former Soviet republics and some Eastern and Central European countries (Anderson et al 2001). Because of their reliance on plebiscitary appeals, the mass public in the Andes tends to perceive populist leaders as more democratic than presidents who prefer traditional mechanisms of political intermediation. This perception is bolstered by a political culture that generally equates democracy with suffrage and elections, and pays far less attention to its liberal, Madisonian dimension (O'Donnell 1994). Thus, and paradoxically, populist leaders frequently use direct democracy mechanisms to undermine the already weak foundations of liberal democracy.

While populist discourse tends to be stridently anti-status quo, the changes that populist leaders seek to enact are not sweeping economic and/or social reform. They are generally political reforms that alter the institutional makeup of the country and change the rules of the game to secure reelection. The adoption of unicameral congresses, the enhancement of presidential prerogatives, the establishment of immediate reelection, the change of electoral laws—all are changes sought after by populist leaders so that they can extend their tenure in office and aggrandize their own power.

The Tortuous Path to Democracy

The Andean countries shared a common history of political instability and lack of democracy for most of the twentieth century. Although Colombia largely avoided military rule, the Andean countries, by the end of the 1950s, looked more similar than dissimilar when comparing their degree of democratic progress. This common trajectory gradually began to change as both Colombia and Venezuela embarked on a serious if somewhat flawed process of democratization. On December 1, 1957, millions of Colombian men and—for the first time ever—women went to the polls to vote in a plebiscite to ratify a set of constitutional reforms. The most significant of these reforms was the creation of the Frente Nacional (National Front), which established a sixteen-year period during which the Liberal and the Conservative parties, until then fierce enemies, agreed to alternate in the presidency and split evenly the spoils of power (Palacios and Stoller 2006; Peeler 1986). With almost unanimous public endorsement, the Colombian parties thus put a formal end to a secular conflict that reached historic proportions in what came to be known as La Violencia, when almost 250,000 people were killed in a civil war.

The Colombian example of pacted democracy was soon followed by Venezuela. On October 31, 1958, Acción Democrática (Democratic Action), COPEI (Political Electoral Independent Organization Committee), and Unión Republicana (Republican Union), Venezuela's most important parties at the time, facing a perilous transition to democracy and anxious to end once and for all military intervention in politics, signed a historic pact, the Pacto de Punto Fijo, to set the parameters of the upcoming civilian administrations (McCoy and Myers 2004). Under the terms of this pact, all parties committed to the defense of the constitutional order and agreed to the adoption of a common governmental platform and a government of national unity.

The successful implementation of these two pacts set the foundations for democratic development in Venezuela and Colombia during the 1960s and 1970s. Bolivia, Ecuador, and Peru, however, continued to endure military rule for most of these years. Bolivia experienced military government for most of the years between 1964 and 1982. Ecuador was ruled by military juntas in 1963–1966 and in 1972–1979. Peru saw military governments in 1962–1963 and again in 1968–1980. By the mid-1970s, the political paths of the Andean countries had clearly bifurcated: one path was of democratic consolidation, the other of deepening instability and authoritarianism. A well-known scholar (Peeler 1986) had no qualms including Colombia and Venezuela in the group of Latin American liberal democracies. By contrast, Bolivia, Ecuador, and Peru became examples of the "new authoritarianism" that swept Latin America in the 1970s (Collier 1979; Malloy 1977).

The transitions to democracy in Ecuador (1979) and Peru (1980) were relatively straightforward affairs, with the military carefully controlling both the timetable and the terms of the transitions. The advent of electoral democracy in Bolivia (1982) had more twists and turns. Presidential elections were held in Bolivia in 1978, 1979, and 1980, and on each occasion the democratization process was aborted by coups and countercoups (Malloy and Gamarra 1988). For a brief period of time between 1980 and 1981, Bolivia was ruled by a predatory military junta headed by General Luis García Meza, which engaged in widespread human rights abuses, including political killings, and rampant corruption and drug trafficking. By the mid-1980s, however, all Andean countries were enjoying civilian and democratically elected governments. But the 1980s would not be kind to either the established or the emerging democracies. In the next section I discuss setbacks and the unraveling of democracy in the Andes that began in the 1980s.

The Unraveling of Political Settlements

Like most Latin American nations, the Andean countries were affected by the severe economic crisis of the 1980s. Although the "lost decade" affected Andean countries in different degrees—for instance, Colombia was largely unscathed by economic troubles—all countries saw the gradual unraveling of the political arrangements that had been laboriously worked out in previous years or even decades.

Let us begin by examining the nascent democracies. Bolivia had to deal with rampant inflation since transitioning to democracy in 1982. The Hernán Siles Suazo administration (1982–1985) inherited a country in virtual bankruptcy and could not find the political formula to deal with an out-of-control inflation that was running at an annual rate of 24,000 percent at the beginning of 1985

(Buckman 2013, 69). Forced to cut his term short—not the most auspicious way to start a democratic transition—the task of bringing Bolivia back to some normalcy fell to Víctor Paz Estenssoro, the historic leader of the Movimiento Nacionalista Revolucionario (Nationalist Revolutionary Movement, MNR). He adopted a drastic stabilization program and began a policy of economic liberalization (Grindle 2003; Sheahan 2006). As expected, the measures were received with anger by the labor unions, and Paz Estenssoro dealt with them harshly. While the repression of labor reduced opposition to what eventually became a successful stabilization policy, it also meant that Bolivian democracy quickly turned against those who had helped to bring it in the first place. In an act of political audacity, and in an effort to broaden his base of support, Paz Estenssoro signed the Pact of Democracy with the former dictator Hugo Banzer and his party, the Acción Democrática Nacionalista (Democratic Nationalist Action, ADN). This pact was the first of a series of pacts and coalitions that brought some political stability to Bolivia during the second half of the 1980s and most of the 1990s (Orias Arredondo 2005). They could not, however, prevent the emergence of a radical indigenous movement that demanded changes in land tenure laws and protested the growing involvement of foreign investors in the exploitation of Bolivia's natural resources. These pacts could also not forestall the increasing activism of coca growers, who rejected the eradication policies demanded by the United States. Social movements and public opinion eventually began to reject the continuation of the free-market reforms that were enacted in the 1980s to deal with the severe economic crisis. Not surprisingly, street protests against tax increases that were decreed to honor the agreement with the International Monetary Fund (IMF) led to the resignation of Gonzalo Sánchez de Lozada in 2003 and the rise of Evo Morales of the Movimiento Al Socialismo (Movement Toward Socialism, MAS) party.

In Peru, another nascent democracy, the economic crisis was compounded by the negative effects of the weather phenomenon known as El Niño, which produced a negative gross domestic product (GDP) growth of 12 percent in 1983 (Sheahan 1999). Fernando Belaúnde, leader of the center-right party Acción Popular (Popular Action), readily embraced the recommendations of the IMF to deal with the crisis. His policy-making style was characterized by the arrogant conviction that only those with vested interests to defend could disagree with the government's efforts to liberalize the economy (Conaghan and Malloy 1994). This policy style was patently epitomized by Manuel Ulloa, an international banker who became Belaúnde's prime minister (technically, the president of the Council of Ministers). While the technocratic policy style diminished the quality of Peruvian democracy, the real threat came from the domestic insurgency led by the bloody Shining Path and the manner in which the Peruvian state confronted it. For most of the 1980s, Peru faced the combination of uncontrollable inflation and political violence. For a while, the election of the young Alan García, leader of Peru's oldest party, Alianza Popular Revolucionaria Americana (Revolutionary Popular America Alliance, APRA), brought some hope. For a brief moment, it seemed that the adoption of heterodox economic policies would provide a viable alternative to the Washington Consensus. Soon, however, the populist economic policy unraveled, as it had done in Argentina and Bolivia, and inflation skyrocketed. At the same time, the widespread human rights violations committed by the Peruvian army fueled rather than stopped an insurgency that had an even lower regard for human life (Degregori 1990; Palmer 1994; Stern 1998). When Peruvians came to the polls to elect a new president in 1990, they were more than inclined to try anybody who was not associated with the traditional political parties. As we will see later, Fujimori stabilized the economy and pacified the country, but in the process he established an electoral authoritarian regime.

The pattern of enacting economic policies without significant consultation with parliament and the dismissive rejection of all criticism was also evident in Ecuador. The election of León Febres Cordero (1984–1988), leader of the conservative Partido Social Cristiano (Social Christian Party, PSC), introduced Ecuador to market-oriented economic policies. Febres Cordero, with much greater fervor than Victor Paz Estenssoro and Fernando Belaúnde, rapidly embraced the recommendations of the IMF while adopting a governing style that was highly confrontational and borderline authoritarian (Conaghan and Malloy 1994). In one instance, Febres Cordero surrounded the Supreme Court building with tanks to prevent new members appointed by Congress from assuming their posts (Buckman 2013, 178). His administration epitomized the tendency of some Latin American governments to combine the liberalization of the economy with a governance style of questionable democratic character. The two administrations that followed were less extreme but not very effective. The center-left Rodrigo Borja (1988–1992) dealt unsuccessfully with the growing economic crisis and ended up mired in political bickering that led to the end of the coalition that supported his candidacy (Gerlach 2003). The center-right Sixto Durán Ballén (1992–1996) ran on promises to deal with the growing inflation and lackluster economic performance. He enacted harsh economic stabilization policies and began a process of economic liberalization. The economy gradually improved, but Durán Ballén committed a number of serious mistakes that dramatically affected the outlook of Ecuadorian democracy. The promulgation in 1994 of a law that reversed the agrarian reform and put an end to the partition of large estates produced a nationwide protest led by indigenous organizations (Guerrero 1996). The indigenous movement already had a significant presence in Ecuadorian politics, but this blatant attack against their hopes of agrarian equity deepened its mobilization and radicalized its outlook. The subsequent accusations of corruption that led to the indictment of Durán Ballén's vice-president only worsened the perception that the country was being run by a self-serving elite (North 2004). The 1996 elections would mark the beginning of a period of political instability and institutional fragility that lasted until the election of Rafael Correa in 2006.

The economic crisis prevented the nascent democracies of Bolivia, Ecuador, and Peru from taking firmer roots and it also undermined Venezuela's long-held democratic stability. Despite the continuous flow of oil revenues, a misguided economic policy that led to the overvaluation of the bolívar generated significant economic troubles in the 1980s (Sheahan 2006). Known as Black Friday, February 18, 1983, marked the day when Venezuela drastically devalued its currency. This was a belated effort to address the overvaluation of the currency in a context of declining oil prices, and is widely believed to have initiated the demise of the Pacto de Punto Fijo democracy. The feelings of economic insecurity that this devaluation caused in vast segments of the Venezuelan population was later replaced by anger in the wake of the 1989 package of economic reforms enacted by Carlos Andres Pérez. When he was campaigning for reelection, Pérez ran on a platform that promised a return to the good old times. When he failed to fulfill his promises and enacted stabilization policies, Carlos Andrés Pérez unleashed a furor rarely before seen in Venezuela. Lootings and street demonstrations were harshly dealt with, and dozens of people were killed as a result of the upheaval (López Maya and Lander 2004). Not surprisingly, when Lieutenant Colonel Hugo Chávez rose against his government in April 1992, the coup attempt was received with tacit sympathy by many. Pérez would eventually be impeached for corruption and removed from office in 1993. The election of Rafael Caldera in 1994 would turn out to be just the prelude to the dramatic unraveling of democracy that Venezuela experienced after the election of Hugo Chávez in December 1998.

In the 1980s, Colombia escaped most of the economic woes that affected other countries in the region, but was affected by a host of other issues. This country entered the 1980s still dealing with the legacy of the National Front that prevented outsiders from gaining the highest office. A serious challenge to the parties' duopoly was registered in 1970 when the former dictator General Gustavo Rojas Pinilla, leader of the Alianza Nacional Popular (National Popular Alliance, ANAPO) came close to winning the presidential election. In fact, many believe that he was the victim of widespread electoral fraud that favored the Conservative candidate Misael Pastrana. A few years later, disaffected activists founded the Movimiento 19 de Abril (known as M-19) and turned to violence to challenge what they saw as an illegitimate government (Sweig and McCarthy 2005). In addition, during the 1980s, Colombia faced another security threat in the form of drug trafficking, which openly challenged the state and the society at large. If the party system did not suffer significant setbacks during these years, it was largely due to the nature of the electoral system, which allowed factions within each party to run their slates of candidates (Ungar Bleier and Arévalo 2004), thus preventing party fragmentation. During the 1990s, the security threats to the state increased as the largest guerrilla organization, the Fuerzas Armadas Revolucionarias de Colombia (Revolutionary Armed Forces of Colombia, FARC) colluded with narco-traffickers and expanded its activities to the city (Sweig and McCarthy 2005, 18). Violence worsened as vigilante groups funded by land owners to fight the guerrillas coalesced and created the Autodefensas Unidas de Colombia (United Self-Defense Forces of Colombia, AUC) in 1997. The sense of insecurity and chaos that this violence generated led to the election of Álvaro Uribe in 2002. This was the first time in Colombia's history that a candidate not belonging to one of the two major political parties was elected to the presidency. The Uribe presidency would significantly change the security situation in Colombia. While for a brief moment Colombia toyed with the populist temptation, democracy persisted.

In sum, all Andean countries had, through different trajectories and with varying intensity, achieved democratic rule by the early 1980s. Unfortunately, the severe economic crisis and its management encouraged the worst political instincts of many presidents in the emerging democracies of Bolivia, Ecuador, and Peru. The economic crisis also undermined Venezuelan democracy. By the mid-1990s, the fragile institutional arrangements in Ecuador and Peru collapsed, and Venezuela and Colombia faced significant challenges. Bolivia escaped unscathed for a while, but in the early 2000s, the laborious elite agreements would eventually collapse. It is in this context that the region was affected by a new wave of populism.

The Revival of Populism in Ecuador and Peru

The election of Jaime Roldós in 1979 in Ecuador was a clear indication that voters' predilection for populism was not moribund. Roldós's party, Concentración de Fuerzas Populares (Concentration of Popular Forces, CFP) was a populist party founded in 1946, which was led at the time by Assad Bucaram, uncle of Roldós's wife. Initially, Roldós presented himself as a surrogate for Bucaram, who was prevented by the new constitution from running. His overwhelming victory in the runoff cemented his populist inclinations, which led him to clash with his old mentor. When Assad Bucaram—who led a majority of seats in Congress—blocked some of his initiatives, Roldós founded his own party, *Pueblo, Cambio y Democracia*. Soon, Roldós found himself attacking the "patriarchs of the sleazy deal" (*componenda*) when his old party leaders joined forces with Leon Febres Cordero's PSC in Congress. His untimely death in 1982 aborted this populist experiment.

The populist trend crystallized in clearer fashion in Peru during the first administration of Alan García (1985–1990), leader of the APRA party. Even though he did not secure the necessary majority to prevent a runoff, he was able to avoid it when his rival—the left-wing candidate Alfonso Barrantes—declined to compete, given the overwhelming electoral advantage that García exhibited at the time. Soon García was enjoying the *calor popular* (people's embrace) in impromptu *balconazos*, extemporaneous speeches delivered from one of the balconies of the presidential palace. García coupled this style with an economic policy that sought to reactivate the economy by using deficit spending. Seeking regional notoriety, he pledged to allocate no more than 10 percent of Peru's export earnings to service the foreign debt (Reyna 2000). García repeatedly contrasted his nationalist policies and government with the egoistical voracity of foreign lenders who wanted to keep exploiting Peru. Echoes of populism's traditional rhetoric that confronted the nation versus the anti-nation were evident during his 1985–1990 administration.

It was during the 1990s, however, that a purportedly new form of populism emerged in the Andes and other Latin American countries. It was argued that presidents such as Fujimori in Peru and Menem in Argentina represented a departure from classical populism, a breed better described with the term neopopulism (Roberts 1995; Weyland 1996). Neopopulists shared with old populists the plebiscitarian style of leadership that seeks to establish direct links with unorganized masses. On the other hand, they departed from old populism by their embrace of neoliberal policies. In the Andes, Fujimori and, to a much lesser extent, Abdalá Bucaram represented this new form of populism. On the other hand, both Fujimori and Bucaram exhibited traits that were consistent with classical populism.

After his surprising second-place finish in the 1990 presidential election, Alberto Fujimori framed the upcoming contest in the runoff as a confrontation between the white elite that had traditionally ruled Peru and the broad-based, racially diverse insurgency that he claimed to represent. As his campaign slogan put it, Fujimori wanted to offer Peruvians a "President like you." The fact that his family and racial background could not be more different than that of the majority of Peruvians did not matter. He successfully framed his campaign in terms of "us" versus "them," the true Peruvians of many colors and backgrounds versus the moneyed, European-looking elite (Carrión 1997). Once in power, Fujimori displayed the four central components of populism described at the outset of this chapter. His personalistic style of leadership was clearly revealed by the fact that he refused to build a serious political organization. In fact, his disregard of any organizational check to his power led him to create a coterie of "parties" for each electoral contest that he faced. He created the Nueva Mayoría party for the 1992 congressional elections, the Vamos Vecinos party for the 1998 municipal contests, and the Frente Perú 2000 for the 2000 presidential election. None of these electoral vehicles had a serious or even ceremonial role in his government. On the contrary, Fujimori closely associated himself with his main security advisor Vladimiro Montesinos (who did not even belong to any of the pro-Fujimori parties) and relied on technocrats with little or no political experience to run his administration (Conaghan 2005).

Personalistic leadership also implies an unmediated relationship with followers. Populist representation is predicated on the portrayal of the leader as savior of the nation who develops a direct, unmediated connection with *el pueblo*, the people (de la Torre 2010). Given that populism thrives in environments in which strong parties do not exist or are in decline, the populist leader finds it easy to portray them as either oligarchical cliques that obstruct the people's wishes or as unnecessary intermediaries between the leader and the people.

Fujimori constantly divided the country between the supporters of "democracy," meaning his government, and the followers of terrorism. Taking advantage of people's rejection of Shining Path and their yearning for social tranquility, Fujimori charged his opponents with a failure to take the terrorist threat seriously, or even accused them of collaborating with it. He attacked the institutions that opposed his policies, such as the Catholic Church and the judiciary. He also criticized the media and traditional parties. Unlike Alan García, his rhetoric did not contrast "the nation" to the "foreigners," but instead juxtaposed the "traditional politicians" to those who wanted peace and tranquility. Fujimori's politics, as one observer put it, was the politics of the anti-politics (Panfichi 1997).

In addition, Fujimori did not only distrust, but openly rejected checks and balances. Soon after taking office, he began a series of confrontations with Congress over issues related to economic and security policies (Kenney 2004). When Congress showed some backbone and rejected the unchecked powers he was demanding, Fujimori announced on April 5, 1992, that he was suspending the constitution and shutting down both Congress and the Supreme Court. This set of measures ended the fragile democracy inaugurated in 1980. Despite the widespread international condemnation of the autocoup, the Peruvian public rallied behind it (Carrión 2006).

In Ecuador, Abdalá Bucaram's short term in office (1996–1997) does not give us much historical evidence to analyze, but in many regards, his populism shares some important similarities with Fujimori's. Like Fujimori, Bucaram came to power after winning a runoff against a candidate who represented the country's elite, Jaime Nebot of the right-wing PSC. As de la Torre (1999) points out, Bucaram framed the electoral contest as a choice between "the people," whom he allegedly represented, and the "evil oligarchy." Although running on a populist platform (his slogan was "First the Poor"), once elected, he announced a far-reaching program of market-oriented reforms that included the privatization of state enterprises and the pegging of the sucre to the dollar (Gerlach 2003). Bucaram also attacked the press and adopted a confrontational stance vis-à-vis Congress, where the opposition held a majority of seats. For instance, on November 8, 1996, Miguel Salem, his cabinet's general secretary, threatened to shut down Congress. His government was also plagued by accusations of widespread corruption. Many believed that Bucaram himself was benefiting from corrupt practices (Gerlach 2003). His populist experiment collapsed, however, when he raised prices of cooking gas and increased taxes on electricity. In protest, a highly successful national strike was held on February 5, 1997. Bucaram was later impeached by the Congress on the grounds of mental incapacity. His removal opened a decade-long period of political instability that gave Ecuador seven different presidents until the 2006 election of Rafael Correa.

Twenty-First-Century Populism

Venezuela

While the content of Fujimori's and Bucaram's policies could not be more different than that of Hugo Chávez of Venezuela, they all share important similarities in their representational style. Chávez ran against the whole political class, claiming that the regime created by the Pact of Punto Fijo had become a "partycracy" and promising to dismantle it if elected (Hawkins 2003). The momentum created by his decisive 1998 electoral victory allowed him to steam-roll his opponents and impose a radical restructuring of Venezuela's political arrangements. Refusing to assume its role as defender of the constitution, the Supreme Court allowed Chávez to call for a "consultative referendum" to see whether a constituent assembly should be established (Coppedge 2003). This ruling opened the way for the radical political restructuring of the country. In April 1999 Chávez won an astonishing victory when 90 percent of voters approved his call for a constituent assembly to draft a new constitution. Soon thereafter, in July of the same year, Chávez secured another overwhelming victory when his electoral coalition obtained 125 of the 131 seats in the National Constituent Assembly (ANC). With full control of the assembly, Chávez's forces drafted a constitution that significantly enhanced presidential powers, created a new "citizens' branch," and removed Congress' powers to approve military promotions (Shifter 2006). Following a trend in Latin America, the new constitution also removed the ban on immediate reelection. The new article allowed Chávez to run not only in 2000, but also in 2006, potentially allowing him to remain in office until 2011.

Unfortunately, Venezuela's Supreme Court did not pose any serious opposition to Chávez's sweeping reformist zeal. Chávez argued that the ANC was sovereign and all powerful, superseding the powers of the legislature and even the judiciary. The Supreme Court, once more, sided with Chávez and recognized the sweeping powers of the ANC, seeking to secure its own survival (Combellas 2010, 155). The Supreme Court acceded to the suspension of Congress while the ANC was in session. According to Corrales and Penfold (2011, 18),

[d]espite having reservations regarding this process of stripping Congress of power this way, the Supreme Court did not feel confident enough to block the wishes of such a popular president. Chávez was enjoying the highest approval ratings of any Venezuelan president since the 1960s. And so began the process of using the power of majorities to bully the various branches of government.

But in siding with the president, the Supreme Court only bought itself extra time, for soon it would succumb to the Chavista hurricane. On December 15, 1999, less than a year after Chávez took office, the new constitution went into effect after being approved by 72 percent of the voters, and the Congress and Supreme Court were dissolved. The ANC rapidly appointed a new Supreme Court, comptroller, and general attorney (Aveledo 2010, 62). Violating the very procedures that had just been approved, the ANC did not end its functions and instead adopted an ad hoc regime that enabled it to continue modifying the other branches of the state and organizing the upcoming elections. It also appointed a "*congresillo*" ("little congress") to assume the legislative duties of the dissolved Congress. This body was composed of fifteen of its own members and another fifteen citizens appointed by the ANC to legislate. During this interim period, the thirty-member *congresillo* passed thirty-two bills, some of them of major consequence. The newly appointed Supreme Court justified this open power grab by arguing that it conformed to the "doctrine of necessary transitoriness" (Combellas 2010, 159). Moreover, the new pro-Chávez court appointed a committee in charge of restructuring the whole judicial branch. By the end of 2003, 80 percent of all judges in Venezuela were "provisional, acting, or interim" (Aveledo 2010, 63).

The mega-elections of July 2000, thus called because presidential, congressional, gubernatorial, and mayoral elections were held on the same day, cemented Chávez's grip over Venezuela when he obtained 59 percent of the vote. In the wake of his reelection, he escalated his verbal assaults against the "rancid oligarchy," as well as against civil society organizations, such as the press, the Catholic Church, and labor unions.

Using his considerable majority in the unicameral Congress—Chávez's Movimiento Quinta República had won 92 of the 165 seats—he demanded powers to rule by decree, which were granted in November 2000. In exercise of these powers, Chávez issued almost fifty decrees affecting important aspects of economic life, including the oil industry (Corrales and Penfold 2007). These decrees were widely repudiated by all sectors of society and, as Buckman writes, they "had the unintended effect of forging an unlikely alliance between FEDECAMERAS, the country's main business lobby, led by Pedro Carmona, and the CTV [the nation's peak labor union]" (Buckman 2013, 389). Chávez's brazen disregard for the content if not the forms of democracy had the effect of polarizing Venezuelan society. Both business and labor organizations called for a twelve-hour general strike on December 2001. The confrontations continued as anti-Chávez forces took to the streets in massive demonstrations to demand his resignation and pro-Chávez groups rallied in his defense. In April 2002, business and labor unions once again called for a one-day strike to demand Chávez's resignation. Since the strike drew much support, the organizers decided to extend it until Chávez resigned. On April 12, a group of Chávez's supporters shot into the crowd at an opposition rally and killed at least seventeen people. The reaction against the killings was immediate, and Chávez was forced to resign in a military coup that same day. As the new government began to shut down Congress and suspend the constitution, support for the coup rapidly evaporated, causing it to collapse. On April 14, 2003, Chávez was reinstated to power by a group of loyal officers led by General Raúl Baduel, who later became his minister of defense (Carroll 2013).

The coup and countercoup further deepened the division among Venezuelans. The opposition started collecting signatures to demand a recall election, a procedure contemplated in the new constitution. The huge pro- and anti-Chávez rallies continued, and the opposition raised the stakes one more time by calling for an indefinite general strike to begin on December 2, 2002. As the strike gained momentum, paralyzing most of the country and, more critically for the regime, the oil fields, Chávez became more confrontational.

When oil workers joined the strike and began affecting Venezuela's output, his government took over the state-owned but independently-run PDVSA (the state oil company). Chávez dismissed a number of board members and fired thousands of oil workers. As the strike continued through the holiday season and the beginning of the summer, it began to lose steam. The organizers ended it in February 2003.

The defeat of the general strike was a significant setback for the opposition, forcing them to switch to what was called at the time "the electoral solution." The opposition largely abandoned big public rallies and turned its attention to collecting the necessary signatures to demand a recall election (Corrales and Penfold 2007). But the "electoral solution" turned out to be as difficult as action on the streets. Chávez made use of his considerable control of the state institutions to stall this effort. What followed was a series of electoral defeats for the opposition. Despite the enthusiasm and organizational prowess displayed by the opposition, Chávez emerged victorious from the recall election, securing 59 percent of the vote. In the wake of this demoralizing defeat, the opposition refused to participate in the December 2005 gubernatorial and congressional elections, which were easily won by the pro-Chávez forces. The significant shift in the correlation of forces between the government and the opposition that this defeat produced was fully appreciated in the 2006 presidential elections. Social spending, bolstered by a booming economy based on the oil bonanza, skyrocketed and with it the government's standing at the polls (Corrales and Penfold 2007). Despite the fact that the opposition was able to manage a single candidate to oppose Hugo Chávez, he easily won a reelection with a record turnout, obtaining 63 percent of the vote.

In the campaign preceding the election, Chávez had announced his intention to steer Venezuela towards "twenty-first-century socialism," which he failed to explain in detail. Soon after his second reelection, some details would emerge. On December 28, 2006, Chávez announced his decision not to renew the broadcasting license of RCTV, the oldest and most-watched television network in Venezuela. If Chávez sought to intimidate or weaken the opposition, the move certainly backfired. University students, who had remained largely apathetic in the previous two years, took to the streets to protest the silencing of the network. The mobilization of college students, which in the Peruvian case sparked a significant grassroots resistance against the Fujimori regime, also proved very important in Venezuela. Students' activism awakened the opposition from the stupor into which it had fallen, but it did not deter Chávez's march into his twenty-first-century utopia. In January 2007, he announced a series of sweeping measures that included the nationalization of oil refineries, the renegotiation of oil contracts, and a set of constitutional reforms. The most important of these reforms was the complete elimination of term limits for the presidential office while setting a one-term limit to all other elected offices. The proposed reforms would also reduce the working day from eight to six hours. It became very clear that Chávez was willing to spend his recently enhanced political capital to force a significant change in the rules of the game, one that would allow him to stay indefinitely in office. As had been his modus operandi before, he appealed to the public to secure approval. The unicameral Congress quickly approved the constitutional reforms and then called for a plebiscite to ratify the changes.

This time, however, Chávez found significant obstacles to his efforts to perpetuate his power. Civil society organizations, as well as the traditional opposition, mobilized against the reforms. Even the ruling alliance split. Por la Democracia Social (PODEMOS, For A Social Democracy), a party that had supported Chávez before, announced its opposition to the reforms and called for a "NO" vote in the referendum. More symbolically perhaps, General Raúl Baduel, the officer who had restored Chávez to power in 2002, publicly rejected Chávez's efforts to change the constitution, accusing him of staging a coup d'état. The referendum, held on December 2, 2007, resulted in a "NO" vote of 50.7 percent, thus defeating Chávez's ambitions. But the initial defeat did not stop him.

In December 2008, against both the spirit and the letter of the constitution, Chávez submitted to Congress a new proposal to reform the constitution in order to remove term limits for all elected offices and not just for the presidency, as the failed 2007 referendum had initially stipulated. The new referendum was held on February 15, 2009, and this time Chávez emerged victorious with 54.9 percent of the vote. The elimination of term limits removed a significant obstacle for the continuation of populist rule because it addressed a significant weakness of this mode of representation, namely that its personalistic character prevented the nurturing of alternative leaders who can continue the legacy through electoral means. Chávez ran for his third reelection in 2012. But this time he faced a far more ominous enemy. In June 2011, his government announced that he had been diagnosed with cancer. For most of 2011 and 2012, Chávez endured a series of treatments and operations in Cuba to treat his condition. With the true condition of his health hidden from public view, voters went to the polls on October 7, 2012, and reelected Chávez with 55 percent of the vote, against Henrique Capriles, a young former governor of the state of Miranda and leader of the unified opposition. On December 8, 2012, before departing for Cuba for yet another treatment, Chávez declared that if something were to happen to him, he would like his vice-president, Nicolás Maduro, to take over his legacy.

Chávez passed away on March 5, 2013. Nicolás Maduro assumed the presidency and hurriedly called for new presidential elections for April 14 of that year, hoping to benefit from the massive wave of grief caused by Chávez's untimely death. The 2013 presidential election exposed the underbelly of *chavismo* in Venezuela. With the disappearance of the charismatic leader, the shortcomings of the regime were in plain view. First, Venezuelans were facing an acute citizen insecurity crisis. Briceño-León, Camardiel and Avila (2012) put the national homicide rate at 73 per 100,000 and at 122 per 100,000 in Caracas, making this city the most dangerous in the Americas and one of the most violent cities of the world. Second, what Kornblith (2013, 55) has described as "the government's waning fiscal and managerial capacity" has produced severe shortages of basic items such as toilet paper, milk, and coffee, and an inflation rate that reached 56.2 percent in 2013 and could exceed 65 percent by the end of 2014. Third, Maduro himself was revealed to be a lackluster candidate, unable to generate the fervor that surrounded Chávez. The opposition, again led by Henrique Capriles, ran an enthusiastic campaign centered on economic and educational issues, while promising to keep Chávez's social programs intact. The regime was barely able to secure a victory—the margin between Maduro and Capriles was a slim 1.49 percentage points—and Maduro struggled to keep the political initiative. The municipal elections of December 8, 2013, showed the difficulties of the regime, with the opposition making significant gains, especially in urban areas, in comparison to the 2008 municipal contest. Parliamentary elections scheduled for December 2015 could deliver even worse news for the Maduro administration.

Ecuador

In Ecuador, the 2006 election of Rafael Correa brought to office a politician who openly embraced "twenty-first-century socialism." Rafael Correa is a middle-class professional who began a career in politics as a technocrat, becoming minister of finance in 2005 in the Alfredo Palacio administration. He did not have a political party and only created one (Proud and Sovereign Fatherland, PAIS) when he decided to run for the presidency. Although he entered into some alliances—initially with the Socialist party and later with a series of small left-wing and civil society organizations when contesting in the electoral runoff—Correa does not really have a party in the manner that Evo Morales in Bolivia does. Nor are Correa's political views similar to those of Morales'. Correa, as an observant Roman Catholic, couches his advocacy for a twenty-first-century socialism in humanistic terms. Morales, on the other hand, advocates a more radical brand of socialism that is infused with nationalistic and indigenous overtones.

After taking office, Correa rallied against the "oligarchy" and the "bigwigs" ("*pelucones*") who were, according to him, sabotaging his efforts to change Ecuador. Since he lacked a majority in Congress, Correa had to rely on his allies (most notably Pachakutik and the Socialist party) to secure approval for his convocation. He was able to radically transform the rules of the game after a series of astonishing developments. Mindful of the Venezuelan experience, Congress approved Correa's call for a referendum to convoke a new constituent assembly, but inserted an article declaring that it could not dissolve the existing Congress (Buckman 2013, 184). The Supreme Electoral Tribunal—composed of Correa's supporters—ruled that the upcoming assembly would indeed be all powerful and sovereign. In retaliation, Congress dismissed the head of the Electoral Tribunal and five of its members. In an unprecedented move, the Electoral Tribunal removed from Congress the fifty-seven representatives who had voted to dismiss its president. More shockingly even, the

Constitutional Tribunal upheld the removal of members of Congress. Those who came to replace the ejected members of Congress turned out to be more compliant with Correa's demands, and the referendum, on the terms that Correa wanted, was allowed to proceed. As in Venezuela, a plebiscite (held on April 15, 2007) legitimatized the call for a new constitutional assembly. Elections for the actual assembly were held on September 30, 2007, and Correa's supporters secured 80 of the 130 seats. As soon as it was inaugurated, the assembly "suspended indefinitely" the Congress and removed a number of high-level officials, including the general attorney. Soon thereafter, both Correa and his vice-president resigned before the assembly and were subsequently reappointed by it. In this fashion, and with the complicity of those who were supposed to defend the 1998 constitution, Correa drastically changed the rules of the game. The new constitution gave him the right to run for immediate reelection.

Correa ran for reelection in 2009. The electoral contest was generally uneventful, and most observers expected an easy victory for the charismatic president. Indeed, on April 26, 2009, voters reelected him with 52 percent of the vote. Correa's plebiscitary presidency (Conaghan 2008) finally put an end to the period of political instability that had started in 1996. But Correa's second term showed that his intent was not to deepen Ecuador's democracy, but to undermine it. His attacks against the media have been relentless, and Correa has used a compliant judiciary in his efforts to silence critical press. The notorious cases of *El Universo* newspaper and journalists Juan Carlos Calderón and Christian Zurita sent a message to independent journalists that his government will not tolerate open criticism. The Committee to Protect Journalists (2011) wrote that Correa "has led Ecuador into a new era of widespread repression by pre-empting private news broadcasts, enacting restrictive legal measures, smearing critics, and filing debilitating defamation lawsuits." Correa's authoritarian traits increased as he faced increasing opposition. In September 2010 he confronted a police strike protesting what they considered a reduction in pay. Correa framed the revolt as a coup after he was detained in a police hospital, where he had been taken into protective custody to treat him for respiratory distress caused by tear gas. He also attacked and clashed with many of the social movements that initially supported him (de la Torre 2013). Anticipating a higher degree of contestation in the 2013 presidential election, the Correa-controlled legislature passed a new electoral law in 2012. The new legislation severely restricted the media from directly or indirectly promoting a candidate or issue. As Buckman (2013, 186) notes, "newspapers could not endorse a candidate, or criticize one, which are hallmarks of a free press in any democracy. Another provision . . . prohibits private citizens or companies from buying political advertising for 90 days before an election."

With the media severely curtailed and all branches of government—including the electoral board—under his control, Correa started campaigning for his second reelection in early 2013. His popularity was very high (bordering on 80 percent before the election), and he used the windfalls of oil to provide welfare benefits to almost one-third of the country (Buckman 2013, 187). For a brief moment, it seemed that Guillermo Lasso, an independent banker, could mount a serious electoral challenge. In the end, however, Correa prevailed with 57.7 percent of the vote. Even if he does not complete his third term in 2017, he is already the longest-serving president in Ecuador's history. The new electoral law has given him a solid majority in the unicameral Congress, transforming the 52 percent of his party's congressional vote into 73 percent of the seats. It is hard not to agree with de la Torre's (2013, 45) conclusion that "[u]nder Correa, democracy has been reduced to voting in elections that are held on an uneven playing field and without independent oversight."

Bolivia

Morales followed a similar path in Bolivia, but his efforts to reshape its politics ran into serious initial opposition. Morales came to power in 2006 after winning an historic election with 54 percent of the vote, thus sparing him the need to go through congressional confirmation—a first since Bolivia's return to democracy in 1982. Morales has led a solid party that has deep roots in the shantytowns that surround La Paz, as well as in the countryside, especially in the coca-growing areas. His MAS party also includes some civil society organizations. In this sense, Morales' government enjoys an organizational strength that was not available to Bucaram and Correa in Ecuador, Fujimori in Peru, or Chávez in Venezuela. As such, his rule is less personalistic and more bounded by intermediate organizations.

With that said, Morales' government exudes the confrontational mentality, exaltation of leadership, appeals to mechanisms of direct democracy, and disregard for institutional checks and balances that one can find in Ecuador and Venezuela today. Evo Morales espouses a nationalistic discourse, but his brand of nationalism, as Mayorga (2006, 10) notes, is heavily influenced by ethnic components. Thus, as Mayorga further argues, there is an inherent tension in Morales' government between its nationalistic and its indigenist rhetoric.

Morales shares other key components of populism. Soon after his overwhelming election, he pushed for the convocation of a constitutional assembly. Congress approved this request, but—cognizant of the situation in Venezuela—established that a qualified two-thirds majority would be required to approve articles of the constitution. When MAS failed to achieve a two-thirds majority in the new assembly, Morales' supporters pushed for a new regulation that would only require a 51 percent majority to approve new articles. Such blatant disregard for the existing rules of the game precipitated a dramatic political crisis. Representatives of the southern and eastern lowland regions (Santa Cruz, Tarija, Pando, and Beni) along with the representation of PODEMOS, the most important opposition party, decided to boycott the proceedings, thus paralyzing the assembly. The dispute deepened even more as residents of Sucre, where the constitutional assembly was meeting, demanded that their city be declared Bolivia's capital. After a year or so of virtual inactivity, the

184 of Julio F. Carrión

MAS forces approved a draft of the constitution in a night-long session, with members of the opposition absent. Again, the strong-arm machinations were denounced by the opposition and, in protest, the lowland regions convoked regional plebiscites to approve autonomy. One after another, massive votes supported the demands for autonomy in these regions, challenging the unity of the state. There was a new constitutional document but no agreement to proceed with its electoral ratification.

The Morales administration once again appealed to mechanisms of direct democracy to keep the upper hand. It convoked a recall election, not only for Evo Morales and his vice-president, but also for the governors of all departments, including the ones that demand autonomy. Morales received a sizeable endorsement at the August 2008 polls, with 67.4 percent of the voters ratifying his rule. Two of the opposition governors were recalled and quickly replaced with Morales' supporters. With renewed political capital, Morales pushed his new constitution by calling for a referendum on the document. But the opposition refused to follow and called for a national strike on the date that Morales had selected for the plebiscite. The turning point in the political stalemate came in the wake of the event known as the Pando massacre. On the night of September 11, 2008, opposition and government supporters clashed in the town of Porvenir (Pando Department) and as a result fifteen people were killed and thirty-seven wounded. Morales accused the Pando governor—a prominent opposition leader—of being behind the attack. The Morales administration not only arrested him and other opposition leaders, but also declared a state of emergency (martial law) in the department, appointing a new governor. This confrontation weakened the opposition, as many rejected the lethal violence employed against supporters of President Morales (Gray Molina 2013). Eventually, Morales and the opposition reached a compromise on some articles of the new constitution and agreed to hold a referendum to ratify the document. The referendum, held on January 25, 2009, approved the new constitution with 61.4 percent of the vote.

The new constitution enhanced presidential powers; allowed for immediate reelection; removed the old practice of having Congress choose the president if no candidate secured a majority, establishing a runoff election instead; and expanded the presidential term from four to five years (Mayorga 2010). But before the next presidential election was held, a new electoral law was needed. The MAS party wanted to reserve fourteen seats for indigenous representation and give Bolivians living abroad the right to vote in presidential elections. The opposition rejected these provisos and demanded instead a new electoral roll, a demand rejected by Morales. Fearing that the scheduled presidential election on December 6, 2009, was in jeopardy due to the lack of an electoral law, Morales went on a hunger strike on April 9, 2009, demanding congressional action on the new electoral law. Eventually, a compromised was reached and elections proceeded accordingly. As expected, Morales cruised to reelection in December 2009, obtaining 64.2 percent of the vote, and his party secured 88 out of 130 seats in the lower house and 26 out of the 36 senate seats (Buckman

2013, 76). For the first time ever, a president in Bolivia gained a second term while in office.

With the newly gained momentum, Morales moved quickly to assert total control of the political system. Unlike the cases of Ecuador and Venezuela, where the regime's supporters were able to appoint new judicial officers outright, the constituent assembly in Bolivia did not have the power to reorganize the judicial branch. To achieve this goal, Morales wrote in the constitution that fifty-six members of the Supreme Court, the Constitutional Tribunal, the Agro-environmental Tribunal, and the Council of Magistrates (the executive office of the judiciary in charge of the hiring and firing of judges) would be elected by voters. Having a national election to select the top echelons of the judicial branch is unusual enough, but to this Morales added a twist: all candidates would have to be selected by Congress (where Morales has an overwhelming majority) and parties would be prevented from endorsing candidates. In fact, neither polls nor campaigns were allowed for this peculiar election. The opposition tactic was to boycott the election, hoping to diminish the legitimacy of the new judges. While the opposition succeeded in undermining the legitimacy of the election, as the void and blank votes outnumbered the valid votes (only 41 percent of the casted ballots were declared valid), they could not prevent the election of the fifty-six judges preferred by the Morales administration.

As in the case of Ecuador, Morales has encountered difficulties in dealing with some of his own supporters. On December 26, 2010, he announced the removal of state subsidies to hydrocarbons, liberalizing prices for diesel and gasoline, which increased by 73 and 82 percent, respectively. Massive mobilizations led by the Bolivian Workers' Central and other organizations ensued, which forced the resignation of some of Morales' ministers. A few days later, Morales backpedaled and announced the repeal of the decree (Gray Molina 2013, 162). Another confrontation with his base occurred as a result of his decision to build a highway through the Isiboro-Secure National Park. Indigenous communities living in the park protested that they were not previously consulted on the road project (as the new constitution required) and started marching toward La Paz. When David Choquehuanca, minister of foreign affairs, went to negotiate with the protestors, he was detained and forced to march with them. After his release, the protestors were violently repressed by the police, ending the march. A serious rift in the government followed, producing "a third wave of political splintering inside the MAS coalition. MAS indigenous deputies threatened to abandon the party and take with them the two-thirds majority votes required for a filibuster-proof majority in the assembly" (Gray Molina 2013, 164).

In late April 2013, the Constitutional Tribunal, composed of the members selected by the pro-Morales assembly and elected with only 41 percent of valid votes, unanimously ruled that Morales was entitled to seek an additional term in the December 2014 election. The reasoning was that the 2009 constitution created a new state in Bolivia and therefore any previous presidential terms did not count for the two-term limit imposed by the constitution. It is clear that the new judiciary, packed now with Morales supporters, does not seem inclined to offer meaningful checks to his power. This is a problematic ruling that could bring Bolivia closer to the electoral authoritarian governments found in Venezuela and Ecuador. It remains to be seen whether the coalition that brought Morales to power in 2006 will stay intact and whether the authoritarian tendencies will deepen. General elections were held on October 12, 2014, and Morales was reelected with 61 percent of the vote, also obtaining a solid majority in Congress. Bolivia is currently enjoying an economic bonanza generated by the export of natural gas.

The Resilience of Democracy in Peru and Colombia

While Bolivia, Ecuador, and Venezuela have significantly damaged the foundations of liberal democracy, post-Fujimori Peru and contemporary Colombia show a countervailing trend. The explosive revelations of corruption led to the rapid demise of the Fujimori regime in Peru. Congress removed him from office after Fujimori had faxed his resignation from Japan. After a short interim government, Peruvians went to the polls and elected Alejandro Toledo for the period 2001–2006. Toledo had led the opposition to Fujimori, and his party, Perú Posible, grew as a result. A man of humble origins and Andean background, he went on to get a Ph.D. in Stanford. Toledo confronted Alan García, who had presided over Peru between 1985 and 1990, and was the leader of Peru's oldest and strongest party. Toledo won the runoff election with 52.7 percent of the vote, winning the majority of Peru's twenty-five departments.

Toledo continued the free-market economic policies of *fujimorismo*, but clearly set Peru into a more democratic path by embracing political pluralism, seeking to clean up the remnants of the Fujimori influence in the army and the judiciary, although with mixed success. His government was received with widespread enthusiasm, but soon his political mistakes led to increasing discontent. By the midpoint of his administration, his approval rate was in the single digits. Although his popularity recovered somewhat toward the end of this presidency, he left office with the perception that his government was a lost opportunity. But Peru did improve both politically and economically during his five-year term. After a difficult first year, Peru's economy grew at impressive rates, setting the stage for what would eventually be the decade of strongest economic growth of the last half-century. Politically, Peru moved from the "partially free" status of the Fujimori years to "free" during the Toledo administration (according to Freedom House). Perhaps St. John (2010, 186) summarizes this administration best when he writes: "Much went right between 2001 and 2006, and much went wrong." Some of the problems of Toledo's administration were due to the fact that Peru really lacks political parties, and Toledo's organization was clearly unprepared for the task of governing (Tanaka 2005). What is undisputable, however, is that when Peruvians went back to the polls to elect a new president in 2006, nobody questioned the cleanliness and fairness of the vote.

The 2006 contest exposed the deep rifts in Peruvian society. Initially, the race pitted two different visions of Peru. On the left, Ollanta Humala, leader of the newly created Partido Nationalista (Nationalist Party), who embraced a Chávez-like rhetoric and promised the "great transformation" of Peru by rejecting the "neoliberal" economic model and revising the free trade agreement with the United States. On the right, Lourdes Flores Nano, leader of the right-wing Popular Christian Party, who exalted the benefits of the economic policy and promised more growth. Surprisingly, however, Alan García at the end was able to nudge Flores Nano from second place, thus earning a spot in the runoff election scheduled for June 4, 2006. According to Vergara (2007, 100), García was able to achieve this feat because he represented a moderate option, occupying the midpoint between the two extremes of Humala and Flores Nano. At the end, García carried the election with 52.6 percent of the vote, but won only eleven (mostly coastal) of Peru's twenty-five departments, while Humala swept the Andean and Amazonian departments.

Alan García's second term enjoyed an unprecedented record of economic growth only briefly affected by the 2008 global meltdown. Perhaps as a way of overcompensating for his disastrous populist first term, García chose to govern from the right (Cameron 2011, 388). He left the economic model untouched, did not increase social spending, and struck alliances with the right-wing National Unity party. Although poverty rates declined during his administration, they did so more as a result of the impressive growth of the economy than any targeted social policy (Cameron 2011, 389). Political democracy continued strong during García's second term (Freedom House kept rating Peru as a "free" country), but severe institutional weaknesses, especially related to the performance of the state bureaucracy and the judiciary, persisted. Public opinion polls show the pervasive political discontent that affects many Peruvians, despite the years of economic growth (Carrión 2009). Levitsky (2013, 286) concludes that "[w]ith ample resources and relative political stability, García had an extraordinary opportunity to combat some of the structural problems that have long plagued Peruvian democracy, such as social inequality and state weakness. Yet, he did not."

The 2011 presidential contest was Toledo's to lose, and his arrogance and inept campaign managed to do so. Toledo's electoral debacle forced Peruvians to choose between Humala and Keiko Fujimori, daughter and political heiress of the fallen dictator. Moving to the center and securing the endorsement of Toledo and other democratic personalities, Humala was able to attract the Lima voters that had rejected him in 2006, thus securing a victory with 51.4 percent in the June 2011 runoff election.

Humala, however, seems to have taken a page of the García playbook. Although initially he formed a government with prominent center-left figures, he has since taken a more conservative turn. Even though he ran on promises of addressing issues of social inclusion and inequality, his policies have not delivered on these pledges. His presidential approval has tumbled as a consequence, barely reaching 26 percent in October 2013. Surprisingly, given Peru's tradition of populism (McClintock 2013), there are no indications that Humala will try to regain public support by embracing a populist path. Although the export-led boom seems to have slowed down, the economy continues to grow at a brisk pace. According to the International Monetary Fund (2014), Peru's GDP grew 5.8 percent in 2013, the third fastest in South America, and it is expected to grow 3.6 percent in 2014. Humala does not seem interested in upsetting this impressive growth. Peru's democracy after the Fujimori years has endured, and it is now approaching the longest-lived period of democratic rule in the country's history (Levitsky 2013, 308). But as Levitsky himself notes, Peruvian democratic institutions are precarious despite the good economic times. A few years ago, I wrote (Carrión 2009, 39) that

> Peru's crisis of public confidence underscores the need to see beyond economics as the sole cause, or cure, of political problems. For too long, decision makers have been obsessed with issues of economic stabilization and growth, all the while neglecting the serious deficit of citizen trust.

In the past, Peruvian democracy suffered because of the irresponsibility of its leaders in managing economic affairs. Today, there is a real danger that Peru's democracy is threatening the elites' excessive preoccupation with macroeconomic stability, neglecting issues of citizen security, social inclusion, and income inequality, which could open the door to anti-systemic actors.

Democracy in Colombia has also survived—even thrived—in the midst of serious challenges. The bipartisan agreements that produced the institutional rigidities that provided the death knell for democracy in Venezuela were instead addressed institutionally in Colombia. It is true that the two-party system in Colombia was never as rigid as the one established in Venezuela (Taylor 2009), but the growing political violence, the increasing citizen dissatisfaction, and the demands for political reform led to the constitutional reform of 1991. The new constitution established a runoff system to guarantee the election of the president by an absolute majority and provided for a more representative senate, with seats reserved for indigenous people and Afro-Americans (Taylor 2009, 89). The 2003 electoral reform introduced significant changes in the system, replacing the Hare quota with the D'Hondt method and creating a hybrid system of open and closed lists (Botero and Rodríguez 2009, 52).

The erosion of the two-party system received its final blow with the election of Álvaro Uribe in 2002. Although not a political outsider (he had been both a governor of the state of Antioquia and senator of the Republic for the Liberal Party), he contested the president as an independent and became the first elected president of recent history who was not the official candidate of either the Liberal or the Conservative party. Uribe made "democratic security" the centerpiece of his campaign. Mason (2003, 392–93) provides some staggering indicators of the security crisis that Colombia faced: there were 5,000 deaths in 2002 as a result of the armed conflict, and two-thirds of the fatalities were civilians; there were over 28,500 homicides that year. In 2002, Mason claims (2003), over 412,000 were displaced by conflict-related violence. Not surprisingly, some began to wonder whether Colombia was on the brink of state failure (DeShazo, Mendelson Forman, and McLean 2009, 10).

Uribe was able to quickly build the authority and capacity of the state to control its territory and protect its citizens. Immediately after taking office, he declared a "state of internal commotion" to issue security-related decrees for an initial period of ninety days (Mason 2003, 397). He also established a one-time-only security tax. The additional resources allowed him to increase the size of the armed forces, which grew by almost 39 percent between 2002 and 2009 (DeShazo, Mendelson Forman, and McLean 2009, 20). The number of professional soldiers increased at even higher rate, from 55,000 in 2002 to 86,000 in 2009 (idem).

As part of his "democratic security," Uribe negotiated a demobilization agreement with the AUC, the main paramilitary organization, which declared a unilateral cease-fire at the end of 2002 (Crandall 2005, 177). A more permanent demobilization happened after the enactment of the 2005 Law of Justice and Peace, which provided a series of benefits (reduced sentences and even amnesty) to the members of paramilitary groups who chose to cease violent activities. This law was criticized by many human rights organizations that claimed it codified impunity. But the results of Uribe's security in reconstituting the authority and capacity of the state were impressive and he was rewarded with very high approval rates.

During his first electoral campaign, Uribe promised that one of his first acts of government would be the convocation of a referendum to approve constitutional reforms against corruption and "*politiquería*" (crass politicking). Uribe, in compliance with the constitution, submitted a bill to Congress that included fifteen questions aimed at reforming certain political practices. The proposed reforms

> included the establishment of a smaller, unicameral legislature; the elimination of alternate delegates (*suplentes*) in the legislature; the requirement of nominal voting in all elected legislative bodies; the abolition of discretionary funds (*auxilios*) used as patronage by politicians; and the strengthening of conditions under which a member of Congress could be removed from office.
>
> (Dugas 2003, 1131–32)

In quite a contrast with the Venezuelan, Ecuadorian, and Bolivian cases, the Colombian Congress did not passively adopt the president's proposal. As Dugas (idem) notes, Congress struck down Uribe's proposal for a unicameral Congress, as well as the possibility of convoking a new Congress before 2006. After congressional approval, the referendum questions were examined by the Constitutional Court, which made further changes in the questions. Uribe had no choice but to accept the final version that eventually came out of the legislative and judicial process. In the end, although voters overwhelmingly favored the questions posed to them in the October 25, 2003, referendum, the reforms could not be enacted because not enough voters showed up to cast a ballot (a 25 percent turnout was required).

The enabling of immediate reelection in Bolivia, Ecuador, Peru, and Venezuela came as a result of a radical remaking of constitutional rules. By contrast, the process that led to the 2006 reelection of Uribe happened under significantly different conditions. A group of pro-Uribe senators introduced a proposal in March 2004 to enable the immediate reelection of both the president and the vice-president. After heated debate in the chambers, a final bill entitled Legislative Act No. 2 of 2004 was approved in December of that year, approving the possibility of reelection. After its passage, the Constitutional Court subjected it to judicial review. Jaime Bermúdez, Uribe's main advisor for communication, wrote later that the court was very close to rejecting the act outright. There was a political tiff with the minister of the interior, who had declared that there were "perverse wishes" against the reelection and alerted that "if the reelection was not sanctioned by the Constitutional Court, the government would not take it quietly" (Bermúdez 2010, 240). In an official response, the court lamented any insinuation of bias and reiterated its commitment to render a verdict with independence and according to the rule of law (idem). Eventually, the Constitutional Court allowed immediate reelection, but it also established a set of rules to regulate the activities of the incumbent during the campaign. Soon thereafter, the Colombian Congress enacted a Law of Guarantees, establishing procedures that the incumbent needed to abide by in seeking reelection, including limits to campaign contributions and providing a set of rights and guarantees to the opposition. Uribe was reelected with 62 percent of the vote in 2006, and no complaints of electoral improprieties were raised.

While the constitutional reform enabling presidential reelection has negatively impacted the balance between the executive and the other branches of government established by the 1991 constitution by giving the president greater powers (Pachón 2010, 65–7; Botero, Hoskin, and Pachón 2010, 59–60), both Congress and the Constitutional Court continue to act as effective checks on presidential power. When Uribe's supporters approved a new law in Congress calling for a referendum that could enable a second reelection, the Constitutional Court—despite Uribe's overwhelming public approval—declared the law unconstitutional. As Posada-Carbó (2011, 138) acknowledges, Uribe "had not much of a choice" as "the Constitutional Court had ruled against some Uribe administration measures, and the president—like his predecessors—had accepted the adverse judgments as valid and lawful." This ruling ended the possibility of a populist regime in Colombia.

Juan Manuel Santos, member of Uribe's party and former minister of defense, was elected president in a landslide, winning 69.1 percent of the vote in the runoff election held on June 20, 2010. His government has initiated peace talks with the FARC guerrillas, and at this writing there is a good possibility that an historic agreement can be reached, thus ending the longest conflict in the Western Hemisphere. Although many, especially former President Uribe, criticized Santos for this peace initiative, he was able to secure reelection in a runoff contest held on June 15, 2014. In September of that year, Santos introduced a constitutional reform in Congress to end presidential reelections in Colombia.

Conclusion

Populism, as it has been shown here, exerts a strong attraction in the Andes. Presidents of different political persuasions and varying commitments to democracy often resort to this type of political representation. The persistence of populism reflects the frailties of the region's political institutions, but it is also a cause of them. The personalistic style of leadership, the distrust of checks and balances, the use of electoral majorities to undermine institutions, and the confrontational mentality that it fosters make populism a clear threat to democracy. Andean democracies are too frequently blind to the demands and hopes of the poor and the indigenous. Populist leaders thus appear as the only ones who really care about them. It is by addressing the poverty and inequality that plague the Andes that one could hope to diminish the appeal of those who claim that a "quick fix" for the poor is available if only they could have all the power.

Bolivia, Ecuador, and Venezuela are still embarked, with varying degrees, in the populist project. Evo Morales faced the most stringent opposition to his desires to change the rules of the game, and although he now enjoys the upper hand, he is facing opposition from some of his own supporters as he tries to balance the realities of free market policies with social demands. But his regime is, at least so far, eschewing the worst authoritarian practices found in Ecuador and Venezuela. Rafael Correa is increasingly looking more like a thin-skinned *caudillo* with socially conservative values than a twenty-first-century transformational figure. He has alienated many of his former supporters and has harshly criticized environmental and indigenous leaders. In Venezuela, Maduro is struggling to contain what seems to be the inevitable collapse of a regime condemned by its own corruption and economic mismanagement. Populism may endure for a while, but it has certainly lost the momentum and allure that it once had. It increasingly looks more like established power than rebellious movement.

Andean nations, as the case of Colombia and post-Fujimori Peru show, are not fatalistically destined to endure populism. When political actors and elites, those running the congresses, electoral boards, and judiciaries—the institutions that embody checks and balances—resist the cries for "quick fixes," democracy can survive. The Colombia experience under Uribe shows that even a phenomenally popular president can be checked when those in charge of defending the constitution decide to do so. All too frequently, the rise of populism is blamed on the strong mass support that some presidents elicit. But we tend to forget that it is not "the masses" who declare constitutions defunct by agreeing to let plebiscites proceed. Those who hide behind "the popular will" to let presidents undermine the liberal foundations of their countries deserve as much blame for the rise of populism as the presidents who seek to aggrandize their power. Mass approval may trigger the populist temptation, but it is ultimately in the behavior of elites where we need to look to understand the success of populist presidents in undermining democracy.

Note

* This chapter is a significantly revised and updated version of "The Persistent Attraction of Populism in the Andes," which appeared in the first edition of this book. I thank Lauren Balasco for her research assistance.

References

Abts, K. and Rummens, S. (2007) "Populism versus Democracy." *Political Studies* 55: 405–24.

Albertazzi, D. and McDonnell, D. (2008) *Twenty-First Century Populism and the Spectre of Western European Democracy*. London: Palgrave Macmillan.

Anderson, R., Fish, M.S., Hanson, S., and Roeder, P. (2001) *Postcommunism and the Theory of Democracy*. Princeton, NJ: Princeton University Press.

Arditi, B. (2007) *Politics on the Edges of Liberalism. Difference, Populism, Revolution, Agitation*. Edinburgh: Edinburgh University Press.

Aveledo, R. (2010) "Consecuencias Institucionales de la Presidencia de Hugo Chávez" in F. Ramos Pismataro, C.A. Romero, and H.E. Ramírez Arcos (eds.), *Hugo Chávez: Una Década en el Poder*. Bogotá: Editorial Universidad del Rosario.

Barr, R. (2009) "Populists, Outsiders and Anti-Establishment Politics." *Party Politics* 15: 29–48.

Bermúdez, J. (2010) *La Audacia del Poder: Momentos Claves del Primer Gobierno de Uribe Contado por uno de sus Protagonistas*. Bogota: Planeta.

Boas, T. (2005) "Television and Neopopulism in Latin America: Media Effects in Brazil and Peru." *Latin American Research Review* 40: 27–49.

Botero, F., Hoskin, G., and Pachón, M. (2010) "Sobre Forma y Sustancia: Una Evaluación de la Democracia Electoral en Colombia". *Revista de Ciencia Política* 30: 41–64.

Botero, F. and Rodríguez, J.C. (2009) "Grande no es Sinónimo de Fuerte. Los Partidos y la Reforma Política", in M. Tanaka (ed.), *La Nueva Coyuntura Crítica en los Países Andinos*. Lima: IEP-IDEA.

Briceño-León, R., Camardiel, A., and Avila, O. (2012) *Violencia e Institucionalidad. Informe del Observatorio Venezolano de Violencia 2012*. Caracas: Editorial Alfa.

Buckman, R. (2013) *The World Today Series 2013. Latin America. 47th Edition*. Lanham. MD: Stryker-Post Publications.

Burbano de Lara, F. (ed.) (1998) *El Fantasma del Populismo: Aproximación a un Tema (Siempre) Actual*. Caracas: Nueva Sociedad.

Cameron, M. (2011) "Peru: The Left Turn That Wasn't," in S. Levitsky and K.M. Roberts (eds.), *The Resurgence of the Latin American Left*. Baltimore: The Johns Hopkins University Press.

Cammack, P. (2000) "The Resurgence of Populism in Latin America." *Bulletin of Latin American Research* 19: 149–61.

Canovan, M. (1999) "Trust the People! Populism and the Two Faces of Democracy." *Political Studies* 47:2–16.

Canovan, M. (2005) *The People*. Cambridge: Polity Press.

Carrión, J.F. (1997) "La Transformación de la Opinión Pública Peruana Bajo el Primer Gobierno de Fujimori: ¿De identidades a intereses?" in F. Tuesta Solvedilla (ed.), *Los Enigmas del Poder*. Lima: Fundación Friedrich Ebert.

Carrión, J.F. (2006) "Public Opinion, Market Reforms, and Democracy in Fujimori's Peru," in J.F. Carrión (ed.), *The Fujimori Legacy: The Rise of Electoral Authoritarianism in Peru*. University Park, PA: Pennsylvania State University Press.

Carrión, J.F. (2009) "Peru's Confidence Gap." *Americas Quarterly* 3: 35–9.

Carrión, J.F. (2013) "Understanding Populist Governance: The Andes in Comparative Perspective." Presented at the Annual Meeting of the American Political Science Association, Chicago.

Carroll . R. (2013) *Comandante. Hugo Chávez's Venezuela*. New York: The Penguin Press.

Collier, D. (ed.) (1979) *The New Authoritarianism in Latin America*. Princeton, NJ: Princeton University Press.

Collier, D. and Mahon, J. (1993) "Conceptual 'Stretching' Revisited: Adapting Categories in Comparative Analysis." *American Political Science Review* 87: 845–55.

Combellas, R. (2010) "La Venezuela de la V República: La Reforma Política y sus Implicancias Institucionales", in M. Tanaka and F. Jácome (eds.), *Desafíos de la Gobernabilidad Democrática. Reformas Político-Institucionales y Movimientos Sociales en la Región Andina*. Lima: IEP, IDRC-CRDI, INVESP.

Committee to Protect Journalists (2011) *Confrontation, Repression in Correa's Ecuador. A Special Report by the Committee to Protect Journalists*. Available at http://cpj.org/reports/CPJ.Ecuador.9.1.11.pdf. Accessed 11/1/2014.

Conaghan, C.M. (2005) *Fujimori's Peru: Deception in the Public Sphere*. Pittsburgh, PA: University of Pittsburgh Press.

Conaghan, C.M. (2008) "Ecuador: Correa's Plebiscitary Presidency." *Journal of Democracy* 19: 46–60.

Conaghan, C.M. and Malloy, J. (1994) *Unsettling Statecraft: Democracy and Neoliberalism in the Central Andes*. Pittsburgh, PA: University of Pittsburgh Press.

Coppedge, M. (2003) "Venezuela. Popular Sovereignty versus Liberal Democracy," in J.I. Domínguez and M. Shifter (eds.), *Constructing Democratic Governance in Latin America. Second Edition*. Baltimore and London: The Johns Hopkins University Press.

Corrales, J. and Penfold, M. (2007) "Venezuela: Crowding Out the Opposition." *Journal of Democracy* 18: 99–113.

Corrales, J. and Penfold, M (2011) *Dragon in the Tropics: Hugo Chávez and the Political Economy of Revolution in Venezuela*. Washington, D.C.: Brookings Institution Press.

Crandall, R. (2005) "From Drugs to Security: A New U.S. Policy Toward Colombia," in R. Crandall, G. Paz, and R. Roett (eds.), *The Andes in Focus: Security, Democracy and Economic Reform*. Boulder and London: Lynne Rienner Publishers.

de la Torre, C. (1999) "Neopopulism in Contemporary Ecuador: The Case of Bucaram's Use of the Mass Media." *International Journal of Politics, Culture, and Society* 12: 555–71.

de la Torre, C. (2010) *Populist Seduction in Latin America. Second Edition*. OH: Ohio University Research in International Studies.

de la Torre, C. (2013) "Technocratic Populism in Ecuador." *Journal of Democracy* 24: 33–46.

de la Torre, C. and Arnson, C.J. (eds.) (2013) *Latin American Populism in the Twenty-First Century*. Washington, D.C. and Baltimore: Woodrow Wilson Center Press—The Johns Hopkins University Press.

de la Torre, C. and Peruzzotti, E. (eds.) (2008) *El Retorno del Pueblo: Populismo y Nuevas Democracias en América Latina*. Quito: FLACSO Ecuador.

de Shazo, P., Mendelson Forman, J., and McLean, P. (2009) *Countering Threats to Security and Stability in a Failing State: Lessons from Colombia*. Washington, D.C.: Center for Strategic & International Studies.

Degregori, C.I. (1990) *El Surgimiento de Sendero Luminoso: Ayacucho 1969–1979*. Lima: Instituto de Estudios Peruanos.

Dornbusch, R. and Edwards, S. (eds.) (1991) *The Macroeconomics of Populism in Latin America*. Chicago: University of Chicago Press.

Dugas, J. (2003) "The Emergence of Neopopulism in Colombia? The Case of Álvaro Uribe." *Third World Quarterly* 24: 1117–36.

Gerlach, A. (2003) *Indians, Oil, and Politics: A Recent History of Ecuador*. Wilmington, DE: Scholarly Resources.

Goertz, G. (2006) *Social Science Concepts: A User's Guide*. Princeton and Oxford: Princeton University Press.

Gray Molina, G. (2013) "Bolivia: Keeping the Coalition Together," in J.I. Domínguez and M. Shifter (eds.), *Constructing Democratic Governance in Latin America. Fourth Edition*. Baltimore: The Johns Hopkins University Press.

Grindle, M. (2003) "Shadowing the Past? Policy Reform in Bolivia, 1985–2002," in M. Grindle and P. Domingo (eds.), *Proclaiming Revolution: Bolivia in Comparative Perspective*. Cambridge, MA and London: Institute of Latin American Studies, University of London, and David Rockefeller Center for Latin American Studies, Harvard University.

Guerrero, A. (1996) "El Levantamiento Indígena de 1994. Discurso y Representación Política en Ecuador". *Nueva Sociedad* 142: 32–43.

Hawkins, K. (2003) "Populism in Venezuela: The Rise of Chavismo." *Third World Quarterly* 24: 1137–60.

Hawkins, K. (2010) *Venezuela's Chavismo and Populism in Comparative Perspective*. Cambridge: Cambridge University Press.

Hermet, G., Loaeza, S., and Prud'homme, J.F. (eds.) (2001) *Del populismo de los antiguos al populismo de los modernos*. Mexico: El Colegio de México.

International Monetary Fund. (2014) *Regional Economic Outlook Update*. Western Hemisphere Department. Fall. Available at www.imf.org/external/pubs/ft/reo/2014/whd/eng/pdf/wreo1014.pdf. Accessed 11/1/14.

Ionescu, G. and Gellner, E. (eds.) (1969) *Populism. Its Meaning and National Characteristics*. New York: Macmillan Company.

Kenney, C. (2004) *Fujimori's Coup and the Breakdown of Democracy in Latin America*. Notre Dame, IN: University of Notre Dame Press.

Knight, A. (1998) "Populism and Neo-populism in Latin America. Especially Mexico." *Journal of Latin American Studies* 30: 223–48.

Kornblith, M. (2013) "Chavismo After Chávez?" *Journal of Politics* 24: 47–61.

Laclau, E. (2005) *On Populist Reason*. London: Verso.

Levitsky, S. (2013) "Peru: The Challenges of a Democracy without Parties," in J.I. Domínguez and M. Shifter (eds.), *Constructing Democratic Governance in Latin America. Fourth Edition*. Baltimore: The Johns Hopkins University Press.

López Maya, M. and Lander, L.E. (2004) "The Struggle for Hegemony in Venezuela: Poverty, Popular Protest, and the Future of Democracy," in J.M. Burt and P. Mauceri (eds.), *Politics in the Andes: Identity, Conflict, Reform.* Pittsburgh, PA: University of Pittsburgh Press.

Malloy, J. (ed.) (1977) *Authoritarianism and Corporatism in Latin America.* Pittsburgh, PA: University of Pittsburgh Press.

Malloy, J. and Gamarra, E. (1988) *Revolution and Reaction: Bolivia, 1964–1985.* New Brunswick, NJ: Transaction Books.

Mason, A. (2003) "Colombia's Democratic Security Agenda: Public Order in the Security Tripod." *Security Dialogue* 34: 391–409.

Mayorga, F. (2006) "El Gobierno de Evo Morales: Entre Nacionalismo e Indigenismo". *Nueva Sociedad* 206: 4–13.

Mayorga, R.A. (2006) "Outsiders and Neopopulism: The Road to Plebiscitary Democracy," in Mainwaring, S., Bejarano, A.M., and Pizarro Leongómez, E. (eds.), *The Crisis of Democratic Representation in the Andes.* Stanford, CA: Stanford University Press.

Mayorga, F. (2010) "Bolivia: El Azaroso Camino de la Reforma Política", in M. Tanaka and F. Jácome (eds.), *Desafíos de la Gobernabilidad Democrática. Reformas Político-Institucionales y Movimientos Sociales en la Región Andina.* Lima: IEP, IDRC-CRDI, INVESP.

McClintock, C. (2013) "Populism in Peru: From APRA to Ollanta Humala," in de la Torre, C. and Arnson, C.J. (eds.), *Latin American Populism in the Twenty-First Century.* Washington, D.C. and Baltimore: Woodrow Wilson Center Press—The Johns Hopkins University Press.

McCoy, J. and Myers, D. (eds.) (2004) *The Unraveling of Representative Democracy in Venezuela.* Baltimore, MD: Johns Hopkins University Press.

Mudde, C. (2004) "The Populist Zeitgeist." *Government and Opposition* 39: 541–63.

Navia, P. and Walker, I. (2008) "Political Institutions, Populism, and Democracy in Latin America," in S. Mainwaring and T. Scully (eds.), *Democratic Governance in Latin America.* Stanford, CA: Stanford University Press.

North, L. (2004) "State Building, State Dismantling, and Financial Crises in Ecuador," in J.M. Burt and P. Mauceri (eds.), *Politics in the Andes: Identity, Conflict, Reform.* Pittsburgh, PA: University of Pittsburgh Press.

Novaro, M. (1996) "Los Populismos Latinoamericanos Transfigurados". *Nueva Sociedad* 144: 90–103.

O'Donnell, G. (1994) "Delegative Democracy." *Journal of Democracy* 5:55–69.

Orias Arredondo, R. (2005) "Bolivia: Democracy under Pressure," in R. Crandall, G. Paz, and R. Roett (eds.), *The Andes in Focus: Security, Democracy, and Economic Reform.* Boulder, CO, and London: Lynne Rienner Publishers.

Pachón, M. (2010) "Reforma Institucional en Colombia: el via Crucis por el Equilibrio entre la Gobernabilidad y la Representación (1991–2006)", in M. Tanaka and F. Jácome (eds.), *Desafíos de la Gobernabilidad Democrática. Reformas Político-Institucionales y Movimientos Sociales en la Región Andina.* Lima: IEP, IDRC-CRDI, INVESP.

Palacios, M. and Stoller, R. (2006) *Between Legitimacy and Violence: A History of Colombia.* Durham, NC: Duke University Press.

Palmer, D.S. (1994) *The Shining Path of Peru.* New York: St. Martin's Press.

Panfichi, A. (1997) "The Authoritarian Alternative: 'Anti-politics' in the Popular Sectors of Lima," in D. Chalmers, C.M. Vilas, K. Hite, S.B. Martin, K. Piester, and M. Segarra (eds.), *The New Politics of Inequality in Latin America.* New York: Oxford University Press.

Panizza, F. (2000) "Neopopulism and Its Limits in Collor's Brazil." *Bulletin of Latin American Research* 19: 177–92.

Panizza, F. (2005) *Populism and the Mirror of Democracy*. London, New York: Verso.

Peeler, J. (1986) *Latin American Democracies: Colombia, Costa Rica, Venezuela*. Chapel Hill, NC: University of North Carolina Press.

Posada-Carbó, E. (2011) "Colombia After Uribe." *Journal of Democracy* 22: 137–51.

Quijano, A. (1998) "Populismo y Fujimorismo", in F. Burbano de Lara (ed.), *El Fantasma del Populismo: Aproximación a un Tema (Siempre) Actual*. Caracas: Nueva Sociedad.

Reyna, C. (2000) *La Anunciación de Fujimori: Alan García 1985–1990*. Lima: Desco.

Roberts, K. (1995) "Neoliberalism and the Transformation of Populism in Latin America: The Peruvian Case." *World Politics* 48:82–116.

Roberts, K.M. (2007) "Latin America's Populist Revival." *SAIS Review* 27: 3–15.

Roberts, K.M. (2013) "Parties and Populism in Latin America," in C. de la Torre and C.J. Arnson (eds.), *Latin American Populism in the Twenty-First Century*. Washington, D.C. and Baltimore: Woodrow Wilson Center Press – The Johns Hopkins University Press.

Roxborough, I. (1984) "Unity and Diversity in Latin American History." *Journal of Latin American Studies* 16:1–26.

Schamis, H.E. (2013) "From the Peróns to the Kirchners: 'Populism' in Argentine Politics," in C. de la Torre and C.J. Arnson (eds.), *Latin American Populism in the Twenty-First Century*. Washington, D.C. and Baltimore: Woodrow Wilson Center Press – The Johns Hopkins University Press.

Sheahan, J. (1999) *Searching for a Better Society: The Peruvian Economy from 1950*. University Park, PA: Pennsylvania State University Press.

Sheahan, J. (2006) "The Andean Economies: Questions of Poverty, Growth, and Equity," in P.W. Drake and E. Hershberg (eds.), *State and Society in Conflict: Comparative Perspectives on Andean Crises*. Pittsburgh: University of Pittsburgh Press.

Shifter, M. (2006) "In Search of Hugo Chávez." *Foreign Affairs* 85: 45–59.

St. John, R.B. (2010) *Toledo's Peru. Vision and Reality*. Gainsville, FL: University Press of Florida.

Stern, S.J. (1998) *Shining and Other Paths: War and Society in Peru, 1980–1995*. Durham, NC: Duke University Press.

Sweig, J. and McCarthy, M.M. (2005) "Colombia: Staving Off Partial Collapse," in R. Crandall, G. Paz, and R. Roett (eds.), *The Andes in Focus: Security, Democracy, and Economic Reform*, Boulder, CO, and London: Lynne Rienner Publishers.

Taggart, P. (1995) "New Populist Parties in Western Europe." *West European Politics* 18: 34–51.

Taggart, P. (2000) *Populism*. Buckingham and Philadelphia: Open University Press.

Tanaka, M. (2005) *Democracia sin Partidos. Perú, 2000–2005*. Lima: IEP.

Taylor, S.L. (2009) *Voting Amid Violence. Electoral Democracy in Colombia*. Boston: MA: Northeastern University Press.

Ungar Bleier, E. and Arévalo, C.A. (2004) "Partidos y Sistemas de Partidos en Colombia hoy: ¿Crisis o Reordenación Institucional?" in M. Kornblith, R.A. Mayorga, S. Pachano, M. Tanaka, E. Ungar Bleier, and C.A Arévalo (eds.), *Partidos Políticos en la Región Andina: Entre la Crisis y la Continuidad*. Lima: International IDEA.

Vergara, A. (2007) *Ni Amnésicos ni Irracionales. Las Elecciones Peruanas de 2006 en Perspectiva Histórica*. Lima: Solar.

Vilas, C.M. (ed.) (1994) *La Democratización Fundamental: El Populismo en América Latina*. Mexico: Consejo Nacional para la Cultura y las Artes.

Weyland, K. (1996) "Neopopulism and Neoliberalism in Latin America: Unexpected Affinities." *Studies in Comparative International Development* 31: 3–31.

Weyland, K (2001) "Clarifying a Contested Concept: Populism in the Study of Latin American Politics." *Comparative Politics* 34: 1–22.

Section III

Domestic and Regional Issues

12 Indigenous Mobilization and Democracy in Latin America

Roberta Rice

Indigenous peoples' interests have long been excluded from the national political agenda in Latin America. That is, until indigenous peoples began to mobilize en masse in defense of their rights in the 1990s. Since that time, indigenous peoples have become prominent social and political actors in the region. They have mobilized on a variety of fronts. Indigenous peoples have participated in protests and demonstrations, civil society coups, and constituent assemblies. In some instances, they have formed their own political parties, contested elections, and even won presidential office in a bid to advance indigenous peoples' demands for identity, territory, and autonomy (Lucero 2008; Madrid 2012; Rice 2012; Van Cott 2008). Indigenous mobilization is challenging the region's exclusionary governing structures and the failure to incorporate, represent, and respond to large segments of the population. The emergence of vibrant indigenous rights movements is one of the few bright spots in Latin America's democratic record.

The chapter broaches the following question: what is the democratic contribution of indigenous peoples' struggles in Latin America? The specter of indigenous political mobilization has divided analysts into those who view it as a threat to democratic stability versus those who see it as an opportunity to improve the quality of democracy. This chapter suggests that indigenous mobilization, on balance, has served to broaden democratic representation and participation. I propose that in the absence of indigenous mobilization, Latin America's political leaders would not have taken up the indigenous question.[1] In much as the same way that worker organization and protest in early-twentieth-century Latin America prompted ruling elites to respond to the social question, indigenous mobilization in the current era marks a new potential period for incorporation of the most excluded sector of society (Collier and Collier 1991; Gargarella 2013). The manner in which states respond to indigenous peoples' demands for inclusion will be highly consequential for the character and depth of Latin America's democratic regimes.

The chapter opens with a brief overview of the rise of indigenous peoples as political actors in the third wave of democratization. The following section looks at the debate in the literature over the impact of indigenous movements on democracy. It finds that indigenous movements have made a mostly positive contribution to democracy in Latin America. The final section of the chapter examines the relationship between indigenous mobilization and democracy in the exceptional case of Bolivia under President Evo Morales. The Bolivian case highlights the region's best efforts in championing indigenous rights, yet it also reveals the challenges of reconciling representative democracy with indigenous peoples' demands and expectations. The chapter concludes with a call for further research on the democratic potential of indigenous governance innovation.

Latin America's Indigenous Peoples

Indigenous peoples are a marginalized majority in Bolivia, Ecuador, Guatemala, and Peru, and a significant minority in most other Latin American countries (Table 12.1).[2] The estimated number of indigenous peoples in the region today ranges from 28 to 40 million, divided among some 671 officially recognized nations or peoples (Andersen 2010, 24; Layton and Patrinos 2006, 25). At the time of European conquest, between 30 and 70 million people inhabited the Americas. Possibly half of the native population died during the conquest. Disease, displacement, and forced labor took the lives of millions more (Prevost and Vanden 2011, 90). Early colonial societies were powerfully marked by racial and class distinctions. European settlers occupied the top rungs of colonial

Table 12.1 Estimated Indigenous Population Size in Latin America, 1990s

Country	Percent of Total Population
Argentina	1.1
Bolivia	50.5
Brazil	0.2
Chile	7.1
Colombia	1.7
Costa Rica	0.8
Ecuador	24.9
El Salvador	1.7
Guatemala	48.0
Honduras	11.9
Mexico	9.5
Nicaragua	7.6
Panama	7.8
Paraguay	2.0
Peru	38.4
Uruguay	0.2
Venezuela	1.5

Source: Deruyttere (1997).

society, while indigenous peoples and imported African slaves were located at the bottom. Nevertheless, indigenous peoples and Africans were positioned differently to the colonial state. Indigenous identity was institutionalized by the colonial order. Indigenous peoples, by virtue of their status as "Indians" within the administrative structure, were required to pay tribute, in the form of labor or goods, to the state in exchange for minimal rights and obligations (Larson 2004; Wade 2010). No such protections existed for Africans. Race, ethnicity, and power continue to overlap in important ways in contemporary Latin American societies. Inequality and exclusion have persisted, despite many attempts at democratization.

Throughout much of Latin America's history, indigenous demands have been oppressed, ignored, and silenced. Indigenous groups, where they have mobilized at all, have traditionally done so around class, partisan, religious, and revolutionary identities as opposed to ethnic ones (Yashar 1998). Latin American states promoted assimilation into the dominant *mestizo* culture. Racial mixing, or *mestizaje*, is regarded as a social process rather than a strictly biological one, based on an individual's degree of acculturation and integration. The fluidity of ethnic identities in the region is a widely held assumption (Roitman 2009). The renouncement of *mestizaje* in favor of newly politicized ethnic identities on the part of indigenous peoples caught many analysts by surprise. The emergence of powerful movements based on indigenous identity and rights in countries as diverse as Mexico, Colombia, Ecuador, and Bolivia has generated an extensive body of scholarship that seeks to explain the sudden and unexpected politicization of ethnic cleavages in the region. By most accounts, a mix of internal and external factors led to the rise of indigenous actors in contemporary Latin America. Such factors include a positive international human rights framework, harmful policies of neoliberal economic adjustment, the availability of transcommunity networks, and the greater associational space afforded by democratization (Albó 2002; Bengoa 2000; Brysk 2000; Maybury-Lewis 2002; Van Cott 2005; Warren and Jackson 2002; Yashar 2005).

The shift to democracy in the 1980s presented indigenous groups with a dilemma: should indigenous movements limit themselves to applying pressure on the political system from the outside, or should they take advantage of opportunities to participate in political institutions and attempt to bring about change from within? A participatory strategy is conventionally assumed to risk the loss of movement legitimacy and autonomy as indigenous groups submit themselves to the rules and regulations of a largely alien political system that had long served as an instrument of their domination. Latin America's indigenous movements have adopted a variety of stances in relation to electoral politics. In some instances, they have remained as social movements, emphasizing political autonomy and the ability to mobilize social pressure on the government in power, both domestically and by way of international allies and agreements (Brysk 2000; Yashar 2005). In other instances, they have opted to align themselves with political parties in order to take advantage of existing political networks and attempt to broaden them to include indigenous concerns (Massal and Bonilla 2000).

Lastly, indigenous movements in a handful of cases have opted to create their own political parties as part of a strategy of "autonomy in participation" by combining protest and electoral politics (Rice 2012). Through the formation of their own electoral vehicles, indigenous peoples have been able to participate in formal politics on their own terms.

Indigenous peoples have turned their backs on electoral politics as a means of advancing the indigenous agenda most notably in Mexico and Guatemala. In Mexico, the indigenous-based Zapatista Army of National Liberation (EZLN) has distanced itself from the state and political parties since the breakdown in negotiations between the two sides in the mid-1990s over issues of autonomy and self-government within indigenous communities. In response, the Zapatistas have turned inward in an attempt to build de facto autonomous communities (Gómez Tagle 2005; Nash 2001). In Guatemala, indigenous communities voted down the proposed amendment to the constitution in the 1999 referendum that included the recognition of indigenous rights. Warren (2002, 163) has suggested that the "NO" vote on the part of Mayan communities reflected their skepticism of the electoral process as an effective means of bringing about change. Instead, Mayas are working to find alternative avenues of political influence by building a grassroots movement based on cultural revitalization.

In Argentina, Brazil, and Paraguay, indigenous groups have attempted to articulate their claims through existing party channels. Indigenous peoples in these countries are geographically dispersed and have little national presence. In Argentina, indigenous organizations have formed their own sections within the major political parties, particularly the Peronist Party (PJ), and have gained a measure of political representation by competing on their party lists (Van Cott 2005, 190). In Brazil, the Workers' Party (PT) initially attracted support from the country's indigenous movement due to its favorable stance on indigenous rights. The PT's 2002 presidential victory raised expectations on the part of indigenous groups for positive change. However, the PT's support for the indigenous cause has so far been more rhetorical than real (Warren 2004, 219). After an unsuccessful bid at launching its own electoral vehicle, Paraguay's indigenous movement also opted to align itself with leftist political parties—in this case, the socialist Party for a Free Native Land (PPL)—in order to compete in elections (Gutiérrez 2000).

Ecuador and Bolivia are home to Latin America's most successful national indigenous-based political parties to date. In addition to their larger indigenous populations, the success of these countries' indigenous movements is the result of a two-pronged strategy based on opposition in the streets and in parliament, as well as their capacity to combine competing class and ethnic-based demands (Collins 2004; Van Cott 2008). In Ecuador, the Movement for Plurinational Unity Pachakutik-New Country (MUPP-NP) party was a major organizational force behind the winning electoral coalition in the presidential race of 2002. Since then, however, the party has lost much of its appeal due to a complex set of factors, including its ill-fated electoral alliance and its perceived shift to a more ethnicist stance (Mijeski and Beck 2011). In

Bolivia, the indigenous-based Movement Toward Socialism (MAS) party led by Evo Morales managed to obtain a majority vote in the presidential election of December 2005, a feat that had not been achieved by any Bolivian party since the transition to democracy in the early 1980s. President Morales has since been reelected by an even wider margin in the December 2009 elections. The MAS's program of state decolonization and societal transformation has redefined indigenous–state relations in Bolivia.

Democratic Threat or Opportunity?

Indigenous peoples are at the forefront of the struggle against neoliberalism in Latin America. The imposition of neoliberal-inspired policies of stabilization and adjustment has had dramatic social, political, and economic consequences. The disarticulation of class-based collective action and the erosion of linkages between political parties and their constituents that took place in the 1990s created a void in interest representation for the popular sectors (Burt and Mauceri 2004; Levitsky and Cameron 2003; Mainwaring 2006). In countries such as Ecuador and Bolivia, indigenous movements have artfully linked indigenous peoples' demands to issues of political and economic inclusion for the masses to produce powerful movements that draw support from a broad spectrum of civil society. In these two countries, indigenous peoples have taken the lead in protest episodes that toppled successive national governments throughout the late 1990s and early 2000s (Rice 2012; Silva 2009). Such actions are suggested to have contributed to institutional weakening by altering political systems through unconstitutional means (Mainwaring, Bejarano, and Pizarro Leongómez 2006; Mayorga 2006). In the case of Bolivia's coca growers, the defense of coca production as part of indigenous culture and tradition in the face of forced eradication programs promoted by the US government has garnered the movement considerable radical appeal as an expression of anti-imperialism.[3] Viewed from this perspective, indigenous mobilization constitutes a threat to democratic legitimacy and stability.

For the most part, however, scholars agree that indigenous mobilization plays a much-needed role in pushing for a more inclusive society and broadening political agendas (Lucero 2008; Madrid 2012; Van Cott 2005). Yashar (2006) has suggested that indigenous mobilization is the product, not the cause, of Latin America's deep-seated political instability. The region has long suffered from exclusionary state structures. A crisis of deteriorating state–society relations has been especially acute in the Andes, where a broadly mobilized indigenous sector feels increasingly alienated from a mono-cultural, distant, and repressive state. The political exclusion of indigenous peoples, especially in countries with substantial indigenous populations, has undoubtedly contributed to the weakness of party systems and the lack of accountability, representation, and responsiveness of third-wave democracies to the needs of the popular sectors. This, in turn, has resulted in situations of increasing political conflict and social unrest in the region. In this view, indigenous movements and their demands for recognition, representation, and reform are a democratizing force.

The impact of indigenous peoples' parties on the quality of democracy and on democratic governance is another topic of debate in the literature. In the context of a hostile political environment, indigenous peoples chose to enter formal politics, not through assimilation, but by politicizing ethnic identities (Glidden 2011). Ethnic parties are widely regarded as having a profoundly negative impact on democracy through the way in which they pit ethnic groups against each other in an attempt to solidify support among co-ethnics (Horowitz 1985; Rabushka and Shepsle 1972). This type of party behavior is expected to worsen ethnic polarization and to increase the likelihood of ethnic violence in a country. Referring to the case of Bolivia, Mayorga (2006) has suggested that the political incorporation of indigenous peoples has undermined representative democracy, governmental capacity, and state unity. In his view, indigenous movements "seek to destroy democratic institutions and replace them with utopian ethnic-based, direct democracy and nationalist populism" (Mayorga 2006, 133). Andersen (2010) has cautioned that the rise of indigenous nationalist leaders in Latin America could potentially lead to civil war as they contest artificially imposed nation-states.

Notwithstanding the literature on ethnic parties and ethnic nationalism, a number of scholars have found indigenous-based parties to have an important stabilizing effect on party systems in Latin America by including marginalized ethnic groups in formal politics (Birnir 2007; Madrid 2005; Van Cott 2000). According to Madrid (2012), the ethnic policies and appeals of indigenous peoples' parties in Latin America tend to be inclusionary rather than exclusionary in nature. All totaled, indigenous parties have improved political participation and support for democracy among indigenous peoples, increased indigenous political influence and representation, helped to reduce ethnic inequality and discrimination, and promoted greater respect for indigenous rights. In a similar vein, Van Cott (2005, 228–32) found that indigenous-based parties have had a mostly positive impact on democracy, including introducing new themes into the political agenda, offering a healthy model of party–society linkage, introducing greater transparency and democratic decision making to politics, and forcing conventional parties to incorporate new issues into their political platforms. The rise of indigenous parties and movements has prompted society to rethink the very meaning of democracy and how best to design political representation and participation in plurinational polities. In short, indigenous mobilization in Latin America presents a historic opportunity to deepen democracy in the region.

The Exceptional Case of Bolivia

Bolivia's first indigenous head of state, President Evo Morales (2006–), has garnered international attention for his pro-poor, pro-indigenous policy orientation. The Morales administration set out to redefine state–society relations to promote a more inclusive polity. According to the preamble to Bolivia's newly drafted constitution, the country has left behind the colonial, republican, and neoliberal state of the past.[4] In its place is a plurinational state with multiple autonomies. Without question, this historic accomplishment was the result of strong and sustained social mobilization. In the words of Exeni Rodríguez (2012, 222), "the most creative democratic moments occur through extrainstitutional mobilization. Important adjustments and expansions in institutions cannot be explained without this 'politics in the streets.'" The constitutional recognition of plurinationality in Bolivia, as well as in neighboring Ecuador, marks a watershed moment in indigenous–state relations in Latin America. It represents an opportunity for governments to reconceptualize their relationship with indigenous peoples as sovereign and self-determining peoples or nations. Plurinationality challenges previous governmental attempts to divide indigenous peoples, to categorize them in ways that obscure their ethnicity, to discount them from national policy debates, and to denigrate them as obstacles to development and democracy. It replaces the unidirectional relationship between the state and indigenous groups with a bilateral or government-to-government relationship based on mutual respect and consideration (Becker 2011; Walsh 2009).

The 2009 Bolivian constitution goes further than any previous legislation in the country, indeed in Latin America, in securing representation and participation for the nation's indigenous peoples. For instance, the new constitution recognizes and protects traditional uses of coca (art. 384), guarantees the right of title to ancestral territories (art. 30), confers the political rights of autonomy and self-determination on indigenous communities (art. 2), and recognizes the practice of indigenous law (art. 190). In addition, it recognizes all thirty-six indigenous languages of Bolivia as official languages of the state (art. 5) and guarantees the right to proportional representation of indigenous peoples in the national legislature (art. 147). The constitution also incorporates mechanisms for direct citizen participation in politics, including recall referendums, town councils, citizen-led legislative initiatives, and the legal-political recognition of civil society groups to contest elections. These governance innovations presuppose that representation and participation occur beyond, and at times outside, the traditional channels of representative democracy (Exeni Rodríguez 2012, 215). As noted by Cameron, Hershberg, and Sharpe (2012), the inclusion of direct, participatory, and communitarian elements may have changed the character of Bolivia's representative democracy, but they need not be seen as undermining it.

There are limits to the degree of autonomy afforded to indigenous peoples by the new Bolivian constitution. For example, the creation of autonomous self-governing indigenous bodies appears to democratize the state by devolving power to indigenous communities. Yet, a highly centralized organization of power in the executive branch tends to work against the application of indigenous rights (Gargarella 2013). This internal contradiction has resulted in significant tensions between the governing MAS party and indigenous groups over issues of natural resource extraction and state-sponsored development projects within indigenous territories. Most recently, clashes have occurred between government forces and lowland indigenous groups over the government's proposed plan to build a highway through the Isiboro-Sécure Indigenous Territory and National Park (TIPNIS) in the department of Beni that would connect the central Andean highlands with the lowlands to the north. The MAS maintains that the road is essential for national development. Local residents balk at the government's lack of good faith in its prior consultation process. Although Bolivia's constitution (art. 30.15) does not establish the right of indigenous peoples to free, prior, and informed consent, but merely to prior consultation, it does stipulate that the consultation process be conducted in good faith and in keeping with local indigenous norms and procedures (Schilling-Vacaflor and Kuppe 2012; Wolff 2012). In light of the controversy over its plans, the government has suspended the highway project until further notice. The TIPNIS conflict reveals the serious gaps between legislation and practice that still exist in Bolivia.

The Morales administration has also faced significant opposition from formerly dominant actors who now find themselves excluded from the state. President Morales' rise to power has polarized the country into regional camps. On the one hand, regional elites centered in the eastern lowland departments desire a lean, neoliberal state that eschews centralism in favor of regional authority. They claim that the central government discriminates against *mestizo* and white populations by only representing the interests of indigenous and poor people (Eaton 2007; Fabricant 2009; Gustafson 2008). On the other hand, government supporters based largely in the western highland departments back a strong centralized interventionist and redistributive state. The result is a highly politicized regional cleavage with racial and class overtones. However, as Madrid (2012, 165) points out, the polarization between supporters and opponents of the Morales regime is more ideological and regional than ethnic in nature. Opposition groups in the eastern lowland departments have resolved not to recognize the new constitution and instead agitate for greater regional autonomy. Having lost their voice in the political system, the regional elites are looking for an exit (Eaton 2007).

In spite of the challenges inherent in constructing an alternative political and economic project for the country, support for democracy in Bolivia has improved dramatically during Morales' time in office, reaching 68 percent in 2008 from a low of just 49 percent in 2005. Satisfaction with democracy has also improved considerably, especially among indigenous peoples. The percentage of Bolivians who reported being satisfied or very satisfied with democracy rose from 24 percent in 2004 to 50 percent in 2009, with 65 percent of self-identified indigenous peoples reporting being satisfied or very satisfied with their democracy (Madrid 2012, 172). Electoral participation rates have also skyrocketed under Morales. The 2010 departmental and municipal elections, the first held under the new constitution, recorded the country's highest electoral turnout of any election in the past thirty years. The participation rate of 87.1 percent even exceeded that of the high-stake presidential race of 2005, which broke previous records with an electoral turnout rate of 84.5 percent (CNE 2010; Romero Ballivián 2007, 45). The empirical evidence indicates that there have been substantial gains in the quality of political representation and participation in Bolivia. There are grounds for optimism.

Conclusion

This chapter has sought to analyze the relationship between indigenous mobilization and democracy in Latin America. Based on an overview of the literature as well as an examination of the case of Bolivia, I have argued that there is a positive correlation between the two. The demands placed on the state by indigenous mobilization provide an opportunity to enhance democracy. More research is needed on the impact of indigenous governance initiatives on the quality and functioning of democracy in the region for a definitive answer. From the current vantage point, however, it is clear that indigenous rights and representation do not undermine democracy or the state; they may in fact strengthen them. The transformation of Latin America's exclusionary governing structures serves the interests of the region's indigenous peoples as well as those of the broader society. States can continue to repress indigenous movements or attempt to co-opt them rather than adequately address their demands. These approaches will surely exacerbate political instability and conflict in the region (Otero and Jugenitz 2003). Only by meaningfully including indigenous peoples in the formal political system will all citizens be able to live in more integrated, egalitarian, and democratic societies.

Notes

1 Postero and Zamosc (2004, 5) define the indigenous question as "the crucial issue of what kinds of rights indigenous people should be granted as citizens of democratic nation-states."
2 Indigenous population size is notoriously difficult to estimate accurately given the fluid and ambiguous nature of ethnic identities in the region (Madrid 2012), as well as the technical complexities involved (Layton and Patrinos 2006). However, the estimates provided by Deruyttere (1997) are generally considered reflective of overall indigenous population sizes in terms of relative proportion to the total population in each country.
3 The coca leaf is considered sacred by indigenous peoples. It is used for rituals and in daily consumption as a means of suppressing hunger and easing altitude sickness. It is also the principal ingredient used in the production of cocaine.
4 Bolivia's 2009 constitution is available for download at http://pdba.georgetown. edu/constitutions/bolivia/bolivia.html. Accessed November 3, 2013.

References

Albó, X. (2002) *Pueblos Indios en la Política*. La Paz: Centro de Investigación y Promoción del Campesinado (CIPCA).

Andersen, M.E. (2010) *Peoples of the Earth: Ethnonationalism, Democracy, and the Indigenous Challenge in "Latin" America*. Lanham: Rowman & Littlefield Publishers.

Becker, M. (2011) *Pachakutik: Indigenous Movements and Electoral Politics in Ecuador*. Lanham: Rowman & Littlefield.

Bengoa, J. (2000) *La Emergencia Indígena en América Latina*. Santiago: Fondo de Cultura Económica.

Birnir, J.K. (2007) *Ethnicity and Electoral Politics*. New York: Cambridge University Press.

Brysk, A. (2000) *From Tribal Village to Global Village: Indian Rights and International Relations in Latin America*. Stanford: Stanford University Press.

Burt, J.-M. and Mauceri, P. (eds.) (2004) *Politics in the Andes: Identity, Conflict, Reform*. Pittsburgh: University of Pittsburgh Press.

Cameron, M.A., Hershberg, E., and Sharpe, K.E. (eds.) (2012) *New Institutions for Participatory Democracy in Latin America*. New York: Palgrave Macmillan.

CNE (2010) "Resultados: Elecciones Departamentales y Municipales." Documento de Información Pública, Corte Nacional Electoral, No. 4.

Collier, R.B. and Collier, D (1991) *Shaping the Political Arena: Critical Junctures, The Labor Movement, and Regime Dynamics in Latin America*. Notre Dame: University of Notre Dame Press.

Collins, J. (2004) "Linking Movements and Electoral Politics: Ecuador's Indigenous Movement and the Rise of Pachakutik," in J.-M. Burt and P. Mauceri (eds.), *Politics in the Andes: Identity, Conflict, Reform* (38–57). Pittsburgh: University of Pittsburgh Press.

Deruyttere, A. (1997) *Indigenous Peoples and Sustainable Development: The Role of the Inter-American Development Bank*. Washington: Inter-American Development Bank.

Eaton, K. (2007) "Backlash in Bolivia: Regional Autonomy as a Reaction Against Indigenous Mobilization." *Politics and Society* 35: 71–102.

Exeni Rodríguez, J.L. (2012) "Elusive Demodiversity in Bolivia: Between Representation, Participation, and Self-Government," in M.A. Cameron, E. Hershberg, and K.E. Sharpe (eds.), *New Institutions for Participatory Democracy in Latin America* (207–300). New York: Palgrave Macmillan.

Fabricant, N. (2009) "Performative Politics: The Camba Countermovement in Eastern Bolivia," *American Ethnologist* 36: 768–83.

Gargarella, R. (2013) *Latin American Constitutionalism 1810–2010: The Engine Room of the Constitution*. New York: Oxford University Press.

Glidden, L.M. (2011) *Mobilizing Ethnic Identity in the Andes*. Lanham: Lexington Books.

Gómez Tagle, S. (2005) "The Impact of the Indigenous Movement on Democratization: Elections in Chiapas (1988–2004)." *Canadian Journal of Latin American and Caribbean Studies* 30: 183–219.

Gustafson, B. (2008) "By Means Legal and Otherwise: The Bolivian Right Regroups." *NACLA Report on the Americas* 41: 20–6.

Gutiérrez, A.C. (2000) "Camino Hacia La Autodeterminación: Movimiento Indígena 19 de Abril." *Revista Acción* 209: 1–4.

Horowitz, D. (1985) *Ethnic Groups in Conflict*. Berkeley: University of California Press.

Larson, B. (2004) *Trials of Nation Making: Liberalism, Race, and Ethnicity in the Andes, 1810–1910*. New York: Cambridge University Press.

Layton, H.M. and Patrinos, H.A. (2006) "Estimating the Number of Indigenous Peoples in Latin America," in G. Hall and H.A. Patrinos (eds.), *Indigenous Peoples,*

Poverty and Human Development in Latin America, 1994–2004 (25–39). New York: Palgrave Macmillan.

Levitsky, S. and Cameron, M.A. (2003) "Democracy without Parties? Political Parties and Regime Change in Fujimori's Peru." *Latin American Politics and Society* 45: 1–33.

Lucero, J.A. (2008) *Struggles of Voice: The Politics of Indigenous Representation in the Andes.* Pittsburgh: University of Pittsburgh Press.

Madrid, R.L. (2005) "Indigenous Parties and Democracy in Latin America." *Latin American Politics and Society* 47: 161–79.

Madrid, R.L. (2012) *The Rise of Ethnic Politics in Latin America.* New York: Cambridge University Press.

Mainwaring, S. (2006) "The Crisis of Representation in the Andes." *Journal of Democracy* 17: 13–27.

Mainwaring, S., Bejarano, A.M., and Pizarro Leongómez, E. (eds.) (2006) *The Crisis of Democratic Representation in the Andes.* Stanford: Stanford University Press.

Massal, J. and Bonilla, M. (eds.) (2000) *Los Movimientos Sociales en las Democracias Andinas.* Quito: Facultad Latinoamericana de Ciencias Sociales (FLACSO).

Maybury-Lewis, D. (ed.) (2002) *The Politics of Ethnicity: Indigenous Peoples in Latin American States.* Cambridge: Harvard University Press.

Mayorga, R.A. (2006) "Outsiders and Neopopulism: The Road to Plebiscitary Democracy," in S. Mainwaring, A.M. Bejarano, and E. Pizarro Leongómez (eds.), *The Crisis of Democratic Representation in the Andes* (132–167). Stanford: Stanford University Press.

Mijeski, K.J. and Beck, S.H. (2011) *Pachakutik and the Rise and Decline of the Ecuadorian Indigenous Movement.* Athens: Ohio University Press.

Nash, J.C. (2001) *Mayan Visions: The Quest for Autonomy in an Age of Globalization.* New York: Routledge.

Otero, G. and Jugenitz, H.A. (2003) "Challenging National Borders from Within: The Political-Class Formation of Indigenous Peasants in Latin America." *Canadian Review of Sociology and Anthropology* 40: 503–24.

Postero, N.G. and Zamosc, L. (2004) "Indigenous Movements and the Indian Question in Latin America," in N.G. Postero and L. Zamosc (eds.), *The Struggle for Indigenous Rights in Latin America* (1–31). Brighton: Sussex Academic Press.

Prevost, G. and Vanden, H.E. (2011) *Latin America: An Introduction.* New York: Oxford University Press.

Rabushka, A. and Shepsle, K. (1972) *Politics in Plural Societies.* Columbus: Charles E. Merrill.

Rice, R. (2012) *The New Politics of Protest: Indigenous Mobilization in Latin America's Neoliberal Era.* Tucson: The University of Arizona Press.

Roitman, K. (2009) *Race, Ethnicity, and Power in Ecuador: The Manipulation of Mestizaje.* Boulder: Lynne Rienner.

Romero Ballivián, S. (2007) *El Tablero Reordenado: Análisis de la Elección Presidencial de 2005.* La Paz: Corte Nacional Electoral (CNE).

Schilling-Vacaflor, A. and Kuppe, R. (2012) "Plurinational Constitutionalism: A New Era of Indigenous-State Relations?" in D. Nolte and A. Schilling-Vacaflor (eds.), *New Constitutionalism in Latin America: Promises and Practices* (347–70). Burlington: Ashgate.

Silva, E. (2009) *Challenging Neoliberalism in Latin America.* New York: Cambridge University Press.

Van Cott, D.L. (2000) "Party System Development and Indigenous Populations in Latin America: The Bolivian Case." *Party Politics* 6: 155–74.

Van Cott, D.L. (2005) *From Movements to Parties in Latin America: The Evolution of Ethnic Politics*. New York: Cambridge University Press.

Van Cott, D.L. (2008) *Radical Democracy in the Andes*. New York: Cambridge University Press.

Wade, P. (2010) *Race and Ethnicity in Latin America*. 2nd edition. New York: Palgrave Macmillan.

Walsh, C. (2009) "Estado Plurinacional e Intercultural, Complementariedad y Complicidad Hacia el 'Buen Vivir,'" in A. Acosta and E. Martínez (eds.), *Plurinacionalidad: Democracia en la Diversidad* (161–84). Quito: Ediciones Abya-Yala.

Warren, J. (2004) "Socialist *Saudades*: Lula's Victory, Indigenous Movements, and the Latin American Left," in N.G. Postero and L. Zamosc (eds.), *The Struggle for Indigenous Rights in Latin America* (217–31). Portland: Sussex Academic Press.

Warren, K.B. (2002) "Voting Against Indigenous Rights in Guatemala: Lessons from the 1999 Referendum," in K.B. Warren and J.E. Jackson (eds.), *Indigenous Movements, Self-Representation, and the State in Latin America* (149–80). Austin: University of Texas Press.

Warren, K.B. and Jackson, J.E. (eds.) (2002) *Indigenous Movements, Self-Representation, and the State in Latin America*. Austin: University of Texas Press.

Wolff, J. (2012) "New Constitutions and the Transformation of Democracy in Bolivia and Ecuador," in D. Nolte and A. Schilling-Vacaflor (eds.), *New Constitutionalism in Latin America: Promises and Practices* (183–202). Burlington: Ashgate.

Yashar, D.J. (1998) "Contesting Citizenship: Indigenous Movements and Democracy in Latin America." *Comparative Politics* 31: 23–42.

Yashar, D.J. (2005) *Contesting Citizenship in Latin America: The Rise of Indigenous Movements and the Postliberal Challenge*. New York: Cambridge University Press.

Yashar, D.J. (2006) "Ethnic Politics and Political Instability in the Andes," in P.W. Drake and E. Hershberg (eds.), *State and Society in Conflict: Comparative Perspectives on Andean Crises* (189–219). Pittsburgh: University of Pittsburgh Press.

13 Crime and Citizen Security
Democracy's Achilles' Heel

Richard L. Millett

Over the past three decades, much of Latin America has witnessed a remarkable transformation from authoritarian regimes to elected civilian governments. Unfortunately, as is often the case, the bulk of these transitions have been accompanied by a notable deterioration in citizen security. Crime, both common local and organized transnational, has become a constant reality for much of the region's population.[1] Policing is usually inadequate, if not incompetent; court systems are overwhelmed; the prison system has become a major source of training and recruits for organized crime; and widespread corruption both undermines efforts to respond and further erodes popular support for elected governments. It is a measure of both the problem's scale and the public's rising frustration that in at least two elections the victors owed much of their support to perceptions that they were serious about combating crime because close relatives had been murdered.[2]

Latin America is by no means alone in facing this dilemma. It is usually present in nations that are emerging from or are still immersed in civil conflicts. It is an ongoing issue in the Balkans, especially in Kosovo. In much of Central Africa, citizen security is largely nonexistent. In Somalia, there is virtually no state to provide security. The situation in Iraq and Afghanistan is too obvious to require further comment.

There are a number of factors that contribute to this situation. One element, of course, is the lingering effect of civil conflicts. This is true whether or not there has been a negotiated end to the conflict. There will be elements that reject the settlement, that feel excluded, deprived, or angered over concessions made to their foes, and these elements often make violent efforts to disrupt the process (Lovelock 2005).

The end to civil conflicts frequently leaves thousands of former combatants from all sides without jobs, land, or education and accustomed to a violent lifestyle. Employment opportunities are scarce, both for former combatants and for emerging generations. Efforts to reincorporate these individuals into society are often inadequate and not sustained, providing ready recruits for criminal organizations. This is further exacerbated by the ready supply of weapons left behind by these conflicts.

In addition, the very process of transition to more democratic and less authoritarian states contributes to the deterioration of citizen security. As Warren

Almand of the Canadian-based International Center for Human Rights and Democratic Development has observed, "Almost every new democracy manifests an overwhelming increase in common crime and delinquency. The result, in many cases, is a groundswell of popular sentiment in favor of a return to authoritarian modes of governance" (Almand 1999). This also feeds growing mass protests over government failure to curb crime and violence, notably in Brazil and Venezuela. With a freer media, government failures to deal with crime gain much more attention and crimes generate more publicity. Revelations of government corruption can reduce individual incentives to obey the law. Police are often poorly trained and poorly paid, and in a democratic transition may have experienced a leadership purge. They are distrusted by the public and unaccustomed to respecting citizens' rights. Confidence in the judicial system is low, and citizens may have neither a tradition of nor faith in the state's capacity to act as an impartial arbiter. Prisons are badly overcrowded, court dockets are overwhelmed, and conviction rates of those finally brought to trial are astonishingly low. Under such conditions, rapid increases in crime rates and the consequent deterioration of citizen security should come as no surprise.

As the state becomes less capable of controlling criminal violence, there is frequently a rapid increase in privatized justice. Those with the economic means turn to private security companies, often controlled by individuals who have been dismissed from the government's security forces for corruption, human rights abuses, or other illicit activities. Overwhelmed police forces make little effort to investigate violent actions perpetrated by these private security firms, giving them virtual immunity and exacerbating their tendencies to use extra-legal violence.

For the poor, this increasingly means resorting to vigilante tactics, hunting down and beating or even killing suspected criminals. Sometimes the poor organize their own militias, which, in turn, abuse citizens' rights and engage in criminal activity. Recent developments in Mexico are an extreme example of this, as in Michoacan and other states private militias have waged open warfare against narcotics cartels and against what they perceive as corrupt government officials. Central government efforts to rein them in and/or incorporate them into legal security institutions have had limited success. All of this is destructive to efforts to establish a credible rule of law (International Crisis Group 2013).

In addition to the rise in common crime, there has been a steady increase in the level of organized transnational criminal activities. This reflects the globalization of trade and communications; the immense wealth generated by illicit trafficking of narcotics, people, arms, and other commodities; and the widespread corruption of public officials. The power and resources available to organized criminal groups often greatly exceed that available to local authorities. These groups find it easy to enlist local youth in their enterprises, providing deadly linkages between transnational and ordinary crime.

Part of this problem relates to the inability of many nations to control their entire national territory. For smaller, weaker states, this includes an inability to control air space and sea frontiers, making them targets of opportunity for those engaged in illegal trafficking. Of greater import are states that cannot control frontier territories, a reality highlighted by the current situation in nations like Pakistan and Colombia. These areas previously had marginalized importance, since events there had little, if any, impact on the rest of the country. But modern communications have made these in many ways ideal locations for criminal activities and for attacks on central government authority. This, in turn, disrupts traditional patterns of local authority in frontier regions and jeopardizes their relations with the central government.

Urbanization contributes to citizen insecurity. It breaks down traditional extended family structures and informal authority mechanisms, and creates growing alienation between those who move to the city and their children. This second-generation phenomenon is the greatest single source of violent crime. Rejecting traditional values, but having little to substitute for them, lacking education and opportunity, they readily form gangs and engage in a wide variety of criminal activities.

While all of these factors are global in scope, they have had a particularly strong impact on Latin America. The respected *Latinobarometro* poll of nearly 19,000 individuals throughout the hemisphere found in 2005 that 41 percent of its respondents knew someone who had been a victim of crime in the previous twelve months. This was up from 33 percent a year earlier.[3] In addition, homicide has become the leading cause of death among Latin American males between the ages of 15 and 44. The murder rate has continued to rise in the twenty-first century, growing by 11 percent from 2000–2010 to a total of over 100,000 annually. Nearly two-thirds of Latin Americans avoid going out at night because of their fear of crime, and over 10 percent reportedly moved in the past decade in search of safer living conditions (*The Economist*, 2013) While the percentage of citizens identifying crime as the major problem facing their nations declined slightly from 2011 to 2013, it remained the first choice of 55 percent of those interviewed for the 2013 *Latinobarometro* survey and was the major concern in all but four of the nations surveyed (Inter-American Development Bank 2013). In 2012 nearly one out of every three Latin Americans was a victim of violent crime (United Nations Development Program 2013). Not surprisingly, all this translates into low levels of confidence in police and in the judiciary, with less than 40 percent of respondents expressing "a lot" or "some" confidence in these institutions (*The Economist* 2006a). As Brazil's Paulo Sergio Pinheiro put it,

> despite democracy, the rule of law—particularly for the majority of poor Latin American children and adolescents—continues to be elusive. The region is struggling with seemingly intractable problems: abusive use of lethal force by the police forces, extra-judicial killings, lynching, torture, abominable prison conditions, and corruption in the criminal justice system.

(Pinheiro 2006)

Testifying before the US Congress, Adolfo Franco of the United States Agency for International Development pointed out that "Latin America has the dubious distinction of being one of the most violent regions in the world with crime rates more than double the world average." He further added "Latin America's per capita Gross Domestic Product would be twenty-five percent higher if the region's crime rates were equal to the world average (Testimony of Adolfo A. Franco 2005).

While the situation varies significantly from country to country, virtually every Latin American nation has at least one of the factors I have enumerated as contributing to the rise of criminal violence and citizen insecurity; most have two or more. A few case studies, including what are arguably the worst, provide examples of the deterioration of citizen security and the consequent undermining of democratic consolidation.

Case Studies

The four northern nations of Central America—Guatemala, El Salvador, Honduras, and Nicaragua—were all caught up in the violent conflicts that swept through the region from the end of the 1970s until the early 1990s. While Honduras escaped much of the direct violence, it experienced some of the consequences, including armed incursions across its borders and a flood of weapons that became widely available. Since the end of the civil conflicts, something achieved in each case by negotiation and internationally monitored political agreements, citizen security has actually declined in El Salvador, Guatemala, and Honduras. These nations occupy three of the top five places on the world's list of murder rates, with Honduras ranking first (CNN Staff 2014). Nicaragua has been an exception, but is increasingly impacted by the situation in its northern neighbors (Cajina 2013). The deterioration in regional citizen security has been confirmed by conversations with Central Americans, especially Salvadorans, living in the United States, who repeatedly declare that "it is more dangerous for me to go back to my country today than it was during the height of the civil conflicts."[4] Guatemala's former vice-president, Eduardo Stein, has declared "democratic governance is in jeopardy . . . because of drug money going into local elections" (Stein 2007). Many regional leaders, notably Guatemala's President Otto Perez Molina, have urged a reexamination of existing drug laws as part of an effort to stem the rising tide of crime.

While transnational criminal activity has greatly expanded in Central America, the impact on the average citizen has been a virtual explosion of common crime associated with violent youth gangs. While exact figures are impossible to come by, estimates of the total number of gang members in El Salvador, Guatemala, and Honduras alone are usually over 60,000.[5] Involved in a host of criminal enterprises, including extortion, contract killings, narcotics and arms trafficking, kidnappings, and robbery, they have emerged as the overriding security issue in each of these nations.

Thousands of mostly young males have been killed in Central America by the gangs. According to Honduras National Commissioner for Human Rights Ramon Custodio, the nation lives on the brink of anarchy with a desperate population pleading for greater security from a police force "incapable of preventing or controlling kidnappings" (El Nuevo Herald 2007).

In the words of Anders Kompass, the former representative in Guatemala of the United Nations High Commissioner for Human Rights, "[T]he nation is a paradise for organized crime. The state apparatus is weak; the impunity rate is very high. This has shown that organized crime has penetrated to a much higher level than we ever thought" (Roig-Franzia 2007). The poor are the most common victims of this criminal violence. On occasion, the army is sent into poor neighborhoods to conduct a sweep against criminal gangs, but when the army leaves, the gangs return. In some areas, desperate citizens have actually put up banners calling for the army's return.

The most powerful gangs are in El Salvador, where they are often led by individuals who had been deported from the United States for criminal offenses. Central Americans attribute much of the gang problem to Washington's policy of deporting aliens convicted of felonies after they complete their jail terms. Prison has often functioned both as an institution for advanced training in criminality and a center for networking between Central American and North American criminal organizations. In El Salvador and in Guatemala, many in the business community, frustrated by government inability to control gang violence, have hired off-duty police, private security companies, and others to eliminate actual and potential gang members. Known as "exterminators," they have significantly contributed to the spiraling homicide rate among young males (EFE 2007).

Despite sharing the heritage of a brutal civil war, having easy access to weapons, and suffering from extreme poverty, Nicaragua has to date escaped the worst effects of gang violence. This may reflect a more effective police force, combined with higher levels of public support for and faith in the administration of justice. Also, Nicaraguan criminal elements have an outlet for their activities in the much more prosperous neighboring nation of Costa Rica.[6]

As difficult as the situation is in Central America, it may be even worse in Haiti. Living in the hemisphere's poorest nation, Haiti's citizens have rarely enjoyed real security. The predatory Tonton Macoutes of the Duvalier era were replaced by the violent repression of a series of military governments. US intervention ended the military regime, but also created a security vacuum that international drug dealers, unemployed former soldiers, and local criminal gangs all rushed to fill. At a 1995 conference in Miami, I had several conversations with Haiti's new justice minister about the problems of trying to establish citizen security and the rule of law among a largely illiterate population that had never had any reason to trust state justice. He readily admitted it was a huge task requiring prolonged public education and that resources for this were nearly nonexistent. In the years that followed, constant political conflict led to another US intervention and, ultimately, the creation of a UN peacekeeping force: United Nations Stabilization Mission in Haiti (MINUSTAH). Despite the United Nations' presence, however, violence continued to spread. The 2003 Annual Report of the Inter-American Commission on Human Rights noted "the existence in Haiti of armed groups who act unlawfully and with impunity, sometimes terrorizing the population" and added that there was "credible information that judges were pressured by armed groups seeking to influence the outcome of certain cases" and decried the "state's failure to guarantee the population's security" (Inter-American Commission on Human Rights 2003). By the start of 2007 the Overseas Security Advisory Council had Port-au-Prince rated as "CRITICAL for crime" adding that "organized gang criminal activity has been on a sharp rise in the past year" and "kidnapping remains the number one criminal activity" (Overseas Security Advisory Council 2007b).

All of this helped produce a 2007 agreement between the Haitian government and MINUSTAH to send the 8,000-man peacekeeping contingent into the capital's slums to combat the worst gangs. In a series of bloody engagements, the gangs were driven from some of their strongholds and a modicum of security restored to the roads in Port-au-Prince. The UN force commander, Brazilian Major General Carlos Alberto da Santa Cruz, pledged that he would "continue to cleanse these areas of the gangs who are robbing the Haitian people of their security" (Lacey 2007).

This progress abruptly ended with the January 2010 earthquake, which killed over 250,000 and allowed virtually all the prisoners in Port-Au-Prince jails to escape. Crime rates surged, and what progress had been made toward improving the police and the courts was largely undone. Between May 2012 and May 2013, over 1,000 Haitians were murdered; there were 972 reported sexual assaults and 72 kidnappings (Agence Frace-Presse 2013). Some progress has been made in restoring the court system and reorganizing the police, but Haiti remains a violent and unsafe place where citizen security is minimal and democratic institutions are fragile at best.[7]

Mexico has long been plagued by both organized and common crime. Much of this involves illegal trafficking of narcotics and people into the United States and of arms from the United States into Mexico. As a result, some of the worst violence and most powerful organized crime groups have been concentrated near the US border.[8] The situation deteriorated steadily in the 1990s, fueled by widespread corruption, the diminished authority of the ruling party (the PRI), and extreme poverty in urban areas, especially parts of Mexico City.

With the election of Vincente Fox as president in 2000, the eight decades of rule by Mexico's Institutionalized Party of the Revolution (PRI) ended. The new administration had pledged to deal with crime, but its efforts were largely unsuccessful. Reports of serious federal crimes climbed from a daily average of 203.1 in 2001 to 300.4 in 2006 (Centro de Estudios Sociales y de Opinion Publica 2007). Kidnappings became a major source of concern, many of them involving Mexico's hoard of unregulated taxis. Suspicions were rife that the police themselves were involved in many of these, something given additional credence in 2006 with the arrest of fourteen police in Baja California for involvement in kidnappings and other crimes.[9] Violence spread as drug cartels fought over transit routes in the states of Michoacan and Guerrero and in states bordering the United States. By 2006 murders attributed to narcotics trafficking had reached 2,100, with over 600 of these in Michoacan alone (*The Economist* 2007). President Felipe Calderon, declaring that in parts of the country "organized crime was out of control," sent the army and the marines out to fight the drug traffickers (Jane's Intelligence Review 2007b).

President Calderon's efforts resulted in the arrest of several leaders of the narcotics cartels and the death of others. The cartels, however, struck back, attacking both newspapers who reported on their activities and government officials who tried to combat them. Attacks on newspapers became so frequent that Reporters Without Borders named Mexico as the world's second most dangerous nation for journalists, led only by Iraq (Root 2007). Mexico seemed to be returning to the nineteenth-century era of Porfirio Diaz when it was said that Mexico was safe for everyone except Mexicans.

By the end of his term, Calderon's efforts seemed to be having some results. The murder rate began to drop, security forces were being professionalized, and judicial institutions strengthened. But the high human and economic costs of his efforts were a factor in the return to power of the PRI with Enrique Peña Nieto's victory in the 2012 presidential election.

Peña Nieto's first months in office produced some spectacular results with the capture or killing of numerous cartel leaders, most notably El Chapo Guzman of the Sinaloa cartel. But it also witnessed the growth of vigilante and private militia groups and the continued diversification of organized criminal activities. These have included everything from stealing petroleum and shrimp, to massive extortion of Mexico's avocado producers (Iaconangelo 2014). While citizen security may be slowly improving, organized and common crime remain the primary concern of much of the population. Government corruption is widespread, confidence in police and courts is low, and criminal activities remain a major issue in relations with the United States and a barrier to effective immigration reform.[10]

While Mexico has a tradition of violent politics and criminal activity, Brazil had longed enjoyed a reputation as a less violent nation, dedicated more to the joys of carnival than to violent crime. Unfortunately, by the latter part of the twentieth century, this was changing as crime spread to the tourist beaches of Rio, the business hub of Sao Paulo, and even to the Europeanized regions of the southern state of Rio Grande do Sul. In part, this stemmed from the extreme poverty in the poor *favelas* around Rio and other cities, and in part from Brazil's lack of effective controls over firearms sales and distribution. But a major aggravating factor was the nation's growing involvement in the international narcotics and arms trades. By the start of the twenty-first century Brazil had become a major transit point for Andean cocaine heading for Europe (BBC News 2003). Some of this went direct and some via Africa, notably through the former Portuguese colony of Guinea Bissau. In return, arms from Brazil flowed to insurgents in Colombia, often via Surinam, and even to organized crime groups in Japan. In 2003 Brazil finally passed legislation to regulate the sale of firearms, but by then there were an estimated 15 million handguns in the country, with 4 million of these possessed by criminals (Manrique 2006, 7).

The practice of drug dealers paying those who facilitated their international trade with narcotics rather than with cash contributed to a growing drug problem in Brazil. Children as young as six were being paid with narcotics to work for local criminal gangs. These gangs became increasingly organized and powerful. Most dangerous was a group known as Primeiro Comando da Capital, which had its origin in a series of 2001 riots protesting conditions in Brazil's overcrowded prisons. In May 2006 this group staged an open uprising in the nation's largest city, Sao Paulo, attacking police stations, burning buses, and bringing business to a virtual halt for five days (*The Economist* 2006b). Ultimately the military had to help restore a modicum of order. While violence declined in Sao Paulo after that, it surged elsewhere. In Rio, gangs attacked police posts and buses, killing at least nineteen. According to the Overseas Security Advisory, by 2007 in much of urban Brazil "violent crimes such as murder, rape, kidnappings, armed assaults, and burglaries have become a part of normal everyday life" (Overseas Security Advisory Council 2007c).

Brazil reacted to this by bringing the military into the streets, by increased police violence, and by longer incarcerations, adding increased tinder to the explosive situation in the prisons, which were often gang controlled. In the *favelas* the poor were left largely to fend for themselves. They began to organize their own militias and to lynch criminals. By 2007 these militias were estimated to control 90 of Rios' 600 *favelas* and were spreading to other cities. But as they gained some ground against the gangs, they began to exhibit criminal behavior of their own, notably extortion (Downie 2007).

With Brazil hosting the World Cup in 2014 and the Olympics in 2016, government concern with citizen security increased. Growing popular protests reinforced this trend. A program of sending the military into the *favelas* and then establishing an enhanced police presence was inaugurated. So, too, were efforts to enlist community support in forming self-defense units to combat the gangs. The program was also supposed to include social investments, but these have lagged. While some reduction in gang activities has occurred, these results remain fragile, and violent confrontations between gangs and security forces are frequent (Wells 2014). Police remain poorly paid, prone to violence, and ineffectively subject to legal sanctions (Barbara 2014). Citizen security remains a major issue in Brazil, and the sustainability of government efforts to improve it after upcoming elections and the Olympics is in doubt.

Colombia long held the reputation as being Latin America's most violent nation. Indeed, before the US invasion of Iraq, it was sometimes seen as the world's most violent state. The homicide rate reached the astonishing level of 81 per 100,000 in 1992. After declining slightly for a few years, it again rose at the end of the twentieth and start of the twenty-first century, reflecting rising conflict between government forces, leftist guerrillas, organized criminal groups, and paramilitary forces (Sanchez, Solimano, and Formisano 2003). Signs along major streets urged citizens to keep their eyes open, as there were violent criminals in the area. By the end of the twentieth century the state appeared to be near collapse as various illegal armed groups fought for control of much of the national territory. Some success in Colombian and US efforts to combat the major narcotics cartels, highlighted by the death of Pablo Escobar, only brought the guerrillas and paramilitaries more directly into trafficking as they made alliances with the smaller, weaker cartels that replaced the earlier organizations. Conflict was increasingly spilling over Colombia's borders into neighboring countries, bringing violence and corruption to previously relatively peaceful areas of Panama, Ecuador, Venezuela, and even Brazil (*The Economist* 2006c).

The 2002 election of Álvaro Uribe as Colombia's president signaled a shift in government policies toward the illegal armed groups. He moved aggressively against the guerrillas, renewed efforts to extradite leaders of the narcotics cartels, and expanded efforts to curb coca cultivation. Negotiation with the paramilitary forces resulted in the disarming and disbanding of much of this force. The guerrillas were driven back to more remote areas, cities such as Bogota became safer than they had been for over a decade, and Colombians even began to venture out on the major highways without fear of being ambushed and robbed or kidnapped.

Progress, however, has had its limits. Colombia is still among the world's more violence-plagued societies. Efforts at coca eradication seem to have stalled, and meanwhile some of the crop has simply moved back to former cultivation areas in Peru and Bolivia (*The Economist* 2006c). Although Colombia has dropped to twentieth place on the index of world homicide rates, violence and common crime continue at extremely high levels. The World Bank estimates that if it were not for the high rate of crime and violence, "Colombia would today have a per capita income on the order of 32 percent higher than it currently has" (Ayres 1998).

Government officials are constantly involved in accusations of links with narcotics cartels and other illegal activities (Cawley 2014). Other criminal activities, including counterfeiting and people smuggling, continue unabated. Interpol estimated that 35,000 Colombian women were being shipped each year from Colombia to other nations as part of the international sex trade (Inter-American Commission of Women 2001). Many of the demobilized paramilitaries have returned to criminal activities, forming new bands known as BACRIMS (Bandas Criminales, Criminal Groups), which operate in nearly a third of the nation's municipalities (Looft 2012). Colombia has made significant progress in reducing the level of homicides and kidnappings and restoring a degree of state authority, but the basic plague of criminal activity, especially as it impacts poor Colombians, is proving much more resistant to change. Ongoing negotiations with Colombia's major guerrilla group, the Revolutionary Armed Forces of Colombia (FARC), have made progress and, if ultimately successful, would significantly enhance citizen security, providing effective provisions were made for demobilized combatants.

Chile has been a major exception to Latin America's crime epidemic. While common crime, especially in Santiago, has been a growing problem, the country remains at or near the lowest level in all of Latin America for all varieties of violent crime and has the lowest homicide rate—less than 5 percent of that of

Honduras. According to the BBC, "Chile is relatively free of crime and official corruption" (BBC News 2007).

This can be explained by a number of factors. While Chile experienced a transition from authoritarian to democratic rule in the 1990s, this was achieved largely without violence. Chile had experienced episodes of severe repression, but had no major internal conflict, no civil war with the consequent proliferation of firearms and the problem of dealing with ex-combatants. Furthermore, Chile had a long tradition of democratic practices and a party structure based more on discipline and ideology than on loyalty to an individual leader. For Chile, the military's rule was an interruption in a long democratic tradition, whereas in many other nations, democratic government represented a break with a long authoritarian tradition.

Chile also experienced the highest economic growth rate in Latin America over the past forty years. Combined with a relatively low rate of population growth, this helped control unemployment, financed government services, and provided legitimate opportunities for Chile's youth. People smuggling is not a significant issue.

Chile's administration of justice is more effective and credible than that in almost any other Latin American nation. According to the Chile 2007 Crime and Safety Report, the *carbineros*, Chile's national police, "are considered to be the most professional police force in Latin America" (Overseas Security Advisory Council 2007a). Much of Chile's public seems to share this assessment: public confidence in the police in Chile is 60 percent in contrast to approval ratings around 30 percent in the rest of Latin America (Manrique 2006, 3). Chile has also enacted important judicial reforms, enhancing defendants' rights and increasing public confidence in the administration of justice.[11]

One final factor must be considered. Chile's geographical position—on the extreme southwest corner of Latin America, separated from Argentina to the east by the towering Andes and from Peru and Bolivia to the north by the arid Atacama desert—was long seen as a major obstacle to national development. But today it insulates Chile from the world of transnational crime. Chile is not a trans-shipment point for narcotics, people, or any other illicit trafficking. It doesn't produce narcotics, nor is it a major arms exporter. History, economy, geography, and national character have all combined to make Chile the greatest exception to Latin America's pattern of violent crime and citizen insecurity.

Conclusion

For most of Latin America's history, citizen security was threatened largely by state repression and by conflicts between governments and insurgent forces. While these issues remain in some cases, they are generally much less serious than was the case a third of a century ago. But negotiated ends to civil conflicts, transitions from authoritarian to more democratic systems, and even growing respect for individual rights within the administration of justice have all too often failed to provide the basic citizen security that is a fundamental obligation of every state. Today the greatest threat comes from nonstate actors, notably transnational criminal groups, local youth gangs, and the growing tendency to privatize security.[12] This, in turn, leads to a loss of public faith in the democratic process and increased demands for hard-line policies, regardless of their impact on individual rights and the rule of law.[13] Organized criminal groups often establish control over geographical areas, some in isolated rural areas, but others in congested urban slums. This further undermines government's credibility in providing citizen security.[14]

The epidemic of crime is both a result of and a contributing factor to Latin America's massive poverty. It hurts economic growth and discourages investment. This in turn contributes to high levels of unemployment, especially among youth, providing a constant source of recruits for criminal organizations.

The World Bank has identified four basic areas in which crime impedes growth and contributes to increased poverty. These include adverse effects on the stock of physical capital, the erosion of the development of human capital, the destruction of social capital, and the undermining of government capacity (Ayres 1998, 7–8). To this list might also be added the loss of faith and credibility in government and the democratic process.

Of all these factors, the most devastating may well be the impact on social capital. As the World Bank study concludes,

> Crime and violence have devastating effects on social capital. Norms of trust and reciprocity are replaced by the "war of all against all." Community-based organizations and other social networks, deemed as critical for growth and poverty reduction, suffer attrition. . . . The increase in crime and violence makes it increasingly difficult for any sort of community organizations, not based on fear and coercion, to function.
>
> (Ayres 1998, 8)

Much of Latin America remains trapped in a descending spiral of crime and citizen insecurity. This exacerbates the very conditions that helped produce this epidemic in the first place, undermines state capacity to respond, and erodes the capacity of civil society to develop the institutions and values that are necessary to support democratic structures and provide economic opportunity. In many cases, it produces a situation of formal peace without security. The concept of "post-conflict society" seems to have little meaning as conflicts continue in a new and often more deadly form.

There are no quick or easy solutions to this situation. The problem is largely beyond the capacity of individual states to resolve. It demands much greater international cooperation and assistance, a much stronger focus on the issues of administration of justice rather than the more formal aspects of democratic development such as elections and media freedom. This is not to say that those are not important, but without citizen security, without state capacity to deal with the most violent and corrupting elements, these have little meaning and may not long endure. Crime and the consequent citizen insecurity is the

Achilles' heel of democratic transitions and economic development in Latin America and in many other areas. Failure to deal with this issue risks devastating consequences for the entire global community.

Notes

1 For a series of essays exploring this issue, see *Crime and Violence in Latin America: Citizen Security, Democracy, and the State*, Joseph S. Tulchin, H. Hugo Fruhling, and Heather Golding eds., Washington, D.C.: Woodrow Wilson Center Press, 2003.
2 This was true in Colombia, where President Uribe's father had been murdered, and in Honduras, where the same fate befell President Maduro's son.
3 Cited on World Bank Private Sector Development Blog, October 27, 2005.
4 My interviews with Central Americans in Washington, DC and in Miami over the past decade have repeatedly elicited comments like this.
5 See, for example, the numbers cited by Saul Eliezar Hernandez in his presentation on "Fenomeno de las Pandillas en la Region Centroamericana y la Importancia de la Cooperacion International" before the Inter-American Drug Abuse Control Commission Meeting, June 17, 2005.
6 Costa Ricans blame most of the crime in their nation on Nicaraguan immigrants.
7 For more details, see "Haiti 2013 Crime and Safety Report," www.osac.gov/pages/Content/Details.aspx?cid=14000.
8 For a detailed description of this, see Sebastian Rotella, *Twilight on the Line: Underworld and Politics at the U.S-Mexico Border*. New York: W.W. Norton & Co., 1998.
9 "Kidnapping Trends: Examining Patterns in Africa and the Americas," *Jane's Intelligence Review*, January 2007, p. 52. Dr. Hal Klepak of the Royal Military College of Canada, himself a victim of a kidnapping in Mexico City, has expressed to me his conviction that police officials were involved.
10 For more information on these issues, see John Bailey, *The Politics of Crime in Mexico: Democratic Governance in a Security Trap*. Boulder, CO: First Forum Press, 2014.
11 For details, see Lydia Brashear Tiede, "Chile's Criminal Law Reform; Enhancing Defendants Rights and Citizen Security." *Latin American Politics and Society* 54(3) (Fall 2012): 65–93.
12 For a detailed description of these threats, see Kees Kooning and Dirk Kruijt, *Armed Actors, Organized Violence, and State Failure in Latin America*. London: Zed Books, 2005.
13 Angelina Snodgrass Godoy, *Popular Injustice: Violence, Community and Law in Latin America*. Palo Alto: Stanford University Press, 2006, focuses on this trend, especially as it manifests itself in Guatemala.
14 See Hal Brands, *Criminal Fiefdoms in Latin America: Understanding the Problem of Alternatively Governed Spaces*. Miami: Western Hemisphere Security Analysis Center, Florida International University, September 2010.

References

Agence France-Presse. (2013) "Violent crime in Haiti claims more than 1,000 lives" published 19 June 2013, http://reliefweb.int/report/haiti/violent-crime-haiti-claims-more-1000-lives.
Almand, W. (1999) "Introduction," in R. Neild, *From National Security to Citizen Security*. Montreal: International Center for Human Rights and Democratic Development.
Ayres, R.L. (1998) *Crime and Violence as Development Issues in Latin America and the Caribbean*. Washington, DC: World Bank Latin American and Caribbean Studies.

Barbara, V. (2014) "Pity Brazil's Military Police." *New York Times.* February 19. Retrieved from www.nytimes.com/2014/02/20/opinion/barbara-reform-brazils-military-police.htm?r=0.

BBC News. (2003) "12 Die in Brazil Drugs Battle." January 10. Retrieved from http://news.bbc.co.uk/2/hi/americas/2647695.stm.

BBC News. (2007) "Country Profile: Chile." June 21. Retrieved from http://news.bbc.co.uk/2/hi/americas/country_profiles/1222764.stm.

Cajina, R. (2013) *Security in Nicaragua: Central America's Exception?* Inter-American Dialogue Working Paper, January.

Cawlely, M. (2014) "Election Results Show Persisting Criminal Influence in Colombia Politics." March 11. Retrieved from http://insightcrime.org/news-briefs/colombia-elections-show-persisting-criminal-influence-in-politics?

Centro de Estudios Sociales y de Opinion Publica. (2007) "Camara de Diputados, Mexico." Report CESOP No. 4, Mexico, DF.

CNN Staff (2014) "Which Countries Have the Highest Murder Rates? Honduras Tops the List." April 12. Retrieved from www.cnn.com/2014/04/11/world/un-world-murder-rates.

Downie, A. (2007) "Brazil's Slums Face a New Problem: Vigilante Militias." *Christian Science Monitor* February 8. Retrieved from www.csmonitor.com/2007/0208/p04s01-woam.html. Accessed November 24, 2014.

EFE. (2007) "Obispo salvadoreno saluda la busqueda de 'exterminadores'" August 6. Retrieved from http://elnuevoherald.com/noticias/america_latina/v-print/story/74675.html.

El Nuevo Herald. (2007) "Honduras vive en anarquia dice funcionario de DDHH." (Miami), March 26.

Godoy, A. (2006) *Popular Injustice: Violence, Community and Law in Latin America.* Palo Alto: Stanford University Press.

Iaconangelo, D. (2014) "Knights Templar Mexican Drug Cartel Makes $152M Per Year Extorting Michoacan Avocado Industry." January 14. Retrieved from www.latintimes.com/knights-templar-mexican-drug-cartel-makes-152m-year-extorting-michoacan-avocado-industry-145066. Accessed November 24, 2014

Inter-American Commission on Human Rights. (2003) "Annual Report, 2003" Chapter IV, sections 49 and 51. Retrieved from www.cidh.org/annualrep/2003eng/chap.4b.htm. Accessed November 24, 2014.Inter-American Commission of Women (Organization of American States) and Women, Health and Development Program (Pan American Health Organization). (2001) "Trafficking of Women and Children for Sexual Exploitation in the Americas." Washington, July. Retrieved from www.oas.org/en/cim/docs/Trafficking-Paper%5BEN%5D.pdf. Accessed November 24, 2014.

Inter-American Development Bank (2013) Retrieved from http://blogs.iadb.org/sinmiedos/2013/11/01/latinobarometro-la-delincuencia-sigue-siendo-la-mayor-preocupacion-de-america-latina-pero/. Accessed November 24, 2014.

International Crisis Group. (2013) *Latin American Briefing #29: Justice at the Barrel of a Gun, Vigilante Militias in Mexico.* Mexico City/Bogota/Brussels, May 28.

Jane's Intelligence Review. (2007a) "Kidnapping Trends: Examining Patterns in Africa and the Americas." January: 52.

Jane's Intelligence Review. (2007b) "Fighting Back: Mexico Declares War on Drug Cartels." April: 7–11.

Kooning, K and Kruijt, D. (2005) *Armed Actors, Organized Violence, and State Failure in Latin America.* London: Zed Books.

Lacey, M. (2007) "UN Troops Fight Haiti's Gangs One Street at a Time." *New York Times.* February 10.

Looft, C. (2012) "Study: BACRIMS Continue Steady Expansion Across Colombia." February 27. Retrieved from www.insightcrime.org/news-briefs/study-bacrims-continue-steady-expansion-across-colombia. Accessed November 24, 2014.

Lovelock, B. (2005) "Securing a Viable Peace: Defeating Militant Extremists," in J. Covey, Dziedzic, M.J., and Hawley, L.R. (eds.), *The Quest for a Viable Peace: International Intervention and Strategies for Conflict Transformation* (123–56). Washington, DC: USIP.

Manrique, L.E. (2006) "A Parallel Power: Organized Crime in Latin America." Real Institute Elcano (Spain), September 28, pp. 1–8.

Overseas Advisory Security Council. (2007a) "Chile 2007 Crime and Safety Report." March 8. www.osac.gov/Reports/report.cfm?contentID=63629. Accessed November 24, 2014.

Overseas Security Advisory Council. (2007b) "Haiti 2007 Crime and Safety Report." January 9. Retrieved from www.osac.gov/Reports/report.cfm?contentID=61647. Accessed November 24, 2014.

Overseas Security Advisory Council. (2007c) "Brazil 2007 Crime and Safety Report: Sao Paulo." February 6. Retrieved from www.osac.gov/Reports/report.cfm?contentID=62452. Accessed November 24, 2014.

Pinheiro, P.S. (2006) "Youth Violence and Democracy in Latin America." Alstair Berkley Memorial Lecture, London School of Economics, May 26.

Root, J. (2007) "Mexico Becoming One of the World's Most Dangerous Countries." *McClatchy Newspapers* September 23.

Rotella, S. (1998) *Twilight on the Line: Underworld and Politics at the U.S.-Mexico Border.* New York: W.W. Norton.

Sanchez, F., Solimano, A., and Formisano, M. (2003) "Conflict, Violent Crime, and Criminal Activity in Colombia." Yale University Research Program of the Economics and Politics of Civil Wars.

Stein, E. (2007) Vice-president of Guatemala, interviewed in *Inter-American Dialogue's Latin American Advisor,* Washington, DC, September 7, p. 1.

Testimony of Adolfo A. Franco, Assistant Administrator, Bureau for Latin America and the Caribbean, United States Agency for International Development, before the Committee on International Relations, U.S. House of Representatives, Subcommittee on the Western Hemisphere, Wednesday, April 20, 2005, http://iipdigital.usembassy.gov/st/english/texttrans/2005/04/20050420161901asrellim0.5433161.html#ixzz3NQQubin9.

The Economist. (2006a) "The Democracy Dividend." December 7, Retrieved from www.economist.com/node/8381789. Accessed November 24, 2014.

The Economist. (2006b) "The Mob Takes on the State." May 20, pp. 39–40. Retrieved from www.economist.com/node/6950391. Accessed November 24, 2014

The Economist. (2006c) "One Step Forward in a Quagmire." March 18. Retrieved from www.economist.com/node/5636088?zid=318&ah=ac379c09c1c3fb67e0e8f d1964d5247f. Accessed November 24, 2014.

The Economist. (2007) "The Tough Get Going." January 27, p. 33.

The Economist. (2013) "Violent Crime in Latin America: Alternatives to the Iron Fist." November 16. Retrieved from www.economist.com/news/americas/21589889-how-prevent-epidemic-alternatives-iron-fist. Accessed November 24, 2014.

Tulchin, J. S., Fruhling, H. H., and Golding, H. (eds.) (2003) *Crime and Violence in Latin America: Citizen Security, Democracy, and the State*. Washington, DC: Woodrow Wilson Center Press.

United Nations Development Program. (2013) *Citizen Security with a Human Face: Evidence and Proposals for Latin America*. New York: United Nations.

Wells, M. (2014) "Gangs Reassert Themselves in Rio's 'Pacified' Favelas." March 28. Retrieved from www.insightcrime.org/news-analysis/gangs-reassert-themselves-in-rios-pacified-favelas?. Accessed November 24, 2014.

14 Economic Development and Democracy in Latin America

Michael J. Ferrantino[1] *and*
Sheila Amin Gutiérrez de Piñeres

Introduction

The performance of Latin American and Caribbean (LAC) exports in recent years has given cause for optimism. After the Great Trade Collapse of 2008–2009 (Baldwin 2009), which was sharper than the Great Recession associated with it, export growth in current dollars accelerated to a 16.9 percent annual rate in 2010–2012, exceeding the 14.6 percent annual rate in the pre-crisis period of 2001–2008. Similarly, real gross domestic product (GDP) growth in Latin America, at 4.1 percent per year over 2010–2012, accelerated from the pre-crisis rate of 3.1 percent during 2001–2008. Moreover, Latin American rates of both export growth and GDP growth after the crisis outpaced the rates for the world as a whole (13.5 percent for current exports, 3.1 percent for real GDP growth in 2010–2012). The road to recovery has not been without bumps—for example, developing countries face challenges retaining mobile capital in the face of more normal financial conditions in the United States and Europe (*The Telegraph* 2013). Nonetheless, there is some cause for renewed optimism.

This renewal of export optimism contrasts sharply with an earlier, widely held view that exposure to international trade could hinder LAC development by inducing a "primary product trap." Countries exporting such products as coffee, copper, beef, or bananas were considered likely to fare poorly in international markets either because of a secular decline in the prices of primary products (e.g., Prebisch 1950), because of "unequal exchange" between primary products and manufactures (e.g., Amin 1977), or because lack of diversification would expose "single-export" countries to excessive volatility in the terms of trade, with associated negative effects on investment confidence (Helleiner 1986). Consequently, schemes of import-substituting industrialization were advocated.

The chapter is an attempt to establish some stylized facts about the economies, trade patterns, and governance indicators in Latin American and Caribbean countries. The data show that there is no simple relationship between economic performance and a specialization in primary products—there are primary product exporters who perform both well and poorly. Similarly, diversification per se is not obviously correlated with economic growth. The quality of governance is more relevant for countries' economic performance than the goods they specialize in, as is the ability to attract foreign direct investment (FDI). However, export diversification is still a useful strategy in that it helps countries to manage the risks associated with price and demand volatility of single products.

These results are offered in a spirit of casual empiricism, suitable for an interdisciplinary audience. They do not attempt to rigorously determine the causes of economic growth in Latin America. Although they are broadly consistent with more rigorous econometric studies using global data (Barro and Sala-i-Martin 1995; Balasubramanyan, Salisu, and Sapsford 1996), the reader who is familiar with such studies will readily identify the many issues omitted in this quick treatment.

Historical Overview

Latin America has a long tradition of economic liberalism dating back to the nineteenth century, punctuated by periodic experiments with import substitution. Maddison (1991), using data for 1913, illustrates that Latin America was much more integrated into the world economy than were the Asian countries. During this period, there was a great deal of foreign investment and growth rates were relatively high in Latin American countries. In addition, "the role of the state in the economy was relatively small, and the bureaucratic apparatus weak. The dominant ideology espoused democracy and laissez-faire" (Urrutia 1991). Trade during this era was predominately with the developed world. Intra-Latin trade was minimal (Maddison 1991).

The change in philosophy came after the world depression of 1929. Trade, migration, and capital restrictions forced Latin American countries to look inward for solutions. The volume of trade fell, as did world prices for Latin American exports (Maddison 1991). The openness of Latin American economies magnified the effect of the US depression on those economies. At this point, Latin America began to diverge from liberalism to a more inward-looking policy approach. Protectionist policies in Latin America continued during the post–World War II years, with largely satisfactory performance in terms of aggregate growth. As Maddison (1991) notes, "Despite supply shortages, the countries had been able to grow successfully and to achieve rather easy import substitution without a large switch of resources to capital formation or any massive effort at universal training." Thus, while the rest of the world was moving back towards liberalism in the post-war period, Latin America saw no reason to diverge away from its policies of import substitution.

An intellectual rationale for inward-looking policies was provided by Raul Prebisch's hypothesis of export pessimism (1959). Prebisch, then president of the UN Economic Commission for Latin America and the Caribbean (ECLAC), expressed doubts about the ability of trade to be an engine of growth and saw declining terms of trade for primary products as hindering the growth of developing countries. Prebisch contended that price instability and declining terms of trade created a primary commodity export dependence that was the cause of slow growth. Subsequent empirical research has not supported the hypothesis of a general declining trend in the terms of trade for developing countries (Grilli and Yang 1988). In addition, while certain export commodities have had highly volatile price swings, the price index of the overall primary commodity basket of Latin American exports has not been particularly volatile (Lord and Boye 1991).

In the 1960s, some effort was made to expand intra-Latin exports of manufacturers through the creation of regional trading blocs such as Latin American Free Trade Association (LAFTA), the Andean Pact, and Central American Common Market (CACM). Given the similarity in resource endowments, these trading agreements only met with limited success (Maddison 1991; Michaely 1994). It was not until the second oil shock of 1979 and the debt crisis of the early 1980s that Latin American economies experienced significant pressure for trade liberalization, induced by the sharp economic contractions of the period.

Simultaneously, individual countries have sought independently to promote their exports. Many countries created export promotion agencies (PROEXPO in Colombia, PROCHILE in Chile, SECOFI in Mexico, APEX in Brazil, and PROMEXPORT in Venezuela) whose sole purpose was to expand export markets and encourage diversification in exports. There has always been recognition of the "desirability of diversifying exports away from primary commodities" (Urrutia 1991). The initial push of these agencies was to expand exports of manufactured goods, which proved to be a failure, as these countries were not able to compete on world markets. Years of import substitution had created inefficient high-cost industries, which had been shielded from any real competition.

In an earlier work (Amin Gutiérrez de Piñeres and Ferrantino 2000) we reported a general trend toward export diversification for the period from the early 1960s to the early 1990s. This trend encompassed periods of economic recovery and crisis, and countries with widely divergent policy stances ranging from liberal and outward looking to state oriented and inward looking. For the most recent period, from 1990 to 2011, we report here a modest reversal of this trend—countries in Latin America have become somewhat more specialized in their export portfolios, although nowhere near the degree that prevailed prior to the debt crisis of the early 1980s.

The current period has also witnessed a divergence of policy stances in the region with respect to foreign trade. Latin American free trade areas are a group of countries that have no internal tariffs between countries, but each country defines its own external tariffs. Countries in a customs union have no internal tariffs and common external tariffs. A common market has no internal tariff, common external tariffs, and free movement of factors of production, such as labor and capital. Finally, an economic union is a common market with a supranational authority and a single monetary system. We consider in our present analysis the nineteen largest economies in Latin America. Of these, ten have free trade agreements with the United States:[2] Chile, Colombia, Costa Rica, El Salvador, Guatemala, Honduras, Mexico, Nicaragua, Panama, and Peru. Most of these countries have pursued networks of free trade agreements both within the region and worldwide. Beginning in 2004 with Venezuela and Cuba, and continuing gradually, countries with a socialist or social-democratic orientation grouped themselves into ALBA-TCP, the "Bolivarian Alliance" in short English, adopting strategies of barter and countertrade as well as a common regional currency for electronic settlement. The countries in our sample belonging to ALBA-TCP are Bolivia, Ecuador, Nicaragua, and Venezuela.[3] (Note that Nicaragua is also part of the CAFTA-DR free trade agreement with the United States.) Occupying an intermediate position are the five members of the customs union MERCOSUR: Argentina, Bolivia, Brazil, Paraguay, and Venezuela (note again the overlap between MERCOSUR and ALBA-TCP). We also consider two Caribbean nations— Jamaica and Trinidad and Tobago—which do not fall in any of the three previous categories.

The preceding brief description does not begin to do justice to the complexity and diversity of trade policies observed within Latin America.[4] The point is to illustrate that countries situate themselves very differently with respect to trade policy, but are affected by common economic trends.

Economic Indicators

Since the 1990s, Latin America and the Caribbean has enjoyed positive, if variable, economic growth, with some countries being caught either in the modest global downturn in 2001, associated with the end of the dot-com bubble in US stock markets, or in the much larger Great Recession of 2008–2009, associated with the end of the US housing bubble and triggered by the failure of Lehman Brothers. It is interesting to note that a majority of the countries considered here maintained positive growth through both of the recent global turndowns.

Table 14.1 presents growth rates for five-year periods from 1993–2007, dividing the most recent period (2008–2012) into two pieces in order to reflect the Great Recession and ensuing recovery. The countries are sorted by their cumulative compound growth rates throughout the period 1993–2012. The countries with the four highest long-run growth rates are all among those that pursued bilateral liberalization with the United States—Panama, Chile, Peru, and Costa Rica. However, Mexico, with the deepest integration with the United States, has one of the slower long-run growth rates.

The table also reports a measure of volatility, which is the standard deviation of the annual real growth rate. Volatility is relatively high for oil exporters, such as Trinidad and Tobago and Venezuela, and for countries with persistent

Table 14.1 Real GDP Growth (as % of GDP)

	1993–1997	1998–2002	2003–2007	2008–2009	2010–2012	1993–2012	Volatility
Country Name							
Panama	3.9%	3.3%	7.9%	6.9%	9.6%	6.8%	2.7%
Chile	7.5%	2.5%	4.9%	1.3%	5.9%	5.3%	2.5%
Peru	7.1%	1.7%	6.5%	5.2%	7.3%	5.2%	2.3%
Costa Rica	4.5%	4.4%	6.6%	0.8%	4.7%	5.0%	2.1%
Trinidad and Tobago	2.5%	6.1%	9.1%	−0.3%	**−1.5%**	**4.6%**	4.4%
Bolivia	4.6%	2.4%	4.1%	4.7%	4.8%	4.5%	1.0%
Argentina	4.4%	−3.2%	**8.9%**	3.8%	6.6%	**4.0%**	4.6%
Guatemala	4.0%	3.7%	4.1%	1.9%	3.2%	4.0%	0.9%
Colombia	3.8%	1.0%	5.5%	2.6%	4.6%	3.9%	1.8%
Ecuador	2.6%	1.7%	4.9%	3.7%	5.4%	3.9%	1.5%
Honduras	3.5%	2.6%	5.9%	1.0%	3.3%	3.8%	1.8%
Nicaragua	3.8%	3.7%	4.3%	0.7%	4.5%	3.7%	1.5%
Uruguay	4.5%	−2.3%	4.8%	4.8%	6.2%	3.3%	3.3%
El Salvador	5.1%	2.7%	3.1%	−1.0%	1.5%	3.3%	2.2%
Venezuela, RB	1.6%	−1.6%	7.5%	1.0%	2.7%	3.1%	3.4%
Mexico	2.3%	3.2%	3.4%	−2.4%	4.5%	3.1%	2.7%
Brazil	4.0%	1.7%	4.0%	2.4%	3.7%	3.1%	1.0%
Paraguay	3.3%	−1.3%	5.1%	0.3%	6.4%	3.0%	3.2%
Jamaica	2.3%	**0.2%**	n/a	−2.2%	−0.2%	**1.2%**	1.8%

Calculations in bold italics reflect missing years:
Argentina 2007, Jamaica 2002–2006, Trinidad and Tobago 2010

macroeconomic difficulties resulting from external shocks to the economy and/or poor government decisions, such as Argentina.

The ability to attract FDI is in part a matter of the larger world community's perception of the long-term viability of the country's economy and its business climate. Table 14.2 reports both the absolute level of a country's FDI and its ratio to GDP. The highest rates of FDI absorption are in the smaller island and entrepôt economies—Trinidad and Tobago, Panama, and Jamaica, followed by Chile. The countries with the lowest FDI/GDP ratios are affiliated either with ALBA-TCP or MERCOSUR—Ecuador, Paraguay, and Venezuela. Ecuador and Venezuela are both oil exporters that have nationalized their oil industries, increasing the perception of risk among other foreign investors. Trinidad and Tobago, by contrast, is an oil exporter with significant foreign presence in its export industry. There is a modest positive relationship between the ratio of FDI stock/GDP and the long-run growth rate—the simple correlation between these two variables is 0.26. This is less formal than a full econometric model of growth and convergence would be, but perhaps illustrative.

We now turn to the most familiar indicators of macroeconomic performance—unemployment and inflation. Unemployment rates are reported in Table 14.3 for the purposes of illustration. However, it should be noted

Table 14.2 Foreign Direct Investment and Ratio to GDP, 2012

	FDI stock, millions U.S.	*FDI stock/GDP*
Trinidad and Tobago	21,782	93.4%
Panama	28,903	79.7%
Jamaica	11,581	78.5%
Chile	206,594	76.6%
Nicaragua	6,476	61.6%
Honduras	9,024	49.0%
Costa Rica	18,713	41.5%
El Salvador	8,635	36.2%
Uruguay	17,900	35.9%
Bolivia	8,809	32.6%
Brazil	702,208	31.2%
Peru	63,448	31.1%
Colombia	111,924	30.3%
Mexico	314,968	26.7%
Argentina	110,704	23.3%
Guatemala	8,914	17.7%
Ecuador	13,079	15.6%
Paraguay	3,936	15.4%
Venezuela	49,079	12.9%

Table 14.3 Unemployment Rate

	1990	*1995*	*2000*	*2005*	*2010*
Argentina	9.20%	16.00%	14.65%	11.58%	7.75%
Bolivia	7.30%	3.60%	7.46%	N/A	N/A
Brazil	3.70%	4.64%	9.20%	9.83%	6.74%
Chile	5.70%	4.70%	8.30%	8.00%	8.34%
Colombia	10.20%	8.70%	20.50%	11.87%	11.75%
Costa Rica	4.60%	5.20%	5.20%	6.60%	7.30%
Ecuador	6.10%	6.90%	9.00%	7.90%	7.59%
El Salvador	10.00%	7.70%	7.00%	7.20%	N/A
Jamaica	15.70%	16.20%	15.50%	11.23%	12.38%
Mexico	N/A	4.70%	1.60%	3.58%	5.35%
Nicaragua	7.60%	16.90%	9.80%	N/A	7.86%
Panama	N/A	14.00%	13.50%	10.33%	N/A
Paraguay	6.60%	N/A	10.30%	N/A	7.24%
Peru	N/A	7.10%	7.90%	9.54%	7.96%
Trinidad and Tobago	20.00%	17.18%	12.20%	8.00%	5.93%
Uruguay	8.50%	10.30%	13.60%	12.18%	6.67%
Venezuela	10.40%	10.30%	14.01%	12.25%	8.51%

Source: IMF & International Financial Statistics
Frequency: Annual

Table 14.4 Inflation, Average Consumer Prices (percent change)

	1990	1995	2000	2005	2010	2011	2012
Argentina	2,313.96	3.38	−0.94	9.64	10.46	9.78	10.04
Bolivia	17.12	10.19	4.60	5.40	2.50	9.88	4.52
Brazil	2,947.73	66.01	7.04	6.87	5.04	6.64	5.40
Chile	26.04	8.23	3.84	3.05	1.41	3.34	3.01
Colombia	29.09	20.89	9.22	5.05	2.27	3.42	3.17
Costa Rica	19.04	23.19	10.96	13.80	5.66	4.88	4.49
Ecuador	48.52	22.89	96.10	2.10	3.55	4.48	5.10
El Salvador	28.29	9.73	2.27	4.69	1.18	5.13	1.73
Guatemala	37.98	8.41	5.98	9.11	3.86	6.22	3.78
Honduras	23.32	29.46	11.32	8.81	4.70	6.76	5.20
Jamaica	24.78	19.91	8.14	15.10	12.61	7.53	7.29
Mexico	26.65	35.06	9.49	3.99	4.16	3.40	4.11
Nicaragua	3,004.10	11.18	7.07	9.20	3.02	7.38	7.93
Panama	0.77	0.94	1.45	2.87	3.49	5.88	5.70
Paraguay	38.16	13.39	8.98	6.81	4.65	8.25	3.79
Peru	7,481.69	11.13	3.76	1.62	1.53	3.37	3.66
Trinidad and Tobago	11.06	5.30	3.50	6.89	10.55	5.10	9.27
Uruguay	112.53	42.25	4.76	4.70	6.70	8.09	8.10
Venezuela	40.66	59.92	16.21	15.96	28.19	26.09	21.07

Sources: IMF, World Economic Outlook (WEO) (April 2013)

that unemployment numbers in Latin America are deceiving in that they represent only data for the formal economy. In many developing countries, the informal economy is a large part of the labor market, and even for the formal economy, methods of measuring the unemployment rate are not standardized. The definition of inflation, however, is more standardized, and Table 14.4 shows a clear trend. The very high rates of inflation observed in many Latin American countries historically, including the 1990s, are now largely a thing of the past.[5] One explanation for this may be that the memory of fiscal austerity imposed from without during the 1980s debt crisis is still actively felt in the region, and such austerity is now being imposed from within in order to avoid external policy constraints such as International Monetary Fund (IMF) conditionality. With smaller government debts, there is less pressure to monetize the debt that cannot be easily marketed, and thus less inflation.

Latin American countries are becomingly increasingly open to trade. The data reveal that both imports and exports as a percentage of GDP are increasing over time. (See Tables 14.5 and 14.6.) This is a positive indicator in that it implies countries have the resources to purchase foreign products and are taking advantage of their comparative advantage. The larger export share, however, also makes the country more vulnerable to external pressures and world economic cycles. Here, the relevant feature of the data is the time trend, not

Table 14.5 Imports (as % of GDP)

	1990	1995	2000	2005	2010	2012
Argentina	4.98%	10.09%	11.64%	19.19%	18.40%	17.40%
Bolivia	23.93%	27.19%	27.32%	32.09%	34.32%	n.a.
Brazil	6.96%	8.78%	11.74%	11.52%	11.90%	13.99%
Chile	n.a.	n.a.	28.87%	31.82%	31.76%	33.85%
Colombia	15.92%	20.96%	16.75%	18.78%	17.76%	19.50%
Costa Rica	41.09%	40.37%	45.77%	53.97%	40.93%	41.80%
Ecuador	n.a.	n.a.	27.34%	28.48%	33.35%	n.a.
El Salvador	31.23%	37.76%	42.43%	44.16%	42.84%	46.61%
Guatemala	26.62%	28.53%	32.47%	40.99%	36.27%	n.a.
Honduras	38.94%	56.24%	66.42%	77.48%	63.68%	69.42%
Jamaica	50.87%	60.92%	48.03%	55.24%	49.55%	n.a.
Mexico	19.82%	23.69%	28.49%	28.55%	31.55%	33.99%
Nicaragua	n.a.	34.67%	51.10%	58.64%	69.67%	n.a.
Panama	68.86%	85.73%	69.82%	69.06%	74.36%	n.a.
Paraguay	n.a.	56.29%	38.15%	46.07%	51.52%	46.68%
Peru	13.83%	18.19%	17.96%	19.17%	22.77%	24.29%
Trinidad and Tobago	31.46%	39.25%	45.34%	38.99%	n.a.	n.a.
Uruguay	n.a.	n.a.	20.02%	28.47%	26.28%	29.66%
Venezuela	20.18%	21.82%	18.11%	20.47%	17.61%	22.95%

Sources: Inter-American Development Bank (IADB) and LATAM Macro Watch Data Tool

Table 14.6 Exports (as % of GDP)

	1990	1995	2000	2005	2010	2011	2012
Argentina	10.61%	9.68%	10.99%	25.07%	21.71%	21.82%	19.71%
Bolivia	22.78%	22.55%	18.27%	35.55%	41.19%	44.12%	n.a.
Brazil	8.20%	7.26%	9.98%	15.13%	10.87%	11.89%	12.56%
Chile	n.a.	n.a.	30.63%	40.27%	38.06%	37.99%	34.21%
Colombia	18.86%	14.53%	15.92%	16.85%	15.94%	18.93%	18.31%
Costa Rica	34.19%	37.56%	48.62%	48.50%	38.17%	37.43%	37.67%
Ecuador	n.a.	n.a.	32.13%	27.62%	29.42%	31.59%	n.a.
El Salvador	18.56%	21.64%	27.40%	25.64%	25.92%	28.03%	28.21%
Guatemala	22.15%	21.60%	22.65%	25.05%	25.80%	27.14%	n.a.
Honduras	38.51%	36.63%	53.97%	59.01%	45.76%	49.93%	49.00%
Jamaica	47.13%	50.64%	37.99%	35.29%	31.31%	30.91%	n.a.
Mexico	18.39%	25.96%	26.76%	27.10%	30.34%	31.57%	32.90%
Nicaragua	n.a.	19.12%	23.89%	28.97%	42.63%	45.85%	n.a.
Panama	75.90%	88.25%	72.58%	75.49%	75.95%	89.50%	n.a.
Paraguay	n.a.	61.54%	46.10%	57.32%	54.63%	48.85%	46.76%
Peru	15.77%	12.50%	16.05%	25.09%	25.50%	28.68%	25.28%
Trinidad and Tobago	47.71%	53.77%	59.22%	65.78%	n.a.	n.a.	n.a.
Uruguay	n.a.	n.a.	16.70%	30.40%	27.19%	27.23%	26.26%
Venezuela	39.45%	27.11%	29.74%	39.66%	28.53%	29.94%	25.79%

Sources: IADB and LATAM Macro Watch Data Tool

the cross-country comparison. Smaller countries, such as Jamaica, are likely to have larger trade/GDP ratios than larger economies such as Mexico or Brazil; thus, the ratio by itself is not a direct indicator of "openness to trade" in the policy sense. However, the upward time trend for most countries does suggest that Latin American economies are affected by the general trend toward globalization.

In Latin America, concentration of exports in primary products (agriculture and food, forestry, fishing, and mining products, including mineral fuels) is still higher than it is for industrial countries. Table 14.7 shows the share of primary products in total exports, ranging from 20 percent in manufacturing-oriented Mexico to 90 percent in oil exporters Ecuador and Venezuela. The relevant question for our purposes is whether there is a problem with primary exports per se, or with a lack of diversity of such exports. As noted earlier, some of the theories popular in earlier decades promoted import-substituting industrialization as a way of avoiding "primary product traps."

The alternative concept of diversification is captured by an indicator known as the Herfindahl index, which is defined as the sum of the squared shares of exports of each industry in total exports for the region under study and takes a value between 0 and 1, with 1 indicating that only a single product is exported. Higher values indicate that exports are concentrated in fewer sectors. The

Table 14.7 Primary Commodity Exports (percentage of the total for each country for each year)

	1995	2000	2005	2010	2011	*Average*
Argentina	61%	64%	66%	62%	63%	63%
Bolivia	53%	59%	81%	86%	85%	73%
Brazil	37%	32%	41%	58%	60%	45%
Chile	41%	43%	49%	42%	41%	43%
Colombia	64%	67%	62%	72%	77%	68%
Costa Rica	73%	34%	34%	38%	38%	43%
Ecuador	89%	91%	92%	89%	91%	90%
El Salvador	58%	51%	21%	22%	26%	36%
Guatemala	70%	65%	41%	54%	56%	57%
Honduras	87%	74%	72%	N/A	N/A	78%
Jamaica	N/A	30%	34%	62%	N/A	42%
Mexico	19%	15%	21%	21%	24%	20%
Nicaragua	74%	87%	84%	79%	76%	80%
Panama	78%	82%	86%	67%	6%	64%
Paraguay	45%	66%	77%	91%	90%	74%
Peru	51%	43%	49%	55%	57%	51%
Trinidad and Tobago	57%	71%	74%	69%	N/A	68%
Uruguay	47%	49%	60%	N/A	N/A	52%
Venezuela	81%	88%	89%	95%	97%	90%

Source: World Integrated Trade Solution (WITS), World Bank

Table 14.8 Export Concentration: Herfindahl Index

	1995	2000	2005	2010	2011	Average
Argentina	0.049	0.068	0.067	0.062	0.066	0.062
Bolivia	0.119	0.090	0.259	0.266	0.286	0.204
Brazil	0.040	0.040	0.046	0.060	0.067	0.050
Chile	0.140	0.129	0.168	0.217	0.198	0.170
Colombia	0.121	0.201	0.171	0.337	0.429	0.252
Costa Rica	0.135	0.134	0.081	0.086	0.105	0.108
Ecuador	0.198	0.297	0.375	0.329	0.354	0.310
El Salvador	0.159	0.079	0.187	0.137	0.120	0.136
Guatemala	0.123	0.086	0.069	0.053	0.054	0.077
Honduras	0.322	0.143	0.109	N/A	N/A	0.191
Jamaica	N/A	0.334	0.406	0.187	N/A	0.309
Mexico	0.117	0.142	0.127	0.131	0.124	0.128
Nicaragua	0.108	0.136	0.079	0.102	0.118	0.108
Panama	0.178	0.157	0.260	0.134	0.103	0.166
Paraguay	0.166	0.157	0.179	0.191	0.202	0.179
Peru	0.110	0.098	0.126	0.159	0.157	0.130
Trinidad and Tobago	0.262	0.442	0.509	0.467	N/A	0.420
Uruguay	0.063	0.070	0.084	N/A	N/A	0.072
Venezuela	0.587	0.743	0.775	0.873	0.934	0.782
Average (15 countries)	0.167	0.178	0.205	0.208	0.221	0.198

Average excludes Trinidad and Tobago and Uruguay.
Source: UN COMTRADE data extracted from WITS

Herfindahl index (see Table 14.8) reveals that most Latin American countries have a diversified portfolio, with the exception of Venezuela who is dependent on oil production. Moreover, diversification is possible even within an overall specialization in primary products. The most diversified exporters in Latin America—Argentina, Brazil, Nicaragua, and Uruguay—all have primary product shares between 40 and 80 percent of total exports. A blend of primary products plus some manufacturers account for this diversification.

There is a virtually no correlation between export concentration (lack of diversification) and higher growth rates, as illustrated in Figure 14.1. This is true whether or not we include the extreme point represented by Venezuela at the far right, with very high concentration and relatively low growth. Even less so is specialization in primary products a hindrance to growth. There is a very slight positive correlation between primary product specialization and economic growth as seen in Figure 14.2. Thus, the simple ideas about primary product specialization, lack of diversification, and economic growth do not apply to today's Latin America, if in fact they ever applied. This does not mean that diversification is not important in shielding the economy from unpredictable shocks—but this is a question we will not examine deeply here.

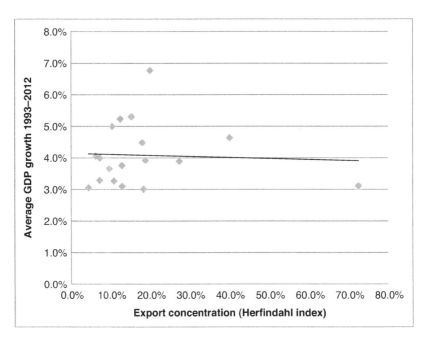

Figure 14.1 GDP Growth vs. Export Concentration

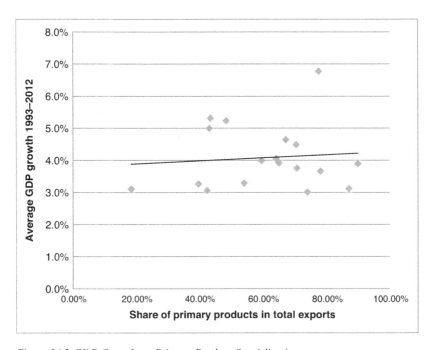

Figure 14.2 GDP Growth vs. Primary Product Specialization

Economic Freedom

One important determinant of the rate of economic growth is the quality of governance. Indicators that measure "institutional quality," "rule of law," and "economic freedom" tend to capture something similar and to rank countries in a similar way. Indicators of economic freedom illustrate the degree to which a country exhibits clear property rights, enforcement of contracts, entrepreneur-friendly laws and regulations, and other institutional features necessary to align economic incentives with productive activity rather than rent seeking. One widely used indicator, the Index of Economic Freedom, is reported in Table 14.9. Higher values mean more economic freedom. An important feature of these data is their tendency to bifurcate over time. Countries with a relatively high degree of economic freedom today, such as Chile, Colombia, and Costa Rica, have tended to show steady improvement over time, while countries with low economic freedom today, such as Venezuela, Ecuador, Bolivia, and Argentina, have tended to get worse over time. In the case of Argentina, the reversal of performance in governance from being one of the most economically free countries in Latin America in 1995 to being one of the least free is striking. The same is true when examining individual components of the index, such as property rights, corruption, or fiscal policy.

Table 14.9   Economic Freedom Index: Overall Score

	1995	2000	2005	2010	2013	Change 1995–2013
Argentina	68	70	51.7	51.2	46.7	−21.3
Bolivia	56.8	65	58.4	49.4	47.9	−8.9
Brazil	51.4	61.1	61.7	55.6	57.7	6.3
Chile	71.2	74.7	77.8	77.2	79	7.8
Colombia	64.5	63.3	59.6	65.5	69.6	5.1
Costa Rica	68	68.4	66.1	65.9	67	−1
Ecuador	57.7	59.8	52.9	49.3	46.9	−10.8
El Salvador	69.1	76.3	71.5	69.9	66.7	−2.4
Guatemala	62	64.3	59.5	61	60	−2
Honduras	57	57.6	55.3	58.3	58.4	1.4
Jamaica	64.4	65.5	67	65.5	66.8	2.4
Mexico	63.1	59.3	65.2	68.3	67	3.9
Nicaragua	42.5	56.9	62.5	58.3	56.6	14.1
Panama	71.6	71.6	64.3	64.8	62.5	−9.1
Paraguay	65.9	64	53.4	61.3	61.1	−4.8
Peru	56.9	68.7	61.3	67.6	68.2	11.3
Trinidad & Tobago	69.2*	74.5	71.5	65.7	62.3	−6.9
Uruguay	62.5	69.3	66.9	69.8	69.7	7.2
Venezuela	59.8	57.4	45.2	37.1	36.1	−23.7

*Score is for 1996.
Source: Heritage Foundation (2014).

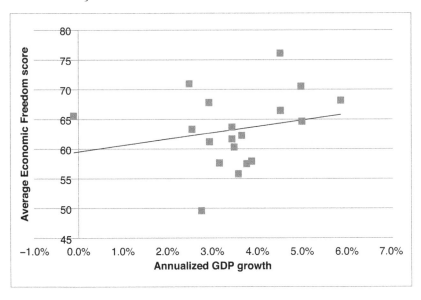

Figure 14.3 GDP Growth and Economic Freedom 1995–2011

Averages exclude 2007 for Argentina, 2002–2006 for Jamaica, and 1995 and 2010 for Trinidad and Tobago due to missing data.

There is a modest positive correlation between economic freedom and real GDP growth over the period 1995–2011 (see Figure 14.3). The simple correlation between the two variables is 0.22, about the same as that between GDP growth and the FDI stock. Similar results are obtained when using the average of the World Bank's World Governance Indicators in place of the Heritage Foundation index. In a more rigorous econometric investigation, taking into account other variables such as investment, education, and the tendency of poorer countries to catch up to rich countries, we expect that this result would be confirmed. However, as noted earlier, such investigations tend to be performed on global data and over long periods in order to obtain a sample size suitable for formal hypothesis testing.

Conclusion

The chapter establishes some stylized facts about the economies, trade patterns, and governance indicators in Latin American and Caribbean countries. The data illustrate that there is no simple relationship between economic performance and a specialization in primary products—there are primary product exporters who perform both well and poorly. Similarly, diversification per se is not obviously correlated with economic growth. However, export diversification is still a useful strategy in that it helps countries manage the risks associated with price and demand volatility of single products. Moreover, diversification is possible even within an overall specialization in primary products. The most

Table 14.10 Economic Freedom Indices: Change from 1996 to 2013

	Overall Score	Property Rights	Corruption	Fiscal	Government Spending	Business	Labor*	Monetary	Trade	Investment	Financial
Argentina	-28	-55	-40	-15.9	-37.3	-24.9	3.5	-17.1	7.6	-30	-40
Bolivia	-17.3	-40	-2	-0.4	-11.2	0.8	-16.9	-14.2	8.9	-60	-20
Brazil	9.6	0	8	3.6	-19.6	-2	-7.4	74.4	12.7	0	10
Chile	6.4	0	22	-12.2	-2.2	-14.5	-3.1	16.6	17	15	20
Colombia	5.3	0	24	-4.3	-24	20.2	16.5	14.6	7.2	0	0
Costa Rica	0.6	0	-2	0.4	-0.4	-11.7	-0.7	3.5	22.1	0	0
Ecuador	-13.2	-30	-3	1.1	-45.2	-3.5	8.2	13.9	7.1	-50	-10
El Salvador	-3.4	-10	-16	2	-6.6	-8.2	-6.1	7.1	6	0	0
Guatemala	-3.7	-20	-23	-4.5	-3	-4.2	-11.9	6.5	16.2	10	0
Honduras	1.8	-20	-4	19.8	-3.5	6	-17.9	10.6	14.1	15	10
Jamaica	0.1	-30	-17	1.3	-8.8	14.3	0.9	23.9	10	15	-10
Mexico	5.8	0	-20	8	-13.7	26.4	-1.7	11.1	17.6	0	30
Nicaragua	2.5	-15	15	0.1	-3.4	-3.8	-10.7	4.7	29.4	-10	0
Panama	-9.3	-20	-17	8.6	-7.4	2.5	-5.1	-12.3	9.8	-5	-20
Paraguay	-6	-20	12	5.8	-7.4	-10.9	-2.5	17.8	13.7	-20	-10
Peru	5.7	-10	4	-1.1	-4.3	17.3	21.2	26.4	30	0	-10
Trinidad and Tobago	-6.9	-40	-18	20.4	-17.1	-14.9	-2.3	-2.2	34.9	-30	-10
Uruguay	6	20	20	1.2	1.4	3.4	-5.2	21.9	19.9	5	-40
Venezuela	-18.4	-45	9	0.4	-25.5	-24.4	2.2	3.2	-6.2	-45	-30

Labor is from 2005 to 2013.

A negative score implies a decline in the index value from 1996 to 2013.

diversified exporters in Latin America—Argentina, Brazil, Nicaragua, and Uruguay—all have primary product shares between 40 and 70 percent of total exports. A blend of primary products plus some manufactured goods accounts for this diversification. There is a virtually no correlation between export concentration (lack of diversification) and higher growth rates. Even less so is specialization in primary products a hindrance to growth; there is a very slight positive correlation between primary product specialization and economic growth. Thus, the simple ideas about primary product specialization, lack of diversification, and economic growth do not apply to today's Latin America, if in fact they ever applied. Yet, the quality of governance is more relevant for countries' economic performance than the goods they specialize in, as is the ability to attract FDI. There is a modest positive correlation between economic freedom and real GDP growth over the period 1995–2011. Stability in governance is important for overall growth, regardless of the export mix.

Notes

1 These are solely the views of the authors and not the views of the US International Trade Commission or any of its commissioners.
2 As well as the Dominican Republic, not included in this analysis. The Colombia and Panama agreements were ratified by the US Congress in 2011, and thus do not directly affect the data presented here.
3 Other members of ALBA-TCP, other than those we analyze, include Antigua and Barbuda, Cuba, Dominica, Saint Vincent and the Grenadines, and Saint Lucia.
4 See Sabatini (2012) for an account of some of the political and economic issues involved in Latin American integration.
5 At the time of writing, Argentina is an exception to this rule, backsliding on its inflation performance. A new government price index, developed in response to criticisms that earlier statistics had been manipulated, showed an annualized inflation rate of 44 percent in early 2014. Critics continue to believe that actual inflation is higher. See *Washington Post* (2014).

References

Amin, S. (1977) *Imperialism and Unequal Development*. Hassocks: Harvester Press.
Amin Gutiérrez de Piñeres, S. and Ferrantino, M.J. (2000) *Export Dynamics and Economic Growth in Latin America: A Comparative Perspective*. Aldershot, UK: Ashgate Press.
Balasubramanyan, V.N., Salisu, M.A., and Sapsford, D. (1996) "Foreign Direct Investment and Economic Growth in EP and IS Countries." *The Economic Journal* 106: 92–105.
Baldwin, R. (ed.) (2009) *The Great Trade Collapse: Causes, Consequences, and Prospects*. Centre for Economic Policy. London, United Kingdom.
Barro, R.J. and Sala-i-Martin, X. (1995) *Economic Growth*. New York: McGraw-Hill.
Grilli, Enzo R & Yang, Maw Cheng. (1988) "Primary Commodity Prices, Manufactured Goods Prices, and the Terms of Trade of Developing Countries: What the Long Run Shows," World Bank Economic Review, World Bank Group, vol. 2(1), pp. 1–47, January.

Helleiner, G. (1986) "Outward Orientation, Import Instability and African Economic Growth: An Empirical Investigation," in S. Lall and F. Stewart (eds.), *Theory and Reality in Economic Development*. London: Macmillan.

Heritage Foundation (2014) *2014 Index of Economic Freedom*. Washington, DC: Heritage Foundation.

International Monetary, *World Economic Outlook: Hopes, Realities, Risks*. Washington, DC. April 2013.

Lord, M.J. and G.R. Boye. (1991) "The Determinants of International Trade in Latin America's Commodity Exports," In *Long Term Trends in Latin American Economic Development*. Edited by M. Urrutia. Washington, D.C.: Inter-American Development Bank.

Maddison, Angus (1991) Dynamic Forces in Capitalist Development: A Long-Run Comparative View Oxford University Press, New York.

Maddison, A. (1991) "Economic and Social Conditions in Latin America, 1914–1950," in M. Urrutia (ed.), *Long-Term Trends in Latin American Economic Development*. Baltimore: Johns Hopkins University Press for the Inter-American Development Bank.

Michaely, Michael. (1994) Preferential Trade Agreements in Latin America: An Ex Ante Assessment (processed). Latin America and the Caribbean Region. World Bank.

Prebisch, R. (1950) *The Economic Development of Latin America and Its Principal Problems*. New York: United Nations Economic Commission on Latin America.

Sabatini, C. (2012) "Rethinking Latin America: Foreign Policy Is More Than Development." *Foreign Affairs* 91(2) (March/April): 8–13.

The Telegraph (2013, August 30) "Capital Flight from Emerging Markets Doubles to $6bn." Retrieved from www.telegraph.co.uk/finance/financialcrisis/10276698/Capital-flight-from-emerging-markets-doubles-to-6bn.html. Accessed 2/18/14.

Urrutia, M. (1991) "Conclusions," in M. Urrutia (ed.), *Long-Term Trends in Latin American Economic Development*. Baltimore: Johns Hopkins University Press for the Inter-American Development Bank.

Washington Post (2014, February 13) "Believe It or Not: Argentina's New Inflation Index." Retrieved from www.washingtonpost.com/world/the_americas/believe-it-or-not-argentinas-new-inflation-index/2014/02/13/47bef98e-94d4-11e3-9e13-770265cf4962_story.html. Accessed 2/19/14.

15 Democratic Governance and Corruption in Latin America[1]

Gerardo Berthin

Introduction[2]

Elections are an important component of democratic governance, but are not the only measure of it. The existence of effective public institutions to meet citizen needs, accountability and transparency in the public policy and decision-making processes, enforcement of the rule of law, checks and balances, and citizen participation are also important components of democratic governance. An overwhelming majority of countries in Latin America have consolidated their electoral component of democratic governance over the past three decades. However, the degree of overall democratic governance performance is divergent. While several countries enjoy high levels of democratic governance performance, the majority find themselves still coping with the challenges of expanding citizens' voice and participation, achieving equity and inclusion, and strengthening transparency and accountability systems.

Many studies show that people in Latin America overwhelmingly prefer democracy to other forms of government.[3] However, there is also evidence showing that a substantial proportion of people in Latin America are not particularly satisfied with how democratic governance is performing.[4] This dissatisfaction has its roots in a number of factors, including lack of checks and balances among the branches of government, centralized decision-making processes, lack of transparency and accountability in the public policy cycle, lack of effective demand and control from citizens and nongovernmental organizations, and the overall inability of the democratic governance system to deliver many of society's most basic needs in key areas such as education, citizen security, and social welfare. A key lesson from Latin America is that democratic governance is not only about gaining legitimacy through competitive elections, but, more importantly, is about strengthening horizontal and vertical accountability systems to provide a comprehensive oversight system. *Horizontal accountability* is exercised within and between government institutions, while *vertical accountability* is exercised by the public vis-à-vis government institutions and officials.

This context provides the framework to understand the persistence of both perceptions of corruption and corrupt practices in Latin America. Despite impressive human and economic development gains in recent years and the existence of an array of anti-corruption actors, tools, and legal frameworks, the level of perceived corruption remains high. The extent of the phenomenon is recognized by a host of international and national organizations and their data, experts, and analysts, as well as civil society organizations. Corruption can be perceived both in everyday dealings with governmental officials (petty corruption) and in major national government contracts and/or the financing of political parties (grand corruption).[5]

The chapter analyzes the evolution of democratic governance and anti-corruption in Latin America over the past two decades. It explores the persistence of both perceptions of corruption and corrupt practices and the effects on democratic governance. Given the complex and multidimensional nature of democratic governance and corruption, the chapter explores potential drivers and factors that can explain the relation and interaction of these two areas. The chapter concludes with a brief discussion of the role of transparency and accountability in strengthening democratic governance and in reducing the prevalence of perceived corruption in Latin America. Overall, the chapter argues that strengthening democratic institutions and improving governmental performance in Latin America necessarily involves effective governmental and citizen strategies and actions against corruption and in favor of transparent and accountable government.

The Evolution of Democratic Governance and Anti-Corruption in Latin America

After the transition from authoritarian to democratic regimes in the 1980s, many Latin American countries began a process of liberalizing political and economic processes. These processes exposed vulnerable areas and raised awareness about the challenges of addressing corrupt practices and behavior under democratic regimes, and fed international and national demands for anti-corruption efforts. As Latin America moved to the global economic stage and intensified its international business competitiveness and trade, governments were pressured to develop and implement effective accountability and transparency systems. A closer examination of this evolution reveals that since the democratic transitions in the 1980s, a number of anti-corruption benchmarks have accompanied the democratic governance process over the past three decades (see Figure 15.1). These were the results of national, regional, and international initiatives (Berthin 2008).

For example, the Declaration of Principles of the First Summit of the Americas held in Miami in December 1994 explicitly forwarded the idea that "[e]ffective democracy requires a comprehensive attack on corruption as a factor of social disintegration and distortion of the economic system that undermines the legitimacy of political institutions."[6] The heads of state in the First Summit also called for a plan of action to confront corruption. The plan of action was drawn and addressed a significant number of issues that were later included in the Inter-American Convention against Corruption (IACC).

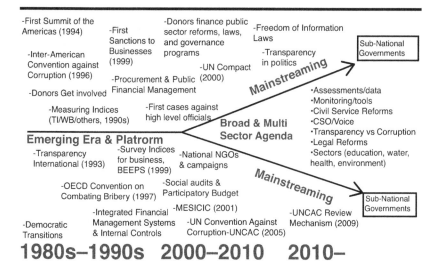

Figure 15.1 Important Anti-Corruption Benchmarks in Latin America

In March 1996, twenty-nine members of the Organization of American States (OAS) adopted the IACC in Caracas, Venezuela. Today, thirty-three countries in the Western Hemisphere have ratified the IACC.[7] In 2001, the Mechanism for Follow-Up on the Implementation of the Inter-American Convention against Corruption (MESICIC) was adopted as a means to monitor and evaluate compliance and implementation.

The IACC was the first international treaty to deal with the issue of corruption. In 1997, the Organization for Economic Cooperation and Development (OECD) approved the Convention on Combating Bribery of Foreign Public Officials in International Business Transactions, and by 2013, a handful of Latin American countries (namely Argentina, Brazil, Colombia, Chile, and Mexico) had ratified it. Almost simultaneously, the United Nations (UN) initiated a process to develop an international treaty for the same purpose, and by a General Assembly resolution the United Nations Convention against Corruption (UNCAC) was adopted in October 2003 and came into force in December 2005. By 2013, with the exception of Barbados, Belize, Montserrat, Surinam, and Saint Kitts and Nevis, an overwhelming majority of countries in the region had ratified the UNCAC.

The birth of Transparency International (TI) in 1993 as a major global nongovernmental movement against corruption, the advent of its Perception Corruption Index (CPI), and the establishment of national chapters marked yet another benchmark in the anti-corruption effort in the Latin American region. In 2014, a majority of countries in Latin America had a TI chapter and/or affiliate.[8] In addition, the CPI became an advocacy tool and influenced the creation of a plethora of additional tools to measure corruption in an effort to facilitate cross-national data and evidence of the determinants and impact of corruption. In the 1990s, the World Bank also explored the use of surveys in Latin America as a means to "measure" corruption, and conducted private- and business-sector surveys as well (the Business Environment and Enterprise Performance Survey, or BEEPS). The World Bank Institute (WBI) Governance Indicators, including one for control of corruption, added yet another tool to measure the quality of governance across countries, including in Latin America (Kaufmann 2010).

Other approaches to measure corruption and compare across Latin American countries followed in the 1990s and the ensuing decade. For example, the Victimization Methodology, which focused on individual direct experience (Seligson 2012); the Global Barometer Survey and the Bribe Payers Survey, with relevant data for Latin America;[9] the International Budget Partnership, which developed a Budget Transparency Index with the help of leading civil society organizations in the region;[10] and the Global Integrity Report that has collected data of more than a dozen countries in Latin America since 2004.[11] Last but not least, at the national level, several organizations in Latin America have also introduced new methodologies and approaches to measure and monitor corruption and integrity in their respective countries, such as social audit, participatory budget, and public service monitoring.[12] All of these efforts have yielded an important body of data, which has helped not only to refine the understanding of the causes and nature of corruption in Latin America, but also, and more importantly, to provide government policy makers and civil society organizations with powerful advocacy and monitoring tools for combating corruption and mainstreaming anti-corruption across sectors.

Efforts to promote reform in the structure and functions of public institutions have also been part of the ongoing evolution of democratic governance and anti-corruption in Latin America. Over the past couple of decades, considerable sums of national and international donor funds have been invested in financial management reform. Initiatives have included internal control frameworks, procurement reform, integrated financial management systems, and e-governance. Another positive trend is that there have been efforts in many countries in Latin America to modernize the state apparatus, including the deconcentration of decision-making processes, simplification of government procedures, and enhancing the delivery of public services.

Another positive sign has been efforts to make government operations more transparent and accountable by strengthening internal mechanisms and facilitating more public access to information necessary for external oversight (UNDP 2011). Ongoing efforts persist in Latin America to strengthen government regulations and procurement, tax collection, the administration of justice, and the electoral and legislative processes. Similarly, at the global and regional levels, the activity of the OAS, the OECD, and the United Nations in anti-corruption has helped to create a common language, prevention tools, and mechanisms to disseminate and combat corruption, and to lay the groundwork for anti-corruption cooperation platforms. There is also an energetic and still-evolving civil society anti-corruption movement and regional networks. In addition, a number of other topics have been part of the evolution of the democratic governance and anti-corruption agenda in Latin America during the past couple of decades, which have broadened the scope and sectors, such as political-party finance systems, freedom of information laws, strengthening of investigation and penalization, and review mechanisms for the IACC and the UNCAC.

The challenge of addressing corruption has been on the agenda for more than two decades in Latin America, and as in other regions and globally, it is an issue of serious interest linked to the quality, legitimacy, and performance of democratic governance. As evidenced by the brief recount of benchmarks and initiatives noted earlier, a number of steps have been taken to detect, prevent, and punish corruption under the context of democratic governance. Generally, the approaches have been multidimensional and have attempted to put in place key elements of good governance to resolve challenges, such as fiscal oversight, resource allocation, professional management, and transparency and accountability. These are still ongoing efforts, and challenges remain, as reflected by a persistent high level of perceived corruption. This is a pernicious issue that continues to constrain the full realization of economic growth, equality, and citizen satisfaction.

Human Development, Economic Growth, and Building Democratic Governance and Anti-Corruption Systems

Over the past couple of decades, an overwhelming majority of Latin American countries have made important strides when it comes to human development (UNDP 2013, 23). According to the latest Human Development Index (HDI),[13] Chile and Argentina are in the very high human development group, and most other countries are either in the high human development group or in the medium human development group. Haiti is the only country in the region in the low human development group. The average HDI value for the region is the second highest in the world (see Figure 15.2).

Similarly, the Latin American region's economies have shown a strong and more balanced economic performance during the last five years. Having weathered the global financial downturn comparatively well, Latin America has been able to post impressive economic growth numbers in the last decade (ECLAC 2012; Rojas-Suarez 2010). The economies of Latin America grew, on average, more than the global economy. Both the International Monetary Fund (IMF) and the United Nations Economic Commission for Latin America and the Caribbean (ECLAC), are forecasting that the region's economy will continue to expand into 2014–2015, although at lower growth rates (IMF 2014; ECLAC 2014)

More recently, there is evidence showing a decrease in the percentage of Latin Americans living in poverty, as much as 15 percent in the first decade of the twenty-first century, while the number of middle-class Latin Americans rose as much as 50 percent (World Bank 2013; Lustig 2012). Increased

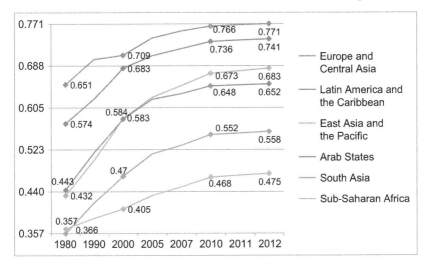

Figure 15.2 Regional Human Development Index Scores 1980–2012

human development trends—in particular, the educational component—and targeted social spending for low-income groups have been credited as key factors of this progress.

Moreover, Latin America has become a region of middle-income-countries (MICs). Haiti is the only country in the region that can be classified as a lower-income country (LIC). Like in many other regions, the middle-income status in Latin America is diverse. It includes resource exporters like Venezuela, Bolivia, Mexico, and Ecuador; diversified economies like Brazil and Chile; post-conflict economies like Colombia and El Salvador; and service-driven economies like Panama and Peru.

Despite impressive progress in human development and economic growth, there are still some signs in Latin America of critical vulnerabilities. For example, the informal sector and the extractive industries remain prominent sources of employment (ECLAC 2012; and Andres & Ramlogan-Dobson 2011) and, as such, are vulnerable to the risks of corruption because informal work lies outside government regulation and extractive industries bring enormous pressures to government regulation and transparency systems. Similarly, while Latin America's middle class has grown and there is evidence that the Gini Index (which measures the degree of inequality in the distribution of family income in a country) might be decreasing, income inequality is still high relative to other regions (Lustig 2012). Twelve of the twenty countries worldwide with the highest levels of inequality are from Latin America (UNDP 2013, 30).

Over the past two decades, progress has been documented on a number of anti-corruption fronts in Latin America, although it varies across countries. For example, countries in Latin America today have greater access to a wide variety of technological, legal, institutional, and administrative tools to prevent and combat corruption. Most countries in the region have made significant improvements in the modernization of their financial and management systems, their procurement practices, and the strengthening of their Supreme Audit Institutions (SAIs) and public prosecutors. In various degrees, many countries have also introduced information and communication technology initiatives (e-government) to improve government efficiency, effectiveness, transparency, and accountability. Moreover, most countries in the region have made progress in improving their constitutional, legal, and institutional frameworks, including constitutional amendments to increase the independence and professionalization of the judiciary. Others have introduced new legislation (freedom of information, transparency laws, career civil service laws), and they have created new institutions such as ombudsmen and anti-corruption agencies and/or specialized anti-corruption offices.

There are also encouraging anti-corruption local and institutional practices that show promise, for example, participatory budgeting, the strengthening of internal revenue services, the modernization of comptroller general offices, enhancing internal control systems, and local social auditing and participatory strategic planning. Awareness of the problem of corruption also has significantly increased in Latin America over the past couple of decades. In contrast to the past, corruption is a problem that is widely and openly discussed as part of policy agenda.

Governments are being forced to address corruption by domestic pressures, as well as by external pressures. The different anti-corruption programs supported by the governments and the international donor community during the past couple of decades have brought new actors to the anti-corruption stage. The private sector is beginning to emerge as a critical partner for anti-corruption activities, including awareness. Civil society and citizen organizations are increasingly improving their technical skills to effectively oversee their government's performance and make it accountable and promote awareness campaigns. Universities are also playing an increasingly important role in analyzing corruption and disseminating their results, training public officials, and making technological applications of information and communication technology. The media has played a significant role in reporting corruption cases and raising awareness about the nature and the scope of the problem.

A number of countries in Latin America have also refined their anti-corruption strategies over the past couple of decades. Anti-corruption covers a much wider range of approaches and themes, with a variety of sectoral and cross-sectoral activities. Some countries, such as Chile, Colombia, and Mexico, have developed and implemented a more systemic, holistic, long-term, and multidimensional anti-corruption approach, covering:

- **Prevention**: To reduce the opportunities and promote greater efficiency, accountability, and transparency in the delivery and administration of public services. This includes initiatives such as civil service reform, access to information legislation, simplification of procedures and regulations through the use of information and communication technologies, and the introduction of financial management systems.

- **Strengthening oversight and control institutions**: To restrain the power of public officials by strengthening institutions such as anti-corruption agencies. Such institutions include an Office of the Comptroller General, Office of the Auditor General, Office of the Ombudsperson, and/or legislative oversight commissions.
- **Engaging citizens and civil society coalitions**: To ensure broad public support, participation, and involvement in the public policy process.
- **Enforcement**: To reduce impunity by promoting greater independence and accountability of the judicial system, strengthening prosecutors and the capacity and integrity of the police, and typifying corrupt practices.

Moreover, a decade ago, it was unthinkable to tackle corruption and transparency issues related to political parties. Today, political corruption is emerging as a key issue. Most Latin American countries have introduced some form of legislation on political parties, in particular, to regulate the sources, flow, and destination of money in politics. Bans and limits in the area of political party campaign finance are being addressed divergently in the region. Public funding is being debated, discussed, and in some cases reformed. Control mechanisms are being created and strengthened to encourage and enforce disclosure of information by political parties. Civil society organizations are becoming increasingly involved in promoting better disclosure and transparency and in lobbying for reform in political party finance.

A majority of the countries have ratified the IACC and UNCAC. Over the past couple of decades, and in response to regional and global conventions, the Latin American region has progressively adopted a number of laws and regulations designed to prevent, control, and punish corrupt practices and increase transparency and accountability, for example, financial disclosure for public officials, illicit enrichment, access to information, administrative procedures, and procurement laws.

In Latin America over the past decade there has also been a focus on clarifying anti-corruption responsibilities, and a number of public institutions are now directly responsible for dealing with anti-corruption efforts. For example:

- Comptroller general offices (*contralorías generales*) are the main control institutions in many countries. The *contraloría* exercises pre-authorization of expenditures and audit oversight of all public institutions.
- Attorney general offices (*procuradurías*) are another institution that has as its primary anti-corruption responsibility investigating and putting together cases to be prosecuted in the judicial system.
- Within the attorney general's office and/or separately, there are also specialized oversight entities (*fiscalías/unidades de investigación*). They generally investigate cases and receive complaints.

- Preventive institutions, usually attached to the executive branch, such as anti-corruption councils/commissions, public ethic offices, and anti-corruption agencies/ministries. Their role is varied and has evolved over the years, particularly to avoid overlaps and/or duplications of functions with other entities.
- The judicial system clearly plays a vital role in anti-corruption, as it is responsible for the detection, prosecution, and punishment of corrupt acts.
- In addition, other entities such as the electoral bodies, ombudsman's offices (*defensorías del pueblo*), and courts of accounts have also acquired a role in the anti-corruption apparatus.
- Because the national legislative assembly/congress has as its mandate legislation and oversight functions, it can also be considered part of the anti-corruption apparatus.

Inequality and Perception of Corruption and Impunity: The New Burden on Democratic Governance in Latin America

Despite the impressive human and economic development trends and the array of anti-corruption actors, tools, and legal frameworks (mentioned earlier), perceptions of corruption over the last decade remain high and pervasive in Latin America (see Figure 15.3). Public officials in Latin America continue to be widely perceived as corrupt. Over 38 percent of respondents said corruption was very common in their country, and nearly 80 percent described corruption

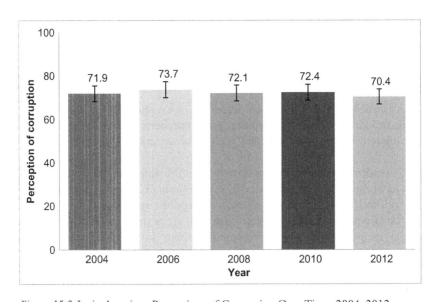

Figure 15.3 Latin American Perceptions of Corruption Over Time, 2004–2012

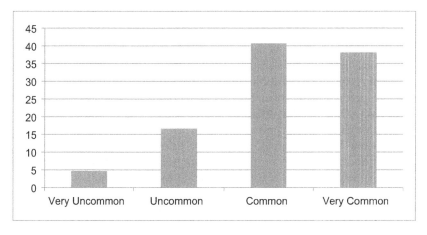

Figure 15.4 Intensity of Perceptions of Corruption in Latin America, 2012

as "very common" and/or "common" (see Figure 15.4). Corruption and "poor government" represent the third most frequently cited problem facing countries in Latin America (Seligson et al 2012, 154).

In general, recent analysis suggests that in Latin America, citizens who perceive their national governments as delivering a strong economy, curbing corruption, and providing security are most likely to support the democratic system (Seligson et al 2012). While there could be mounting trust in core democratic governance and institutions, the broader issue of democratic governance legitimacy is still a work in progress in Latin America, and the persistent perception of corruption is a key ingredient in understanding the lack of legitimacy. Specific elements of legitimacy in Latin America, such as low trust in the judiciary system, high perceptions of impunity, high citizen insecurity, low interpersonal trust, high perceptions of economic injustices, and opaque decision-making processes are all working to lend less-than-optimal support to the overall democratic governance system and, in turn, they feed perceptions of corruption (Berthin and Sandin 2011).

Latin America has some general characteristics that should be taken into account when considering the phenomenon of corruption. One is that the region is not poor, but it has not been able to tackle poverty. Latin America is also one of the most unequal regions in the world. While the average gross domestic product (GDP) is US$8,952,[14] there are marked differences ranging from US$15,260 in Chile to US$1,370 in Haiti. Within countries, economic inequality runs deeper. For example, the richest 10 percent of the population has 48 percent of the income, while the poorest 10 percent of the population has only 1.6 percent of the income. According to the First Regional Human Development Report of the United Nations Development Programme (UNDP), inequality in Latin America is so high and so persistent that it is passed from one generation to another (UNDP 2010).

Similarly, for more than two decades, almost all countries in Latin America have enjoyed democratically elected governments. However, the region faces serious challenges that have led to a deep, popular dissatisfaction with how democratically elected governments are governing. An inability to translate economic growth into better livelihoods and mobility, persistent inequalities, and the perception of corruption are undermining confidence in electoral democracy (OAS/UNDP 2010).

It can be said that corruption has been so profound and traditionally present in the region, that during past decades, the visions that attributed corruption to a cultural background in Latin America became widely accepted. Traditional phrases used by the region's population to describe, and even celebrate, the existence of corruption, such as "today for you, tomorrow for me," "they steal millions and I am only stealing a chalk," "he who does not cheat does not get ahead," and "play smart, everybody does it" are well-known mottos in the region.

In addition, during the last couple of decades there have been highly publicized corruption scandals in Latin America. For example, in 1991, President Fernando Color de Mello (Brazil) was constitutionally charged with bribery and removed from office as president; in Venezuela, in 1993, President Carlos Andres Pérez was charged, along with some of his ministers, with embezzlement and fraud; in Chile in 1994, after the dictatorship of General Augusto Pinochet, million-dollar payments to the general's son were discovered in transactions made by the armed forces; in Mexico, in 1995, there was a case involving the brother of President Raul Salinas de Gortari, with accusations of murder and illicit enrichment; in Ecuador, in 1997, President Abdala Bucaram was accused of corruption and deposed by Congress; in Peru, in 2000, President Alberto Fujimori was accused of crimes against humanity and corruption—he fled to Japan and then to Chile, where he was extradited to Peru and is now serving time; in Argentina, in 2001, former President Carlos Saul Menem was accused of corruption and arms trafficking to Ecuador and Croatia; and in Nicaragua, in 2002, Arnoldo Aleman's case in which the former Nicaraguan president was accused of embezzlement and misappropriation of US$100 million in public funds (UNDP 2012).[15]

More recently, there have been the wave of corruption scandals in Brazil in 2011, which forced President Dilma Rousseff's cabinet ministers to resign;[16] a Bolivian government's top anti-corruption cop arrested in 2013 in Miami and accused of extorting a former Bolivian airline owner;[17] and an array of cases throughout 2013 involving Mexican governors (Humberto Moreira of Coahuila, Mario Ernesto Villanueva Madrid of Quintana Roo, and Andres Granier Melo of Tabasco).[18] These and previous scandals, allegations, and investigations provoke discontent and indignation in Latin America and help nourish and spread perceptions about corrupt practices.

Several indicators show that the overall public perceptions of corruption in Latin America have improved slightly in recent years. Nonetheless, those perceptions are still high compared to other regions in the world. Transparency

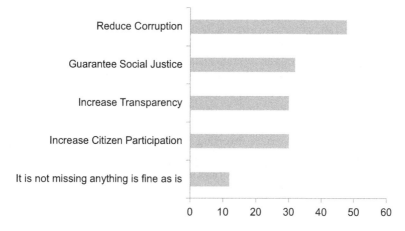

Figure 15.5 What Is Missing in Latin American Democracy?

International's 2012 analysis showed that 60 percent of Latin American countries do not even make it to the middle of the global ranking in terms of the CPI.[19] Within Latin America, perceptions of corruption are also divergent. While in Chile and Uruguay these perceptions are relatively low, in Paraguay and Haiti they are relatively high (UNDP 2012). Corruption remains a major concern and risk for Latin American democratic governance. For example, the *Latinobarometro* Survey asked what was missing in Latin American democracy. As can be seen in Figure 15.5, the first three answers in order were 1) reduce corruption, 2) guarantee more social justice, and 3) increase transparency (*Latinobarometro* 2011).

While data trends in current perceptions beyond Transparency International's CPI suggest that perceived levels of corruption in Latin America might be falling, other indicators provide clues to the issues that continue to shape perceptions of corruption and/or encourage corrupt practices. For example, the Latin American Public Opinion Project (LAPOP) Survey shows that the percentage of individuals who report being targeted for a bribe again increased in 2012 in Latin America, after a slight drop in 2010 (Seligson 2012). In 2012, one in five people reported that they had been asked for a bribe. While actual levels of bribery corruption have remained the same or increased in 2012, levels of perceived corruption have decreased. One explanation for this is that overall, the economic perspectives in Latin America are looking brighter, and people are less likely to perceive corruption in government when they also perceive economic progress.

According to interviews, corruption assessments, and other reports, public attitudes to corruption remain somewhat illusive in the Latin American region.[20] On the one hand, while slightly falling perceptions about corruption as a problem persist, on the other, impunity is seen as another major challenge. Beyond the more high-profile cases, evidence suggests that in much of Latin

America, corruption permeates daily life (Blake and Morris 2009, 2). From various bureaucratic processes (licenses, permits, legal notices) to routine traffic violations, corruption is often the rule rather than the exception. A major component of these is impunity and/or the lack of consequences. Indeed, impunity remains remarkably high throughout the region. Despite the many cases of corruption that are made public, and even while some public officials may get investigated, they are rarely prosecuted. Cases involve illegal campaign funds and expenditures; bribing members of congress; multimillion-dollar fraud and kickbacks; and bribes involving government contracts, state concessions, and the privatization of state-owned enterprises; and judges getting paid for their verdicts or for closing cases (Blake and Morris 2009). Impunity emboldens corrupt individuals and fosters disappointment and apathy among citizens when justice is not served.

Many people in Latin America also identify many forms of corruption as a routine way of doing business. In 2012, a study in fourteen countries in Latin America surveyed corporate executives in a broad cross-section of US and Latin American-based companies about corruption. Half of all respondents believed that their company had lost business to competitors making illicit payments in Latin America. Furthermore, 44 percent said corruption was a significant obstacle to doing business. Just 28 percent of respondents believed anti-corruption laws were effective in the Latin American countries where they worked. Last but not least, when respondents were asked to rank the sectors according to levels of risk for corrupt practices to occur, the police, customs, legislative branch, municipal/local governments, the judicial branch, and the executive branch were mentioned (Miller Chevalier and Matteson Ellis et al 2012 2012).

Unpacking Democratic Governance in Latin America and Making the Link with Corruption and Inequality

Having weathered the global financial downturn of 2008 to 2009 comparatively well, the region has been able to post impressive human development progress and economic growth numbers over the past two decades. A key lesson to keep in mind is that economic growth and the progress of human development do not necessarily translate automatically into more equal opportunities for people.

Citizens in Latin America perceive their national governments as not delivering economic opportunities, curbing corruption, or providing security. As such, they are less likely to support the democratic governance system (IDB 2012). Similarly, citizens in Latin America are not confident about the capacity of governments to manage public resources transparently and provide services efficiently. When persistent inequality is added to the mix and linked to the quality of democratic governance, it further nourishes among citizens perceptions of "bad governance"—for example, the poor quality of political representation (affecting oversight and accountability), unequal access to influence specific public policies (affecting transparency), lack of systematic public opposition to corruption (affecting attitudes), and the institutional shortcomings and/or vulnerabilities (leading to state corruption and capture). These *systemic* factors mean that the democratic governance dynamics in place could actually be exacerbating, instead of mitigating, the reproduction of corrupt practices and inequality. Thus, when unpacking the current state of democratic governance in Latin America and its anti-corruption component, it is important to understand the complex relationship between the day-to-day operation of the democratic governance system as a whole and the objective and subjective indicators of inequality and corruption.

Every democratic governance system offers opportunities for certain irregular and illegal practices, such as bribery, clientelism, state capture, corruption, and institutional weakness. At the same time, every democratic governance system has different capacities to prevent, manage, and punish these irregular and illegal practices. That link is important to understanding the relationship between inequality and corruption in Latin America. When people in democratic governance perceive that only one sector of society uses its power and resources to promote measures and public policies that benefit their narrow interests, such as tax cuts or exemptions, judicial impunity, operating permits, or access to privileged information, among other prerogatives, they also tend to associate this situation with corruption and on that basis render judgments on the entire democratic governance system. In turn, there is evidence that shows that inequality and the lack of transparency and accountability in public policies can reduce people's motivation and resilience towards corrupt behaviors, which, in turn, leads to lack of action, lack of interpersonal trust, and persistent skepticism about democratic governance, and perpetuates the structural and behavioral elements that nourish inequality (Uslaner 2010).

There is growing cross-national evidence that as democratic governance evolves beyond elections, equality and open and accountable government stand at the beginning of a virtuous causal chain that shapes perceptions (Charron and Lapuente 2010). Both are necessary to create trust in public policies and in promoting more citizen involvement and oversight in the public policy cycle and, most importantly, to combat corruption. Perceptions about corruption matter because citizens base their actions on their perceptions, impressions, and views. If citizens believe that the courts are inefficient in punishing evidence-based cases or they need to bribe to obtain access to health services, they are unlikely to value the overall benefits of democratic governance systems.

Thus, it is difficult to pinpoint specific issues that determine corruption risks in Latin America. Rather, corruption is the result of a combination and/or interplay of a number of actors and factors. Also, in a region as diverse as Latin America, it could be difficult to generalize corruption trends and challenges. The incidence, perception, and/or risk of corruption in Latin America vary from country to country. In some cases, it might be easier to identify, prevent, and manage corruption risks. In other cases, corruption risks are more complex, multidimensional, and systemic, with a multitude of actors, institutions, and sectors involved. Thus, rather than focusing on identifying specific issues that determine corruption, for Latin America, it makes more sense to understand the policy challenges that need to be addressed in order to prevent, reduce, and punish corrupt practices. These include:

1. **Checks and oversight on executive decision-making process:** While there are ongoing strengthening efforts, oversight, and control institutions (ministries, anti-corruption offices, ombudsmen, general comptrollers, attorney generals, and legislative and justice systems), checks and oversight remain a challenge. Most of these mechanisms are dependent on the executive branch, which continues to concentrate power in the presidency, and the degree of autonomy and independence of oversight and control institutions remains low. Similarly, in spite of judicial reforms (penal codes, retraining of judges, and the creation of oversight institutions), judicial systems in many Latin American countries do not yet have the full capacity to prosecute and punish corrupt officials. Not only do judges still retain enormous discretion, but the system is overwhelmed and people, particularly the poor, are deterred from using it. This contributes to the perception of impunity.

2. **The lack of transparency and accountability in government operations, in particular, public expenditures and budgets:** There is still a lack of autonomy in control and regulatory institutions charged with monitoring public policies, including budgets and use of resources. While ministries of finance and/or their equivalents have stepped up efforts to be more transparent and accountable, legislatures, congresses, and parliaments are still perceived to be ineffective, particularly in overseeing the executive. In spite of access to information laws, legislatures are generally unable to debate budget issues "openly" with constituencies and the public at large. The budget cycle process is often flawed by ambiguity between the executive and legislative roles and weak monitoring and reporting systems, resulting not only in an opportunity for discretion in the use of public funds, but also in opacity of public funding allocations and spending. Integrated financial management systems have been implemented throughout the region, but these are still not being used widely to improve public-sector legitimacy, produce timely and efficient accounting for public resources, and increase government accountability and transparency.

3. **Public service delivery**: While there are more resources and policies in place to expand social services to the poorest sectors of society, the capacity and articulation of systems and/or institutions have not been strengthened sufficiently. In most Latin American countries, the transition to a more professional civil-service career that rewards merit more than patronage is still a work in progress. Moreover, cumbersome legislation, overlapping responsibilities of different government agencies, legal confusion, and face-to-face transactions all contribute to increasing the discretionary power and unethical behavior of public officials. This also blurs the lines of policy

direction and accountability and creates unnecessarily large bureaucratic barriers, which can serve to multiply opportunities for bribes and ineffective service delivery. Complex and excessive bureaucratic procedures and regulations in public services (health, education, social services, legal, and justice) encourage petty corruption and adversely affect potential business development, particularly small and medium enterprises. There is inconclusive evidence of the role that decentralization processes are playing in preventing and/or managing corruption risks in Latin America. While not all countries have undergone deeper decentralization reforms, most have varying degrees of delegation and deconcentration of functions. The jury is still out on whether these efforts have improved service delivery and increased transparency and accountability.

4. **Social and citizen oversight and voice:** Even though the number of civil society organizations that work in the area of transparency has grown in Latin America, most of their efforts have concentrated more on awareness-raising activities than on forming coalitions, generating greater pressure for reforms, and/or prosecuting corrupt officials and in promoting an "ethical culture" in and out of government. Citizen groups and networks remain fragmented and face many challenges, such as lack of adequate technical capacity to process and analyze information released by the government and/or to gain access to information using freedom of information legislation. In addition, they have limited capacity to translate advocacy activities into broad (governmental and nongovernmental) coalition-building strategies for change. Also, in some cases, governmental and political interests have captured and/or purged many of these organizations (including the media), in effect neutralizing their capacity to voice dissenting and critical opinions. Moreover, citizens and/or civil society organizations do not use complaint systems, either because they perceive them as ineffective and/or out of fear of retaliation, as no country in the region to date has whistleblower protection laws and/or norms. Furthermore, since a majority of countries in Latin America have passed access-to-information legislation, civil society groups and citizens have not been able to transcend beyond the right to request information. This has not ensured a more proactive access-to-information movement that demands open government and participatory budgets, among other things, and in turn articulates and/or works with other accountability mechanisms.

Conclusions

The current evidence suggests that despite progress in human development and economic growth in Latin America, perceptions of corruption and impunity persist in most countries. These challenges have to be balanced with a central premise that like most democratic governance reforms, anti-corruption efforts are long-term projects and results are not always evident in the short run. Many now recognize that a well-designed anti-corruption reform strategy requires a long-term vision and a clear understanding that fundamental change can begin to take place now, but can only come to fruition within one or two generations (Thacker 2009). Added to the challenge of the perception of corruption and impunity in Latin America is the prevalence of inequality, in spite of economic growth. These narratives help to explain in great part, not only the nexus between democratic governance and anti-corruption in Latin America today, but also the corrosive implications that persistent high perceptions of corruption and impunity can have on democratic governance and its support among citizens.

While it may be too early to judge the effectiveness of the array of anti-corruption actors, tools, and legal frameworks that have been put in place in Latin America in the last couple of decades, it may be possible in the short term to analyze in more detail the effect of these in the incidence of corruption perceptions and corrupt practices. Similarly, analyzing the resilience of current democratic governance structures against corrupt practices may be able to yield clues as to the new and old factors and/or variables that might be making the current democratic governance structures vulnerable. A key question would be what is constraining the various horizontal and vertical accountability actors, tools, and frameworks to prevent, detect, and/or punish corruption.

At this stage, more cross-national and national research on the dynamics of corruption and data collection efforts should be a priority for Latin American countries. An understanding that goes beyond perceptions, the enabling environment, individual behavior/choices, and causal dynamics and drivers of corrupt practices will continue to provide inputs to enhance the understanding of causes and consequences on democratic governance.

The efforts that have been made by a majority of Latin American countries over the past couple of decades to prevent, detect, and punish corrupt practices should offer a glimpse of hope. However, promoting a more integrated and multidimensional approach to enhancing democratic governance in Latin America, and not just as an anti-corruption effort, needs buy-in from citizens and civil society organizations. While citizens and civil society organizations have played an important role in anti-corruption efforts, they have not transcended beyond awareness. Because economic growth does not translate fully into equality of opportunities, citizens may tend to accept corrupt behavior as a survival strategy, rather than be more proactive in demanding more transparency and accountability. It would be costly to Latin American democratic governance if citizens and civil society organizations did not demand a better rule of law and enforcement of current laws and norms. Viewing and accepting corrupt practices as normal and not deviant behavior could be detrimental to the quality of democratic governance. Although civil society complains about corrupt practices and even recognizes it as a problem, it needs to transcend this into more systemic and sustained action directed not only at political and governmental actors, but also at citizens themselves. Any reform focusing on increasing transparency must be accompanied by measures for strengthening citizens' capacity to act and to make the right ethical choices.

Despite the difficulties identified in this chapter in preventing and punishing corrupt practices, progress has been made. Corrupt practices are found in all societies (rich and poor, democratic and authoritarian). However, countries, particularly those that adhere to democratic practices, show different degrees of capacity to prevent and punish corrupt practices. As such, evidence of recurring corrupt practices and high perceptions of corruption can shape beliefs, attitudes, behavior, and individual and collective responses to the problem. In general, countries with high transparency and low corruption indicators tend enjoy greater prosperity, opportunity, and individual liberty. Ensuring that democratic governments are capable of dealing effectively (in prevention, enforcement, and punishment) with the threats of corruption has to be seen as an investment in a key public good. Inequality will only decline in Latin America if the democratic governance is robust and can prevent and punish corrupt behavior.

Notes

1   The opinions expressed in this chapter are those of the author and do not necessarily reflect the position of the organizations he was, and is currently affiliated with.
2   The author would like to thank Camila Bozzo, a student of the Master Program in Public Policy at the University of Edinburgh, for her research and assistance in the preparation of this chapter.
3   See Pérez's Chapter 3 in this volume.
4   See, for example, Seligson et al (2012), the Organization of American States/ United Nations Development Programme (2011), Mainwaring and Scully (2009), and Millett et al (2009).
5   See Transparency International Corruption Perception Index, the World Bank's Governance Indicators, the four rounds of reporting under the MESICIC of the Organization of American States, and Seligson et al (2012).
6   See complete text of the Declaration of Principles signed by the heads of state and government participating in the First Summit of the Americas (www.summit-americas. org/i_summit/i_summit_dec_en.pdf). Since then, the Summits of the Americas have become institutionalized and have opened spaces to tackle corruption and promote accountability and transparency. They have been held in 1994 (Miami, United States), 1996 (Santa Cruz, Bolivia), 1998 (Santiago, Chile), 2001 (Quebec City, Canada), 2004 (Monterrey, Mexico), 2005 (Mar de Plata, Argentina), 2009 (Port of Spain, Trinidad and Tobago), and 2012 (Cartagena, Colombia).
7   See State Parties of the IACC at www.oas.org/juridico/english/Sigs/b-58.html.
8   See information of chapters and affiliates at www.transparency.org/whoweare/ organisation/our_chapters.
9   See Transparency International tools section at www.transparency.org/whatwedo/ publications.
10 See the International Budget Partnership Initiative at http://internationalbudget. org/.
11 See the Global Integrity web page at www.globalintegrity.org/report.
12 For example, the Good Governance Index in Mexico and the Integrity and Transparency Index in Colombia.
13 This is based on the Human Development Index, which is a composite indicator that is calculated on the basis of three dimensions: 1) health measured by life expectancy at birth; 2) overall knowledge level as measured by the adult literacy rate

combined with the gross enrollment ratios of students in primary school through the university level; and 3) standard of living measured with the gross domestic product per capita in purchasing power parity in US dollars. The HDI facilitates instructive comparisons of the experiences within and between different countries. The HDI was introduced in the first Human Development Report in 1990 as an alternative to purely economic assessments of national progress. For more information, go to http://hdr.undp.org/en/statistics/hdi/.

14 According to the IMF, 2011.
15 In many cases, after extensive litigation, the direct participation of these senior officials in corruption acts could not be proved; at times, their cases were overturned due to withdrawal or death of witnesses, or because the higher courts accepted appeals and overturned the accusations. Whatever the case, a perception of corruption and impunity was left in the public opinion.
16 "Brazilian President Faces Corruption Scandals." *Los Angeles Times.* July 12, 2011. Retrieved from http://articles.latimes.com/2011/jul/08/world/la-fg-brazil-cabinet-20110708.
17 "Bolivian Anti-Corruption Chief Charged with Extorting Airline Executive in Miami." *Miami Herald,* September 14, 2013. Retrieved from www.miamiherald.com/2013/09/05/3607301/bolivias-anti-corruption-chief.html.
18 "Official Corruption in Mexico, Once Rarely Exposed, Is Starting to Come to Light," *New York Times,* June 23, 2013.
19 "The Americas: Economies Grow, Democracies Shrink. What Does Corruption Have to Do With It?" December 5, 2012, Transparency International. Retrieved from http://blog.transparency.org/2012/12/05/the-americas-economies-grow-democracies-shrink-what-does-corruption-have-to-do-with-it/.
20 Seligson (2012), *UNDP (2012),* and *Transparency International (2012).*

References

Andres, A. and Ramlogan-Dobson, C. (2011) "Is Corruption Really Bad for Inequality? Evidence from Latin America." *Journal of Development Studies* 47(7): 959–76.

Berthin, G. (2008) "Towards Incorporating Transparency Policies: Lessons from Latin America." *Reforma & Democracia* 41 (July):141–72.

Berthin, G. and Sandin, L. (2011) "Does Transparency Have a Payoff for Democratic Governance and Human Development? Exploring Initial Evidence from the Case of Latin America and the Caribbean." Working Document. Panama: UNDP Regional Service Centre for Latin America and the Caribbean.

Blake, C.H. and Morris, S.D. (2009) *Corruption and Democracy in Latin America.* Pittsburgh: University of Pittsburgh Press.

Charron, N. and Lapuente, V. (2010) "Does Democracy Produce Quality of Government?" *European Journal of Political Research* 49: 443–70.ECLAC. (2014) *Economic Survey of Latin America and the Caribbean: Challenges to Sustainable Growth in a New External Context.* Santiago, Chile: ECLAC.

ECLAC. (2012) *Social Panorama of Latin America.* Santiago, Chile: ECLAC.

Inter-American Development Bank. (2012) The *Governance of Citizen Security in Latin America and the Caribbean: Challenges and Strategic Management Priorities.* Washington, D.C.: IDB.

IMF (2014) *Regional Economic Outlook Update.* Washington D.C.: IMF Western Hemisphere Department.

Kaufmann, D., et al. (2010) "The Worldwide Governance Indicators: Methodology and Analytical Issues." Brookings Institute Paper.

Latinobarometro. (2011) *Latinobarometro 2011*. Santiago, Chile.

Lustig, N. (2012) "The Impact of Taxes and Social Spending on Inequality and Poverty in Argentina, Bolivia, Brazil, Mexico, and Peru: A Synthesis of Results." Working Paper 311. Washington, D.C.: Center for Global Development.

Mainwaring, S. and Scully, T.R. (eds.). (2009) *Democratic Governance in Latin America*. Stanford, CA: Stanford University Press.

Miller & Chevalier Law Firm and Matteson Ellis Law Firm. (2012) Latin America Corruption Survey. Miller & Chevalier Chartered & Matteson Ellis Law PLLC.

Millet, R.L. et al. (eds.) (2009) *Latin American Democracy: Emerging Reality or Endangered Species?* NY: Routledge.

Organization of American States/United Nations Development Programme. (2011) *Our Democracy*. Washington, D.C.: OAS/UNDP.

Rojas-Suarez, L. (2010) "The International Financial Crisis: Eight Lessons from and for Latin America." Washington, D.C.: Center for Global Development.

Seligson, M. et al. (eds.) (2012) *The Political Culture of Democracy in the Americas 2012: Towards Equality and Opportunities*. Nashville, TN: LAPOP/Vanderbilt University.

Thacker, S.C. (2009) "Democracy, Economic Policy, and Political Corruption in Comparative Perspective," in C.H. Blake and S. Morris, *Corruption and Democracy in Latin America* (25–45). Pittsburgh: University of Pittsburgh Press.

Transparency International. (2012) *Corruption Perception Index 2012*. Berlin: Transparency International.

UNDP. (2010) *Regional Human Development Report for Latin America and the Caribbean*. New York: UNDP.

UNDP (2011) *Access to Public Information in Central America and Mexico: Assessment and Recommendations*. Panama: UNDP, Regional Service Centre for Latin America and the Caribbean.

UNDP. (2012) *Anticorruption Programmes in Latin America and the Caribbean. Study on Anti-Corruption Trends and UNDP Projects*. Panama: UNDP, Regional Service Centre for Latin America and the Caribbean.

UNDP. (2013) *Human Development Report 2013. The Rise of the South: Human Progress in a Diverse World*. New York: UNDP.

Uslaner, E.M. (2010) *Corruption, Inequality and the Rule of Law*. Cambridge: Cambridge University Press.

World Bank. (2013) *Shifting Gears to Accelerate Prosperity in Latin America and the Caribbean*. Washington DC: The World Bank Group.

16 Chinese Influence on Latin America

Challenges and Opportunities

R. Evan Ellis

Introduction

During the past decade, the expanding activities of the People's Republic of China (PRC) and Chinese commercial actors in Latin America and the Caribbean have significantly impacted the dynamics of the region. In the process, it has spawned an array of scholarship, including general accounts of what was happening (Dunbaugh and Sullivan 2005; Jubany and Poon 2006; Ellis 2009), studies of the economic relationship (Blázquez-Lidoy et al 2006; Devlin et al 2006; Jenkins and Peters 2009; Gallagher and Porzecanski 2010; Fornés and Butt Philip 2012), and multiple compiled volumes focusing principally on country-specific studies (Aranson et al 2008; Roett and Paz 2008; Jilberto and Hogenboom 2010; Hearn and León-Manríquez 2011; Straus and Armony 2012; Dussell et al 2013).

The new engagement is a by-product of both globalization and the reemergence of China as a major economic and political actor on the world stage. Even before the end of the Cold War, and accelerating in the twenty-first century, revolutions in areas such as container shipping and information technology have made international, transoceanic supply chains economically viable, and have made it possible to manage associated production, personnel, and financial challenges. These developments, in turn, have enabled the PRC to successfully pursue a development strategy of global proportions, initially leveraging its comparative advantage in labor to become a world manufacturing hub. With guidance and assistance from the Chinese state, the PRC has used associated foreign investment, technology, and revenue to grow domestic producers in strategically valued industries, who, with time, have begun to project themselves into foreign markets such as those of Latin America and the Caribbean.

Beyond looking to the region as a market, the expansion of industrial production in the PRC also pushed its companies toward Latin America as a source of the primary products to fuel its industries and industrialization, and agricultural commodities such as soy and fishmeal to feed its 1.35 billion people. The "go out" strategy (*zou chuqu*), contained in the 2002 tenth 5-year plan of the Chinese Communist Party, was an official blessing for Chinese companies to build the new overseas relationships and presence to secure access to new markets and necessary technologies and sources of supply.

At the same time, globalization was driving Latin America and the Caribbean to diversify their economic and political relationships. On the commercial side, Latin American traders began to discover the profitability of importing goods from Asia, while increasingly powerful companies based in the region (the "multilatinas") begun to outsource their production to factories in China's new booming coastal zones such as Dailan, Shanghai, Shenzhen, and Tianjin. In a region disappointed by the development produced by its long-standing economic ties with the United States and Europe, politicians, businessmen, and others began to dream of selling their products to a market of over a billion Chinese.

Within little more than a decade, PRC trade with Latin America and the Caribbean grew from being an almost insignificant actor for most countries of the region to being one of the top three trading partners for most of its states (International Monetary Fund 2013). If China became the dominant new economic relationship for the region, however, it was only one of a series of new relationships that the region was forging as it built new commercial relationships with Europe and other nations of the Pacific.

Phases of Chinese Involvement

Chinese engagement in Latin America and the Caribbean has not only grown dramatically in recent years, but has fundamentally changed in nature. Prior to 2001, China's limited interactions with the region were primarily political and cultural in character, concentrating on advancing China's diplomatic recognition and building goodwill. The 2001 admission of the PRC into the World Trade Organization (WTO) was a key milestone for takeoff of a new commerce-driven relationship with the region. It was the November 2004 visit by Chinese President Hu Jintao, however, that called the attention of mainstream Latin American business and political elites to the possibilities offered by doing business with China. As President Hu and his entourage stopped in Brazil, Argentina, and Chile on his way to the summit, they publicly announced the possibility of tens of billions of dollars in possible new investment projects at a time in which the region had just hit a historical low in terms of foreign direct investment.

Although the period following China's ascension to the WTO was characterized by exponential growth in China's trade with Latin America and the rest of the world, there were almost no Chinese companies or personnel in the region during this time, except for long-standing Chinese ethnic communities in places like Peru and Panama, and a handful of businessmen and government officials from the PRC negotiating the trade deals. Chinese primary product purchases from the region were relatively simple, if large, transactions, requiring relatively few people. Similarly, most Chinese products entering the region during this period were imported by Western companies or traders.

Behind the scenes, however, domestic Chinese companies were growing in size and sophistication, while businessmen and government personnel on both sides of the Pacific were building relationships and creating financial and legal infrastructures that would soon support a more significant Chinese physical presence.

In both symbolic and economic terms, the weight of the PRC in Latin America and the Caribbean expanded significantly in 2007–2008 as the global financial crisis forced deep reductions in US and European purchases of goods from the region and prevented Western financial institutions from investing substantial capital in the region. In this environment, sustained demand from China was the factor that saved countries like Peru, Chile, and Brazil from serious economic contraction (Maciel and Nedal 2011, 246). In addition, taking advantage of the paralyzed financial state of the competition, Chinese companies accelerated major acquisitions of mining and petroleum companies in the region, setting the stage for a new Chinese presence on the ground in Latin America in these sectors, as the new owners subsequently brought in their own teams, and Chinese subcontractors, to develop the assets they had acquired.

At roughly the same time, Chinese construction companies began to make significant advances in the region with projects self-financed by loans from Chinese banks, even while Chinese product manufacturers began, for the first time, to expand retail outlets and open assembly facilities in the region, and other Chinese service companies began to establish a visible position in the region.

The New Chinese Presence on the Ground

The developments described in the previous section were transformative, producing a new physical presence of Chinese companies and personnel on the ground in the region in four areas: (1) primary product industries such as mining, petroleum, timber, and agriculture; (2) construction; (3) final assembly and sales of consumer goods; and (4) telecommunications, space, banking, and other strategic service sectors.

In petroleum and mining, Chinese companies have purchased or injected capital into companies with developmental rights in order to obtain access to the associated resources. Key early deals include the 2005 China National Petroleum Corporation (CNPC)-led acquisition of the Canadian firm Encana, with petroleum holdings in Ecuador; the 2006 acquisition by China Metallurgical Corporation of rights to the Sierra Grande iron mine in Argentina; the 2007 acquisition of the Omai bauxite mine in Guyana by Bosai Minerals Group; and China Aluminum's acquisition of Peru Copper the same year, including rights to Toromocho, one of Peru's biggest copper deposits. The emphasis shifted to petroleum in 2010 with Sinopec's acquisition of a majority stake in the Brazilian operations of Repsol through a $7.1 capital injection, followed in December of the same year by its $2.45 billion acquisition of Occidental Petroleum, with significant assets in Argentina, China National Offshore Oil Corporation's (CNOOC $3.1 billion purchase of Bridas, and Sinochem's $3.1 billion acquisition of the Brazilian assets of the Norwegian firm Statoil in 2011.

In some deals, Chinese firms have only acquired a minority stake, giving them a "seat at the table," while minimizing high-profile approval processes. Major examples include CNPC's 2003 acquisition of a 45 percent interest in PlusPetrol Norte, Sinopec's $5.2 billion acquisition of a 30 percent stake in Galp Energy, and China International Trust and Investment Corporation's (CITIC) $1.95 billion acquisition of a 15 percent stake in Companhia Brasileira de Metalurgia e Mineracao (CBMM). Even with a minority stake, the relationship has created opportunities for Chinese engineering and petroleum service companies to win support contracts, expanding the Chinese physical presence in Latin America.

Beyond buying companies with existing resource development rights, Chinese firms have also negotiated and competed for new rights. The first such initiatives were in politically sympathetic countries, such as Venezuela, which in 2010 agreed to partner with CNPC on a $16.4 billion project to develop the Junin-4 block of the Orinoco oil belt, and has gone on to negotiate similar agreements for Junin-1, Junin-8, Junin-10, and the Marisal Sucre gasfields. More impressive was the case of Brazil, where in October 2013, CNPC and CNOOC won a role in the development of the massive new Libra oil field (Blount and Lorenzi 2013).

In agriculture, companies such as Chongquing Grain, Sanhe Hopeful, and Beidahuang have sought to set up agricultural production complexes in the region, including storage and processing facilities, albeit with limited success. In forestry, companies such as Bai Shan Lin and China Timber Resources in Guyana and the China Greenheart Group in Suriname have come to control significant quantities of timberland by buying up smaller companies with timber rights (Ellis 2013b; "Bai Shan Lin . . ." 2013).

In construction, Chinese companies such as China Harbor, Sinohydro, China Railway Road, CITIC, and China Water and Electric have won major projects in the region, leveraging the ability to self-finance the work with funds from Chinese banking partners. To date, most work has been in the nations of Bolivarian Alternative for the Americas (ALBA) and the Caribbean basin, reflecting willingness by these governments to negotiate package deals giving the projects to Chinese companies in exchange for Chinese financing. Initiatives have included railroads (Venezuela); ports, airports, and road infrastructure (Jamaica, Suriname, Guyana, and Costa Rica); and major hydropower projects (Ecuador, Bolivia, and Argentina). Chinese companies have also won some projects in countries with more competitive public procurement processes, including Brazil, where a subsidiary of Sinopec built the Gasene pipeline ("Sinopec Signs . . ." 2008), and Colombia, where Sinohydro is in the first phase of a major water control project for the Magdalena River (Ellis 2012b).

Chinese companies are even winning self-financed construction projects in countries that do not diplomatically recognize the PRC, including the Patuca III dam in Honduras and the Jaguar power plant in Guatemala ("Central

America-China Ties . . ." 2011). These are overshadowed, however, by a possible $40–$80 billion canal across Nicaragua, as well as new rail, highway, and port infrastructure projects across Guatemala and Honduras ("Jumping on the Interoceanic Bandwagon" 2013).

Finally, Chinese groups are also beginning to invest their own capital in major projects in the region, with the work done by Chinese companies. Examples include the $3.5 billion Baha Mar resort in the Bahamas; a smaller resort in Bacholet Bay, Grenada; and the north-south toll road in Jamaica.

In the retail sector, as Chinese companies expand their sales to Latin American and Caribbean countries, they are building retail networks and final assembly facilities in the region to avoid import taxes and better serve local customers. Examples include Haier and Gree appliance manufacturing plants in Brazil; Jialing, Jincheng, and AKT motorcycle assembly facilities in Colombia; automotive plants by Chery (Uruguay, Venezuela, and Brazil) and FAW (First Automobile Works), (Colombia); and heavy equipment facilities in Brazil by Sany, Xuzhou Construction Machinery Group (XCMG), and Zoomlion ("The First Excavator . . ." 2011; "Chinese Giant XCMG . . ." 2012).

In telecommunications, the Chinese companies Huawei and Zhongxing Telecommunications Equipment Corporation (ZTE) have made significant advances, both in selling consumer products such as telephones, modems, routers, and data access devices, and in constructing new communications infrastructure for commercial and government telecom companies in the region (Ellis 2013c; Hulse 2007).

In banking, Chinese companies have established a presence in the region to facilitate trade and transactions by Chinese companies, including establishing large currency swap deals to facilitate international transactions with Brazil ($30 billion) and Argentina ($10 billion). They have also begun to enter consumer banking with the 2011 acquisition of Argentina's Standard Bank by the Industrial and Commercial Bank of China (ICBC), and have signed agreements to integrate the Chinese "UnionPay" financial network into Western networks to facilitate activities by Chinese businessmen and tourists in the region ("Land of Opportunity . . ." 2012).

In the space services sector, China has developed and launched two satellites for Venezuela and one for Bolivia, with plans to launch a satellite for Nicaragua in 2016.

The China–Latin America Military Relationship

The Chinese military presence in Latin America is modest, yet is strategically significant and growing. Such activities, openly mentioned in China's 2008 white paper toward Latin America ("China's Policy Paper . . ." 2008), allow the PRC to develop strategic relationships with Latin American militaries, which are some of the region's most important institutions.

Although the PRC has long provided nonlethal gear and small arms to select countries in the region, Venezuela provided the first opportunity for Chinese military companies to sell sophisticated end items. The Venezuelan purchase of Chinese K-8 light fighters in 2010 paved the way for the sale of six K-8s to Bolivia. Similarly, Venezuela's purchase of JYL-1 air defense radars facilitated China's sale of JYL-2 radars to Ecuador (Ellis 2011b).

Chinese arms companies are also increasingly acting with commercial sophistication resembling their Western counterparts. Firms like Norinco, China Aviation Industry Corporation (AVIC), China National Aero-Technology Import & Export Corporation (CATIC), and Poly Technologies are regular participants in the region's defense trade fairs, such as the Latin American Aerospace and Defense (LAAD) conference in Brazil, International Air & Space Fair (FIDAE) in Chile, and Salón Internacional de Tecnología para la Defensa y Prevención de Desastres Naturales (SITDEF) in Peru. Chengdu Aircraft Corporation is marketing its FC-1 fighter to Argentina by offering to manufacture part of it in that country (Fisher 2013), while Poly Technologies responded to losing a bid in Peru for an air defense system with a legal protest that successfully blocked award of the contract to its competitor (Hearn 2012).

The Chinese military has also expanded institutional cooperation with its counterparts in the region, including visits by leaders and institutional delegations, as well as professional military education and training exchanges. Virtually every military in Latin America and the Caribbean has sent officers to the Defense Studies Institute in Beijing, with some also attending programs at the People's Liberation Army (PLA) navy and ground forces schools, as well as Shijiazhuang and other locations. Relatively few PLA personnel have gone to Latin America for military training, although the Colombian defense forces have hosted Chinese in areas such as riverine operations, sharpshooting, and jungle survival (Ellis 2011b).

The PLA has also conducted a limited number of military operations in the region, often under the rubric of peacekeeping or humanitarian assistance. From 2004 through 2012, the PLA sent a modest military police contingent to United Nations Stabilization Mission In Haiti (MINUSTAH), the UN peacekeeping operation in Haiti. In November 2010, it conducted a small humanitarian relief exercise with the Peruvian military, and in December 2011, the PLA sent its new hospital ship, the *Peace Arc* to the Caribbean (Ellis 2013e). In 2013, the PLA sent a naval flotilla to South America, where it conducted joint exercises with the Chilean navy ("Plan's Taskforce . . ." 2013) and subsequently the Brazilian navy ("China, Brazil . . ." 2013).

Chinese Soft Power

Although the PRC has not established exclusive political alliances in Latin America and the Caribbean, the expansion of its commercial and other activities has contributed to and benefitted from its "soft power" there. Discussions of US influence in the region generally refer to US companies, affinity for US culture, or regional elites who have attended American universities (Nye 1990; Nye 2004).

By contrast, Chinese soft power in the region is largely based on the future, including hopes for loans from Chinese banks or the expectation of China's future importance on the world stage. For some, such as the countries of ALBA, the PRC offers a vehicle for escaping from dependence on Western companies, banks, and political institutions (Ellis 2011a). Overall, in the 2012 *Americas Barometer* survey, in 100 percent of the countries surveyed, the average respondent perceived the PRC to have at least "a little" influence in the country, if not much more (Faughnan and Zechmeister 2013).

Despite such leverage, China's soft power in Latin America is limited in important ways. Relatively few people in the PRC speak Spanish or Portuguese or understand its business, political, and cultural dynamics well enough to conduct business effectively. At lower levels, the language barrier leads workers and managers to isolate themselves rather than interacting with the local community. At senior levels, few Chinese executives have the local knowledge or contacts to assess local political risks, choose local partners wisely, or steer projects free of difficulties.

Chinese firms are also frequently regarded with suspicion, even while their investment is wooed by local governments and would-be partners. In battles for contracts in industries such as construction, competitors frequently use perceptions of Chinese corruption, mistreatment of workers, or other presumed bad practices to block awards of projects to Chinese companies ("CJIA Expansion" 2012).

Challenges for Chinese Firms

As Chinese companies expand their physical presence in Latin America, the challenges that they face resemble those confronted by Western multinationals, including winning and successfully completing projects; managing personnel and supply chains; providing security for their operations and personnel; and dealing with local governments, communities, competitors, and project opponents. Particularly for the Chinese, however, the previously mentioned impediments of language, culture, and trust multiply opportunities for problems and impede the ability to successfully resolve such challenges.

The challenges faced by Chinese companies in Latin America and the Caribbean start at market entry. A number of Chinese attempts to acquire assets in the region have been blocked over concern regarding Chinese ownership, including in 2004, when Minmetals was blocked from purchasing the Canadian minerals firm Noranda, and in 2009, when the Bahamas prevented Hutchison Whampoa from acquiring the Grand Bahamas Port Authority (Smith 2009). Similarly, the Argentine government delayed approval of the acquisition of Standard Bank by ICBC for more than a year, and Sinopec's $7.1 billion bid for Pan American Energy collapsed over shareholder concerns.

Chinese firms have also had difficulty with losing project work. Examples include a failed bid by Sinohydro for the Hidroituango hydroelectric project in Colombia (Ellis 2012b) and the collapse of the Amaila Falls hydroelectric project in Guyana.

Attempts by Chinese firms to take major investment projects forward in Latin America have also been fiercely resisted. Examples include attempts to block the Dragon Mart retail/wholesale complex in the Mexican state of Quintana Roo (Guthrie 2013), protests against the Chinese mining firm, Tongling, the collapse of a project by Beidahuang to build a soy production complex in the Argentine province of Rio Negro ("Proyecto Suspendido" 2011), and Ecuador's revocation of a dam construction contract from the Chinese company Tiesjiu ("Ecuador's Senagua . . ." 2013).

Once operating, Chinese firms have also experienced difficulties with local laborers and subcontractors, opposition from local communities and environmentalists, difficulties with actions by host governments, and security issues from crime to political kidnappings to protesters blocking and overrunning facilities.

Fifty-seven percent of those polled in an *Americas Barometer* survey perceive that Chinese businesses in the region have labor problems (*Americas Barometer* 2012). In addition to strikes, such as those seen at Marcona and Sierra Grande, there are a number of cases of contractors working for Chinese publicly disputing payments, including in Jamaica (Balford 2012), Trinidad (Swamber 2012), and Peru ("Empresarios Loretanos Paralizan . . ." 2011).

For communities, a common protest theme is the failure of the Chinese company to hire the expected number of local workers. Protesters have taken to the streets against Shanghai Construction Group in Guyana ("Opposition Pickets . . ." 2013) and against China Harbour in Jamaica (Matthews 2010), among others, over their hiring practices. In 2007 in Orellana, Ecuador, protests against Petroriental for not hiring enough local workers led to the death of thirty persons and the declaration of a state of emergency ("Heridos 24 Militares . . ." 2007).

Beyond Orellana, Chinese firms face constant challenges to the security of their operations, particularly given that petroleum and mining operations in which their activities are concentrated often occur in remote areas, with extractive operations impacting communities, and even insurgents and criminals found there. Major incidents to date include violent protests against the Rio Blanco mine in Piura, Peru ("Piura Pobladores . . ." 2011), Cerro Dragon in Argentina ("Chubut . . ." 2012), the Colquiri mine in Potosí, Bolivia ("Colquiri aún Dialoga . . ." 2012), and the Bosai bauxite mine in Linden, Guyana. Protesters also took over a Chinese-operated oilfield in Tarapoa, Ecuador, in 2006, while in Olancho, Honduras, in June 2013, the Chinese company Sinohydro was forced to cease work on the Patuca III hydroelectric facility because of threats received against its workers ("Estancadas las Obras . . ." 2013). In Caquetá, Colombia, the oil operations of Chinese-owned Emerald Energy were subject to multiple attacks, culminating in the kidnapping of three Chinese workers in June 2011 ("Emerald Energy Suspends Operations . . ." 2012).

In addressing such security challenges, Chinese companies face a dilemma, in that they do not yet have close relationships with Latin American security forces to protect their operations and personnel, yet are just beginning to learn how to effectively work with private security companies in the region.

Beyond challenges directly affecting Chinese companies and nationals, PRC trade and commercial activities in the region have increased the visibility of Chinese ethnic communities living there, while also creating new opportunities for smuggling Chinese immigrants through the region. Chinese communities are noticed more in smaller states of the Caribbean basin in particular, and are perceived to be growing rapidly, feeding suspicions and resentment toward them by other residents (Ellis 2013a). Chinese shopkeepers have been victimized by ethnic violence in Maracay and Valencia in Venezuela (Reyes 2004) and in Papitam and Maripaston in Suriname (Ellis 2013b). In July 2013, residents of Santo Domingo staged major protests against the city's Chinese shopkeepers (Santana 2013).

To date, the Chinese government has not openly acted to protect PRC companies, nationals, or ethnic Chinese in the region. Indeed, because the Chinese style of pursuing interests is different from that of the West, and because the PRC is sensitive to the US reaction as it operates in the region, it will probably continue to avoid directly challenging partner nations and other actors as it pursues its interests. The PRC's 2010 decision to stop importing soy oil from Argentina in the face of that nation's continuing restrictions against Chinese consumer goods is instructive (Malena 2011, 265). While the PRC government never called its action a response to Argentine protectionism, the loss of $1.4 billion per year in soy revenue prompted a visit by the Argentine foreign minister, and subsequently its president, to the PRC. Within months, the Argentine government committed over $10 billion in railway modernization work to Chinese companies, and soy imports were quietly resumed shortly thereafter ("China Agrees . . ." 2010).

Impacts on the Region

Beyond the challenges for Chinese companies, ethnic Chinese, and the PRC government, Chinese engagement is changing the dynamics of the region in important ways, including driving changes to its economic composition, physical infrastructure, educational institutions, and even its political divisions.

With respect to economic structure, Chinese goods are displacing local manufacturers in the region or forcing them to outsource parts of their production chain to survive. Simultaneously, commodity exports, bolstered by Chinese loans and investments, are expanding the role of industries such as mining and petroleum in the economies of the region (Gallagher and Porzecanski 2008; Gallagher and Porzecanski 2010). In a similar fashion, the composition of agricultural production is changing as countries such as Argentina, Brazil, and Paraguay plant millions of hectares of soy and other cash crops in response to Asian demand.

The physical infrastructure of the region has also evolved to accommodate the demands of the new trans-Pacific commerce, including expansion and modernization of Pacific-facing ports from Manzanillo and Lazaro Cardenas in Mexico, to Iquique and Valparaiso in Chile, as well as rail and other projects connecting those Pacific coast ports to the rest of the continent (Ellis 2009). The greater volume of trans-Pacific commerce, and the new generation of larger ships built to carry it, has also been a significant driver behind the expansion of the Panama Canal, and a contemplated new canal going through Nicaragua, as well as the previously mentioned transcontinental rail links crossing Guatemala, Honduras, and Colombia. In the Caribbean, the new patterns of commerce were a factor behind the Chinese-built Freeport container port and contemplated new ports at Berbice in Guyana and Goat Island in Jamaica (Browne 2013). Even in Uruguay, expanding commerce with Asia is a key driver behind the contemplated new La Paloma mega-port, likely to be built by Chinese companies ("Uruguay Sees . . ." 2013).

Such changes in physical infrastructure not only affect patterns of commerce in the region, but also alter where wealth is produced and bring people together in new ways by connecting previously isolated communities in the interior with the new trading hubs.

Within the region's educational institutions, China-oriented language, business, and social science programs are flowering. This includes the twenty-one universities across the region, which host a Confucius Institute for officially sanctioned Chinese language education, as well as business- and policy-oriented China studies programs in an increasing number of others.

A less desirable consequence of the growing trade with and investment from the PRC has been the expansion in trans-Pacific criminal activities, including human smuggling, drugs and precursor chemicals, contraband, and money laundering. Criminal organizations such as Red Dragon bring Chinese immigrants to the United States through multiple points in Latin America and the Caribbean, collaborating with or paying off the transnational organized crime groups, which control the routes over which their "cargo" must pass (Ellis 2012a). In addition, Chinese (and Indian) companies sell precursor chemicals such as ephedrine and pseudo-ephedrine to transnational criminal organizations in Latin America to make methamphetamines and other synthetic drugs, while Latin American cartels increasingly export cocaine to the PRC. Contraband merchandise from the PRC is imported by Chinese traders, while metals stolen or mined informally in areas such as Madre de Dios in Peru or Michoacán in Mexico are acquired by intermediaries and ultimately sold to Chinese companies (Ruvulcaba 2013; Ellis 2012a).

In the political arena, the PRC has established relations with the region's multilateral institutions, participating as an observer in the Organization of American States, joining the Inter-American Development Bank (IADB) and Caribbean Development Bank, and developing ties with Union of South American Countries (UNASUR), Community of Latin American and Caribbean States (CELAC), and ALBA.

By contrast, the region has failed to develop a coordinated approach toward the PRC. Indeed, an ideological split has emerged regarding how to most effectively engage with the PRC. On one hand, the nations of the newly formed "Pacific Alliance" (Chile, Peru, Colombia, and Mexico) emphasize a market-oriented, rules-based approach focusing on achieving a level playing field with transparency, efficiency, and respect for contracts and private property. By contrast, the countries of ALBA are pursuing a state-centered approach built around government-to-government deals, including Chinese loans for social programs and infrastructure projects, ultimately repaid through the export of commodities.

Beyond these different visions, the PRC has played an important role in the survival of the ALBA regimes. As of October 2013, Venezuela had received $41 billion in loans from China, including a new $5 billion renewal of its heavy investment fund, and was negotiating to renew its $20 billion "Long-Term, Large Volume Fund." It has used such funds not only to keep the energy and other infrastructures supporting its petroleum industry functioning, but also for social programs that sustain its support base, such as the purchase of 2 million Chinese Haier appliances, sold at a discount to the country's poor during the run-up to the 2012 national elections ("Programa Mi Casa . . ." 2012). Similarly, Ecuador has received $10.8 billion in loans from China, including $1.4 billion in the months prior to Ecuador's own February 2013 national elections (Gill 2013), as well as a key Chinese role in the country's $12 billion Refinery of the Pacific (Hall 2013).

On the other hand, the PRC has also been key to the economic success of Pacific Alliance countries, including over $3 billion of Chinese mining investments in Peru ("Inversiones de China" 2012), plus significant purchases of Chilean copper and Colombian coal and petroleum.

For Mexico, particularly since the June 2013 visit of Chinese President Xi Jinping, engagement with China has become an important vehicle for the administration of President Peña Nieto to distance himself from the "war on drug cartels" of his predecessor, while moving Mexico away from its economic dependence on the United States.

Impact on US-Latin American Relations

The position of the United States in Latin America and the Caribbean has also been affected by expanding PRC activities in the region. Aside from impacts on US companies in the region, the principal effect has been to weaken leverage for the US government to promote its agenda on free trade, Western-style democracy, human rights, and other matters. Specifically, the availability of the PRC as an alternative source of loans, investment, and export revenue have undercut the interest of many states in the region in following the proscriptions of Western-dominated institutions such as the International Monetary Fund (IMF), World Bank, and IADB—particularly the ALBA regimes. The United States has not necessarily become "less liked" so much as less relevant to the future of the region. In the process, even the United States is forced to rethink its relationship with the region, focusing on how to be an effective partner and promote its agenda in a context in which it can no longer count on political, economic, and ideological domination of the region to do so.

Conclusion

China's engagement with Latin America and the Caribbean, while principally economic in nature, is profoundly impacting the dynamics of the region, creating both new challenges and new opportunities. It is changing the structure of commerce; patterns of human interaction; political dynamics; and literally, what its politicians, business leaders, and others think about on a daily basis.

On the Chinese side, the new patterns of engagement are forcing the Chinese government to rethink the meaning of "nonintervention in the affairs of foreign countries" as it confronts the imperatives to defend them and promote their interests, including such basic questions as *who* is to be protected and *how?*

For Latin America and the Caribbean, by contrast, engagement with the PRC has dislocated long-standing patterns of commerce and interaction, while producing both new conflicts and resources for change. It has also altered relationships with traditional partners such as the United States and among member states. In short, engagement with the PRC has created the opportunity for the region to reimagine its future, although with no guarantee of the ultimate results.

References

Americas Barometer. (2012). Latin American Public Opinion Project (LAPOP). Available at www.LapopSurveys.org. Accessed on November 7, 2014.

Aranson, C., Mohr, M., and Roett, R. (eds.) (2008) *Enter the Dragon: China's Presence in Latin America.* Washington, D.C.: Woodrow Wilson International Center for Scholars.

"Bai Shan Lin Boss Denies Violating Forestry Laws." (July 14, 2013) *Stabroek News.* Georgetown, Guyana. Retrieved from www.stabroeknews.com. Accessed on 11/7/14.

Balford, Henry. (Dec. 16, 2012) "China Harbour/Union Dispute Brewing." *Jamaica Observer.* Retrieved from www.jamaicaobserver.com. Accessed on 11,7,14.

Blázquez-Lidoy, J., Rodríguez, J., and Santiso, J. (2006) *Angel or Devil? Chinese Trade Impacts on Latin America.* Paris: OECD Development Center.

Blount, J. and Lorenzi, S. (Oct. 23, 2013) "Petrobras-Led Group Wins Brazil oil Auction with Minimum Bid, Many Stay Away." *Reuters.* Retrieved from www.reuters.com. Accessed on 11,7,14.

Browne, R. (Sept. 13, 2013). "History Suggests US in Control of Jamaican Property Sought by China—Goat Islands, Vernamfield Foreign Policy Conundrum." *The Jamaica Gleaner.* Retrieved from http://jamaica-gleaner.com/gleaner/20130913/business/business5.html#disqus_thread. Accessed on 11/7/14.

"Central America-China Ties to Deepen." (May 2011) *Latin America Monitor.* Retrieved from www.latinamericamonitor.com. Accessed on 11/7/14.

"China Agrees to Reopen Market to Argentine Soybean Oil Imports, People Say." (Oct. 11, 2010) *Bloomberg.* Retrieved from www.bloomberg.com. Accessed on 11/7/14.

"China's Policy Paper on Latin America and the Caribbean (full text)." (Nov. 2008) Government of the People's Republic of China. Retrieved from http://english.gov.cn/official/2008-11/05/content_1140347.htm. Accessed on 11/7/14.

"Chinese Giant XCMG Takes German Schwing." (April 24, 2012) *Construction Week Online.* Retrieved from www.constructionweekonline. Accessed on 11/7/14.

"China, Brazil Holds Joint Naval Drill." (Oct. 29, 2013) *Global Times.* Retrieved from www.globaltimes.cn. Accessed on 11/7/14.

"Chubut: Pan American Energy Dijo que Acudirá a la Conciliación con los 'Dragones'." (July 5, 2012) *Clarín.* Retrieved from www.ieco.Clarín.com. Accessed on 11/7/14.

"CJIA Expansion Works to Await Review of World Bank Sanction." (June 23, 2012) *Stabroek News.* Retrieved from www.stabroeknews.com. Accessed on 11/7/14.

"Colquiri aún Dialoga y Denuncian más Tomas." (June 9, 2012) *Los Tiempos.* Retrieved from www.lostiempos.com. Accessed on 11/7/14.

Devlin, R., Estevadeoradal, A., and Rodríguez-Clare, A. (2006). *The Emergence of China: Opportunities and Challenges for Latin America and the Caribbean.* Cambridge, MA: Harvard University Press.

Dumbaugh, K. and Sullivan, M.P. (2005). *China's Growing Interest in Latin America.* Congressional Research Service. Library of Congress. RS22119. Washington D.C.

Dussel Peters, E., Hearn, A.H., and Shaiken, H. (eds.) (2013) *China and the New Triangular Relationship in the Americas.* Mexico City: Universidad Nacional Autonoma de Mexico.

"Ecuador's Senagua Cancels Chone Project Contract with Chinese-led Consortium." (June 4, 2013) *Business News Americas.* Retrieved from www.bnamericas.com. Accessed on 11/7/14.

Ellis, R. Evan. (2009) *China in Latin America: The Whats and Wherefores.* Boulder, CO: Lynne Rienner Publishers.

Ellis, R. Evan. (2011) "Chinese Soft Power in Latin America: A Case Study." *Joint Forces Quarterly.* 60(1st Quarter): 85–91.

Ellis, R. Evan. (2011b) "China–Latin America Military Engagement." Carlisle Barracks, PA: U.S. Army War College Strategic Studies Institute. Retrieved from www.strategicstudiesinstitute.army.mil/pubs/. Accessed on 11/7/14.

Ellis, R. Evan. (2012a) "Chinese Organized Crime in Latin America" *Prism* 4(1): 67–77.

Ellis, R. Evan. (2012b) "Las Relaciones China-Colombia en el Contexto de la Relación Estratégica Entre Colombia y los Estados Unidos.", in B. Creutzfelt (ed.), *China en América Latina.* (295–325). Bogota, Colombia: Universidad Externado.

Ellis, R. Evan. (2013a) "Chinese Commercial Engagement with Guyana: The Challenges of Physical Presence and Political Change." *China Brief* 13(19): 13–16.

Ellis, R. Evan. (2013b) "Suriname and the Chinese: Timber, Migration, and the Less-Told Stories of Globalization." *SAIS Review* 32(2): 85–97.

Ellis, R. Evan. (2013c) "The Strategic Dimension of Chinese Activities in the Latin American Telecommunications Sector." *Revista Científica 'General José María Córdova* 11(11): 121–40.

Ellis, R. Evan. (2013e) *The Strategic Dimension of China's Engagement with Latin America* William J. Perry Paper. Washington DC: Center for Hemispheric Defense Studies.

"Emerald Energy Suspends Operations in Southern Colombia Following Rebel Attacks." (March 6, 2012) *Colombia Reports*. Retrieved from http://colombiareports.com. Accessed on 11/7/14.

"Empresarios Loretanos Paralizan Obra de Alcantarillado de Iquitos por Abuso de Empresa China." (Jan. 11, 2011). *La Voz de la Selva*. Retrieved from http://Radiolvs.cnr.org.pe/ninterna.html?x=10229. Accessed on 11/7/14.

"Estancadas las Obras en la Represa Hidroeléctrica Patuca III en Honduras." (June 9, 2013) *La Prensa*. Retrieved from www.laprensa.hn. Accessed on 11/7/14.

Faughnan, B.M. and Zechmeister, E.J. (2013) "What Do Citizens of the Americas Think of China?" Americas Barometer Project. Retrieved from www.AmericasBarometer.org. Accessed on 11/7/14.

Fernandez Jilberto, A.E. and Hogenboom, B. (eds.) (2010) *Latin America Facing China: South-South Relations beyond the Washington Consensus*. New York, NY: Berghahn Books.

Fisher, R.D. (June 23, 2013) "Argentine Officials Confirm Joint-Production Talks over China's FC-1 Fighter." HIS Jane's 360. Retrieved from www.janes.com/article/23497/argentine-officials-confirm-joint-production-talks-over-china-s-fc-1-fighter. Accessed on 11/7/14.

Fornés, G. and Philip, A.B. (2012). *The China-Latin America Axis: Emerging Markets and the Future of Globalisation*. London: Palgrave Macmillan.

Gallagher, K and Porzecanski, R. (2008) "China Matters: China's Economic Impact in Latin America." *Latin American Research Review* 43(1): 185–200.

Gallagher, K. and Porzecanski, R. (2010). *The Dragon in the Room*. Stanford: Stanford University Press.

Gill, N. (Aug. 26, 2013) "Ecuador Receives $1.2 Billion Loan from China for Budget." *Bloomberg*. Retrieved from www.bloomberg.com. Accessed on 11/7/14.

Guthrie, A. (Jan. 17, 2013) "China Plan Raises Ire in Mexico." *Wall Street Journal*. Retrieved from http://online.wsj.com. Accessed on 11/7/14.

Hall, S. (June 10, 2013) "China's CNPC Nears Ecuador Refinery Deal." *Wall Street Journal*. Retrieved from http://online.wsj.com. Accessed on 11/7/14.

Hearn, A.H. and Marquez, J.L.L. (eds). (2011) *China Engages Latin America: Tracing the Trajectory*. Boulder, CO: Lynne Rienner Publishers.

Hearn, K. (May 27, 2012) "China-Peru Military Ties Growing Stronger." *Washington Times*. Retrieved from http://www.washingtontimes.com/news/2012/may/27/china-peru-military-ties-grow-stronger/?page=all. Accessed 12/27/2014.

"Heridos 24 Militares en Incidentes en Protestas en Orellana." (July 5, 2007) *El Universo*. Retrieved from www.el-universo.com. Accessed on 11/7/14.

Hulse, J. (2007) "China's Expansion into and US Withdrawal from Argentina's Telecommunications and Space Industries and the Implications for US National Security." US Army War College Strategic Studies Institute. Carlisle Barracks, PA.

International Monetary Fund. *Direction of Trade Statistics Quarterly*. September 2013.

"Inversiones de China en Nuestro país Totalizan 3,000 Millones de Dólares." (April 24, 2012) *La Republica*. Retrieved from www.larepublica.pe. Accessed on 11/7/14.

Jenkins R. and Dussel Peters, E. (eds.) (2009) *China and Latin America: Economic Relations in the 21st Century*. Bonn, Germany: German Development Institute.

Jubany, F. and Poon, D. (2006) "Recent Chinese Engagement in Latin America." *Canadian Foundation for the Americas*. Retrieved from http://focal.ca/pdf/china_latam.pdf. Accessed on 11/7/14.

"Jumping on the Inter-Oceanic Bandwagon." (June 27, 2013) *LA News*. Retrieved from www.lanews.com. Accessed on 11/7/14.

"Land of Opportunity." (May 24, 2012) *China Daily*. Retrieved from www.chinadaily.com. Accessed on 11/7/14.

Maciel, R.T. and Nedal, D.K. (2011) "China and Brazil: Two Trajectories of a 'Strategic Partnership,'" in A.H. Hearn and J.L.L. Marquez (eds), *China Engages Latin America: Tracing the Trajectory* (235–55). Boulder, CO: Lynne Rienner Publishers.

Malena, J.E. (2011) "China and Argentina: Beyond the Quest for Natural Resources," in A.H. Hearn and J.L.L. Marquez (eds), *China Engages Latin America: Tracing the Trajectory* (pp 257–78). Boulder, CO: Lynne Rienner Publishers.

Matthews, Kimmo. (Sept. 22, 2010) "Angry Protesters Demand Jobs on Palisadoes Project." *Jamaica Observer*. Retrieved from www.jamaicaobserver.com. Accessed on 11/7/14.

Nye, J.S., Jr. (1990) *Bound to Lead: The Changing Nature of American Power*. New York: Basic Books.

Nye, J.S., Jr. (2004) *Soft Power: The Means to Success in World Politics*. New York: PublicAffairs.

"Opposition Pickets Marriott over Hiring Practices." (Feb. 14, 2013). *Stabroek News*. Retrieved from www.stabroeknews.com. Accessed on 11/7/14.

"Piura: Pobladores Agredidos en Protesta Antiminera Exigen Justicia." (Nov. 16, 2011). *El Comercio*. Retrieved from http://elcomercio.pe/peru. Accessed on 11/7/14.

"PLAN's Taskforce Conducts Maritime Joint Exercise with Chilean Navy." (Oct. 14, 2013) *People's Daily Online*. Retrieved from http://english.people.com.cn/90786/8434317.html. Accessed on 11/7/14.

"Programa Mi Casa Bien Equipada ha Vendido 850 Mil Equipos." (Feb. 7, 2012). *El Universal*. Retrieved from www.eluniversal.com. Accessed on 11/7/14.

"Proyecto Suspendido." (Nov. 24, 2011) *La Nación*. Retrieved from www.lanacion.com.ar. Accessed on 11/7/14.

Reyes, Y.O. (Nov. 11, 2004) "Ciudadanos Chinos Reciben Protección." *El Universal*. Retrieved from http://www.eluniversal.com/2004/11/11/imp_pol_art_11106F. Accessed 12/27/2014.

Roett, R. and Paz, G. (eds.) (2008) *China's Expansion into the Western Hemisphere*. Washington, D.C.: Brookings Institution Press.

Ruvalcaba, H. (Aug. 20, 2013) "Asian Mafias in Baja California." *Insight Crime*. Retrieved from www.insightcrime.org/news-analysis/asian-mafia-in-mexico. Accessed on 11/7/14.

Santana, O. (July 30, 2013) "Protestan contra "Nuevos Comerciantes Chinos." *Diario Libre*. Retrieved from www.diariolibre.com. Accessed on 11/7/14.

"Sinopec Signs Brazil Pipeline Deal with Petrobras." (Jan. 21, 2008) *Downstream Today*. Retrieved from www.downstreamtoday.com. Accessed on 11/7/14.

Smith, I. (Oct. 29, 2009) "Gov't Told 'Block Hutchison." *Jones Bahamas*. Retrieved from www.jonesbahamas.com. Accessed on 11/7/14.

Strauss, J.C. and Armony, A.C. (eds.) (2012) *From the Great Wall to the New World: China and Latin America in the 21st Century*. Cambridge, MA: Cambridge University Press.

Swamber, K. (May 22, 2012) "Chinese Firm, Local Company Try to Settle Lawsuits." *Trinidad Express.* Retrieved from www.trinidadexpress.com. Accessed on 11/7/14.

"The First Excavator Rolled Off the Production Line in Sany Brazil." (Feb. 25, 2011) Sany, Inc. Official Website. Retrieved from www.sanygroup.com. Accessed on 11/7/14.

"Uruguay Sees Deepwater Port as Regional Master Plan." (Oct. 22, 2013) *UPI.* Retrieved from www.upi.com. Accessed on 11/7/14.

17 Conclusion

Slow Progress and False Promises

Orlando J. Pérez and Jennifer S. Holmes

An enduring reality or an endangered species? That is the question that has framed the discussion of Latin American democracy in this volume. As evidenced by the analysis in the preceding chapters, answering this question is not easy. The best response is perhaps the proverbial, "it depends." The answer varies according to institutions, issues, and particular countries. For some citizens in Latin America, stable democratic governance is a reality, but for far too many, it remains an unattained dream. In this chapter, we will endeavor to weave the contributors' arguments and present a cohesive assessment of the state of democratic governance and prospects for stability in contemporary Latin America.

The good news about democracy in Latin America is that all countries, with the notable exception of Cuba, are governed by elected leaders. Competitive elections are now seen as the only legitimate means of selecting those who will lead and represent the citizenry in the halls of power. Elections, of course, are not the sole measure of institutional democracy, but they are an important component. In many countries, the electoral mechanisms have improved, with significant advancements in the development of independent electoral management institutions and increased popular accountability and transparency. Even in countries such as Venezuela and Haiti, where the conduct of elections has been questioned, political power has been determined through electoral contests. In the past decade, most countries have witnessed alternation in power between opposing political parties through the ballot box rather than the barrel of a gun. Democracy in practice, however, is far from perfect. In Venezuela, the opposition has been harassed and jailed. Protests have turned violent. Corruption concerns in Panama have increased. In the Dominican Republic, the high court started a debate over the definition of citizen when it ruled to revoke the citizenship of children of undocumented immigrants. This ruling had major implications for many of the children of Haitian immigrants. The parliament later acted to provide legal residence to people born in the Dominican Republic, with a path to naturalization. If one observes the scores from Freedom House, we find a significant persistence of democracy, albeit imperfect, in Latin America. In 2006, among the thirty-five countries in the Americas, thirty-three were classified as electoral democracies.

Only two—Cuba and Haiti—were listed as not free. By 2013, Cuba was the sole country rated as not free, but ten of the democracies were listed as partly free. As Holmes points out, citizens expect more out of their democracies other than electoral processes.

Another positive indicator is that Latin American citizens express overwhelming support for the idea that democracy is the best form of government, despite its many difficulties. The acceptance of the "Churchillian" notion that democracy may have problems, but it is the best form of government is essential to guarantee democratic legitimacy in the midst of economic, social, and political problems. In addition, as shown by Pérez in Chapter 3, substantial majorities in most countries of the region identify democracy with intrinsic and normative values, such as liberty and freedom. The combination of these two factors is important because legitimacy is rooted in the belief by citizens that democracy is better than the alternative regimes. Latin America has historically experimented with many different political and economic regimes; many citizens no longer recall the repression of the military-led governments of the 1960s and 1970s, and thus may easily fall victim to the siren call of authoritarian alternatives, particularly of a populist nature, if they are promised quick solutions to the nation's problems. However, to the extent that citizens are willing to support democracy based on normative values and look beyond immediate problems, democracy will have a stronger footing in the region. Nonetheless, we must point out that while support for democracy as a system of government is high, satisfaction with the way democracy is working is rather low. Thus, there is a dichotomy between the idea of democracy and the actual experience of citizens with the way democratic governments operate. This difference in attitudes is a troubling fact for many countries in Latin America.

Dissatisfaction with the performance of democracies appears to be the cause of this difference in attitudes. Rojas Aravena points out the low level of confidence in the institutions, as well as the impact of corruption, crime, and economic inequality on the public's assessment of democratic performance across the region. Maisto's chapter points to the inability of the inter-American regional system to uphold democratic norms consistently. As Maisto points out, the Organization of American States (OAS) has failed to enforce the provisions of the Inter-American Democratic Charter in such cases as Venezuela and Ecuador. Holmes' chapter on democratic consolidation highlights that only in Argentina, Ecuador, Nicaragua, and Uruguay do at least 50 percent express satisfaction with democracy. Why? There is ample evidence of scant progress on key concerns. Corruption scores are troublesome in countries such as the Dominican Republic, Guatemala, Honduras, Nicaragua, Paraguay, and Venezuela. In terms of human development, large differentials exist in child mortality among income and indigenous groups, especially in countries like Brazil and Bolivia. High levels of gender inequality exist in Panama, Haiti, and Guatemala. Millett discusses the growing problem of crime and violence, its undermining of citizen security in the region, and its effect on poverty and the economy.

Despite the stereotype of Latin American *machismo*, Martínez Rosón points out that in spring 2014, three Latin American countries had women presidents. This is promising for a region that historically has had significant gender disparities and inequality in government, especially at the lower levels. The region is also innovative in terms of experimenting with various policy interventions to change this. She focuses on Latin American women legislators to examine issues of women's representation. Some countries, like Bolivia, have almost reached gender parity in representation, while others, like the Dominican Republic, lag far behind. Interestingly, Martínez Rosón examines the disparity in representation by level and position, and by the degree of power and authority. The traditional lack of women in office has been a focus of many reforms, most notably the use of the quota. In Latin America, fifteen countries use one type of quota or another to address concerns about gender disparity in legislatures. She examines different factors, both in the details of the quota and the general context of the electoral system, that may influence the effectiveness of these policies. Beyond proportions, she also provides a profile of the type of woman who has been elected. More often than not, they tend to be single, well educated, and have similar levels of policy experience, although less political experience. Martínez Rosón also examines whether or not having more women in parliament has an impact on policy preferences.

Moscovich examines local governments as rich arenas for deepening democracy in decentralization efforts. She illustrates how local politics have impacted national politics and the numerous examples of policy innovation. Decentralization has been pursued in the region as an effort to address the typical unevenness of state presence and the predominance of the executive and the capital city. The results of decentralization vary in terms of resources available to local governments, their ability to raise their own revenue, and even the success of local taxation efforts. She examines the balance of power among different levels and the incentives for politicians to see the outcome. Decentralization can also be reversed.

Indigenous groups have historically suffered political exclusion throughout the region, but have been able to politically mobilize in this wave of democratization. Rice describes the recent indigenous mobilization as "one of the few bright spots of Latin America's democratic record." Some have characterized mobilization along newly politicized ethnic identities as a possible threat to democracy, but Rice argues that, on average, democracy will benefit from these new challenges to long-standing inequality and exclusion. She discusses the many pathways to change, from social movement and autonomous communities, through working with or within existing political parties. She discusses the Bolivian reforms to include direct, participatory, and communitarian elements in order to include the numerous indigenous groups in the country. Although some tensions have increased within the country, overall, democracy, and satisfaction with democracy have increased. She warns that attempts to co-opt or repress indigenous mobilization would be more combustible than tensions that may arise from their new mobilization.

Economically, until recently, one of the main lines of research was between regime type and economic performance. It was also assumed that a reliance on primary commodities was not a good bet for long-term economic growth. However, Latin American economic performance has been more robust and resilient than what most expected after the global economic crisis. Ferrantino and Gutiérrez de Piñeres argue that there is no simple relationship between a specialization in primary exports and economic development. This contrasts with much of the conventional wisdom of the past that associated a reliance on primary exports with an increasing gap between industrialized and developed countries. This view led to policies such as import substitution industrialization. In contrast, they find that since the lost decade of the 1980s, in general, Latin America has experienced positive growth and a modest specialization in their export portfolios. They conclude that there is no clear pattern between either export specialization or diversification and economic growth. They conclude that platitudes about primary product specialization, lack of diversification, and economic growth are too simplistic and may have never accurately described economic development in Latin America.

As we mentioned earlier, Latin American democracies face some serious challenges. Among the most important is the increasing level of crime. According to the UN Office on Drugs and Crime, the Americas has doubled the homicide rate than the world average. Even this average masks reality. In general, South American homicide rates (with a notable exception of Venezuela) have declined, whereas Central American homicide rates have rapidly increased. As described by Richard Millett in his chapter, organized and transnational criminal networks are a major threat to political stability in the region. Organized crime undermines the legitimacy of governments by challenging the authority of the state to control and manage sectors of the national territory and significant areas of major cities. Criminal networks also increase corruption by using their vast financial wealth to buy policemen, judges, and public officials. Public opinion evidence shown in Chapter 3 of this volume illustrates the extent to which crime undermines public support for democracy. As criminal activity increases and governments are unable to stop it, the public's confidence in government wanes and their susceptibility to authoritarian solutions increases. Moreover, the response to the wave of crime may also undermine democracy as governments are increasingly pushed toward harsher measures, the so-called "*mano dura*" approach, which may satisfy the public's hunger for tough actions, but erode democratic accountability and civil rights.

The threat of military coups is, for most countries in the region, a thing of the past. The armed forces have accepted a subordinate role to the elected civilian authorities. Reductions in budget and personnel have turned historically dominant institutions into small forces focused almost exclusively on internal development and security issues. Even in cases where the military has stepped forward to replace extant governments, such as in Ecuador and Bolivia, they have done so by following the established constitutional line of authority. And in the cases where the military retains high levels of authority, such as

Guatemala, they do so behind the scenes and recently did nothing to prevent a left-leaning candidate, Alvaro Colom, from becoming president. However, we must point out that military subordination has often been bought at the expense of high levels of institutional autonomy for the armed forces. Diamint and Tedesco examine civil military relations from a broad perspective, including attention to the formulation of defense policy, control over the police, and *mano dura* policies and their implications for society. They highlight the thin line between military and police force and the resultant militarization of public security. In many countries, the military dominates defense policy-making and is increasingly involved in internal security matters, which tend to undermine police authority. In addition, civilian oversight, particularly by the legislature, remains weak and ineffective. Civilian knowledge of and attention to defense matters is woefully inadequate to assure effective control of the armed forces. Too often civilian dominance is exercised exclusively by the president. Ultimately, however, given the history of direct military intervention in the political process of Latin America and that thirty years ago the region was governed almost exclusively by military officers, the fact that the armed forces have accepted a back seat, albeit within earshot of the driver, must be celebrated as a significant advance.

Corruption is seen as a major concern across the region. Berthin's chapter explored the persistence of both perceptions of corruption and corrupt practices and the effects on democratic governance. Corruption undermines trust in government institutions and negatively affects economic development. While significant efforts have been made by international development organizations and national governments, lack of transparency and accountability are problems that still affect too many countries in Latin America. Berthin argues that strengthening democratic institutions and improving governmental performance in Latin America necessarily involves effective actions against corruption.

Governing is a challenge in the region. In the past, presidents were strong and able to impose laws and policies. Now, it is more common to have divided legislatures and presidential rule by decree, as Rojas Aravena points out. As a result, there have been at least sixteen interrupted presidencies between 1992 and 2013 signaling serious instability, as presidents have not been able to maintain support or finish their original terms. Siavelis discusses the prospect for Latin American democracy in light of the historical preference for presidential systems and the system's possible hindrance of stability in the Latin American context dominated by multiparty systems. Further complicating matters, presidents tend to be anti-system and at least initially very popular because of their stance against traditional parties. The dominance of traditional party systems has crumbled in countries such as Brazil and Chile. New leaders struggle with an uncomfortable strategic environment that does not always give them free rein in either choice of policy or implementation. Legislative-executive conflicts have created many crises, such as impeachment proceedings, but are sometimes resolved without major impact. The record of Latin American presidentialism is mixed, with presidential success linked to factors other than institutional design.

Rule of law remains tenuous in the region. In her contribution, Nagle focuses on the impediments to rule of law: corruption, dysfunctional judiciaries, shortcomings in legal education, organized crime and terrorism, and the increasing influence of foreign states in the region. Corruption and bureaucratic malaise persist despite a generally highly educated technocrat class. Old patronage systems remain in the background, despite modern facades. She describes a reality of rule by law rather than rule of law. However, she warns that progress will only be secure when both citizens and leaders change from expecting personal favors and instead expect merit-based rewards. This is not an easy transition, given the colonial and post-colonial practices and history of inequality and social exclusion that continue to influence contemporary societies. In many countries, she describes a situation of dysfunctional and corrupt judiciaries that have low levels of independence and are, as a result, weak and failing. She also expresses doubt about the efficacy of quick-fix solutions imported from advanced industrialized societies. Misguided reform efforts based on the Anglo-American adversarial system have further undermined reform possibilities for the Latin American legal foundation and its unique legal culture. On a positive note, their progress is partially due to the work of the OAS, activist judiciaries (such as in Colombia that have been willing to challenge the historically dominant executive branch), and changing expectations of citizens.

Carrión's chapter focuses on the reemergence of populism as a major political force in the region and on the challenges this poses to democratic governance. While the reasons for the rise of populism vary, from the disintegration of historical political party systems, the rise of charismatic leaders, the crisis of representation from the collapse of corporate intermediary organizations, and deep economic crises stemming from the exhaustion of the neoliberal model, there are six specific factors that help characterize populist regimes and explain their unique challenge to democracy. First, the existence of an anti-politics lexicon, where rejection of traditional political participation appears as one of the key issues. This discourse finds fertile ground in those societies where political parties and traditional forms of participation are regarded poorly by a large part of the population. Chávez and Fujimori came to power in their respective countries after deep social disillusionment with politicians, who were accused of being inept and corrupt. Second, populism uses the mass media to promote a direct link between leader and people. Regular or traditional forms of mediation between the population and the government are set aside; instead, a direct dialogue between the leader and his supporters is established via the skillful use of traditional and new media. Television in particular becomes a key tool to carry the message of the leader to the masses and to mobilize supporters. Third, there is a bias toward mobilization rather than participation. Important sectors of the population are required to provide support for the leader's agenda. When in power, the discretional use of public resources promotes the support of social groups that become visible in the streets, giving voice to the *caudillo*, as happened with the "Peronist" masses in Argentina of the 1940s and 1950s or as happened in contemporary Venezuela with Chávez's "Bolivarian Circles" and multiple mass rallies. Fourth, populists use nationalistic rhetoric and symbols to mobilize popular support. The appeal to nationalistic sentiment is one of the emotional links that populist leaders establish with the people. Hugo Chávez and his successor, Nicolás Maduro, have sought to legitimate themselves through historical references, particularly as the political and ideological heirs of Simón Bolívar. Also, populist leaders seek external enemies to rally popular support. Often, these enemies are in the form of transnational corporations, international financial institutions, or wealthy industrialized nations, particularly the United States. Moreover, in some cases, such as Venezuela, the enemy can be a neighbor—in this case, Colombia, which Venezuelan leaders perceive as close to the United States and a regional military and economic rival. Fifth, populism employs the notion of the leader as the embodiment of the people. The link is direct and organic. The discourse of the *caudillo* is not that of a statesman in the sense of being one who rules and directs in a democratic fashion; the *caudillo* demands unconditional support and party discipline; the names vary from country to country, but the concept remains the same: follow blindly and unconditionally. The populace is exhorted to follow the leader in the achievement of objectives that are not always coherent. It is charisma and the personal qualities of the leader that represent key elements in the construction of a populist regime. Sixth, populism is characterized by a deep mistrust of liberal democratic institutions. Populist leaders seek to dismantle the institutional mechanisms and structures that mediate between the population and the government. In so doing, they destroy or undermine what Guillermo O'Donnell calls "horizontal accountability." That is, the network of institutions that provides the checks and balances so necessary for a liberal democracy to operate. Populist leaders seek to construct a version of direct democracy they call "participatory," but which, unfortunately, often degenerates into manipulating popular participation and weakening vital institutions such as the judiciary, legislature, and other independent agencies. In the end, populism weakens the basic institutional structures of representative democracy without building strong and genuine popular democracy either.

Although citizens may be frustrated with the slow and uneven pace of improvement, the international environment is more supportive of democracy than in the past. The geostrategic situation and steps toward regional economic integration have reduced external threats or the possibility of intrastate conflicts.[1] The Organization of American States' Charter of Democracy precludes recognition of any governments that come to power via extra-constitutional means. The United States has not directly intervened to destabilize a democratic Latin American regime since the 1980s in Central America. The last direct intervention was overthrowing Panama's Noriega in 1989. Rojas Aravena points out that US influence is still strong in the northern part of the region, but is less decisive in the south. Furthermore, he stresses that the vast majority of Latin Americans do not support the United States' strategic choices in the war on terror, which added to historical concerns about US imperialism. According to him, the divide among Latin American countries in regard to the Washington Consensus and how to engage globalization is wide and growing.

As shown by Ellis' chapter, China's engagement with Latin America, while principally economic, is profoundly changing the dynamics of the region, creating both new challenges and new opportunities. For Latin America, engagement with China has dislocated long-standing patterns of commerce, while producing both new conflicts and increasing resources. It has also altered relationships with traditional partners such as the United States. As the United States' focus on the region wanes, China is stepping forward as a major player, challenging long-standing geopolitical dynamics and economic relations. How both Latin American countries and the United States handle such changes will go a long way in determining the region's economic and political future.

Conclusion

Despite heavy pressures, Latin American democracies persist. Since the first edition of this volume, the region withstood better than most the global economic crisis of 2008–2009, and electoral processes have endured everywhere except Cuba. Even in countries where crime has undermined the ability of the state to supply citizen security, such as Honduras and Guatemala, competitive elections and democratic transfer of power have prevailed. The people of Latin America generally prefer democracy over authoritarianism. However, corruption, crime, economic inequality, and other problems challenge the stability of democratic governance and provide an opportunity for authoritarian "solutions" to gain ground. A common theme throughout the book is that of a "*falsa promesa*" (false promise) that can come from populist or simplistic solutions that pledge quick results but that may be nothing more than a debilitating illusion. Slow, steady progress is more sustainable than rash attempts, but will democracy be able to withstand growing frustration, impatience, and disillusionment, or will countries fall prey to the "*falsa promesa*" of authoritarianism?

Note

1 We must add a caveat to this statement related to the Colombia-Ecuador-Venezuela conflict over Colombia's handling of their internal civil conflict and the effects on its neighbors. While an escalation of tensions ensued after Colombia's military incursion into Ecuadorian territory in early 2008, with Venezuela and Ecuador mobilizing military forces to the border area, the fact remains that multilateral mechanisms were used successfully to deescalate the conflict. While tensions remain, the thought of a full-scale war between the countries remains a remote possibility.

Index

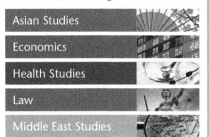